Second Edition

Contemporary
Music
Education

Second Edition

Contemporary Music Education

Michael L. Mark
Towson State University

SCHIRMER BOOKS
A Division of Macmillan, Inc.
NEW YORK

Collier Macmillan Publishers
LONDON

To my mother, Ruth Mark

Copyright © 1978 by Schirmer Books
A Division of Macmillan Publishing Co., Inc.

Copyright © 1986 by Schirmer Books
A Division of Macmillan, Inc.

Schirmer Books
A Division of Macmillan, Inc.
866 Third Avenue, New York, N. Y. 10022

Collier Macmillan Canada, Inc.

Printed in the United States of America

printing number
  2 3 4 5 6 7 8 9 10

Library of Congress Cataloging in Publication Data

Mark, Michael L.
    Contemporary music education.

    1. School music—Instruction and study—United
States. I. Title.
MT3.U5M32 1986   780'.7'2973   85-13794
ISBN 0-02-871220-X

Contents

List of Illustrative and Teaching Materials

Preface to the Second Edition

The period between the publication of the first and second editions has brought changes to music education that make new kinds of demands on music educators. As always, they must practice their art with the greatest skill, insight, wisdom, and aesthetic sensitivity. It is unlikely that anything less will ever be acceptable. Changes in American society, however, have impacted in many ways on the profession of music education. In order to develop a broad and realistic view of the profession, music educators need to look beyond its boundaries to examine the social, political, and economic structure of the society that supports it. For that reason, the second edition includes material that helps define the interrelationships between music education and society. By learning about the social environment of the profession, the music educator will better understand why things are as they are, and can make better-informed choices for the future.

The second edition touches on many areas, but emphasizes developments in music education. Although music educators are encouraged to look beyond their profession for deeper understanding, they will achieve their greatest success and satisfaction by knowing as much as possible about children and music, and by applying that knowledge effectively in order to develop and maintain music education programs of the highest quality.

M.L.M.
Towson State University

Preface to the First Edition

It is always important for educators to be aware of recent developments and trends in education. It is especially important at this particular time, when American education is in a state of intense, and in some cases overwhelming, change. Busy educators find it difficult to keep up with "what's new," and almost impossible to find the time to digest the origins, mechanics, and implications of trends. Every current trend does not directly affect every educator, but change in general does. Educators owe themselves, their students, and their profession a commitment to the present and the future. In order to fulfill that commitment it is imperative to understand what is happening now and to try to formulate implications for the future.

Music educators need to be aware of trends because the modes of response to society's educational needs change as society does. Because of the changing nature of music, music educators must be informed of how the profession remains contemporary and viable. In recent years changes in music education philosophy and methodology have brought happy results. Music educators who take the trouble to keep up with current trends and events do so with pride and hope for the future of the profession.

M.L.M.
1977

Acknowledgments

My sincerest thanks for their contributions of ideas, criticism, and various other forms of assistance go to the following people: Dr. Abraham Schwadron, University of California at Los Angeles; Willard H. Markey, Malmark, Inc.; Dr. Ronald Lee, Syracuse University; Dr. Edwin Gordon and Dr. John Holahan, Temple University; Sr. Lorna Zemke, Silver Lake College; Rosemarie Cook, Music Consultant, Los Angeles County Public Schools; Dr. Sue Gilvin, Silver Burdett Company; John J. Warrener, Director of Music, Brimfield, Massachusetts Public Schools; Madeleine Carabo-Cone; Dr. Philip Tacka, Georgetown University; Dr. Anthony L. Barresi, University of Wisconsin; Don Muro; Dr. Paul Gayzagian, University of Lowell; Dr. Roger Phelps, New York University; Dr. Keith Thompson, The Pennsylvania State University; Dr. George Heller, The University of Kansas; Betty Betton, National Association of Jazz Educators; Jeanne Knorr, Towson State University; Alice Beer, the Peabody Conservatory of Music; Dr. Charles Gary and Dr. Robert Garofalo, The Catholic University of America; Adele Chwalek, The Catholic University of America Library; Dr. Leon Burton, University of Hawaii; Dr. Norman Dello Joio, Boston University: Eoline Kukuk, Project ARTS, Montgomery County Public Schools (Maryland); Dr. Terrell Stackpole, Division of Arts Education, Pittsburgh Public Schools; and Dr. Karen Lofgreen, Weber State College.

The Foundations of Contemporary Music Education

Part I

1

Historical Foundations of Music Education

When the Pilgrims and the Puritans arrived in the New World in 1620 and 1630, they brought with them the sophisticated and refined music culture of England. Their music served an important purpose because of its use in worship. Life in the New World was difficult, however, and they had little time to maintain musical skills. Life was a constant and continuing struggle for survival against starvation, bitter winters, and hostile natives. Needless to say, the ability to make aesthetically satisfying music declined in such an environment. Succeeding generations may have had somewhat easier circumstances, but the quality of their lives retained many of the harsh realities of earlier times. It was difficult to maintain skills through succeeding generations in that kind of society, and each new generation was less musical than the one before it.

Education was important in the colonial period. The Massachusetts Bay Colony, the educational leader of that time, passed early school laws. The first, the "Massachusetts School Law of 1642," required town officials to compel parents to provide their children with an elementary education. The law did not establish schools; it merely set up minimum essentials of education and allowed each town to comply in the best way possible. The second law, the "Massachusetts School Law of 1647," required that every township of at least fifty families appoint a teacher for the children, and that reading and writing be taught. Towns of 100 or more families were required to "set up a grammer schoole, the master thereof being able to instruct youth so farr as they may be fited for the university [sic]" (Harvard College was founded in 1636). Under this law, taxation for the purpose of paying a teacher was made legally permissible. The "Massachusetts School Law of 1648" was more specific about what should be taught, and why.

Forasmuch as the good education of children is of singular behoof and benefit to any Common-wealth; and whereas many parents and masters are too indulgent and negligent of their duty in that kinde. It is therefore ordered that the Select men of everie town, in the severall precincts and quarters where they dwell, shall have a vigilant eye over their brethren and neighbours to see, first that none of them shall suffer so much barbarism in any of their families as not to indeavor to teach by themselves or others, their children and apprentices so much learning as may inable them perfectly to read the english tongue, and knowledge of the Capital lawes; upon penaltie of twentie shillings for each neglect therein. Also that all masters of families doe once a week (at the least) catechize their children and servants in the grounds and principles of Religion. . . . And further that all parents and masters do breed and bring up their children and apprentices in some honest lawfull calling, labour or imployment, either in husbandry, or some other trade profitable for themselves, and the Common-wealth, if they will not or can not train them up in learning to fit them for higher imployments.[1]

The legislatures of Connecticut, Plymouth, and New Hampshire followed suit within a few decades.

Obviously, early American education was geared to practical needs (which included the needs of the church). Music was not considered a proper subject for study in the tax-supported schools at that time, and would not be until the first half of the nineteenth century.

The music used for worship and recreation was learned by listening to it. People did not learn to read music because a written music tradition had not yet developed in the New England colonies. Since the transmission of musical knowledge was oral, with each succeeding generation the ability to sing the psalms used in church services accurately, with good tone quality, diction, and musicality, declined. By the turn of the eighteenth century, genuine concern for the quality of congregational singing was expressed by many people, especially ministers. Alice Morse Earle wrote:

Of all the dismal accompaniments of public worship in the early days of New England the music was the most hopelessly forlorn—not only from the confused versifications of the Psalms which were used, but from the mournful monotony of the few known tunes and the horrible manner in which these tunes were sung.[2]

Reverend Thomas Walter wrote in 1721:

The tunes are now miserably tortured and twisted and quavered in our churches, into a horrid medly of confused and disorderly voices. Our tunes are left to the mercy of every unskilled throat to chop and alter, to twist and change, according to their infinitely diverse and no less odd humours and fancies. I have myself paused twice in one note to take a breath. No two men in the congregation quaver alike or together. It sounds in the ears of a good judge like five hundred tunes roared out at the same time, with perpetual interfearings with one another.[3]

The response to the agitation caused by the critics of musical quality was the beginning of public music education in this country. It was in the form of the "singing school," a movement in which itinerant singing masters provided their services to cities, towns, and villages for a fee. Classes were held in schools, churches, taverns, homes, or any other place where space was available. The singing masters taught the rudiments of music and their classes learned to read music from notation. Singing schools lasted from a couple of weeks to several months, after which the singing master traveled to the location of his next singing school. The students were children and adults. Entire families sometimes attended every time a singing school was held in their community. A fee was charged for each student, and the singing master earned additional income by selling tunebooks, most of which were compiled by themselves or other singing masters.

Singing schools were highly regarded and successful because they satisfied an expressed need of the people. They served both musical and social purposes. People enjoyed singing and appreciated the pleasant social atmosphere created by learning music and singing together.[4] The singing schools and other kinds of "night schools" (there were many to fulfill the need for practical education not yet met by public schools), including those for language, navigation, surveying, sewing, and cooking, probably came closer to true accountability than any public school system in the second half of the twentieth century. The eighteenth century night schools existed only because people wanted them to, and teachers were able to earn their livelihoods (at least in part) because they were considered both necessary and effective by their students. If the need for a particular subject did not exist, or if a teacher had not been successful in the past, then economic support was not forthcoming. No tax money was spent in support of the movement.

The singing schools did indeed help to improve the quality of singing in the churches. The singing school movement existed from the 1720s to the second half of the nineteenth century, and some even existed in isolated rural areas well into the twentieth century. They provide an important lesson for contemporary educators in that they served a practical purpose and existed because of popular demand. It was a self-perpetuating movement—as people came to enjoy music more, the demand for singing schools increased.

There was no formal methodology of teaching, but a balance between pedagogy and music was achieved that satisfied the public. Also, the earliest American school of composers, the "Yankee tunesmiths" (Billings, Read, Holden, among others), were singing masters, and for that period in our history the best composers were also the teachers. The composers and their music were close to the people and appreciated by them. They served a utilitarian purpose that affected the lives of many people. Later generations of Americans found themselves separated from composers, who were often put on a pedestal, revered, and known only to the part of the public that went to concert halls. The Contemporary Music Project (see chapter 2) of the late 1950s and the 1960s provided a historic service by placing composers and performers in public school situations in order to make contemporary music a part of children's lives.

Music was taught in schools in various parts of the country starting at the beginning of the nineteenth century. It was not taught so that children would know about music, but so they could use it in church and for recreation. In 1838 Lowell Mason persuaded the Boston School Committee (board of education) to include music in the curriculum of the public schools as a regular subject. It was a major step forward because for the first time the teaching of music was supported by public taxes just as were the other subjects. The School Committee report that recommended the addition of music in the schools justified its action with three reasons: music, like the other school subjects already in existence, had to meet the criteria of being intellectually, morally, and physically beneficial to children. The report carefully explained how music was beneficial for children in each of the three ways.[5] Many other reasons were also given, including recreation, worship, and discipline. The conclusion of the report describes the effects that the study of music was expected to produce:

In the language of an illustrious writer of the seventeenth century, "Music is a thing that delighteth all ages and beseemeth all states, a thing as seasonable in grief as joy, as decent being added to actions of greatest solemnity, as being used when men sequester themselves from action." If such be the natural effects of Music, if it enliven prosperity or soothe sorrow, if it quicken the pulses of social happiness, if it can fill the vacancy of an hour that would otherwise be listlessly or unprofitably spent, if it gild with a mild light the chequered scenes of daily existence, why then limit its benign and blessed influence? Let it, with healing on its wings, enter through ten thousand avenues the paternal dwelling. Let it mingle with religion, with labor, with the homebred amusements and innocent enjoyments of life. Let it no longer be regarded merely as the ornament of life. Let it no longer be regarded merely as the ornament of the rich. Still let it continue to adorn the abodes of wealth, but let it also light up with gladness, the honest hearth of poverty. Once introduce music into the common schools and you make it what it should be made, the property of the whole people. And so as time passes away, and one race succeeds to another, the true object of our system of Public Education may be realized, and we may, year after year, raise up good citizens to the Commonwealth, by sending forth from our schools, happy, useful, well instructed, contented members of society.[6]

Music education has been very successful in some ways since 1838. The performance program has produced choruses, bands, orchestras, small ensembles, and soloists that can be described only in the most positive and enthusiastic terms. Many teachers have been very successful with general music classes. However, music education, as a formal discipline within the public education structure, has not yet succeeded in making the United States a musical nation by producing an adult population that is musically literate, appreciative, and participatory. The most important reason needs to be discussed at this time because it provides a point of reference for readers of this book. Music education has not always been presented musically, and for musical purposes. In other words, music educators have not always been true to music. This is not because of the motives or abilities of music educators; they, like other teachers, must conform to the rules, regulations, and practices of the school systems that employ them, and are often restricted in their approach to music instruction. There have been notable exceptions, of course, and the fact that some areas have strong musical cultures is due, to some extent, to effective aesthetically based music education programs.

Around the end of the nineteenth century, a pedagogical battle took place between music teachers who thought that the teaching of music reading should be a rote process, and those teachers who advocated a pure reading approach. The battle was beneficial to the profession because it made teachers think about methodology. In considering method, one must consider what is to be taught. Preceding that is the most basic consideration—why should the subject be taught at all? When the smoke of battle began to clear around the turn of the twentieth century, some music educators began to realize that the "why" had never received proper consideration before teaching methods were developed. It had been assumed that teaching children to read music in order to enable them to sing the great choral literature (which was a major goal at that time) was sufficient justification for music in public education. At the beginning of the twentieth century, when the child-centered movement in American education was taking hold, music educators finally began to agree that music education could be justified only in terms of helping children to enjoy music so it could become an important part of their lives. Samuel Cole said at a 1903 meeting of the National Education Association:

The real purpose of teaching music in the public schools is not to make expert sight singers nor individual soloists. I speak from experience. I have done all these things and I can do them again; but I have learned that, if they become an end and not a means they hinder rather than help, because they represent only the abilities of the few. A much nobler, grander, more inspiring privilege is yours and mine; to get the great mass to singing and to make them love it.[7]

The time was right because the new child-centered approach valued the arts in education. The work of Friedrich Froebel, John Dewey, and Maria Montessori affected education in ways favorable to music and the other arts. Music appreciation was introduced into the curriculum, as were music literature, history, and theory. Instrumental music assumed an increasingly important place in the schools. Why, then, has music education not produced a musical American public? The reason is the lack of musicality in music education and comprises several factors.

1. Methodology continued to be a problem even after the child-centered curriculum was implemented in the early part of this century. Method continued to get in the way of learning. Music teachers had to conform to a broader school philosophy and curriculum. Silberman states:

> The normal school movement viewed teachers as technicians rather than as autonomous professionals, and trained them accordingly. This view was solidified in the first few decades of this century, when superintendents of schools were caught up in the national fervor for "Scientific Management." Slavishly imitating the way they (sometimes mistakenly) thought corporate executives operated, superintendents tried to control the most minute details of school operation . . . teachers were production line workers whose every move had to be controlled and checked.[8]

Teachers who had so little freedom to function were often unable to implement successfully a child-centered aesthetic approach to music education. Music was taught from any of the great number of texts published in this century, and students demonstrated their learning in public performances. The demonstrations have almost always been successful. But most of the attention was given to the process, rather than the product. Teachers did the jobs expected of them. They taught children about music, and in many cases helped them develop a true love of music, but sometimes this was more or less incidental. Most of the elementary graded music series, the music appreciation books, and the instrumental method books, based on process rather than product, stressed cognitive learning and psychomotor development. The music in the books was not usually of high musical quality. Much of it was devised for educational purposes, and often consisted of songs and other musical forms to which most children did not relate. Throughout most of this century the authors of educational music materials have, for the most part, failed to take advantage of the great body of excellent music that represents the classical, folk, and popular traditions.

The student's performance itself often was considered to be the educational product. It is a fact, however, that most music students do not continue to perform after graduation from school, nor do they become consumers of classical music in adulthood.

2. The population of the United States is extremely diversified; it is comprised of people from virtually every national and ethnic background. Until recently, American education has not respected differences in heritages. When the United States was considered to be a "melting pot" until around 1930, American education was one of the strongest forces in assimilating people of varying backgrounds. Although the melting pot concept has always been considered an American virtue, we have also come to value the social, ethnic, and cultural diversity of American society. Since the 1960s American schools have attempted to teach about ethnicity, and the curriculum now is structured to reflect various cultural values and traditions. Until the 1960s, music teachers utilized a rather parochial body of music literature and attempted to "teach up" to a "cultured" level, that is, the level of the upper economic class. Western classical music was considered to be the best music, and teachers thought it proper to encourage students to aspire to it. Countless people of a variety of cultural heritages learned to love Western art music, but music educators excluded ethnic, folk, and popular music from the curriculum. Their failure to recognize what was most meaningful to students and their families and communities turned many people away from art music, which requires knowledge, experience, and sophistication for most people to appreciate.

3. The United States had become a nation of listeners. The days of the singing school were healthy, musically speaking, because people participated in music. The music was not especially refined and performance standards for the participants were probably not high. If people wanted music, however, they had to make it themselves because there were few places to go to hear it. And so they did make it. During the nineteenth century, however, European concert artists discovered America. They came here and toured, and Americans loved them. Recitalists, opera companies, and orchestras traveled here and introduced millions of Americans to the best European art music in excellent performances. Performers like Jenny Lind and Ole Bull became national heroes to Americans. American tours to cities, towns, and villages were very profitable for European musicians. Their example helped American professional music performance to improve, and Americans eventually had the opportunity to hear many excellent American touring organizations, such as the Theodore Thomas Orchestra and the Gilmore and Sousa bands.

As a result, however, the "listeners'" participation in music became passive rather than active. Music was now a connoisseur art heard in concert halls, rather than an integral part of everyday life. School performing organizations later did much to change this, at least with children, throughout the twentieth century, but most of the children who performed did not continue to do so after completing school. For a time (until the 1930s) it was common for industry to sponsor choruses, bands, and orchestras comprised of their own employees; some industrial music ensembles still exist. This was a generous and humanistic aspect of some American industrial corporations, but as industry continued to grow and become more impersonal, and world economic and political conditions changed societal behavior, normal human relations suffered in the increasingly industrialized society. Music performance by co-workers became uncommon. It has been replaced in many instances by piped-in "canned" music, which is selected for its ability to create an environment that is conducive to greater productivity by the people who work in the "musical" atmosphere. In some European countries, there are still large numbers of industrially sponsored musical organizations.

Music has become readily accessible to the American public in the form of records, radio, television, and public concerts, creating generations of music lovers who take advantage of the almost endless availability of music. However, little of the music on which Americans spend money is that which music educators have aspired to have their students appreciate. The public listens to what has not, until recently, been considered worthy material for music education. By definition, popular music is the music of the people, and it is not surprising that it is loved by the masses. Yet, even with popular music, people do not always listen—it is often "wallpaper" or "elevator" music—part of the environment that is not noticed until it is turned off.

4. Throughout most of this century, there has been great emphasis on performance in school music. This statement may appear to conflict with the previous discourse on America as a nation of listeners, but student performers have usually become listeners after leaving their school ensembles. The quality of performance in American music education is excellent, and we have set an example for the rest of the world in that regard. Large ensemble performance, however, is somewhat restrictive to individuals who learn to play second violin parts, third clarinet parts, tuba parts, and so forth to the best of their abilities. The participants in the Yale Seminar (chapter 2) pointed out that this does not necessarily constitute music learning. The student musician who can play one particular part to a major symphony or a Sousa march does not necessarily know anything else about the music, and has not necessarily developed much musical independence by playing that part in the ensemble. In that regard, performance in a chamber ensemble might be of more benefit in developing musicality. Large ensemble participation may be extremely gratifying to the student, especially if the ensemble performs for an appreciative audience or receives a high festival rating. The individual students are happy, proud, satisfied, and have derived pleasure from the experience. Yet they may not have learned much about music from it.

Despite the problems discussed above, American music education has helped millions of American children to learn about music, to participate in it, and to enjoy it. There are many other people, however, whose lives have not been touched by music, despite the fact that they received music instruction in the school. Change is taking place now, and that change is the subject of this book. The contemporary era of music education is a time when music teachers are very much concerned about children's affective response to music; when individual backgrounds are recognized, respected, and utilized in selecting suitable musical materials; when more people than ever (adults and children) are participating in music making; and when there is more freedom for teachers to experiment with new methods, materials, and styles of education. While there is no way of ensuring that the future adult population will be more musical than those of the past and present, American music educators seem to be more concerned about the future musical behavior and attitudes of their students than were previous generations of music teachers. That concern is often reflected in their planning. As will become evident in this book, there are signs that the contemporary era of music education is quite capable of producing an adult population that is musically literate, appreciative, and participatory.

CHANGING ATTITUDES TOWARD EDUCATION

The 1950s

American education in the 1950s was characterized by turmoil. World War II had forced us to assume the dual role of helping to rebuild those countries that had been destroyed by the war, as well as to continue our own social and economic growth. The Cold War and the Korean conflict created not only tension in all aspects of American life, but also a divisiveness in American society that was reflected in the educational structure. We feel the results of that divisiveness even now.

Fluctuating world and national conditions were so precarious that it was not possible to define the kind of world for which our schools were educating students. Sand and Miller stated:

1. Contemporary society is changing fundamentally and rapidly. It is changing so fundamentally and rapidly that we have difficulty fitting ourselves in to the present and projecting ourselves into the future. . . .
2. The almost incredible explosion of knowledge threatens to overwhelm us unless we can find, and quickly, some intelligent solutions to problems created by the new and growing wealth of information. . . .

3. Significant discoveries are being made about people and learning—
discoveries that emphasize the vast range of differences among and within
individuals and point to the great variety of ways in which people can learn.
At a time when there is so much to be learned, and so urgent a need to
learn it, we must create new teaching methods and adapt old ones to
accelerate and enrich the teaching-learning process.[9]

Throughout the 1950s the schools were attacked by both rightists
and leftists, each charging the entire educational system with anti-
intellectualism. As the decade progressed, industrial, military and
educational leaders became increasingly aware of the fact that educational change was needed if the demands of society were to be met.
A climate of urgency developed and was greatly intensified when, in
October 1957, the Soviet Union launched Sputnik I. This was a shock
for the American people; it told them that the Soviet Union had
overtaken the United States in space technology. Thus the need for
improved education was not only based on the requirements of
improved living standards, but also on a struggle for national survival.
Starting in 1958, the rate of change in American education accelerated
dramatically.[10] An analysis of change in the New York State public
schools indicated that the rate of innovation more than doubled in the
fifteen months following the launch of Sputnik I. Change was spurred
by vocal and provocative education critics, such as Vice Admiral Hyman
G. Rickover, who directed the development of the United States Navy
atomic submarine program. Rickover's influence in forcing American
education to prepare students for needs of a technological age was
strong:[11]

Russia has built an educational system in record time which produces exactly
the sort of trained men and women her rulers need to achieve technical
supremacy. . . . Russia has no substandard teachers . . . students are
studious, polite, well-disciplined, and earnest. . . . [Students] have no
competing attractions, no comfortable homes, no playrooms, no jukeboxes,
no senior proms, no dating, hardly any radio or TV, and no hot rods.

Rickover was aware that the lack of intellectual freedom in the
Soviet Union was the cause of its second-rate art, literature, and theatre,
but he felt it was more important to produce scientists and engineers.
The fact that the Soviet Union had overtaken the United States in
the space race indicated weakness in our society. To remedy the
weakness, it was necessary to accord the highest status in our society
to scientists and engineers, and to reorganize American education to
strengthen science education. Rickover compared American and European education and found the American system lacking. European
education, as he perceived it, provided the essential intellectual, cultural,
and physical requirements. Students who were unable to meet
requirements were given vocational training. To him, the American

system wasted precious resources by attempting to educate everyone, regardless of ability. Such activities as field trips, assemblies, artistic endeavors, and extracurricular activities were further evidence of waste in education. He strongly recommended that more money be spent on education, that science and math offerings be strengthened, and that all frills be eliminated from the curriculum.

Another influential education critic was Dr. James Bryant Conant, formerly president of Harvard University, who stressed the need for stronger academic preparation. Conant's view was somewhat broader than that of Rickover. Conant stressed the need for stronger math and science programs, but he recommended that students be urged to include art and music in their high school elective programs. However, little emphasis was placed on this recommendation, which was one of many that he made for improving American high schools.[12]

Rickover, Conant, and other critics brought awareness of the importance of what were considered to be the most basic subjects—reading, mathematics, science, and foreign languages.

National attention to education was further magnified by the increased involvement of the federal government. In 1960 President Eisenhower appointed eleven distinguished Americans to the Commission on National Goals. One of the areas addressed by the commission was education. The final report, "National Goals in Education," known as the Gardner Report (prepared by John W. Gardner, president of the Carnegie Corporation), was a strong statement of educational philosophy and goals that served as a basis for change in American education. In 1961 President Kennedy established the White House Panel on Educational Research and Development (an advisory board to the U.S. Office of Education, the National Science Foundation, and his own science adviser) to help improve American education. The panel determined three goals for itself. The immediate goal was to address the issue of urban education, which was failing miserably in preparing urban students for American society. The second goal was to improve instruction through new and daring curricula, and was to be paralleled by more effective recruiting and training of teachers. The third goal was to attempt to solve the problems caused by lack of understanding of the nature of learning.[13]

An important event in American education in 1959, when the Woods Hole (Massachusetts) Conference took place. The purpose of this conference was to discuss the problems of science education and to recommend solutions. The conference was convened by the Education Committee of the National Academy of Sciences and was supported by the Academy, the U.S. Office of Education, the Air Force, and the Rand Corporation. The ten-day conference was attended by educators, historians, physicists, biologists, psychologists, and mathematicians.

This was the beginning of an educational trend—the unified efforts of distinguished people in varied fields addressing themselves to the general improvement of education.[14]

The Woods Hole Conference generated many curriculum studies in academic subjects. A 1962 study listed ten projects in science, eleven in mathematics, one in language arts, two in foreign languages, and four in social studies. In 1961 the National Education Association sponsored a large-scale "Project on Instruction," which involved scholars in all disciplines.[15]

The federal government strongly supported change in education. The Cooperative Research Branch of the Office of Education disbursed approximately $10 million a year from 1956 to 1961 for 407 research projects. The National Science Foundation granted $159 million in 1960, $34 million of which went to teacher improvement institutes that served 31,000 teachers. In 1961 more than half of all funds granted by large foundations went to educational enterprises.[16]

The vast amounts of resources that were poured into education in the late 1950s and early 1960s were mostly for the improvement of curricular areas directly related to the perceived needs of the postindustrial technological society. The arts were not excluded from the movement, but neither did they receive generous support from it. The attention of the nation was focused on what were considered to be the basic subjects. The arts were often thought of as educational frills that contributed little to the needs of children. Some school systems went to extremes to create a sharp dichotomy between what was considered the solid courses and those deemed extraneous:

One school system labels as "food for thought" content of mathematics, science, English, history, and foreign language courses. Electives are called "desserts" and are used mainly to tempt the appetites of students who are not college bound.[17]

The implications of an unbalanced curriculum were clear to many educators. One group that was disturbed by the growing apathy to the arts in education was the American Association of School Administrators (AASA). In 1959 the AASA issued the following statement:

The American Association of School Administrators commends the president, the Executive Committee, and the staff for selecting the creative arts as the general theme for the 1959 convention. We believe in a well-balanced school curriculum in which music, drama, painting, poetry, sculpture, architecture, and the like are included side by side with other important subjects such as mathematics, history, and science. It is important that pupils, as a part of general education, learn to appreciate, to understand, to create, and to criticize with discrimination those products of the mind, the voice, the hand, and the body which give dignity to the person and exalt the spirit of man.[18]

The arts received support from the Project on Instruction, sponsored by the National Education Association. The project report stated:

Priorities for the schools are the teaching of skills in reading, composition, listening, speaking (native and foreign languages), and computation . . . ways of creative and disciplined thinking . . . competence in self-instruction and independent thinking . . . fundamental understanding of the humanities and the arts, the social sciences and the natural sciences, and in literature, music, and the visual arts . . . health education and physical education.[19]

Concern was also voiced by scientists who were alarmed by the curricular imbalance. The Panel on Educational Research and Development was an advisory body of nongovernmental experts that recommended action to the National Science Foundation, the U.S. Office of Education, and the President's Office of Science and Technology.

Certain members of the Panel were convinced that there was a degree of correlation between excellence in scientific achievement and the breadth of an individual's human experience. The best scientists, it was thought, were not necessarily those who had devoted themselves singlemindedly to their own field; somehow, familiarity with the arts and humanities sharpened a good scientist's vision.[20]

The 1960s

The events of the 1950s led to significant changes in American education during the 1960s. The increased attention given to what were considered the "basic" subjects helped to increase scores on the Scholastic Achievement Tests (SAT). In 1957 the mean math SAT score was 496. It rose to an all-time high of 502 by 1963. The support for arts education voiced by administrators, scientists, and education critics was effective, and the arts retained a fairly strong position in American education. Economically, the 1960s was a time of strength for education because the "baby boom" that followed World War II generated high enrollments. The maturation of that generation, combined with the social reform movements of the 1960s, changed the character of American education. The youth movement of the 1960s led to the development of a stronger voice in the making of educational decisions by young people. This in turn led to an enlargement of the curriculum, resulting in numerous courses of study being offered in elementary, junior high, and high schools in "soft" areas, i.e., decision making, attitudinal development, surveys of areas of interest to students, etc. Such expansion was accompanied by an enrollment decline in the traditional areas of the curriculum, including math, science, English foreign languages, classical studies, and the arts. The competition for students between the various curricular areas contributed to a general lowering of standards that continues into the 1980s. Another contributory factor to the decline was the need to prepare enough teachers to staff the newly enlarged schools. It is generally recognized that standards of teacher education also declined. Combined with traditionally low teacher salaries, this tended to discourage people of the highest ability from entering the teaching profession.

By the end of the 1960s, portents of future problems were appearing. Like the period immediately preceding the Great Depression of 1929, it was a time of plenty for education. Unlike the Great Depression, the deterioration of quality in education was gradual and insidious. The SAT scores had begun a downward trend. The American public somewhat uneasily supported the curricular trend away from traditional subjects. It was thought that the new technological society required that education attend more than ever to the needs and desires of individuals. School personnel and their boards of education in all parts of the country agreed that the schools had become more humanistic, and accepted that as a trade-off for the lack of strong behavioral and intellectual discipline in the schools. The change in direction was at least partly in response to the rise in juvenile delinquency, which had become an increasingly severe problem all over the country. Delinquency was often related to the drug culture that had developed during the 1960s. These problems were taken by many to be evidence of the dangers of the dehumanized technological society, and the response was to attempt to humanize the curriculum by making it more responsive to student desires. In many cases, the result was that students were encouraged to "get in touch with their feelings" and "discover themselves." This attitude was manifested in the curriculum in the form of courses in which students learned about subjects, but did not actually learn much content in the various disciplines. The wisdom of hindsight tells us that it was an experiment that did not work, but the exigencies of American society and education during the 1960s led inexorably to those developments. By the end of the sixties, however, standards had not yet sunk to the point where alarm was being expressed by educators and the public—that was to happen a decade later.

The 1970s

Education in the 1970s was characterized by decline. During the early part of the decade, world economic conditions were severely affected by greatly increased oil prices. The ensuing inflation seriously hampered the ability of local school districts to maintain previous levels of funding. The states were faced with similar problems and were unable to make up for the shortages faced by local school districts. The federal government, which had been highly supportive of education for over a decade, was faced with new problems in social policy, foreign affairs, and economics. Attention was shifted from education, as was federal support.

School enrollments were also down because the "baby boom" following World War II had provided only a temporary boost during the 1960s. To meet that upsurge, school resources had expanded in the 1960s. New buildings were constructed and faculties were increased to staff them. When the student population decreased in the 1970s, fewer teachers were needed, and it was often the music positions that were discontinued. The number of music teaching positions declined significantly, as did positions in art and other subjects.

One of the ways in which boards of education cut costs was to reduce the number of periods in the school day, thus reducing the number of electives that could be taken by students. This, too, had the effect of reducing both the number of music teaching positions and the availability of music courses as electives for students. Declining enrollments also caused many schools to be closed, and the student bodies of two or more underenrolled schools to be consolidated; this was another cause of the reduced number of music teaching positions.

By the end of the decade, it was generally recognized that the quality of education was at such a low level that the nation had to deal with it quickly and effectively. In 1980 the average math SAT score had plunged to an all-time low of 466. Juvenile crime, drugs, and other social problems had created even more problems for the schools than they had experienced a decade earlier, when they had been considered extremely serious. Equally important was the fact that public confidence in the nation's schools had dropped precipitously.

Earlier in the seventies, as awareness of the situation was beginning to grow, an accountability movement developed. Various accountability devices in many school districts were implemented as a panacea for declining performance by students and teachers. Although it did not prove to be a cure, the movement helped to clarify the goals and objectives of education and provided a needed tool to measure the educational growth of individuals and the effectiveness of the educational system. Later in the decade, as the public became increasingly aware of the continuing decline of its educational system, there began to be heard calls for reform from educators and from spokespersons for business, industry, the military, and the general public. The desire for reform developed into a "back-to-basics" movement, a somewhat nebulous attempt to restore the schools to their old practices of requiring study of "basic subjects," eliminating "frills," and expecting reasonably high standards of students and teachers. In fact, history was being repeated because the back-to-basics movement was strikingly similar in many ways to the public outcry for higher educational standards after the launch of Sputnik I in 1957. Even the aspect of alarm raised after the Soviet Union took the lead in the space race was repeated in the 1983 report of a major panel charged with examining the educational system and making recommendations. It was titled "A Nation at Risk: The Imperative for Educational Reform."

The 1980s

By the turn of the decade, there was general recognition that something had to be done to improve American education. Although the problem was national in scope, education has usually been a local and state matter. Despite the concern expressed by the President of the United States and the Congress, practical decisions are made by state and local boards of education and superintendents. The greatest part of educational funding is provided by states and localities. Because there are approximately 16,000 school districts in the United States, it is virtually impossible to achieve uniformity of quality on a national scale. All that can be done is to identify the problems, recommend solutions, and hope that the states and localities find the will and the resources to bring about reform.

A number of factors contributed to the problems in American schools in addition to the ones discussed above. The fifty years leading to the 1980s saw a drop in the number of school districts from 130,000 to 16,000. The percentage of classroom teachers in the total school staff declined from 96 percent to 86 percent, and the amount of school support from local governments declined from 83 percent to 43 percent. During the same period, the population almost doubled, and the per student cost increased almost 500 percent.[21]

NATIONAL REPORTS ON AMERICAN EDUCATION

In 1983, following years of increasingly harsh rhetoric about poor educational quality, several reports were released to inform the public about various studies that had been completed and their recommendations for proposed solutions to the problems. Some of the more significant reports are discussed briefly here.

The National Commission on Excellence in Education

The National Commission on Excellence in Education, a presidential commission, released a report entitled *A Nation at Risk: The Imperative for Educational Reform* in April 1983. It echoed the calls for reform heard in 1957:

If an unfriendly foreign power had attempted to impose on America the mediocre educational performance that exists today, we might well have viewed it as an act of war. As it stands, we have allowed this to happen to ourselves. We have even squandered the gains in student achievement made in the wake of the Sputnik challenge. . . .

The report listed numerous defects in the educational system, making the point that, by any of a number of measures, the quality of American education had declined significantly. The current level of mediocrity was unlikely to produce an educated adult population capable of living productive and satisfying lives in the increasingly technological world community. As other nations overtook us in educational matters, the United States could be expected to fall behind economically, thus leading to a lower quality of life. The findings of several sociological and economic studies have indeed shown that several nations have surpassed the United States in quality of life. The commission reported on the following problems.

CURRICULUM

"Secondary-school curricula have been homogenized, diluted, and diffused to the point that they no longer have a central purpose. In effect, we have a cafeteria-style curriculum in which the appetizers and desserts can easily be mistaken for the main course. . . . " It was pointed out that only 31 percent of recent high school graduates complete intermediate algebra, 13 percent French I, 16 percent geography, and 6 percent calculus. "Twenty-five percent of the credit earned by general-track high school students are in physical and health education, work experience outside the school, remedial English and math, and personal service and development courses, such as training for adulthood and marriage."

TIME IN CLASS

"(1) Compared to other nations, American students spend much less time on school work; (2) time spent in the classroom and on homework is often used ineffectively; and (3) schools are not doing enough to help students develop either the study skills required to use time well or the willingness to spend more time on homework."

TEACHING

"Too many teachers are being drawn from the bottom quarter of graduating high school and college students. . . . The teacher-preparation curriculum is weighted with courses in 'educational methods' at the expense of courses in subjects to be taught." The report also indicated that teachers' salaries were too low and that there were shortages of teachers of math, science, and foreign languages and for the gifted and talented, language minority, and handicapped students. Also, a large proportion of mathematics, science, and English teachers were unqualified to teach those subjects.

CONTENT

Among the recommendations of the commission were the following:

At a minimum, all students seeking a diploma be required to lay the foundation in the Five New Basics by taking the following curriculum during their four years of high school:

(a) four years of English
(b) three years of mathematics
(c) three years of science
(d) three years of social studies, and
(e) one-half year of computer science

For the college-bound students, two years of foreign language was recommended. "A high level of shared experience in these basics, together with work in the fine and performing arts and foreign languages, constitute the mind and spirit of our culture. . . . ."

Two of the specific recommendations also mention the arts:

7. The high school curriculum should also provide students with programs requiring rigorous effort in subjects that advance students' personal, educational, and occupational goals, such as the fine and performing arts and vocational education. These areas complement the New Basics, and they should demand the same level of performance as the basics.
8. The curriculum in the crucial eight grades leading to the high school years should be specifically designed to provide a sound base for study in those and later years in such areas as English language development and writing, computational and problem solving skills, science, social studies, foreign language, and the arts. These years should foster an enthusiasm for learning and the development of the individual's gifts and talents.

Other recommendations were made to (1) increase standards and expectations of students; (2) improve the preparation of teachers, the quality of their work, the amounts of their salaries, and offer substantial economic and professional incentives for outstanding teachers; and (3) hold elected officials and educators responsible for providing the leadership to bring about reform.

Making the Grade: The 20th Century Fund Task Force on Federal Elementary and Secondary Education Policy

The 20th Century Fund Task Force released its report in May 1983. The task force called on "the executive and legislative branches of the federal government to emphasize the need for better schools and a better education for all young Americans." It recommended that: (1) a national master teacher program be established to recognize and reward excellent teachers; (2) "the federal government clearly state that the most important objective of elementary and secondary education in the United States is the development of literacy in the English language"; (3) various actions be taken by the federal government to improve science, math, and foreign language education and special education programs; to fund education; and to utilize research to improve education. No mention was made of music and arts education. Whether the report alluded to arts education can only be inferred from the following quotation.

While we strongly favor maintaining the diversity in educational practices that results from the decentralization of the schools, we think that schools across the nation must at a minimum provide the same core components to all students. These components are the basic skills of reading, writing, and calculating; technical capabilities in computers; training in science and foreign languages; and knowledge of civics, or what Aristotle called the education of the citizenry in the spirit of the polity.

As we see it, the public schools, which constitute the nation's most important institution for the shaping of future citizens, must go further. We think that they should insure the availability of large numbers of skilled and capable individuals without whom we cannot sustain a complex and competitive economy. They should foster understanding, discipline, and discernment, those qualities of mind and temperament that are the hallmarks of a civilized polity and that are essential for the maintenance of a domestic tranquility in a polyethnic constitutional democracy. And they should impart to present and future generations a desire to acquire knowledge, ranging from the principles of science to the accumulated wisdom and shared values that derive from the nation's rich and varied cultural heritage.

The National Task Force on Education for Economic Growth

The National Task Force was created by the Education Commission of the States and composed of state government and education leaders. Its report was released in June 1983. The focus of the report was the relationship between national economic and business stability and education. The task force recommended higher teacher salaries, longer school days combined with more homework, revision of state teacher certification rules (to permit qualified people from business and industry to teach), and an increased partnership between public schools and industry.

The National Science Board Commission on Precollege Education in Mathematics, Science and Technology

The Commission, a panel of the National Science Foundation, published its report in September 1983. It was entitled "Educating Americans for the 21st Century: A plan of action for improving mathematics, science and technology education for all American elementary and secondary students so that their achievement is the best in the world by 1995." The report urged the federal government to take a leadership role in education, warning that the United States "must not become an industrial dinosaur," and stated: "The nation that led the world into the age of technology is failing to provide its own children with the intellectual tools needed for the 21st century." The report also recommended a longer school day, more required courses for high school graduation and admission to college, and higher teacher pay. Although not supporting arts education in terms as strong as those used by scientists after the launch of Sputnik I, the report stated:

The Commission recognizes . . . the interrelationships among all areas of learning, and that there are also glaring deficencies in the teaching and learning of English and foreign languages, history, political science, the classics, art, music and other areas of study important for life in the 21st century. Plans and programs to meet these problems are vital. The commission hopes such plans and programs will be developed with the same time schedule in mind.

The College Board Study

The document that offered the greatest support to arts education, and one of the most practical of all the reports in terms of implementation, was "Academic Preparation for College: What Students Need to Know and Be Able To Do," published in 1983 by the College Board. The College Board publishes tests and provides other educational services for students, schools, and colleges. It is highly influential in such areas as college admissions and high school curriculum. The report is a part of the Educational Quality Project, "a ten year effort of the College Board to strengthen the academic quality of secondary education and to ensure quality of opportunity for postsecondary education for all students."

The report first identified the desired outcomes of precollegiate education and then the basic academic competencies. They are reading, writing, speaking and listening, mathematics, reasoning, and studying. Included among the basic academic subjects are English, the arts, mathematics, science, social studies, and foreign languages. Because of its potential importance, a major section of the arts section is quoted here.

WHY?

The arts—visual arts, theater, music, and dance—challenge and extend human experience. They provide means of expression that go beyond ordinary speaking and writing. They can express intimate thoughts and feelings. They are a unique record of diverse cultures and how these cultures have developed over time. They provide distinctive ways of understanding human beings and nature. The arts are creative modes by which all people can enrich their lives both by self-expression and response to the expressions of others.

Works of art often involve subtle meanings and complex systems of expression. Fully appreciating such works requires the careful reasoning and sustained study that lead to informed insight. Moreover, just as thorough understanding of science requires laboratory or field work, so fully understanding the arts involves first-hand work in them.

Preparation in the arts will be valuable to college entrants whatever their intended field of study. The actual practice of the arts can engage the imagination, foster flexible ways of thinking, develop disciplined effort, and build self-confidence. Appreciation of the arts is integral to the understanding of other cultures sought in the study of history, foreign language, and social sciences. Preparation in the arts will also enable college students to engage in and profit from advanced study, performance, and studio work in the arts. For some, such college-level work will lead to careers in the arts. For many others, it will permanently enhance the quality of their lives, whether they continue artistic activity as an avocation or appreciation of the arts as observers and members of audiences.

WHAT?

Students going to college will profit from the following preparation in the arts.

- The ability to understand and appreciate the unique qualities of each of the arts.
- The ability to appreciate how people of various cultures have used the arts to express themselves.
- The ability to understand and appreciate different artistic styles and works from representative historical periods and cultures.
- Some knowledge of the social and intellectual influences affecting artistic form.
- The ability to use the skills, media, tools, and processes required to express themselves in one or more of the arts. College entrants also will profit from more intensive preparation in at least one of the four areas of the arts: visual arts, theater, music, and dance. . . .

If the preparation of college entrants is in *music*, they will need the following knowledge and skills.

- The ability to identify and describe—using the appropriate vocabulary— various musical forms from different historical periods.
- The ability to listen perceptively to music, distinguishing such elements as pitch, rhythm, timbre, and dynamics.
- The ability to read music.
- The ability to evaluate a musical work or performance.
- To know how to express themselves by playing an instrument, singing in a group or individually, or composing music.[22]

The Paideia Proposal

The Paideia Proposal, the result of the work of the Paideia Group, was written by Mortimer Adler. It proposed that there be no electives in the curriculum, and that all students take the same three-part course of study. The three parts do not correspond to specific separate courses:

1. acquisition of organized knowledge by means of didactic instruction, lectures and responses, textbooks, and other aids in three subject areas—language, literature, and the fine arts; mathematics and natural science; and history, geography, and other social studies.
2. development of intellectual skills and skills of learning by coaching, exercises, and supervised practice in reading, writing, speaking, listening, calculating, problem solving, observing, measuring, estimating, and exercising critical judgment.
3. enlarged understanding of ideas and values by means of Socratic questioning and active participation in the discussion of books and other works of art and involvement in artistic activities such as music, drama, and visual arts.[23]

The Carnegie Foundation for the Advancement of Teaching

The Foundation released its report, written by its president, former United States Commissioner of Education Ernest Boyer, in 1983. It was entitled *High School: A Report on Secondary Education in America*. Boyer identified one of the major problems of education as a sense of powerlessness among teachers: "A welter of routine procedures and outside interruptions . . . often dominate life . . . and, in the end, restrict learning." Discipline problems, low teacher pay, and insufficient teacher discretion in selecting textbooks and developing lesson plans were also identified as problems. Boyer recommended that the first two years of high school be dominated by a core curriculum of required courses, including the arts. Electives and specialized studies would be permitted during the final two years. According to Boyer, "The arts are an essential part of the human experience. They are not a frill. We recommend that all students study the arts to discover how human beings use nonverbal symbols and communicate not only with words but through music, dance, and the visual arts."[24]

A Place Called School

A Place Called School, by John Goodlad, strongly supports arts education. Goodlad proposes that from 10 to 15 percent of each student's program be in the arts. Another 10 to 20 percent should be reserved for the development of student interests and talents; much of this time would be used for arts activities by those students who so wish. Goodlad refutes the argument that there is not enough time in the school day for all of the subjects that need to be offered in a curriculum of high quality. He points out the ways in which a great deal of time is wasted because of current practices, and recommends how subjects can be scheduled more efficiently and effectively.

Horace's Compromise: The Dilemma of the American High School

Theodore Sizer, former Dean of the Harvard Graduate School of Education and Headmaster of Phillips Academy, created the fictional Horace Smith, a composite character representing all high school English teachers. Although motivated to teach well, he knows that it is impossible to do so because of the barriers created by the educational system. There is not sufficient time to present the material that he considers important, nor is there time to prepare effectively for teaching. The students do not care; they are in school because that is where they are expected to be. Receipt of a diploma makes possible their release from the deadly and ineffective educational system.

Sizer believes that secondary education should consist of more than the development of minimum competencies in reading, writing, math, and civics. In fact those competencies should be developed prior to beginning high school. He recommends a four-part curriculum consisting of inquiry and expression, mathematics and science, literature and the arts, and philosophy and history. Teachers would utilize the Socratic method, by which they could assist students in discovering knowledge, rather than feeding them random bits of information as in the traditional teaching role.

"Horace's Compromise" is the first installment of a five-year study sponsored by the National Association of Independent Schools and the National Association of Secondary School Principals.[26]

Summary of National Reports

Although each report emphasizes a particular point of view, there are areas of commonality among them. In general, they agree that the goals of education need to be clarified. Those commissions interested in particular disciplines, such as math and science, tend to recommend goals that support science and technology. Commissions that perceive education primarily as preparation for work tend to downplay the importance of education for personal fulfillment. There is agreement "that schools must continue to develop academic competencies, foster vocational skills and awareness, contribute to personal fulfillment and cultivate civic responsibility."[27]

There is also general agreement that all students should be required to complete a core curriculum. Little call is made for single-subject curricula, or single-method solutions to curriculum problems. Extraneous areas of the curriculum, those presented in "soft, nonessential courses," should be eliminated. There is disagreement about the meaning of "core curriculum," however. Some groups consider the core to be courses that should be required, and others to be a common set of concepts, principles, skills, and ways of knowing. Another area of disagreement is the relative importance of various components of the curriculum.

There is some agreement on the importance of the mastery of language. Literacy is a primary prerequisite for the study of all other subjects. Most of the reports recognized the extent of problems concerning mastery of language, and recommended that they be addressed.[28]

Arts educators were pleased to note that most of the reports, specifically the ones that were based on careful research and reflection rather than simple reaction to the national situation, were supportive of arts education. Probably the greatest disappointment to arts educators was *A Nation at Risk*, in which the arts are supported, but are subordinated to what the National Commission on Excellence in Education identifies as the basic subjects. Paul Lehman stated:

I wish that the press coverage and the public discussion of this document had reflected the emphasis it places on the arts. At the same time, I am deeply disappointed that the Commission assigned the arts to a second tier of priorities, clearly subordinate to the highest ranked fields of study. In this respect, "A Nation at Risk" is sharply at odds with most other major reports, which have included the arts among the basics.[29]

Responses to National Reports and Critics

Responses to the flurry of reports on the state of American education and their recommendations were many and varied. In general, they were fairly repetitious of the responses of two decades earlier. There was widespread agreement on the nature of the problems, and healthy discussion of the possible solutions. Having learned the danger of immediate and strong reaction from the experiences of the 1960s, numerous leaders urged that reforms be reasonable and well-planned. Fred Hechinger wrote, "The mass of proposals and contradictory remedies could well neutralize each other. A confused public may grow impatient with all the talk and counter-talk and tune out again. Then, nothing would happen beyond some minor cosmetic readjustments."[30] Diane Ravitch warned about the ineffectiveness and danger of panaceas meant to improve education. In her history of American education from 1945 to 1980, she described the equal opportunity movement as the main focus for reform at all levels of education:

Probably no other idea has seemed more typically American than the belief that schooling could cure someone's ills. As a result, sometimes schools have been expected to take on responsibilities for which they were entirely unsuited. When they have failed, it was usually because their leaders and the public alike had forgotten their real limitations as well as their real strengths.

She also wrote of her distress when an educational movement "made it possible to implement something less than the best for everybody, or to lower our ideals; but at least our ideals ought to be good ones. I think I end up finally impressed with the idea that anything that smacks of a panacea should be immediately suspect."[31]

Ravitch's warning is supported by a number of studies from the 1960s to the 1980s, which indicate that there is little relationship between the amount of money spent for education and improvement in the quality of education. Admiral Hyman Rickover, by this time retired, reiterated some of his recommendations from two decades earlier and added others. In 1983 he recommended that (1) more academically solid courses be required of all students; (2) all talented students be assured of the opportunity to achieve their intellectual potential; and (3) the system of recruiting, training, and compensating teachers be radically modified.[32]

The effect of all the reports on education was similar to that of the post-Sputnik era. The attention of the public was drawn to a few issues, often to the neglect of basic and traditional educational needs. The problem posed to the arts in such a situation is two-pronged. First, so much attention is given to English, math, the sciences, and foreign languages that the arts are neglected. Neglect leads to contempt. Slowly and insidiously, the value of the arts declines in the general perception as the problem areas grow in importance. Second, when smaller school budgets are divided among curricular areas, there is a tendency to increase support for the problem areas, thereby making less money available for the neglected ones. As arts programs weaken, their quality declines, and this provides the temptation to educational decision makers to abandon them because they are not of the highest quality. Or, as is sometimes the case, the programs are not abandoned. Instead, a lower level of quality is accepted because it is less costly, and that level then becomes the qualitative norm. This is what happened to the subject areas identified as problems in the early 1980s (English, mathematics, science, etc.) after about fifteen years of neglect and refusal to face the problem in its early stages. It is imperative that this does not happen to music education and to the other arts areas. Music educators must constantly be aware of the necessity to provide the best possible music instruction to as many students as possible, and must keep the public informed of why music is of basic importance in education. Warning of the danger of overreaction to the wave of criticism of education, John Mahlmann wrote:

. . . No one denies that the need for attention to our educational process is long overdue. The danger lies in the overreaction or "knee-jerk" reactions to certain deficiencies. If not carefully analyzed to allow sensible judgements to be made, proposed solutions could offer little improvement; indeed, they conceivably could even worsen the present situation, which has been diagnosed as inadequate.

Stated more bluntly, we cannot allow the deafening roar of the educational critics to drown out the sounds of music in the schools. The report, *A Nation at Risk*, provides a balanced picture. However, in our haste to take remedial action to combat the "rising tide of mediocrity," which, the report charges, is eroding the allocational foundations of our society, it is possible that our good intentions can cause some serious oversights.

So while we are "at risk" we will further exacerbate the situation, increase the risk, and stunt the chances for success if we are guilty of answering the call unaware of its emphasis on the important role of the arts in the education process. The real "risk" is not of failure to meet the challenges but in the dangers of overzealously attacking the system's balance of skill, knowledge and appreciation in all areas of learning.[33]

THE BEGINNINGS OF THE CONTEMPORARY ERA OF MUSIC EDUCATION

Music education in the early 1950s had changed little since the 1930s in terms of content and method. Music had been an important and successful subject in the progressive education curriculum, but, when the progressive movement waned in the 1940s, music education lost an important base of support. Because no new, comprehensive philosophy was forthcoming to guide American education, music educators did not alter their programs significantly. No new direction was indicated for curricular development; thus music education, as well as other curricular areas, remained static. Music retained a strong and secure place in the curriculum in the early 1950s, but the force of change that had overtaken American society and education after World War II was not yet spent. It gradually became obvious that music educators could not continue to offer a 1930s curriculum in a time of fast and radical societal change.

The entire school curriculum needed to be updated, but the problem was approached in a fragmented manner. Each subject area was developed as its specialists saw fit, and the growth in the various areas was uneven. This was a step backward from the holistic approach to curriculum development of the progressive education movement, which, if not entirely successful, at least perceived the entire curriculum as a single entity. Each subject area was an integral part of an overall educational pattern. Gordon Lee explains:

This climate encouraged a blurring of distinctions between the strictly academic phases of the school program and those with more obvious psychological overtones or implications. Indeed, the tendency to assess every aspect of the life of the school in terms of its impact upon the general development of personality made it difficult, if not impossible, to advance any curricular hierarchy, to support, for example, the contention that English or chemistry was more (or less) valuable than typing or home economics or basketball. On the contrary, the teacher was assumed to be operating within the bounds of a commitment to teaching itself as holistic and integrated, so that "citizenship" in the English class held a status almost as high as that accorded the performance in English, and sometimes higher.[34]

The problems created by this approach to curriculum planning and design became apparent in the late 1940s, when it was found that people recruited into the armed forces had little functional knowledge of mathematics and science. The problem was compounded by the information explosion, which forced educators to the realization that the schools would have to find more effective means of providing basic education in mathematics and science. As the amount of information continued to increase at an ever-quickening pace, so too did the process of obsolescence. Jobs that had not existed ten years earlier suddenly had to be created because the information explosion required new kinds of occupations. Many of those new jobs became obsolete as new information (and its applications) brought about even newer requirements in the job market. Quickly changing conditions required people and institutions to be extremely adaptable. Thus, another force began to work on the schools, and it continues to exert itself to the present.

It was natural that the problem of implementing immediate educational reform on a national scale would be approached by means of the subject matter itself rather than by the organizational structure of American education. Because education is controlled at the state and local levels, it was impossible to consider meaningful reform that would require the consent of thousands of educational decision-making organizations (state and local boards of education and legislative bodies). Change came about by means of curriculum development, which did not disturb the organizational framework of school systems. Curriculum development in the various subject areas began to depart from the previously favored child-centered approach to subject, or discipline-centered, approaches. It became common for curriculum developers to favor conceptual approaches to the various disciplines. The old way of imparting a body of facts to children was not sufficient at a time when so many new facts were being discovered that it was virtually impossible to choose the data that would be meaningful both in the near and distant future. Instead, curriculum came to be organized around concepts, principles, and modes of inquiry, which would make it possible for students to know how to learn what would be important for their own individual needs. The ability to think inductively in order to be able to resolve unfamiliar problems became the curriculum planners' goal for students.[35]

An important aspect of the reform movement was that its leaders were mostly from outside the education establishment. The curriculum developers were, for the most part, university professors in the various disciplines. Another significant aspect was that financial support came not from the education establishment, but from private foundations and the federal government.

The resultant problems of the fragmented approach to curriculum structure of the late 1950s and the 1960s became apparent and pressing. The emerging technological society needed an educational system that could develop in young people the ability to perceive relationships, rather than isolated fragments of knowledge, in order to be able to pull together the almost overwhelming developments in all fields of knowledge. According to Goodlad,

The curriculum and the students of tomorrow may be better served by subjects and subject combinations other than those deemed important today. But curriculum planning takes place in such a piecemeal fashion that across-the-board examination of the total school experience of children and youth is not likely to occur. In all probability, new accretions and formulations will occur in the traditional school subjects if the curriculum revision procedures of the past decade continue. But ongoing inquiry in fields not now firmly established in the curriculum is likely to go unnoticed unless we concentrate on the aims of schooling rather than on the organization of specific subjects.[36]

The "core curriculum," which had existed for some time, was emphasized in the late fifties in response to the need. Language arts, social studies, and some areas of the humanities were treated as one subject, known as "core." The core curriculum was widely adopted throughout the United States during the late 1950s, but by the middle 1960s it too had lost popularity because of its many problems, not the least of which was an inadequate supply of capable teachers. Few teachers were able to develop sufficient expertise in so broad a subject.

American education has continued to develop in a fragmented manner to the present, despite many attempts to integrate the curriculum. Although new and promising work is being done in various school systems, it is unlikely that true curricular unity will come about in the near future except in isolated schools or school systems. Disciplinary autonomy has become so firmly ingrained, and so many fundamental changes would have to be made in the organizational structures of schools and colleges that prepare teachers, that profound change is virtually impossible.

Music education experienced a certain amount of growth, development, and evolutionary change, but such activity was usually confined to individual programs because there were no effective means of broadening the impact of small-scale innovation. The lack of a central philosophy of music education restricted the development of the profession during the time that postwar America was rapidly becoming the world's first technological society.

The history of music education since the middle of the century has roughly paralleled that of other subject areas, and it is only against the background of developments in general education that change in music education can be understood. Despite the fact that change and growth have been sporadic, sometimes ill-founded and misguided, much healthy progress has been made. Many music educators have come to see the music curriculum as a microcosm of the ideal integrated general curriculum. The traditional concept of compartmentalization within the music program is beginning to give way in some places to a broader view of music as a subject of study. The areas of music performance, theory, history, and composition are being viewed by increasing numbers of music educators as a single subject, rather than as individual and independent curricular areas within the music program.

NOTES

1. Sol Cohen, ed. *Education in the United States: A Documentary History*, vol. 1 (New York: Random House, 1974), pp. 394–95.
2. Alice Morse Earle, *The Sabbath in Puritan New England* (Scribner's, 1896), quoted in Edward Bailey Birge, *History of Public School Music in the United States*, 2nd ed. (Washington, D.C.: Music Educators National Conference, 1966), p. 4.
3. William Arms Fisher, *Notes on Music in Old Boston* (Oliver Ditson, 1918), quoted in Birge, *History of Public School Music*, p. 5.
4. Alice Morse Earle, *The Sabbath in Puritan New England*, quoted in Birge, p. 4
5. "School Committee's Report," *Boston Musical Gazette*, no. 16 (5 December 1838), p. 123; also reported in Birge, *History of Public School Music*, pp. 40–50.
6. "School Committee's Report," *Boston Musical Gazette*, no. 18 (26 December 1838), p. 137.
7. Birge, *History of Public School Music*, pp. 61–62.
8. Charles E. Silberman, *Crisis in the Classroom* (New York: Random House, 1970), pp. 437, 438.
9. Ole Sand and Richard I. Miller, *Schools for the Sixties*, Report of the Project on Instruction, National Education Association (New York: McGraw-Hill, 1963), pp. vii–viii.

10. Matthew B. Miles, "Educational Innovation: The Nature of the Problem," in *Innovation in Education*, edited by Matthew B. Miles (New York: Bureau of Publications, Columbia University Teachers College, 1964), p. 8.

11. "Rickover, in Book, Attacks Schools," *New York Times*, 30 January 1959, p. 10.

12. James B. Conant, *The American High School Today* (New York: McGraw-Hill, 1959), p. 48.

13. Jerome S. Bruner, ed. *Learning about Learning: A Conference Report* (Washington, D.C.: U.S. Department of Health, Education and Welfare, Office of Education, 1966), p. iii.

14. A. Theodore Tellstrom, *Music in American Education: Past and Present* (New York: Holt, Rinehart, and Winston, 1971), p. 243.

15. Miles, *Innovation in Education*, p. 3.

16. Ibid., pp. 3–4.

17. Gordon Gardner, Leonard Grindstaff, and Evelyn Wenzel, "Balance and the Selection of Content," in *Balance in the Curriculum* (Washington, D.C.: Association for Supervision and Curriculum Development, 1961), p. 95.

18. American Association of School Administrators, *Official Report for the Year 1958*; including a Record of the Annual Meeting and Work Conference on "Education and the Creative Arts" (Washington, D.C.: American Association of School Administrators, 1959), pp. 248–49.

19. Ole Sand, "Current Trends in Curriculum Planning," *Music Educators Journal* 50, no. 1. (September 1963): 101. Reprinted by permission of Music Educators National Conference.

20. Irving Lowens, "MUSIC: Juilliard Repertory Project and the Schools," *The Sunday Star*, Washington, D.C., 30 May 1971, p. E4; this is a report of the Yale Seminar working group on "Repertory in its Historical and Geographical Contexts."

21. Milton Friedman, "Busting the State Monopoly," *Newsweek*, 5 December 1983, p. 96.

22. *Academic Preparation for College: What Students Need To Know And Be Able To Do*, copyright © 1983 by the College Entrance Examination Board, New York, Reprinted with permission.

23. Education Commission of the States, *A Summary of Major Reports on Education* (Denver: Education Commission of the States, 1983), p. 22.

24. Ernest L. Boyer, *High School: A Report on Secondary Education in America* (New York: Harper & Row, 1983), p. 304.

25. John I. Goodlad. *A Place Called School:* Prospects for the Future. St. Louis: McGraw-Hill, 1983.

26. Theodore A. Sizer. *Horace's Compromise: The Dilemma of the American High School* (New York: Houghton Mifflin, 1984).

27. *A Summary of Major Reports on Education*, p. 3.

28. Ibid.

29. Paul R. Lehman, "The Great Debate on Excellence in Education: What About the Arts," Seventh Annual Loyola Symposium, Loyola University, New Orleans, 1984.

30. Fred M. Hechinger, "Caution: Avoid Confusion on School Reforms," *Bulletin*, American Association for Higher Education 36, no. 1 (September 1983):10.

31. Diane Ravitch, *The Troubled Crusade: American Education, 1945–1980* (New York: Basic Books, 1983).

32. H. G. Rickover, "We Have Lost That Realistic Sense of Purpose," *The Washington Post*, 19 June 1983, p. B8.

33. John J. Mahlmann, "Don't Let the Education Critics Drown Out Music," *School Board News*, 21 September 1983, p. 2.
34. Gordon C. Lee, "The Changing Role of the Teacher," in *The Changing American School*, Sixty-fifth Yearbook of the National Society for the Study of Education, part II, edited by John I. Goodlad (Chicago: University of Chicago Press, 1966), p. 171; used by permission.
35. John I. Goodlad, *The Changing School Curriculum* (New York: Fund for the Advancement of Education, 1966), pp. 14–16.
36. Ibid., pp. 17–18.

BIBLIOGRAPHY

Birge, William Bailey. *History of Public School Music in The United States*. Washington, D.C.: Music Educators National Conference, 1966.

Broudy, Harry S. "How Basic is Aesthetic Education? or Is 'RT the Fourth R?'" *Bulletin*, Council for Research in Music Education, no. 57, Winter 1978, pp. 1–10.

Bruner, Jerome S., ed. *Learning about Learning: A Conference Report*. Washington, D.C.: U.S. Department of Health, Education and Welfare, 1966.

Bulletin, Council for Research in Music Education, Special Issue: Accountability, no. 36, Spring 1974.

Cohen, Sol, ed. *Education in the United States: A Documentary History*, vol. 1. New York: Random House, 1974.

Friedman, Milton. "Busting the State Monopoly." *Newsweek*, 5 December 1983, p. 96.

Gardner, Gordon; Grindstaff, Leonard; and Wenzel, Evelyn. "Balance and the Selection of Content." *Balance in the Curriculum*. Washington, D.C.: Association for Supervision and Curriculum Development, 1961.

Goodlad, John I. *The Changing School Curriculum*. New York: Fund for the Advancement of Education, 1966.

Hechinger, Fred M. "Caution: Avoid Confusion on School Reforms." *Bulletin*, American Association for Higher Education 36, no. 1 (September 1983).

Henry, Nelson B., ed. *Basic Concepts in Music Education*, Fifty-seventh Yearbook of the National Society for the Study of Education, part I. Chicago: University of Chicago Press, 1958.

Lee, Gordon C. "The Changing Role of the Teacher." In *The Changing American School*, Sixty-fifth Yearbook of the National Society for the Study of Education, part II. Edited by John I. Goodlad. Chicago: University of Chicago Press, 1966, pp. 9–31.

Leonhard, Charles. "Toward A Contemporary Program of Music Education." *Bulletin*, Council for Research in Music Education, no. 63, Summer 1980, pp. 11–19.

Mahlmann, John J. "Don't Let the Education Critics Drown Out Music." *School Board News*, 21 September 1983, p. 2.

Miles, Matthew B. "Educational Innovation: The Nature of the Problem." *Innovation in Education*. New York: Bureau of Publications, Columbia University Teachers College, 1964.

Ravitch, Diane. *The Troubled Crusade: American Education, 1945–1980*. New York: Basic Books, 1983.

Rickover, Hyman. "We Have Lost That Realistic Sense of Purpose." *The Washington Post*, 19 June 1983, p. B8.

Sand, Ole; and Miller, Richard. *Schools for the Sixties.* New York: McGraw-Hill, 1963.

Silberman, Charles E. *Crisis in the Classroom.* New York: Random House, 1970.

Tellstrom, A. Theodore. *Music in American Education: Past and Present.* New York: Holt, Rinehart, and Winston, 1971.

National Reports on Higher Education

Adler, Mortimer Jerome. *The Paideia Proposal.* New York: Macmillan, 1982.

Boyer, Ernest L. *High School: A Report on Secondary Education in America.* New York: Harper & Row, 1983.

Business-Higher Education Forum. *America's Competitive Challenge: The Need for A National Response.* Washington, D.C., 1983.

College Entrance Examination Board. *Academic Preparation for College: What Students Need to Know and Be Able to Do.* New York: The College Board, 1983.

Goodlad, John I. *A Place Called School: Prospects for the Future.* St. Louis: McGraw-Hill, 1983.

Lake, Sara. *The Educator's Digest of Reform: A Comparison of 16 Recent Proposals for Improving America's Schools.* Redwood City, Calif.: San Mateo County Office of Education, 1984.

National Commission on Excellence in Education. *A Nation at Risk: The Imperative for Educational Reform.* Washington, D.C.: U.S. Government Printing Office, 1983. Stock L065-000-00177-2.

National Science Board Commission on Precollege Education in Mathematics, Science and Technology. *Educating Americans for the 21st Century.* Washington, D.C.: National Science Foundation, 1983.

Sizer, Theodore A. *Horace's Compromise: The Dilemma of the American High School.* New York: Houghton Mifflin, 1984.

Southern Regional Education Board. *Meeting the Need for Quality: Action in the South.* Atlanta: Southern Region Education Board, 1983.

Task Force on Education for Economic Growth. *Action for Excellence: A Comprehensive Plan to Improve Our Nation's Schools.* Denver: Education Commission of the States, 1983.

2
Curricular Foundations of Music Education

THE CONTEMPORARY MUSIC PROJECT

The contemporary period of music education might be said to have begun in 1957, when the profession found itself caught up in the wave of change sweeping American education in general. In that year, the Ford Foundation began to explore the relationship between the arts and American society.[1] The philanthropic foundation solicited ideas from leaders in the arts, one of whom, composer Norman Dello Joio, suggested that a union be formed between composers and public school music programs:

Having lived the precarious life of a composer of serious music, I proposed the idea of putting young men of proven talent to work, doing what they should be doing, which was to write music.

Since there were school situations in the country that offered outlets, such as choruses, bands, orchestras, and related performing groups, it seemed logical that placing someone in this setting to serve their needs and writing for the particular and specific groups would serve to give young men an outlet, bring to the young students a needed exposure to music of our time, stimulate teachers to expand their interests in a fresher repertory, and make a general community aware of the fact that composers were living beings, functioning right in their midst.[2]

Dello Joio's suggestion resulted in the founding of the Young Composers Project in 1959. The purpose of the project, which was funded by the Ford Foundation and administered by the National Music Council, was to place young composers (not over 35 years of age) in public school systems to serve as composers-in-residence. As expressed

35

by Dello Joio, this activity was expected to benefit both the composer and the school music program. The composers, who were paid $5,000 per year, would have the opportunity to write music for specific performance media and levels of experience and proficiency, with the assurance that their music would be learned, and probably performed as well. This kind of experience would, of course, provide a healthy impetus to a young composer's career. The school systems would benefit by having available someone to write music tailored to the students and to specific occasions. A large body of new music would be added to the school repertoire. It was also anticipated that the students for whom new music would be written would develop respect and appreciation for contemporary music, and, in time, a high regard for music of the past. When that happened, many young people might no longer be satisfied with the trite, low-quality music that had long been a staple of school music programs. Students and teachers, it was believed, would come to know composers as people functioning in their midst, not elevated on a pedestal or hidden away in an ivory tower. At the same time, composers would have the opportunity to know the students and teachers not only as musicians, but also as people.

During the first year of the Young Composers Project, twelve composers were placed in school systems across the country. From 1959 to 1962, thirty-one composers participated in the program. Its success made those involved cognizant of its potential for serving both music education and composers. The composers, however, discovered that many music educators were poorly prepared to deal with contemporary music, and their reluctance to become involved with it had been passed on to their students. Yet teachers and students who gained first-hand experience with contemporary music from their young composers-in-residence were most receptive to new music. It became apparent that music educators not involved in the Young Composers Project would benefit from a training program that would enable them to use contemporary music effectively in their own programs.

In 1962 the Young Composers Project was elevated in status from a pilot program to one of the ten major programs of the Ford Foundation. The Music Educators National Conference (MENC) submitted a proposal to the Ford Foundation that the project be continued, that it be expanded to include seminars and workshops on contemporary music in the schools, and that pilot programs be established in public schools. The Ford Foundation accepted the proposal, and in 1963 awarded to MENC a grant of $1,380,000 to organize what was named the Contemporary Music Project for Creativity in Music Education (CMP). The Young Composers Project was continued under the title Composers in Public Schools. By 1968, forty-six more composers had been matched with public school systems. The five-fold purpose of the Contemporary Music Project, as stated in the proposal accepted by the Ford Foundation, was:

1. To increase the emphasis on the creative aspect of music in the public schools
2. To create a solid foundation or environment in the music education profession for the acceptance, through understanding, of the contemporary music idiom
3. To reduce the compartmentalization that now exists between the profession of music composition and music education for the benefit of composers and music educators alike
4. To cultivate taste and discrimination on the part of music educators and students regarding the quality of contemporary music used in school
5. To discover, when possible, creative talent among students.[3]

One of the first activities of the Contemporary Music Project was the establishment of sixteen workshops and seminars, held at various colleges throughout the country, to help teachers better understand contemporary music through analysis, performance, and pedagogy. Six pilot projects were also established in elementary and secondary schools to provide authentic situations for the teaching of contemporary music.

Three of the projects took place in the Baltimore, San Diego and Farmingdale, New York schools. The programs in Baltimore and San Diego were designed to serve as in-service seminars for teachers by using pilot classes at selected grade levels in various types of schools. The seminars were conducted by composers, and involved studying and analyzing contemporary music and working on musical composition assignments. The pilot classes served as laboratories for experimentation with methods and materials. The objectives of the project were to determine effective means of using contemporary music in various grades, to experiment with techniques for providing creative experiences for children and identify contemporary music that could be used for such experiences, and to serve as in-service education for teachers.

In the Baltimore project, weekly seminars were held for music teachers to improve their understanding of, and ability to use, various aspects of contemporary music, and to identify a body of music literature that could be used with children. The pilot classes were held in classes of several grades in different schools: one school in a poor section of the inner city, another in an old section of the city with average incomes, a school in a wealthy residential area, and an affluent suburban area school. There were two pilot classes in each school. The children listened and responded to, analyzed, improvised, and composed contemporary music. At the end of the pilot classes, the musical growth of the children and their attitudes toward contemporary music were considered to be substantially positive. Most of the seminar participants were music teachers, but most of the daily musical experiences of the children were the responsibility of classroom teachers. Therefore, the program was extended for one year in order to provide seminars for classroom teachers. Three seminars on creativity were held during the 1964–65 school year. The topics were "Sounds Around Us," "Creative Interpretation of Contemporary Music," and "Improvisation and Composition." The purpose of the seminars was to show teachers how to encourage and guide children to compose in a free style and rearrange, or change, a given element of music to compose a piece.

The organization of the San Diego project included a two-hour weekly seminar for teachers and three pilot classes to implement the work of the seminars. The pilot schools included an upper-lower-class elementary, an upper-middle-class elementary, and a lower-class junior high. The highest priority was given to the "development of creative approaches to the presentation of recorded contemporary music." The work of the seminars and pilot classes resulted in the following conclusions:

1. Music in the twentieth century idiom is appropriate for and interesting to children at any age level. The earlier it is presented, the more natural the enthusiasm is likely to be. Young children should be exposed to the sound of contemporary music before they are able to intellectualize about it.
2. Activities related to contemporary music, such as compositions for percussion instruments, synthetic scales, and new sound sources provide a unique medium for creativity. The student with little or no background in theory and harmony can "create" with enthusiasm and success and, thus, gain a first-hand contact with music that he might otherwise miss.
3. Active involvement with the elements or compositional techniques employed contributes to a more effective listening experience for students at all age levels.
4. Basic goals and teaching techniques for the use of contemporary music at these levels do not differ appreciably from those used for the successful presentation of any music. Thus, a skillful teacher of music who possesses or acquires some knowledge of contemporary music literature should be able to apply it in the classroom situation. Greater emphasis on twentieth century music at the level of teacher education would help teachers feel more secure in presenting this music to children.
5. A background in "traditional" music is not necessary as a prerequisite for listening to twentieth century music; however, approaches need to be adapted to the background of the group.
6. One of the major goals in presenting twentieth century music to children should be to help them grow in listening discrimination, in order that they will gradually be able to be selective in their choice of contemporary music.
7. Additional contemporary selections that are short in length and simple in structure need to be located or composed, in order that they might be incorporated into the larger program of music education.[4]

The Farmingdale, New York approach was unique in that it involved thirty-one musically talented children from grades 6 through 8. The purposes of this project, held in the summer of 1964, were to demonstrate experimental techniques in twentieth-century musical idioms and to develop musical resources through rhythmics, singing, improvisation, and composition. The students were divided into two groups. One explored musical creativity using current techniques. The other explored musicianship through rhythm studies and movement, based on the ideas of Emile Jaques-Dalcroze. This group learned from intrinsic, rather than extrinsic, sources. The approaches used in the two groups were not compared; no assumption was made concerning the superiority of either. Rather, attention was focused on the interrelationship of the two approaches; it was concluded that the best method would be a combination of the two.

In 1965 the Seminar on Comprehensive Musicianship was held at Northwestern University. Its purpose was to develop and implement means of improving the education of music teachers, one of the most important functions of the Contemporary Music Project. The seminar provided the impetus for the development of comprehensive musicianship, which soon became one of the most dynamic aspects of change in music education. As William Thomson stated:

[There is] a quiet but certain revolution that now is pledged to strip the accumulation of words and procedures in our music teaching down to the true essentials, matters that are as relevant to all music, and with that as a beginning, to build up a new body of information and sets of techniques which may enable the novice musician to develop as an intelligent and concerned listener, producer, and teacher of music—music of the past, present, and future.[5]

The Northwestern University seminar established basic principles for comprehensive musicianship. Methodology and materials, however, remained to be developed. This was done at six regional Institutes for Music in Contemporary Education that conducted experimental programs in thirty-six educational institutions.

In 1967 a symposium was held at Arlie House, in Warrenton, Virginia to discuss means of evaluating comprehensive musicianship. The resultant document, *Procedures for Evaluation of Music in Contemporary Education*, offers guidelines for the evaluation of techniques and attitudes acquired through comprehensive musicianship studies. (Comprehensive musicianship is discussed more thoroughly in Chapter 5).

In 1968 the Ford Foundation gave MENC a grant of $1,340,000 to administer the Contemporary Music Project for an additional five years. MENC contributed $50,000 per year. From 1968 to 1973 the Contemporary Music Project consisted of three programs: Professionals-in-Residence to Communities, the Teaching of Comprehensive Musicianship, and Complementary Activities.

The Professionals-in-Residence to Communities program was similar to the Young Composers Project, except that composers were assigned to communities rather than to school systems. Thirteen composers served communities of various sizes and locations for two to three years, not only as composers, but also as catalysts for cultural and artistic change and growth. Many new compositions were created for these communities.

The purpose of the Teaching of Comprehensive Musicianship program was to develop approaches that could be used by teachers of comprehensive musicianship. Twenty-one teachers received grants to write curricula and develop materials and methods of teaching comprehensive musicianship at all educational levels. Several of these teachers have exerted considerable influence on music education through their publications, workshops and clinics.

The Complementary Activities program implemented and publicized the work of the Contemporary Music Project through consultative services to educational institutions at conventions and conferences, and through publications. These activities introduced thousands of music teachers all over the country to Contemporary Music Project philosophy, materials and methods. The purpose of the second national conference of this program was to identify the needs of the profession and to relate the continuation of the Contemporary Music Project to those needs. As a result, a new program, Forums on Contemporary Musicianship, was established. The Forums program attempted to bring together representatives of all aspects of the music profession in order to make plans for influencing the future of music. The forums were both local and national in scope.

When the Contemporary Music Project ended in 1973, its purpose had been fulfilled: "to provide a synthesis, a focus, for disparate activities in music, in order to give them a cohesion and relevance in our society, to its cultural and educational institutions and organizations.[6] The Contemporary Music Project had given direction, provided challenges, developed methodology and materials, and made the music education profession more open-minded toward change and innovation.

Louis G. Wersen, President of MENC, summarized the four main issues that represented to him the essence of all CMP programs.

1. The role of the teacher transcends the mere technical training of his students, and encompasses the development of their inner musicality.
2. The student should be encouraged to assume responsibility for his own musical growth, and in some cases the best thing for the teacher to do is simply to avoid inhibiting that growth.
3. The development of the teacher's musicality must be accomplished in his own schooling, and must continue in his subsequent career as a teacher.
4. The bringing together of a variety of musical and educational points of view to formulate the CMP programs is an exemplary technique to be followed in future efforts to improve music education.[7]

THE YALE SEMINAR ON MUSIC EDUCATION

The Yale Seminar on Music Education took place at Yale University 17–28 June 1963 to consider the problems facing music education and to propose possible solutions. The initial impetus of the seminar was the National Science Foundation, which had sponsored science curriculum development in the late 1950s when the United States lagged behind the Soviet Union in space technology. The success of the National Science Foundation in science education was one of the factors that led to President Kennedy's appointment of the Panel on Educational Research and Development. Some of the members of the panel expressed reservations about the heavy emphasis on the sciences in the then-emerging school curriculum. They felt that serious study of the arts and humanities would enhance excellence in science. It was recognized that students would be stronger in science if they were exposed to the view of human experience as seen through the arts. That so many successful scientists were also accomplished musicians was seen as evidence of this. The panel recommended that the kindergarten through twelfth grade (K–12) music curriculum of previous decades be examined to discover why public school music programs had not produced a musically literate and active public. The recommendations of the panel resulted in a grant awarded to Yale University by the U.S. Office of Education Cooperative Research Program (established in 1954). Claude V. Palisca, professor of music at Yale University, was appointed director of the Yale Seminar. Participants in the seminar included thirty-one musicians, scholars, and teachers who were concerned with the improvement of music education. The seminar participants identified two areas—music materials and musical performance—that required close examination, and about which recommendations would be made. The following discussion is taken from the proceedings of the seminar.

Musical Materials

The changes that took place in American education from the late 1950s on had had little effect on music education. Generally, the profession of music education had granted only limited recognition to contemporary music in its various innovative forms. Because little communication existed between musicologists and music educators, early Western and non-Western musics were seldom included in music education programs. The specific criticisms of the materials in use were as follows:

1. It is of appalling quality, representing little of the heritage of significant music.

2. It is constricted in scope. Even the classics of Western music—such as the great works of Bach, Mozart, Beethoven—do not occupy the central place they should in singing, playing, and listening. Non-Western music, early Western Music, and certain forms of jazz, popular, and folk music have been almost altogether neglected.

3. It stunts the growth of musical feeling because it is so often not sufficiently interesting to enchant or involve a child to whom it is presumed to be accessible. Children's potentials are constantly underestimated.

4. It is corrupted by arrangements, touched-up editions, erroneous transcriptions, and tasteless parodies to such an extent that authentic work is rare. A whole range of songbook arrangements, weak derivative semipopular children's pieces, and a variety of "educational" recordings containing music of similar value and type, are to be strongly condemned as "pseudo-music." To the extent artificial music is taught to children, to that extent are they invited to hate it. There is no reason or need to use artificial or pseudo-music in any of its forms.

5. Songs are chosen and graded more on the basis of the limited technical skills of classroom teachers than the needs of children or the ultimate goals of improved hearing and listening skills. This is one of the causes of the proliferation of feeble piano and autoharp accompaniments and of "sing-along" recordings.

6. A major fault of the repertory of vocal music stems from the desire to appeal to the least common denominator and to offend the least possible number. More attention is often paid to the subject matter of the text, both in the choice and arrangement of material, than to the place of a song as music in the educational scheme. Texts are banal and lack regional inflection.[8]

Despite the availability of a wealth of excellent music, the youth of America still preferred to listen to current popular music that lacked the inherent musical content of art music. School music education had done little to improve the situation. The materials of music education were not appreciably different from what they had been thirty years prior to the Yale Seminar.

Performance

Standards of musical performance had been elevated greatly in the decades before the Yale Seminar. The performance aspects of American school music programs were excellent. However, there was a surplus of competent, energetic musicians who could not be absorbed into the musical professions. The seminar participants considered it important to find a way to utilize these musicians in teaching, in performance, or in other related professions so they would not be forced into nonmusical occupations.

The instrumental music program in American education had been extremely successful and contributed much to the growth of music in American culture. The ability to develop musical skills in children had been demonstrated by teachers many times over. Increasing sales of student-model musical instruments indicated that parents and children valued musical participation. Many instrumental music programs resulted in artistic maturity for individual students and collective groups of students in ensembles. Too often, though, superficial showmanship and mass activity dominated the objectives of programs. Such objectives produced excellent performances, but did little to increase the musicality and musical appreciation of individual musicians. The participants in the Yale Seminar, therefore, considered it necessary to stimulate individual musical initiative and independence, rather than teamwork and technique.

Recommendations of the Yale Seminar

DEVELOPING MUSICALITY

The basic goal of the K–12 music curriculum should be the development of musicality. This can be accomplished through performance, movement, musical creativity, ear training and listening. Creativity, stressed by the participants as a means of developing musicality, includes the performance of original student compositions.

BROADENING THE MUSICAL REPERTORY

The school music repertory should be broadened to include the best of Western and non-Western music of all periods, as well as jazz, folk, and contemporary music. Less emphasis should be placed on music that is artificial in concept. The ability of children to perceive and appreciate a wide variety of authentic music should not be underestimated. An enlarged repertory should be made available in useful formats, perhaps in kits or packages that would include manuals and audiovisual aids.

MUSIC AS A LITERATURE

Guided listening to worthwhile music literature deserves a secure place in the music curriculum. Sequential listening experiences need to be developed for elementary and junior high school students. High school students should be offered music literature courses that provide intensive experiences with representative works. The goal should be to provide students with the tools to listen effectively and appreciatively to a variety of musical genres.

PERFORMANCE ACTIVITIES

Performance activities in schools should include ensembles for which an authentic and varied repertory has been developed. This would include symphony, string and chamber orchestras, concert bands, and various sizes of choruses. Marching and stage bands should also be included to encourage students to participate in other ensembles, rather than as ends in themselves. Small ensembles are especially importnt because they require more intense participation and are relevant for future adult musical activity. Keyboard instruction should also be available free of charge, and should be accompanied by basic musicianship and theory courses.

COURSES FOR ADVANCED STUDENTS

Advanced theory and literature courses should be available to students who can benefit from them. Advanced theory courses should be exploratory and should be structured so that students learn by discovery to understand the materials of musical composition. Advanced literature courses should not be general surveys but should concentrate on the analysis of a selected body of literature. Such music should be studied in the light of other functionally and historically related music.

MUSICIANS-IN-RESIDENCE

The increasing disparity between professional and school music should be reduced by bringing musicians, composers and scholars into the schools. Students should be given insights into how professionals think and work, and professionals should be given opportunities to help develop musicality in young people. This kind of program would also provide a link between schools and contemporary developments in the world of music.

COMMUNITY RESOURCES

School music programs should take advantage of community music resources. Such resources include professional and highly competent amateur musicians who might serve in various capacities, and community-centered ensembles that can lend support and assistance to school programs. Such support can be mutually beneficial. Community libraries of materials and research literature should also be used in conjunction with school music programs.

NATIONAL RESOURCES

Opportunities for advanced music study in metropolitan centers should be made available to all talented students throughout the country. To serve these students, such a program should set up regional cadres of teachers, a chain of state or national academies of music, drama, and dance, urban high schools of performing arts, and educational activities in community arts centers.

AUDIOVISUAL AIDS

Greater use can be made of audiovisual aids in music education in classrooms and in individualized instruction. Films, recordings, and television all have important uses in school music programs. A national research institute might develop and implement audiovisual aids for music education.

TEACHER TRAINING AND RETRAINING

The curriculum revisions suggested by the Yale Seminar cannot be implemented successfully without a related plan for teacher training and retraining. Teachers who are not musicians should be schooled in music; musicians who are not teachers should receive teacher education; music teachers should be retrained. Some means of bringing this about might be realized in university institutes and regional workshops. In addition, undergraduate and graduate music programs need to be broadened to train music teachers who can meet the demands of a curriculum that emphasizes creativity and literature.

After the Yale Seminar

The Yale Seminar participants proposed an idealistic and innovative music curriculum that was not out of step with then-recent developments in science and mathematics education. The seminar participants found that the school music program had failed to keep pace with twentieth-century musical developments. It was recommended that music be learned through its structure so that it could be truly understood. This would be done by means of studying musical elements and by performing, reacting to and listening to music.

Several of the recommendations of the seminar were already in operation in existing school music programs. For example, the development of musicality had long been a goal of American music education. Elementary music programs were commonly structured in a manner similar to that recommended; in practice, however, the philosophy was often unfulfilled. Conscientious music educators could not deny the problems of the profession that were identified by the seminar, nor could they deny the wisdom of many of the suggestions. The time was right for change.

Not all of the changes that began to occur after the Yale Seminar should be attributed to the recommendations of the seminar. Innovations in music education also came from other parts of the United States and from abroad. The value of the Yale Seminar was its contribution to the development of a climate that was conducive to change, in which the music education profession could be free of the restraints of the traditional curriculum so that serious consideration could be given to other modes of teaching. To be sure, not everyone accepted change. However, the profession in general recognized the voice of the seminar as one of wisdom, and one that articulated some of the most serious needs of the profession to help it remain viable in a society undergoing a period of rapid and radical change.

Some of the recommendations of the seminar did come to fruition. They are identified here; their manifestations are described in later chapters. Recognition by the profession of the need to place musicality at the heart of the music program was demonstrated by the widespread acceptance of new curricula, especially the techniques of Kodály, Orff, and Suzuki, and, to a lesser extent, those of Manhattanville and Carabo-Cone. Each curriculum is different, and no one student can receive the benefits of all of them. In keeping with the nature of American music education, however, adaptations have been made and are continually being made to incorporate the best aspects of all approaches into individual school music programs.

School music repertory began to improve during the second half of the 1960s. This development came about partly as a result of the germinal work of the Yale Seminar—its recommendations provided a philosophical base for the Juilliard Repertory Project (this chapter). Since the time of the seminar, and even more so since the Juilliard Repertory Project, publishers have provided books, materials and audiovisual software for the teaching of all of the categories of music recommended by the seminar. Furthermore, the music education repertory has expanded to encompass the various styles of music that had been neglected earlier.

Teaching tools, in the form of educational media, have been refined and sophisticated to a remarkable degree since the Yale Seminar. Students can now see and hear excellent performances through audiovisual programs. The wealth of media that is available to schools now, thanks to funds allocated by the federal government during the 1960s and early 1970s, has given students a wide range of musical experiences. Technology has also made retrieval of a vast amount of information accessible to students in all parts of the country.

Although no cadres of teachers, and only a few regional academies, have come into existence, quality music instruction is available in almost all parts of the country. What might be lacking in supportive resources for music instruction is often made up for by excellent materials and media, which can bring professional musical performance and innovative teaching methods to any community.

Performing arts high schools, which existed in a few major cities at the time of the Yale Seminar, have now been established in many school systems, or in some cases, under the sponsorship of states. The recommendation that professional musicians and music educators cooperate has also been fulfilled to a degree. Professional musicians now visit American schools frequently. It is not unusual for students to hear professional performances of symphonic music, chamber music, folk music, opera, and jazz in their own schools. Nor is it unusual for students to travel to concert halls to hear live music as part of their school music program. Students also have the opportunity to speak with the musicians and to know them as people, rather than only as performers. State arts councils make such opportunities available to many students in all parts of the country at nominal cost. Organizations such as Young Audiences, Inc., give professional performances in schools at reasonable cost, and the Artists in Schools Program of the John F. Kennedy Center for the Performing Arts in Washington, D.C., offers another source of professional artists for the public schools throughout the nation.

The recommendations for music literature have not been satisfied as completely as some of the other seminar recommendations, but there has been a gradual trend in many school systems toward including music literature as part of the music curriculum. Graded sequential listening experiences are presented, and in some places advanced literature and theory courses are offered.

One of the greatest areas of concern for the seminar, performance activities, has never been stronger than it is now. Although much artificial and synthetic music is still used, the repertoire of all school performance organizations has expanded dramatically to encompass a sizable body of excellent music of all periods and styles. Keyboard instruction is also increasing in American music education. Many school systems now offer group instruction via electronic piano laboratories.

Teacher training and retraining has changed radically in the United States, partly because of changing state certification requirements and partly because teacher education institutions have made serious efforts to provide their students with the best possible tools with which to practice their profession.

Because the many new school music curricula that have been implemented since the Yale Seminar require well-trained teachers to present them successfully, numerous workshops and courses for new and in-service teachers have been offered in colleges and special institutes all over the country. That so many teachers take advantage of this type of educational opportunity indicates that music educators feel the need for continuing education and are willing to invest their time, effort, and money to satisfy this need.

THE JUILLIARD REPERTORY PROJECT

An important result of the Yale Seminar was the Juilliard Repertory Project. Shortly after the conclusion of the Yale Seminar, Dean Gideon Waldrop of the Juilliard School of Music submitted an application for a grant to the U.S. Office of Education. The grant would enable Juilliard to develop a large body of authentic and meaningful music materials to augment and enrich the repertory available to teachers of music in the early grades. The application was approved, and the Juilliard Repertory Project was established in July 1964 with the composer Vittorio Giannini as project director.

At first there was opposition from music educators, who feared that Juilliard was planning a curriculum and method that would be promoted as the most effective means of teaching music. However, the music education profession was assured that the intention was to develop a library of first-rate music that would help any teacher, regardless of the method used; MENC indicated its support in the *Music Educators Journal.*

The purpose of the Juilliard Repertory Project was to research and collect music of the highest quality that could be used for teaching music from kindergarten through sixth grade. Keeping in mind the Yale Seminar criticism of the quality of music literature used for music education, the project planners and developers accepted music into the Juilliard repertory only after it was evaluated and approved by school music teachers.

The repertory was compiled by three groups: research consultants (musicologists and ethnomusicologists), educational consultants (music educators), and testing consultants (public school elementary music teachers). To develop the Juilliard Repertory Library, the entire music repertory was divided into seven categories. The research consultants appointed for each category were Gustave Reese (pre-Renaissance), Noah Greenberg (Renaissance), Claude Palisca (Baroque), Paul Henry Lang (classical), Alfred Wallenstein (romantic), Norman Dello Joio (contemporary), and Nicholas England (folk music). The contemporary music category presented difficulties; little music existed that could be used by school children. Therefore, composers were invited to write music designed for use in the schools.

After the research consultants had selected appropriate and authentic music, the approved materials were submitted to a panel of distinguished music educators—Allen P. Britton, Sally Monsour, Mary

Ruth McCulley, and Louis G. Wersen—for further consideration. The panel decided which pieces should be tested in practical classroom situations. Only those pieces that all of the consultants considered unsuitable were rejected. The tests were conducted in four moderate-size communities (Amarillo, Texas; Ann Arbor, Michigan; Boulder, Colorado; and Elkhart, Indiana), two large cities (New York and Philadelphia), and one small town (Winfield, Kansas).

Of the more than 400 compositions tested, 230 vocal and instrumental works were ultimately included in the Juilliard Repertory Library. The collection was published in two formats by the Canyon Press (Cincinnati, Ohio). The Reference/Library contains a complete copy of all of the works and is divided into vocal and instrumental sections that are further divided into seven style categories (pre-Renaissance, Renaissance, Baroque, Classical, Romantic, Contemporary, and Folk). Because of the cost and size (384 pages) of the Reference/Library, the collection is also published in eight separate volumes of vocal music and four volumes of instrumental music. Although there is no overlap of content, each volume contains a cross section of the entire collection.

The Juilliard Repertory Library Project satisfied not only the Yale Seminar requirement for high quality and authentic music for school music programs, but also the recommendation that scholars and teachers join together to upgrade music education.

In 1976, Canyon Press, Inc., with a small grant from the U.S. Office of Education, sponsored a program called "Music '76 for Young Americans" in honor of the nation's Bicentenary. Units of the Juilliard Repertory Library were offered to schools for the cost of handling and shipping. Performing groups were then asked to send Canyon Press a tape recording of one or more selections from the Juilliard Repertory Library. Through the Arts and Humanities Program of the Office of Education, a recording of the outstanding performances by the student musicians was prepared for distribution in the United States and abroad.

THE TANGLEWOOD SYMPOSIUM

The Tanglewood Symposium took place from 23 July to 2 August 1967 in Tanglewood, Massachusetts, the summer home of the Boston Symphony Orchestra. It was sponsored by MENC in cooperation with the Berkshire Music Center, the Theodore Presser Foundation, and the School of Fine and Applied Arts of Boston University. The purpose of the symposium was to discuss and define the role of music education in contemporary American society at a time when society was faced with rapid social, economic, and cultural change. It was also the intention of the participants to make recommendations to improve the effectiveness of music instruction.

The profession of music education needed to define its place in American society. In order to develop a realistic viewpoint, participants were selected as representatives of several facets of American society—sociologists, scientists, labor leaders, educators, representatives of corporations, musicians, and people involved with other aspects of music.

Background of the Tanglewood Symposium

Position papers had been published in the March and April 1967 issues of *Music Educators Journal*. The papers served as bases for discussion at the 1967 MENC Divisional Conferences and for the Tanglewood Symposium itself. Three broad questions were identified in the papers:

1. What are the characteristics and desirable ideologies for an emerging postindustrial society?
2. What are the values and unique functions of music and other arts for individuals and communities in such a society?
3. How may these potentials be attained?

The first week of the symposium was devoted to discussions of value systems as they relate to the role of the arts in society, characteristics of contemporary society, contemporary music, the role of behavioral science, creativity, and the means of cooperation between aspects of society that would allow music education to become more effective.

The week's activities were followed by a postsession. Participants were limited to music educators and consultants. The postsession participants formulated implications of the symposium, identified critical issues, and recommended appropriate actions.

The Symposium

During the first week, the participants explored many areas of the arts and society. Broad topics, called "Basic Issues," were examined and several papers delivered (see Outline 2.1).

Every participant in the postsession met with one of five groups, each of which explored specific issues. The committees submitted reports on the following topics: "A Philosophy of the Arts for an Emerging Society," "Music of Our Time," "Impact and Potentials of Technology," "Economics and Community Support for the Arts," and "The Nature and Nurture of Creativity."

OUTLINE 2.1—THE TANGLEWOOD SYMPOSIUM

The following is an outline of the activities of the Tanglewood Symposium:

FIRST WEEK—BASIC ISSUES

The Role of the Arts in a Changing Society
Potentials for the Arts in the Community
Toward the Year 2000
Prospects for the Future: Television, Symphony, Opera
Perspectives on Music and the Individual
Economics and Community Support: Perspectives
Music of Our Time

SECOND WEEK—POSTSESSION TOPICS

   I. A Philosophy of the Arts for an Emerging Society
      A. Values: Music as Means and Ends
      B. Music in the Emerging Society

   II. Music of Our Time

   III. Impact and Potentials of Technology

   IV. Economics and Community Support for the Arts

   V. The Nature and Nurture of Creativity

   VI. Problems and Responsibilities
      A. Critical Issues
         1. Music and the Inner City
         2. Music Study for All Students in the High School
         3. Music for Teen-agers
      B. Implications for Music in Higher Education and the Community
         1. College Admission, Testing, and the Musically Talented
         2. Relations with Other Disciplines—Inter- and Intra-Musical
         3. Music in the General Education of the College Student
         4. Goals of Aesthetic Education
         5. Creative Teaching of Music
         6. The Need for Highly Trained Specialists in Music
         7. Music and Libraries
         8. Continuing Education in Music

OUTLINE 2.1 (con't.)

   C. Implications for the Music Curriculum
      1. The Music Curriculum for Children
      2. The Music Curriculum for Adolescents
      3. The Other Musics—Their Selection and Use
   D. Implications for the Educational Process and for Evaluation
      1. Identification and Preparation of the Professional Music Educator
      2. Effective Utilization of New Technologies and Approaches in the Educative Process
      3. Improvement of the Teaching Process in Group Instruction
      4. Measurement of Musical Behavior
      5. Accommodating Individual Differences in Learning
      6. Curriculum Must Assume a Place at the Center of Music

 VII. The Tanglewood Declaration

VIII. General Recommendations

The committee that reported on "A Philosophy of the Arts for an Emerging Society" was charged with the consideration of values and music and of music in the emerging society. Specific issues, for which recommendations would be proposed, were defined. Some of the issues were social change, the need to strengthen human values in the midst of change, and the use of change to support constructive values. Other issues, directed more specifically to the place of music education in social change, concerned the arts as a means of transition to new values, the need for higher quality music, education as preparation for leisure, and music experiences for people of all ages. Another group of issues, concerning the relationship of the music education profession to society, included the consideration of a new aesthetic compatible with the music of a technological society, the need to keep traditions and history alive while serving an emerging society, and the need for MENC to reexamine its various functions.

The committee addressed itself to several aspects of change in American life. Rising incomes were providing people more opportunity to participate in and enjoy the arts. Shorter working hours and longer lives were giving Americans more leisure time to devote to music and other arts. Clearly, music education could become a long-term activity, with school constituting only an early stage. Because Americans had become globally oriented, they were receptive to music of other cultures. The new technology had also helped people to become aware of new sounds and new kinds of music. Technology had provided new means for music educators to carry on their activities.

Increasing technology, however, afforded people few opportunities for individual development. By their very nature, the arts promote individual development. Individual development is closely related to basic human values, which also must be one of the considerations when determining the relationship between music education and society. Such values include the realization of what is important to individuals in terms of happiness, satisfaction, and well-being in the context of society. Values are neither taught nor imposed on people—they are developed as the individual relates new experiences and perceptions to old ones. Education should help the individual to be able to explore, identify, and develop new humanistic values throughout life.

The nature of contemporary society forces us to realize that music that is new (electronic) or new only to Western listeners (music of exotic cultures) is aesthetically valid for large segments of the population. An aesthetic theory for contemporary society not only must encompass new music but also must be sufficiently precise to serve a society that is based in many ways on precise scientific principles and measurements.

Prior to the new aesthetic, art works were considered in terms of form, matter, and purpose, as well as the relationship among these three aspects. Music of the new aesthetic cannot be understood by traditional criteria. Instead, each work must be analyzed and evaluated per se. The new aesthetic has definite implications for music educators: (1) the attention of the listener is directed to the art work; (2) the listener is encouraged to develop the capacity to hear detail and to be able to express it in a consistent and creative symbolic language; (3) the development of descriptive–evaluative skills places the work of the general music student on the same level as the skill of the performer. It is imperative for the future of music that audiences have these descriptive–evaluative skills. Music educators must deal with the factual and measurable content of music in order to develop under-standing in students, who then may or may not develop appreciation for the work.

The role of the music educator in helping students to know a work places music in the academic program of the school. Music must be part of formal education because it is part of our cultural and social heritage. It is related to human nature and is one of the great challenges to the human mind.

Music educators need to prepare for tomorrow by anticipating future conditions—a different value system, a freer state of the art of music, a different kind of teaching and performing technology, and a higher level of student sophistication.

The needs of this emerging society require education to extend beyond the public school level. Increasing affluence will provide opportunities for adults to study and participate in the arts. Therefore, an additional role of the music educator will be in the field of adult education. Music can also help individuals to discover and understand themselves in a changing world.

Music and music education must be viewed as they relate to each other and to society. Four roles can be defined in the process of music— creators, distributors, consumers, and educators. Each role must be examined carefully to determine its place in the social structure. The committee concluded its report with several recommendations:

1. There should be a mechanism that allows the profession of music education to establish ongoing communication with all other relevant disciplines and interests.
2. MENC should bring to music teacher training the results of research in philosophy and the social sciences.
3. The profession of music education should direct itelf to the subject of leisure.
4. MENC should adopt a set of official positions as a basis for communication, policymaking, and guidance.
5. MENC should establish informal relationships with the Adult Education Association of the United States of America in order to foster cooperative activity and understanding.
6. MENC should direct its attention to studies of audiences, and such studies should be related to the relationship of school and community.
7. A national commission on music education should be established to confront the issues treated by the symposium.

The committee that considered the topic "Music of Our Time" was charged with the task of identifying, describing, and examining aspects of pluralism and music in American life. Music means many things to many people today. Art music has undergone a revolution. We now have not only traditional art music, but also aleatory, electronic, and serial music. Jazz has evolved into many forms, including ragtime, dixieland, big band swing, bop, funky jazz, third stream jazz, hard rock, and soul rock. Between art music and jazz is environmental, or functional, music. We also have church music, musical theatre, film and television music, social protest folk music, and ethnic and national music from all over the world.

The committee acknowledged that Americans want and need music and that there is a diversity of musical tastes in America. Music has so many dimensions now that new value judgments are needed. Educators and musicians are obliged to know and communicate new facts, to raise issues, and to study new problems. Yet, because new music proliferates so rapidly and because tastes change so fast, the question is raised of whether or not a hierarchy can and should be assigned to various kinds of music.

The committee on "Impact and Potentials of Technology" was asked to consider the changes brought about by the explosion of knowledge. Expanded technology has offered much more to education than educators have so far used. The speed of technological change often outstrips our ability to update education as new possibilities arise. The committee made the following recommendations:

1. MENC should establish a committee on Advanced Educational Technologies, whose duties would be to keep the membership informed of new developments as they apply to music education and to bring the needs of music educators to the attention of industry.

2. Selected people from MENC should learn about computer concepts to enable them to evaluate projects and provide leadership; a training program in computer technology should be made available to music educators.

3. The Educational Resources Information Center (ERIC) proposals should be put into operation as quickly as possible.

4. MENC should be concerned with the preparation of new teaching and in-service experiences in educational technology for working teachers.

The committee on "The Nature and Nurture of Creativity" discussed the nature of creativity and its manifestations in individuals. Creativity is an important part of human life. The committee report stated that "living life to the fullest suggests providing an environment for acquiring the skills needed for creative living." Creativity is latent in the human at birth. The environment of the child can stimulate or suppress its development. It is the responsibility of the school to establish an environment that encourages creativity and provides outlets for it. To do this, teachers must themselves be creative.

Music is taught and experienced in a variety of settings. Facilities and equipment must suit specific educational needs if music is to be taught creatively. The only limitations on the use of new technology in teaching music creativity should be the teacher's imagination and willingness to keep up to date. Creativity should be stressed in preservice and in-service teacher preparation programs.

The second broad area in which several committee reports were developed was "Problems and Responsibilities." The reports are identified in Outline 2.1.

The "Critical Issues" committee dealt with music in inner city schools and music in general education. It recommended that teacher education programs in music be modified or expanded to include the special skills and attitudes needed for teaching inner city children and that a new music teacher education curriculum be formulated that would attract teachers to inner city schools. Such people should be trained in actual community situations.

The committee also recommended that a commission be established to develop content and instructional processes that would make high school music education comparable in quality to other subject areas and that teacher education programs be reformed to prepare music education majors to teach music as a part of general education. Also recommended were commissions to consider the various aspects of music education for specific age groups.

The committee on "Implications for Music in Higher Education and the Community" stated that rigid admission policies sometimes deny talented students the privilege of advanced study. It recommended that the music education profession promote the recognition of precollege music study by higher education admission boards and that college admission standards be made more flexible to recognize and honor creative efforts. It was also recommended that MENC establish liaison committees with composition, musicology, and performance disciplines to encourage the exchange of ideas. Creative scholars from other fields should be included in professional music education meetings in order to provide interaction with composers, performers, and master teacher.

Some of the recommendations for music in continuing education were as follows:

1. Emphasis should be placed on music's role in the development of the whole person.
2. Humanities courses in secondary schools should be encouraged, and such courses should be required for college admission.
3. Music educators should assume leadership in developing continuing music opportunities for their communities.
4. Teacher education programs should be developed for adult and continuing music education.

The committee on "Implications for the Music Curriculum" recommended that a new elementary level music curriculum place major emphasis in four areas of music experience: (1) understanding many types of music through guided listening or performance; (2) studying music through singing, playing instruments, movement, and combinations of these; (3) arranging and composing; and (4) understanding and using music notations. Concerning the quality of music teaching, it was recommended that MENC officially take the position that a teacher with strong music preparation is needed for each school dealing with children of ages 3 through 11.

It was also recommended that all junior high school students be required to take a general music course and that all high school students be required to take at least one arts course, even those who participate in performing ensembles. In the area of instrumental music, instruments other than the standard orchestral instruments, especially social instruments, such as the guitar, should be taught.

The committee on "Implications for the Educational Process and for Evaluation" recommended that music educators establish a means of early identification of potential music educators and that this be done in conjunction with guidance personnel. MENC should develop materials to assist high school counselors to identify potential music educators and to help the students understand the advantage of an early commitment.

The Tanglewood Declaration

The Tanglewood Symposium is summarized in the statement entitled "The Tanglewood Declaration." Because it provides a philosophical basis for future developments in music education, it is quoted in its entirety in chapter 3.

THE GOALS AND OBJECTIVES PROJECT

The Goals and Objectives (GO) Project of MENC was the first step toward realizing the recommendations of the Tanglewood Symposium. The GO Project identified the responsibilities of MENC as they pertain to future professional needs.

The project began in 1969. A steering committee was appointed along with eight subcommittees, each of which was charged with the investigation of, and recommendations for, specific aspects of music education. The following topics were considered:

1. Preparation for Music Educators
2. Musical Behaviors—Identification and Evaluation
3. Comprehensive Musicianship—Music Study in the Senior High School
4. Music for All Youth
5. Music Education in the Inner City
6. Research in Music Education
7. Logistics of Music Education
8. Fact Finding
9. Aesthetic Education
10. Information Science
11. Music for Early Childhood
12. Impact of Technology
13. Music in Higher Education
14. Learning Processes
15. Musical Enrichment of National Life

16. MENC Professional Activities

17. Professional Organization Relationships

18. Music of Non-Western Cultures[9]

Each committee summarized its views on its subject. On the basis of the summaries, the committee chairpersons drafted statements for the National Committee of MENC in March 1970. The eighteen reports were abstracted and condensed, and a draft statement of goals and objectives was issued by Paul Lehman, director of this phase of the project. The statement was then subjected to further revisions by the presidents of federated and associated organizations and the chairpersons of the subcommittees. In October 1970 the MENC National Executive Board made final revisions and adopted the statement of goals and objectives that was published by MENC. In broad terms, the goal of MENC was to conduct programs and activities to build a vital musical culture and an enlightened musical public. The goals of the profession were to carry out comprehensive music programs in all schools, to involve persons of all ages in learning music, to support the quality preparation of teachers, and to use the most effective techniques and resources in music instruction.[10]

Of the thirty-five objectives listed below, the MENC National Executive Board identified eight top priority objectives on which MENC would focus its efforts on the immediate future (they are identified by an asterisk). The goals and objectives of MENC were as follows:

*1. Lead in efforts to develop programs of music instruction challenging to all students, whatever their sociocultural condition, and directed toward the needs of citizens in a pluralistic society

*2. Lead in the development of programs of study that correlate performing, creating, and listening to music and encompass a diversity of musical behaviors

*3. Assist teachers in the identification of musical behaviors relevant to the needs of their students

*4. Advance the teaching of music of all periods, styles, forms, and cultures

5. Promote the development of instructional programs in aesthetic education

6. Advocate the expansion of music education to include preschool children

7. Lead in efforts to ensure that every school system requires music from kindergarten through grade 6 and for a minimum of two years beyond that level

8. Lead in efforts to ensure that every secondary school offers an array of music courses to meet the needs of all youth

9. Promote challenging courses in music for the general college student

10. Advocate the expansion of music education for adults both in and out of school

*11. Develop standards to ensure that all music instruction is provided by teachers well prepared in music

12. Encourage the improvement and continual updating of preservice and in-service education programs for all persons who teach music

*13. Expand its programs to secure greater involvement and commitment of student members

14. Assist graduate schools in developing curricula especially designed for the preparation of teachers

15. Develop and recommend accreditation criteria for the use of recognized agencies in the approval of school and college music program and in the certification of music teachers

16. Support the expansion of teacher education programs to include specializations designed to meet current needs

*17. Assume leadership in the application of significant new developments in curriculum, teaching–learning patterns, evaluation, and related topics, to every area and level of music teaching

18. Assume leadership in the development of resources for music teaching and learning

19. Cooperate in the development of exemplary models of desirable programs and practices in the teaching of music

20. Encourage maximum use of community music resources to enhance educational programs

*21. Lead in efforts to ensure that every school system allocates sufficient staff, time, and funds to support a comprehensive and excellent music program

22. Provide advisory assistance where music programs are threatened by legislative, administrative, or other action

23. Conduct public relations programs to build community support for music education

24. Promote the conduct of research and research-related activities in music education

25. Disseminate news of research in order that research findings may be applied promptly and effectively

26. Determine the most urgent needs for information in music education

27. Gather and disseminate information about music and education

28. Encourage other organizations, agencies, and communications media to gather and disseminate information about music and education

29. Initiate efforts to establish information retrieval systems in music and education and to develop data bases for subsequent incorporation into such systems

30. Pursue effective working relationships with organizations and groups having mutual interests

31. Strengthen the relationships between the conference and its federated, associated, and auxiliary organizations

32. Establish procedures for its organizations' program planning and policy development

33. Seek to expand its membership to include all persons who, in any capacity, teach music

34. Periodically evaluate the effectiveness of its policies and programs

35. Ensure systematic interaction with its membership concerning the goals and objectives of the conference[11]

As a result of the GO Project, MENC appointed two commissions to help implement the recommendations. The MENC National Commission on Organizational Development was established "to prepare recommendations of needed changes in the organization, structure, and function of the conference including all of its federated and affiliated units."[12] The MENC National Commission on Instruction was established "to plan, manage, and coordinate a wide variety of activities, following the operational pattern that has proved highly successful for the Commission on Teacher Education."[13]

The work of the National Commission on Instruction resulted in the publication of an important work entitled *The School Music Program: Description and Standards*. The book provides: (1) a description of a quality school music program against which laypeople and professionals can compare the programs in their own schools, and (2) a set of standards with respect to requirements for curriculum, staffing, scheduling, facilities, and equipment, for use in determining proper levels of support.[14]

The School Music Program offers a measure of standards and has been used in some states for program evaluation. It was a response to the suggestion of the Tanglewood Symposium that MENC provide leadership in the development of high quality music programs in all schools.

Many of the objectives of the GO Project did not require the appointment of new committees or commissions because they could be handled by such existing bodies as the Music Education Research Council, the Publications Planning Committee, the *Music Educators Journal*, and the public relations program.[15]

In the years following the GO Project, MENC engaged in a large number of activities and projects. Not all were generated by the project, but many were influenced by it. During the 1970s, the majority of members of the MENC National Executive Board stated that they were influenced in varying degrees in their decision making by the GO Project. According to one board member,

the GO Project provided a forum for "brainstorming," in consideration of the needs of American society and our youth in particular, related to aesthetic enrichment through music. Whereas Tanglewood was the germinal definition of direction, the GO Project became the catalyst for reaction and action—a pragmatic focus.[16]

SUMMARY

The Yale and Tanglewood conferences took place when music education was in a state of flux. They identified the outdated practices, mistakes and shortcomings of the past, helped define the changes taking place, and suggested a course for the future. The Contemporary Music Project, which existed before, during, and after these conferences, proved that change could be brought about if it was based on well-defined needs and was well planned and supported by adequate personnel, facilities, and financial resources. The Contemporary Music Project, actually a laboratory for change, provided many of the ideas that were considered at Yale and Tanglewood. The Yale Seminar came at the beginning of the transitional period and accentuated the need for greater change than was taking place at the time. Although both conferences were catalysts for change, their most important function was to help define a philosophy for the profession that would guide it through the difficult transitional period by establishing goals for the future.

The Yale Seminar followed the lead of the Woods Hole Conference, which had addressed itself to the problems and solutions of science education. The Yale participants carefully defined the problems of music education and suggested remedies, some of which were implemented. A serious weakness of the seminar was that it included few representatives of MENC, the only vehicle by which broad and sweeping changes could be attempted realistically. The participants represented an impressive array of school and university teachers and administrators, professional musicians, and composers, but few of them were directly involved in school music education. Many were unfamiliar with the content and methods of music education. The Yale Seminar lacked the means and the leadership to carry out its proposals. Because little publicity was given to the seminar, its recommendations reached very few people. Furthermore, many school music educators were unhappy that public funds were used to support the seminar, which was an evaluation of the problems of the profession by people outside of the profession. Reaction to the seminar by music educators was not especially positive for the most part, and the necessity for a conference controlled by professional music educators (the Tanglewood Symposium) was felt.

The Tanglewood Symposium was sponsored by MENC, which provided the leadership for its planning, implementation, and follow-up. Thus, the symposium had the varied resources of a large and influential organization and the means to implement the resulting proposals. Effective use was made of MENC publications, committees, and conventions to bring the work of the symposium to the profession.

The scope of the Tanglewood Symposium was broad. Before considering the problems facing music education, it examined the relationship of music and music education to American society. Input received from nonmusical representatives helped the participants establish a realistic viewpoint of music in contemporary America. The next step was to determine how the music education profession could fulfill the musical needs of the nation. The recommendations of the various symposium committees served as guidelines for MENC in planning its directions and activities for the next several years.

The most important result of the Tanglewood Symposium was the establishment of a unified, eclectic philosophy of music education for an emerging society. In this respect, it completed the work begun at the Yale Seminar. The two conferences disagreed on a major point. The Yale Seminar attempted to bring American youth in touch with what was considered "good" music. For example, it recommended that stage and marching bands be included in the curriculum in order to expose students to better music. Stage and marching bands, however, were not considered to be ends in themselves. The Tanglewood Symposium not only recommended the acceptance of all kinds of music in the curriculum, but recognized that all types of music have aesthetic validity and should therefore be offered as ends in themselves. This was a reflection of the change in adult attitudes toward the younger generation in the late 1960s. As a result of extensive agitation by the "youth culture," the education establishment came to recognize and respect the rights of young people in matters of general lifestyle, including music.

Using all of its resources, MENC addressed itself to the job of translating recommendations into reality. Entire issues of the *Music Educators Journal* were devoted to single topics that had been treated as issues by the symposium. They included such topics as youth music, electronic music, music in urban education, and music in special education. Many sessions of national, regional, and state conferences brought to music educators ideas and methods for practical approaches to fulfillment of contemporary philosophy as they apply to various specific teaching situations. MENC established its Goals and Objectives Project, which functioned from 1969 to 1970. The GO Project resulted in the official adoption of objectives for MENC, many of which related directly to instruction. In 1971 the National Commission on Organizational Development and the National Commission on Instruction were appointed and charged with the responsibility for planning, organizing, and supervising activities that would help to realize the objectives. The Committee on Instruction replaced the National Commission on Instruction a few years later. Its purpose is to identify issues relating to goals and objectives and to develop position statements concerning the issues. The position statements are acted on by the MENC National Executive Board. The committee produced a book, *Selected Instructional Programs in Music*, which identified exemplary programs in thirty-seven areas of music education throughout the United States.[17]

CONCLUSION

The willingness of music educators to consider and accept new approaches may be attributed largely to the Yale and Tanglewood conferences and the Contemporary Music Project, all of which helped pull the profession together on the philosophical issue of a higher quality, more relevant education for both children and adults. By doing so, the profession gained higher stature among education leaders in all fields.

The topic of the American Association of School Administrators annual conference in 1969 was the relevance of the arts in education. Fred T. Wilhelms, Executive Secretary of the Association for Supervision and Curriculum Development, in discussing the curriculum revolution, said, "[An] area deserving criticism is the failure of schools to use literature and art to the best advantage. . . . They are the best media for clarifying values and the significance of life—'the highest form of school activity.'"[18]

Charles L. Gary, Executive Secretary of MENC, stated in a 1975 article published in the *Bulletin* of the National Association of Secondary School Principals:

For fifty years, music educators have proclaimed "Music for Every Child, Every Child for Music" through their professional organization, the Music Educators National Conference. However, many teachers, as well as principals, have focused on a narrower purpose: the highest possible performance skill to be developed in a few selected students.

Today, this limited purpose—appropriate for professionals—has little relevance to the needs of high school boys and girls in a changing society. The purpose of music education in our time is clear: to reveal to students what music can do for their lives and to offer as many opportunities for musical learning as they desire and are capable of assimilating.[19]

The above statements leave little doubt that the attitudes of music educators and other educators toward music education changed radically during the 1960s. In 1975 the Council on Basic Education (CBE), an organization dedicated to the improvement of public education in those subjects that it considers basic, added the arts to the list of subjects that it supports. The acceptance of the arts as a basic subject by CBE indicates the degree of impact of the changes of the 1960s and early 1970s.

Not all of the topics discussed in the following chapters have roots in the Yale and Tanglewood conferences or the Contemporary Music Project; in fact, most do not. That they were openly received, evaluated, and put into practice reflects the enlightened attitudes of music educators during the 1960s. It is reasonable to attribute that attitudinal change to the events described in this chapter.

NOTES

1. Much change in several curricular areas of American education was stimulated by philanthropic industrial foundations, rather than by educators.

2. Norman Dello Joio, letter to author, 6 February 1977.

3. "CMP in Perspective," *Music Educators Journal* 59, no. 9 (May 1973):34.

4. *Experiments in Musical Creativity: CMP 3* (Washington, D.C.: Music Educators National Conference, 1966), pp. 60–61. Reprinted by permission of Music Educators National Conference.

5. William Thomson, "New Math, New Science, New Music," *Music Educators Journal* 53, March 1967, p. 30. Reprinted by permission of Music Educators National Conference.

6. "Contemporary Music Project: Comprehensive Musicianship," *Music Educators Journal* 59, no. 9 (May 1973):47.

7. Louis G. Wersen, "New Directions for Music Education," *Music Educators Journal* 54, no. 7 (March 1968):66–67. Reprinted by permission of Music Educators National Conference.

8. Irving Lowens, "Music: Juilliard Repertory Project and the Schools," *The Sunday Star*, Washington, D.C., 30 May 1971, p. E4. This is a report of the Yale Seminar working group on "Repertory in Its Historical and Geographical Contexts."

9. "The GO Project: Where Is It Heading?" *Music Educators Journal* 40, no. 6 (February 1970):44–45. Reprinted by permission of Music Educators National Conference.

10. Ibid.

11. "Goals and Objectives for Music Education," *Music Educators Journal* 57, no. 4 (December 1970):24–25. Reprinted by permission of Music Educators National Conference.

12. "MENC Forms Two Commissions," *Music Educators Journal* 57, no. 8 (April 1971):47–48. Reprinted by permission of Music Educators National Conference.

13. Ibid., p. 47.

14. National Commission on Instruction, *The School Music Program: Description and Standards* (Vienna, Va.: Music Educators National Conference, 1974), p. ix.

15. "MENC Forms Two Commissions," p. 47.

16. James A. Middleton, letter to author, July 1979. Quoted in "The GO Project: Retrospective of a Decade." *Music Educators Journal* 67, no. 4 (December 1980):42–47.

17. Music Educators National Conference, National Committee on Instruction, *Selected Instructional Programs in Music* (Reston, Va.: Music Educators National Conference, 1977).

18. "The Most Popular Word: Relevancy," *AASA Convention Reporter* (Washington, D.C.: American Association of School Administrators, 1969), p. 11.

19. Charles L. Gary, "Why Music Education?" NASSP *Bulletin* (Reston, Va.: National Association of Secondary School Principals, 1975), p. iii. Reprinted by permission of National Association of Secondary School Principals.

BIBLIOGRAPHY

The Contemporary Music Project

Music Educators Journal 54, no. 7 (March 1968). A section entitled "Contemporary Music Project: Comprehensive Music Education" includes articles and reports about several aspects of the CMP.

Music Educators Journal 59, no. 9 (May 1973). A section entitled "Contemporary Music Project: Comprehensive Musicianship" describes the philosophy, history, and uses of comprehensive musicianship.

Publications of the Contemporary Music Project (CMP)

CMP 1. *Contemporary Music for Schools* (1966). A catalogue of works written by composers participating in the Young Composers Project, 1959–64.

CMP 2. *Comprehensive Musicianship* (1965). A report of the seminar sponsored by the Contemporary Music Project at Northwestern University, April 1965.

CMP 3. *Experiments in Musical Creativity* (1966). A report of pilot projects sponsored by the Contemporary Music Project in Baltimore, San Diego, and Farmingdale.

CMP 4. *Creative Projects in Musicianship* (1967). A report by Warren Benson of pilot projects sponsored by the Contemporary Music Project at Ithaca College and the Interlochen Arts Academy.

CMP 5. *Comprehensive Musicianship: an Anthology of Evolving Thought* (1971). A discussion of the first ten years of the Contemporary Music Project, particularly as they relate to the development of comprehensive musicianship.

CMP 6. *Comprehensive Musicianship and Undergraduate Music Curricula* (1971). A discussion by David Willoughby of curricular implications of comprehensive musicianship as derived from 32 experimental college programs.

CMP 7. *Source Book of African and Afro-American Materials for Music Education* (1972). James A. Standifer and Barbara Reeder provide lists of books, articles, recordings, and other materials dealing with African and Afro-American music traditions.

CMP Library Catalogs

Volume I, Works for Band
Volume II, Works for Orchestra
Volume III, Works for Chorus

The Yale Seminar

Arberg, Harold; and Palisca, Claude V. "Implications of the Government Sponsored Yale Seminar in Music Education," *College Music Symposium* 4 (1964):113–24.

Beglarian, Grant. Review of *Music in Our Schools* by Claude V. Palisca. In *Journal of Music Theory* I (1965):187–89.

Bulletin, Council for Research in Music Education, no. 60, Fall 1979. Entire issue consists of articles on the Yale Seminar.

Lehman, Paul. Review of *Music in Our Schools: A Search for Improvement*. *Notes* 22 (1965):728–30.

Palisca, Claude V. *Music in Our Schools: A Search for Improvement*. Report of the Yale Seminar on Music Education. Washington, D.C.: U.S. Department of Health, Education and Welfare, Office of Education, OE-33033, bulletin 1964, no. 28.

"Seminar on Music Education: Musicians Meet at Yale University." *Music Educators Journal* 50, no. 1 (1963):86–87.

The Tanglewood Symposium

Choate, Robert A. "Music in American Society." *Music Educators Journal* 53 (1967):38–40.

——, ed. *Documentary Report of the Tanglewood Symposium.* Washington, D.C.: Music Educators National Conference, 1968.

Jones, William M. "Functions of Music in Music Education Since Tanglewood." *Bulletin,* Council for Research in Music Education, no. 63, Summer 1980, pp. 11–19.

Murphy, Judith; and Sullivan, George. *Music in American Society.* Washington, D.C.: Music Educators National Conference, 1968.

Music Educators Journal 55, no. 1 (1968). Includes several articles on the Tanglewood Symposium.

Schwadron, Abraham. "The Tanglewood Symposium Summons." *Music Educators Journal* 26 (1968):40–42.

The GO Project

"Goals and Objectives for Music Education." *Music Educators Journal* 57, no. 4 (December 1970):24–25. Reprinted by permission of Music Educators National Conference.

"The 'GO' Project: Where Is It Heading?" *Music Educators Journal* 50, no. 6 (February 1970):24–25. Reprinted by permission of Music Educators National Conference.

Hoffman, Mary E. "Goals and Objectives for the Eighties." *Music Educators Journal* 67, no. 4 (December 1980):48–49, 66.

Mark, Michael L. "The GO Project: Retrospective of A Decade." *Music Educators Journal* 67, no. 4 (December 1980):42–47.

3

Philosophical Foundations of Music Education

It is only in recent years that music educators have recognized the need for a unified philosophy of music education. Although the profession has long recognized the value of a philosophical base, actual music education practices are not, and have not been, much affected by profession-wide philosophical foundations. The process of developing a unified philosophy is complicated by the fact that music, like the other arts, operates in the curriculum somewhat apart from the other subjects, and a realistic philosophy would have to reconcile the divergent segments of the school curriculum. There is no single philosophical basis for American education today. What is needed is an eclectic philosophy that encompasses all viewpoints. The Tanglewood Declaration provided a basis for an eclectic philosophy. The need for such a philosophy has become more apparent as society continues to change. The societal turmoil of the 1960s, the economic exigencies of the 1970s, the drive for excellence in education of the 1980s, and the problems caused by the impact of technology on society have forced educators to serious introspection in order to develop a set of basic values upon which to base educational principles and practices. Reimer wrote:

The need for a philosophy exists at two levels. First, the profession as a whole needs a formulation which can serve to guide the efforts of the group. The impact the profession can make on society depends in large degree on the quality of the profession's understanding of what it has to offer which might be of value to society. There is an almost desperate need for a better understanding of the value of music and of the teaching and learning of music. An uncomfortable amount of defensiveness, of self-doubt, of grasping at straws which seem to offer bits and pieces of self-justification, exists now in music education and has always seemed to exist. It would be difficult to find a field so active, so apparently healthy, so venerable in age and widespread in practice, which is at the same time so worried about its inherent value. . . . The tremendous expenditure of concern about how to justify itself—both to itself and to others—which has been traditional in this field, reflects a lack of philosophical "inner peace." . . . [1]

THE TANGLEWOOD DECLARATION

The Tanglewood Declaration summarized the philosophical aspects of the Tanglewood Symposium recommendations. It provides the basis for an effective eclectic philosophy. Because it is a seminal document on contemporary music education, it is quoted here in its entirety:

The intensive evaluation of the role of music in American society and education provided by the Tanglewood Symposium of philosophers, educators, scientists, labor leaders, philanthropists, social scientists, theologians, industrialists, representatives of government and foundations, music educators, and other musicians led to this declaration:

We believe that education must have as major goals the art of living, the building of personal identity, and nurturing creativity. Since the study of music can contribute much to these ends, WE NOW CALL FOR MUSIC TO BE PLACED IN THE CORE OF THE SCHOOL CURRICULUM.

The arts afford a continuity with the aesthetic tradition in man's history. Music and other fine arts, largely nonverbal in nature, reach close to the social, psychological, and physiological roots of man in his search for identity and self-realization.

Educators must accept the responsibility for developing opportunities which meet man's individual needs and the needs of a society plagued by the consequences of changing values, alienation, hostility between generations, racial and international tensions, and the challenges of a new leisure.

Music educators at Tanglewood agreed that:

1. Music serves best when its integrity as an art is maintained.
2. Music of all periods, styles, forms, and cultures belongs in the curriculum. The musical repertory should be expanded to involve music of our time in its rich variety, including currently popular teen-age music and avant-garde music, American folk music, and the music of other cultures.
3. Schools and colleges should provide adequate time for music in programs ranging from preschool through adult or continuing education.
4. Instruction in the arts should be a general and important part of education in the senior high school.
5. Developments in educational technology, educational television, programmed instruction, and computer-assisted instruction should be applied to music study and research.
6. Greater emphasis should be placed on helping the individual student to fulfill his needs, goals, and potentials.
7. The music education profession must contribute its skills, proficiencies, and insights toward assisting in the solution of urgent social problems as in the "inner city" or other areas with culturally deprived individuals.

8. Programs of teacher education must be expanded and improved to provide music teachers who are specially equipped to teach high school courses in the history and literature of music, courses in the humanities and related arts, and music teachers equipped to work with the very young, with adults, with the disadvantaged, and with the emotionally disturbed.[2]

THE HISTORICAL BASIS OF MUSIC EDUCATION PHILOSOPHY

Music education has been discussed throughout Western intellectual history not only by those who taught music, but, more important, by intellectual, religious, political, and educational leaders. From the time of ancient Greece until the nineteenth century, the great majority of writings about the philosophy of music education with which we are familiar is that of societal leaders. Plato's ideal society, described in the *Republic* and *Laws*, depended heavily on music education to maintain and continue what Plato felt were critical cultural values and traditions. He wrote in *Protagoras:*

The music masters by analogous methods instill self-control and deter the young from evil-doing. And when they have learned to play the lyre, they teach them the works of good poets of another sort, namely the lyrical, which they accompany on the lyre, familiarizing the minds of the children with the rhythms and melodies. By this means they become more civilized, more balanced, and better adjusted in themselves and so more capable in whatever they say or do, for rhythm and harmonious adjustment are essential to the whole of human life. . . . [3]

Aristotle also concluded that education in music served the citizen well:

It is clear then that there are branches of learning and education which we must study merely with a view to leisure spent in intellectual activity, and these are to be valued for their own sake; whereas those kinds of knowledge which are useful in business are to be deemed necessary, and exist for the sake of other things. And therefore our fathers admitted music into education, not on the ground either of its necessity or utility, for it is not necessary, nor indeed useful in the same manner as reading and writing, which are useful in money-making, in the management of a household, in the acquisition of knowledge and in political life, nor like drawing, useful for a more correct judgement of the works of artists, nor again like gymnastic, which gives health and strength; for neither of these is to be gained from music. There remains, then, the use of music for intellectual enjoyment in leisure; which is in fact evidently the reason of its introduction, this being one of the ways in which it is thought that a freeman should pass his leisure. . . .

It is evident, then, that there is a sort of education in which parents should train their sons, not as being useful or necessary, but because it is liberal or noble. Whether this is of one kind only, or of more than one, and if so, what they are, and how they are to be imparted, must hereafter be determined. Thus much we are now in a position to say, that the ancients witness to us; for their opinion may be gathered from the fact that music is one of the received and traditional branches of education. . . . [4]

Throughout the long span of Western history, the unique values of music were recognized by those who advocated music education. However closely music was related to the sciences in the traditional quadrivium of the Middle Ages, or to mysticism in numerology and astrology, its aesthetic impact was recognized and utilized for its own unique value to society.

Early American music education continued the deeply seated tradition of utilitarianism. The teaching of music could not have existed for the sole purpose of aesthetic development. Spanish and French explorers, in what are now the southwestern and north central United States, were quickly followed by teachers from their own countries, who were responsible for introducing the natives to the European cultures of the conquerers. This was accomplished, in great part, by means of music education. The improvement of music in worship to make possible church services of higher quality was the reason for the establishment of the singing school movement along the eastern seaboard early in the eighteenth century. When Lowell Mason's advocacy efforts finally succeeded and music was adopted by the Boston School Committee as a curricular subject in 1838, it was because music had met the same requirements as other school subjects—it had been judged in terms of potential for developing children morally, physically, and intellectually. The report made by a special committee of the Boston School Committee led to the acceptance of music in the curriculum for extramusical reasons that were based on the unique nature of music. The report stated:

Judged then by this triple standard, intellectually, morally, and physically, vocal Music seems to have a natural place in every system of instruction which aspires, as should every system, to develop [sic] man's whole nature. . . . Now the defect of our present system, admirable as that system is, is this, that it aims to develope the intellectual part of man's nature solely, when for all the true purposes of life, it is of more importance, a hundred fold, to feel rightly, than to think profoundly."[5]

The fact that music was judged by the same moral, physical, and intellectual standards as other subjects and was believed to be capable of making a unique contribution to each area is significant. The aesthetic impact of music was thought to be of utilitarian value in the education of the citizen. Throughout the nineteenth century and into the twentieth, music was introduced into public school systems across the country on essentially the same justification that was used in Boston in 1838.

When John Dewey's philosophical system took hold in American education early in the twentieth century, music assumed an even stronger position in public schools. Progressive education changed music instruction radically and granted it a secure place in the curriculum, in part because of its effectiveness in the development of socialization skills in children.

THE DEVELOPMENT OF AN AESTHETIC
PHILOSOPHY OF MUSIC EDUCATION

It was not until approximately the middle of the twentieth century that music educators themselves became the most vocal champions and defenders of their profession. From that time to the present, there has been a more or less steady movement from a utilitarian philosophy to an aesthetic basis for the profession of music education. A significant development occurred in 1954, when the Commission on Basic Concepts was organized by MENC. The commission resulted from a growing awareness that a soundly based theoretical foundation should be developed not only by music educators but also by persons from outside the profession. The work of the commission resulted in a decision by the National Society for the Study of Education to devote its 1958 yearbook to music education. Articles were contributed by a group of distinguished authors in disciplines related to music education. They were published in 1958 under the title *Basic Concepts in Music Education.*[6] This was the first attempt to publish guidelines for the development of a philosophy. The book includes articles on the various philosophical systems upon which American education is based and also on subjects related to the development of a philosophy of music education. Allen Britton cited historical justification for music education, but criticized the practice of referring to ancillary values of music instruction as a basis for justification in our own time:

Music, as one of the seven liberal arts, has formed an integral part of the educational systems of Western civilization from Hellenic times to the present. Thus, the position of music in education historically speaking, is one of great strength. Unfortunately, this fact seems to be one of which most educators, including music educators, remain unaware. As a result, the defense of music in the curriculum is often approached as if something new were being dealt with. Lacking the assurance which a knowledge of history could provide, many who seek to justify the present place of music in American schools tend to place too heavy a reliance upon ancillary values which music may certainly serve but which cannot, in the end, constitute its justification. Plato, of course, is the original offender in this regard, and his general view that the essential value of music lies in its social usefulness seems to be as alive today as ever.[7]

Bennett Reimer later wrote, "If music education in the present era could be characterized by a single, overriding purpose, one would have to say this field is trying to become 'aesthetic education.' What is needed in order to fulfill this purpose is a philosophy which shows how and why music education is aesthetic in its nature and its value."[8] In Charles Leonhard's words,

When we speak of a philosophy of music education, we refer to a system of basic beliefs which underlies and provides a basis for the operation of the musical enterprise in an educational setting. . . . The business of the school is to help young people undergo meaningful experience and arrive at a system of values that will be beneficial to society. . . . While reliance on statements of the instrumental value of music may well have convinced some reluctant administrator more fully to support the music program, those values cannot stand close scrutiny, because they are not directly related to music and are not unique to music. In fact, many other areas of the curriculum are in a position to make a more powerful contribution to these values than is music.[9]

Except for the works of Britton, Leonhard, Reimer, and Abraham Schwadron, relatively little was published on the subject of music education philosophy from the fifties to the late seventies. According to Schwadron,

The *real* problems in contemporary music education which are daily concerns are to a considerable extent value-centered. We are coming to realize that a new or alternate approach is needed for the construction of value-oriented curricular designs. The context of this emerging curriculum will focus on issues relevant to the nature of music and to the lives of the students. It will lead students to ask fundamental questions, to engage in intriguing musical activities, and to seek answers based on personal reflection, inquiry, discovery, and research; it will help them formulate their values of music on both logical and introspective levels.

Does it not follow that educators should themselves be encouraged to explore these matters for both general or practical classroom purposes and the self-examination of personal value systems, prejudices, tolerances, etc.? . . . It seems very odd that the why of music has been investigated by those like Dewey, Mursell, Langer, and Meyer and yet categorically avoided by those directly responsible for daily musical instruction. . . . [10]

In the late 1970s controversy over the utilitarian-versus-aesthetic philosophy reemerged. The problems that national economic conditions created for music education provided a basis for rethinking the subject. Some music educators have advocated a moderate position that would reconcile the two extremes, thereby providing a justification to the public for its continued support of music education and to the profession for basing its values on the aesthetic aspect of music. The philosophical statement of the Bergenfield, New Jersey, music education program is an example of a utilitarian approach:

The PHILOSOPHICAL PURPOSE of the music department is to dedicate itself, first and foremost, to the support and furtherance of the GENERAL PHILOSOPHY of the Bergenfield Board of Education and the individual schools particularly in the phases of character education and the development of better citizenship, preparing young people for life in a free, democratic society in which they will have the opportunity and the responsibility to make choices.[11]

The philosophical statement is followed by the goals and objectives of the music department, which describe an aesthetic approach to the teaching of music. The Bergenfield music educators carried forth the justification that supported music during the years of progressive education, when music education was highly valued as a component of the curriculum—a view stated much earlier by several respected music educators:

The general aim of education is to train the child to become a capable, useful, and contented member of society. The development of a fine character and of the desire to be of service to humanity are results that lie uppermost in the minds of the leaders of educational thought. Every school subject is valued in proportion to its contribution to these desirable ends. Music, because of its powerful influence upon the very innermost recesses of our subjective life, because of its wonderfully stimulating effect upon our physical, mental, and spiritual natures, and because of its well-nigh universality of appeal, contributes directly to both of these fundamental purposes of education. By many of the advanced educators of the present day, therefore, music, next to the "three R's" is considered the most important subject in the public school curriculum.[12]

Because of the decentralized nature of education in the United States, it is doubtful that there will ever be an absolute reconciliation of the two philosophic positions. While it is possible that they will eventually be used to complement each other in philosophical statements developed by a large number of school music programs (in a manner similar to that of the Bergenfield schools), it is more likely that the subject of philosophy will remain controversial and that new positions will evolve in time. The lessons of history teach us that a stagnant philosophy is counterproductive and dangerous. Therefore, continuing discussions and disagreements, resulting in appropriate compromise, are probably the most healthful patterns for the music education profession.

NOTES

1. Bennett Reimer, *A Philosophy of Music Education* (Englewood Cliffs, N.J.: Prentice-Hall, Inc., 1970), p. 3.
2. Robert A. Choate, ed., *Documentary Report of the Tanglewood Symposium* (Washington, D.C.: Music Educators National Conference, 1968), p. 139. Reprinted by permission of Music Educators National Conference.
3. Plato, *Protagoras*, from *The Collected Dialogues of Plato*, ed. Edith Hamilton and Huntington Cairns (Bollingen Foundation, distributed by Pantheon Books, Princeton University Press, 1961), p. 322.
4. Aristotle, *Politica*, book VIII, from W. D. Ross, ed., *The Works of Aristotle*, vol. X (London: Oxford University Press, 1921), 1338:10–35.

5. Report of the select committee of the Boston School Committee, 24 August 1937.
6. Nelson B. Henry, ed., *Basic Concepts in Music Education*, Fifty-seventh Yearbook of the National Society for the Study of Education, part I (Chicago: University of Chicago Press, 1958).
7. Allen Britton, "Music in Early American Public Education: A Historical Critique," in *Basic Concepts in Music Education*, ed. Nelson Henry (Chicago: National Society for the Study of Education, 1958), p. 195.
8. Bennett Reimer, *A Philosophy of Music Education* (Englewood Cliffs, N.J.: Prentice-Hall, Inc., 1970), p. 2.
9. Charles Leonhard, "The Philosophy of Music Education—Present and Future," in *Comprehensive Musicianship: The Foundation for College Education in Music* (Washington: Music Educators National Conference, 1965), pp. 42, 43, 45.
10. Abraham A. Schwadron, "Philosophy in Music Education: Pure or Applied Research?" *Bulletin* of the Council for Research in Music Education, no. 19, Winter 1970, p. 26.
11. "Music Thrives in Bergenfield, N.J.," program of presentation at the Music Educators National Conference Eastern Division In-service Conference, Kiamesha Lake, New York, 31 March 1981.
12. Horatio Parker, Osbourne McConathy, Edward Bailey Birge, and W. Otto Miessner, *The Progressive Music Series*, Teacher's Manual, vol. II (Boston: Silver, Burdett and Company, 1916), p. 9.

BIBLIOGRAPHY

Birge, William Bailey. *History of Public School Music in the United States.* Washington, D.C.: Music Educators National Conference, 1966.
Coates, Patricia. "Alternatives to the Aesthetic Rationale for Music Education." *Music Educators Journal* 69, no. 7 (March 1983):31, 32.
Elliott, Charles A. "Behind the Budget Crisis, A Crisis of Philosophy." *Music Educators Journal* 70, no. 2 (Oct. 1983):36, 37.
Goodlad, John I. *The Changing School Curriculum.* New York: Fund for the Advancement of Education, 1966.
Harvey, Arthur W. "James L. Mursell: A Developmental Philosophy of Music Education." *Bulletin,* Council for Research in Music Education, no. 37, Spring 1974, pp. 1–21.
Henry, Nelson B., ed. *Basic Concepts in Music Education,* Fifty-seventh Yearbook of the National Society for the Study of Education, part I. Chicago: University of Chicago Press, 1958.
Knieter, Gerard L. "Aesthetics for Arts' Sake." *Music Educators Journal* 69, no. 7 (March 1983):33–35, 61–64.
Lee, Gordon C. "The Changing Role of the Teacher." In *The Changing American School,* Sixty-fifth Yearbook of the National Society for the Study of Education, part II. Edited by John I. Goodlad. Chicago: University of Chicago Press, 1966.
Mark, Michael L. "The Evolution of Music Education Philosophy from Utilitarian to Aesthetic." *Journal of Research in Music Education* 30, no. 1 (Spring 1982):16–21.
———. "The Need for a Utilitarian Philosophy of Music Education." *International Music Education: Tradition and Change in Music and Music Education.* Edited by Jack Dobbs. Papers of the 15th International Conference of the International Society for Music Education, Bristol, England, 1982, pp. 84–89.

Phillips, Kenneth H. "Utilitarian vs. Aesthetic." *Music Educators Journal* 69, no. 7 (March 1983):29, 30.

Reese, Sam. "Teaching Aesthetic Listening." *Music Educators Journal* 69, no. 7 (1983):36–38.

Schwadron, Abraham A. *Aesthetics: Dimensions for Music Education.* Washington, D.C.: Music Educators National Conference, 1967.

———. "Philosophy in Music Education: Pure or Applied Research?" *Bulletin* of the Council for Research in Music Education, no. 19, Winter 1970, pp. 22–29.

Silberman, Charles E. *Crisis in the Classroom.* New York: Random House, 1970.

Tellstrom, A. Theodore. *Music in American Education: Past and Present.* New York: Holt, Rinehart, and Winston, 1971.

4

Public Policy and Arts Education

It is important for music educators to understand the relationship between their profession and the numerous and complex facets of government. Public education is mandated by means of state constitutional authority, and implemented according to large and complex bodies of law derived from federal, state, and local constitutions.

American education is organized and operated according to policies created to implement laws and statutes. Laws are passed by legislative bodies and administered by executive agencies. For example, although the United States Constitution leaves the subject of education to the states, it reserves a number of powers that affect education for the federal government. It is the responsibility of the U.S. Congress to approve legislation that supports the powers granted to the federal government by the Constitution. Legislation, in the form of laws, is then administered by federal agencies that operate within the executive branch of the government. Most, but not all, federal education matters are the responsibility of the U.S. Department of Education (DOE), which establishes policies to govern those aspects of education over which it has authority. When DOE distributes federal money to states for support of such programs as school lunches, affirmative action, education for the handicapped, it is the state education law, created by the state legislature, that determines how the money is to be distributed and utilized within the state (in keeping with federal guidelines and policies).

Local school boards are established by state laws. They are assigned specific responsibilities by state education law, and are limited by that body of laws to particular areas of authority and specific kinds of actions. For example, a local board of education has the authority to appoint a superintendent, who is responsible for the administration of the school system. Upon the recommendation of the superintendent, the board approves the budget, appoints teachers and administrators, approves capital projects, approves policies by which the school system operates, and so on.

Arts education may be mandated by state or local education law or policy, or may be offered simply because the board considers it sufficiently important to be included in the curriculum. Arts education may include music, visual art, drama, dance, and others; it may be any one subject or a combination. Depending on the operational policy, arts instruction may be of such a nature that it is provided by general classroom teachers at the elementary level, and by secondary teachers primarily responsible for other subjects, but who have additional or extracurricular assignments in the arts. Ideally, arts education is provided by specialists in the various art areas; that, too, is determined by public policy.

The term "arts education," rather than "music education," is utilized in this chapter because most public policy matters that affect music education are addressed to arts education in general. For this reason, much advocacy for arts education at the local, state, and federal levels is by coalitions representing the various arts. Not only do arts education coalitions represent the subjects addressed by legislators and/or government administrators, but they have the political clout of the combined number of arts education professionals. Advocacy efforts are usually more effective if a larger number of constituents is represented.

The relationship between arts education and government is extremely complex and requires knowledge of political systems and processes. Most art educators, by nature of their interests, education, and training, are not especially familiar with the topic. Yet, because of the impact of public policy on their professional lives, and because it is possible to influence public policy, arts educators can benefit greatly by understanding the democratic process as it applies to education.

THE FEDERAL GOVERNMENT AND ARTS EDUCATION

Because of the manner in which responsibility is assigned to federal agencies, there is virtually no federal policy that applies to arts education at this time. The arts are the responsibility of the National Endowment for the Arts, and education is the responsibility of DOE. One or both of the agencies might be expected to support arts education, but neither does.

Because of the budgeting and funding structure of the federal government, responsibility for an area of national activity is assigned to a specific agency. If the national activity does not fall conveniently within the purview of a single agency, it is assigned to several, each with a piece of the responsibility. "The arts," for example, are assigned to the National Endowment for the Arts, and "arts education" is assigned to the Department of Education. . . . Although arts education belongs to both the world of the arts and the world of education, . . . it does not receive assistance from several federal agencies; in fact, it receives meaningful assistance from none. The major reason for this is that the nation's schools and colleges have traditionally been considered the responsibility of state and local governments, and the federal agency to which education has been assigned, the Department of Education, offers only supplementary assistance to state and local education authorities.[1]

There is reason for optimism, however. In 1983 Frank Hodsell, the Chairman of NEA, indicated in a speech to arts education leaders that he wanted to explore the feasibility of having NEA become more involved with arts education. The next year, in cooperation with the National Assembly of State Arts Agencies, NEA held a series of five regional meetings "to help identify and disseminate techniques, strategies and resources for promoting arts education from kindergarten through 12th grade."

The goal is to find exemplary efforts that improve and promote arts education in schools all across the country. These efforts might be at the state, local or classroom level, and might relate to programs, school board policies or legislative mandates. Using specific examples, the Endowment plans to publish the results of the meetings' findings to serve as a practical guide for encouraging and increasing quality arts programs for all young people.[2]

Historical Background of the Relationship Between the Government and Arts Education

The involvement of the federal government in education began almost two centuries ago with the Northwest Ordinance of 1787, which provided federal land grants for the establishment of educational institutions. From that time until the 1950s, federal aid to education was offered infrequently because educational funding was considered to be a function of state and local government. From the second half of the nineteenth century to the 1950s, federal aid was granted for such purposes in the form of vocational and agricultural education programs and facilities, rehabilitation and training of war veterans, school lunch programs, and health service education.

Throughout its history, federal involvement in local education has been viewed with suspicion and equated with federal interference in state and local matters. Attitudes began to change, however, when the growing discontent with public education in the late 1950s was heightened by the successful flight of Sputnik. Yet even before Sputnik, the federal government had begun to perceive the need for its involvement in education. The National Advisory Committee on

Education Act of 1954 established a committee charged with the responsibility of recommending areas of national concern that might be addressed by the U.S. Office of Education, which was a branch of the Department of Health, Education, and Welfare. (Under President Carter, the U.S. Office of Education was elevated to cabinet-level department status with the name U.S. Department of Education. The Department of Health, Education, and Welfare, which formerly contained USOE, became the Department of Health and Human Services.) Music was identified as a "critical subject" of national concern and was therefore eligible to receive support from the National Defense Education Act (NDEA) of 1958. The NDEA also sponsored, among other things, experimentation and dissemination of information on the effective utilization of media for educational purposes. Public Law (P.L.) 87-474 established grants for the construction of educational television

---

OUTLINE 4.1—NATIONAL DEFENSE EDUCATION ACT–1958

OUTLINE OF TITLES

Title II
Authorized loans to college students with the provision that up to 50% of the amount would be forgiven at the rate of 10% a year for each year that the student taught in the public schools.

Title III
Authorized matching grants for public schools and loans to private schools for the purchase of equipment used in teaching science, mathematics, and foreign languages.

Title IV
Authorized 5,500 three year graduate fellowships for students enrolled in new or expanded programs.

Title V
Provided state education agencies with funds for guidance, counseling, and testing and for guidance and counseling training.

Title VI
Authorized a program for the development of educational utilization of television and related communications media.

Title VII
Expanded vocational education by providing funds to the states for training skilled technicians in science-related occupations.

broadcasting facilities. The numbering system of public laws signifies which Congress passed the legislation and the number of the specific bill. Thus, P.L. 87-474 was passed by the 87th Congress, and was the 474th bill to be passed into law by that Congress.

In the late 1950s and early 1960s, the Ford Foundation Fund for the Advancement of Education also provided a great deal of financial support for educational television. The foundation financed a variety of experiments to develop television as a functional educational tool that could reach more students with fewer teachers because there was a shortage of qualified teachers at that time. The Higher Education Facilities Act of 1963 provided grants and loans for new educational facilities, including electronic music studios.

The U.S. Office of Education

The administration of federally funded programs is a massive undertaking. The agency responsible for most of the education programs is DOE. Because most of this discussion concerns the events of the 1950s and 1960s, however, the previous title of DOE, the U.S. Office of Education, is used here. USOE was comprised of several bureaus, including the Bureau of Elementary and Secondary Education; the Bureau of Adult, Vocational, and Library Programs; the Bureau of Education for the Handicapped; and the Bureau of Research, now the National Institute of Education (NIE). (In 1970 the Bureau of Research was replaced by the National Center for Educational Research and Development; in 1972 it was succeeded by NIE. All research and development projects sponsored by the center were transferred to NIE.)[3]

The Bureau of Research conducted basic and applied research, handled the dissemination of research results, and sponsored research training. The dissemination of research funding and results was considered a sufficiently important function for USOE to develop and maintain the Educational Resources Information Center (ERIC). ERIC provides policy, coordination, training, funds, and general services to clearinghouses at universities and other institutions throughout the country, each of which is responsible for a specific area of education. Music topics are handled within the social studies area. Each clearinghouse acquires, abstracts, indexes, and analyzes educational information appropriate to its area and reports materials to ERIC for publication and dissemination. Materials are announced in two monthly publications—*Research in Education* (RIE), a journal of abstracts, and *Current Index to Journals in Education* (CIJE), an index to more than 600 education journals. The clearinghouses also prepare bibliographies and interpretative summaries of reviews of new and important documents in education.

The Elementary and Secondary Education Act of 1965

A significant piece of legislation for American education, the Elementary and Secondary Education Act (ESEA) of 1965 (P.L. 89-10), was important for arts education and provided much support specifically for music education. The law authorized more than $1.3 billion to be channeled into classrooms to accomplish the following goals: (1) to strengthen elementary and secondary school programs for educationally deprived children in low-income areas; (2) to provide additional school library resources, textbooks, and other instructional materials; (3) to finance supplementary educational centers and services; (4) to broaden areas of cooperative research; and (5) to strengthen state departments of education. The ESEA consisted of several sections, called "titles," each of which was concerned with a different aspect of education. The most significant section to music education was Title I, which was prefaced as follows: "An ACT to strengthen and improve educational quality and educational opportunities in the Nation's

---

OUTLINE 4.2—ELEMENTARY AND SECONDARY EDUCATION ACT-1965

OUTLINE OF TITLES

Title I
Established a three year program of grants to local education agencies for the education of disadvantaged children. The distribution formula allocated 50% of each state's average expenditure per school age child (5–17) to school districts in which at least 3% of the enrollment, or 100 children, came from families with an annual income less than $2,000.

Title II
Authorized a five-year program to purchase library resources, texts, and other instructional materials for the use of children and teachers in public and private schools.

Title III and Title IV
Authorized grants directly to local and regional organizations for the establishment of supplementary educational centers and regional laboratories. Title IV also provided for university related research and development centers.

Title V
Established grants to strengthen state departments of education.

elementary and secondary schools."[4] Until 1973, under the terms of Title I, school districts all over the country received funds (matching funds, in most cases) with which to establish programs to equalize educational opportunities for children of low-income families. Many school districts were able to hire music teachers and purchase instruments and equipment for schools in low-income areas, which were identified by means of well-defined guidelines. Funds were allocated only to those particular schools, and the educational experiences they made possible were supplementary to the services already provided by the individual school districts. Title I enabled great numbers of children to participate in music and the other arts. During fiscal year 1966, approximately one-third of the 8.3 million children participating in the program were involved in music or art.[5]

In 1973 USOE revised the terms of Title I to provide greater support for the development of basic skills, especially in reading and mathematics. Most state education departments interpreted this to mean remedial aid in those areas. Music and art were usually approved for Title I funding in most states if they related somehow to the development of reading, writing, or mathematics skills. The effect of the new interpretation was a greatly reduced involvement of music and art in Title I programs.

ESEA Title III authorized funds for supplementary educational centers and services. Its three basic functions were: (1) to improve education by enabling a community to provide services not then available to the children who lived there; (2) to raise the quality of educational services already offered; and (3) to stimulate and assist in the development and establishment of high quality elementary and secondary school educational programs that could serve as models for regular school programs.[6]

An example of an ESEA Title III program is the Interrelated Arts Program (IAP), formerly an ESEA Title III Elementary Arts Teacher Training Project, which was established in the Montgomery County, Maryland, public schools. The following is a statement of the goals for the original project:

The primary goal of the Title III Arts Project is to train classroom teachers in the arts and to provide in-class support which will enable them to more fully meet their responsibilities for the education of their students.
    The training of classroom teachers is designed to:
1. Build the teachers' confidence in the arts, increase their aesthetic awareness, and develop their understanding of arts processes, concepts, and skills through active involvement in the arts;
2. Develop the teachers' understanding of how the arts contribute to the child's emotional, intellectual, and physical development and how the arts relate to each other and to other subject areas;
3. Develop the teachers' skills in designing and providing classroom activities which incorporate the arts.

The arts teams will demonstrate and encourage educational practice in which:

1. The student will be actively involved in perceptual and kinesthetic experiences;

2. The student–teacher relationship will be one of coauthorship. The teacher will welcome the unexpected response; the teacher will be an active listener;

3. The teacher will avoid judging students' artistic expression as "right" or "wrong";

4. The teacher will consider the wide range of possible alternatives which may arise from the activities provided.[7]

When the funding for the Title III Arts Project expired, it was renewed for a second period. Upon the second expiration, the Board of Education, recognizing the value of the program, voted to continue it with local funding. Its current activities are as follows:

FOR TEACHERS:

1. In-class integrated arts demonstration lessons related to teacher-identified objectives

2. Instructional support packages typically containing arts lesson plans with accompanying print and nonprint materials based on curriculum areas

3. Advanced teacher workshops providing in-depth arts experiences for teachers familiar with the Interrelated ARTS Program

4. Total school participation service: a team of four IAP members providing training, resources, and support for an entire faculty

5. An "Arts in the Classroom" in-service course (3–4 credits) taught three times a year

FOR STUDENTS:

The TAPESTRY (Time for Arts and Performance Experiences for Specially Talented and Ready Youngsters) program is a partnership among selected schools, the IAP, and the instructional planning personnel for the gifted and talented program. Students identified as possessing talent in dance, drama, visual art, or music are provided one hour of concentrated instruction in their art discipline each week.

FOR TEACHERS AND THEIR STUDENTS:

The Interrelated Arts Program is housed at an arts/science/math/computer center. Integrated arts student workshops, called ABCs (Arts in the Basic Curriculum) are developed and published in a catalogue. The catalogue is mailed to every elementary school in the school system. Teachers request classes appropriate to their professional needs and interests. After attending a workshop conducted by IAP, teachers

OUTLINE 4.3—ESEA TITLE III ELEMENTARY ARTS TEACHER TRAINING PROJECT MONTGOMERY COUNTY (MARYLAND) PUBLIC SCHOOLS

OUTLINE OF ACTIVITIES
PHASE I

Fall/Spring 1974–75

Two Arts Teams - - ┐- - -

Support 12 Pilot Schools (110 K–3 teachers)
(each team supports 6 schools from 3 administrative areas)
- conduct monthly arts workshops for the principals, K–3 teachers, and arts specialists from 12 pilot schools, and for participants from the 1973 Street 70 Creativity Workshop
- Individual team members visit participating K–3 teachers in their classrooms an average of 2 half-days per month
- conduct workshops at PTA meetings in pilot schools

Each pilot school receives Title III funds for one eight-hour teacher assistant.

Conduct In-Service Training for Arts Specialists
- conduct 3 countrywide workshops—1 each for art, music, and physical education specialists
- consult with specialists in pilot schools when possible

Support Private School Programs (7 K–3 Teachers)
- teachers from St. John the Evangelist attend monthly workshops and are visited regularly by arts team

Collect Arts Activities for Bank
- publish a newsletter
- design framework for arts activities

Design a Staff Development Program
- define instructional goals for participating teachers

Phase I Outcomes:
13 Schools' K–3 staff received training
2 Arts teams trained
Arts activities collected; preliminary framework designed for activities bank.

OUTLINE OF ACTIVITIES
PHASE II

Summer, 1975

4-Week Workshop, Interrelated Arts in the Classroom
Conducted by 2 arts teams
Participants:
- at least 2 K–3 teachers from each of the 12 new pilot schools
- interested K–3 teachers from original pilot schools
- interested arts specialists from pilot schools
- other MCPS K–3 teachers and arts specialists (total 31 participants)
- 40 K–3 children
Principals of pilot schools will attend 1 week of workshop

Fall/Spring, 1975–76

Three Arts Teams

Support 18 Pilot Schools (est. 127 K–3 Teachers)
- Conduct fall in-service interrelated arts course for K–3 teachers and arts specialists from pilot schools.
- Conduct 1½-hour arts workshops monthly in each pilot school.

(cont.)

OUTLINE 4.3 (CONT.)

- Visit participating K–3 teachers in their schools regularly.
- Visit each pilot school approximately 4 consecutive days once during year.
- Conduct workshops for Title III arts teacher assistants.

Each of 6 new pilot schools receives Title III funds for one three-hour teacher assistant.

Each of 12 original pilot schools receives MCPS funds for one three-hour teacher assistant.

Conduct arts workshops for interested non-pilot schools

Conduct in-service training for arts specialists
- conduct workshops
- consult regularly with specialists in pilot schools

Support Private School Programs
(2 schools, 14 K–3 teachers)
- fall in-service course conducted by teams include K–3 teachers from private schools
- consult with school staffs to design follow-up training

Develop Arts Activities Bank
- continue publishing newsletter
- define learner objectives for K–3 integrated arts program
- develop bank of 50 sample arts activities

Design a Staff Development Program
· 3 programs designed, based upon instructional goals previously defined

Phase II Outcomes:
24 Schools' K–3 staff have received training
 3 Arts teams trained
18 Teacher assistants trained
Preliminary arts activities bank developed
Preliminary staff development program designed

OUTLINE OF ACTIVITIES
PHASE III

Summer, 1976

4-Week Institute, Interrelated Arts in the Classroom
Conducted by 6 arts team members and consultants
Participants
· Interested K–6 teachers from 18 pilot schools
· Interested specialists from pilot schools
· Other MCPS K–6 teachers and specialists
(total 40 participants)
· 60 K–6 children
Elementary principals invited to sessions

4-week Curriculum Development Workshop
Curriculum writer/evaluator and 4 arts team members
Refine staff development objectives and assessments
Develop model for arts package development

(cont.)

OUTLINE 4.3 (CONT.)

Fall/Spring 1976–77

Three Arts Teams

Support 18 Pilot Schools (est. 150 K–6 teachers)
- Conduct fall in-service interrelated arts course
- With each participating school staff, develop project goals for year.
- With each participating teacher, co-design, and deliver services.
- Conduct monthly, centralized workshops for 2nd and 3rd year teachers.
- Identify school staff members to assist in training teachers.
- Consult regularly with arts specialists.

Each pilot school receives MCPS funds for one three-hour teacher assistant (pending budget approval of County Council).

Conduct arts workshops for teacher assistants in pilot schools.

Conduct orientation sessions for MCPS staff, community groups (est. 30 sessions).

Conduct arts workshops for interested non-pilot schools related to school staff goals (est. 30 schools).

Conduct workshops for arts specialists.

Conduct workshops for MCPS Administrators (est. 115 administrators).

Support Private School Programs (est. 2 schools, 20 K–6 teachers)
- Conduct fall in-service interrelated arts course
- Consult with school staff to design additional services

Refine and Pilot Arts Activities Bank

Develop Arts Support Materials for at least 2 existing MCPS curriculum guides.

Disseminate Information on Project
- design and distribute brochure
- conduct out of county workshops
- design and develop training video-tapes, slide packages, and film.

Establish Contacts with Community Arts Resources
- Assess local needs and resources
- Assist schools in working with local artists and art groups

Refine Staff Development Program
- Define objectives and assessments for classroom teacher training in arts.
- Describe procedures and necessary supports for implementation
- Evaluate effectiveness of program
- Write final report and suggest method for expanding program to secondary level

Phase III Outcomes

Over 50 schools K–6 staff have received training

115 MCPS administrators participated in workshops

18 teacher assistants trained

3 arts teams trained

Arts activities bank published and piloted

Arts supported materials developed

Introductory brochure distributed

Training materials developed

Staff development program defined, evaluated

Final report written and published

Source: Montgomery County Public Schools, Rockville, Maryland, under ESEA, Title III. Reprinted by permission.

accompany their students to the ABC class, where lesson plans and follow-through suggestions are provided the teachers.

FOR ADMINISTRATORS, SPECIALISTS, AND TEACHERS

The Arts Resource Center (ARC) is a multimedia resource center containing books, periodicals, art prints, film strips, recordings, and kits on dance, music, visual art, and drama. ARC is staffed and maintained by the Interrelated ARTS Program. Any educator in the school system can borrow ARC materials.

ESEA Title IV amended the Cooperative Research Act of 1954. It authorized $100 million over a five-year period for national and regional research facilities, expansion of existing research and development programs, and a training program for educational researchers. Title IV affected music education as well as other education areas. The Special Training Project in Research in Music Education, sponsored by the Music Education Research Council (MERC), a component of MENC, was held 11–14 March 1968 in Seattle during the MENC national convention.

Title IV also created regional laboratories to develop and implement research data. Two of the laboratories, the Central Atlantic Regional Educational Laboratory (CAREL) in Washington, D.C. and the Central Midwestern Regional Educational Laboratory (CEMREL) in St. Louis, Missouri, were especially concerned with aesthetic education. Their goals and operations were somewhat similar to those of IMPACT (Interdisciplinary Model Programs for Children and Teachers), which is discussed later in this chapter.

ESEA supported many other arts projects in addition to the ones discussed above. In 1966 the USOE Arts and Humanities Program sponsored forty-eight research projects in music, forty-six in art, eighteen in theatre and dance, four in the arts in general, and eleven in the humanities.[8] Some of the projects sponsored in music included the Yale Seminar, the Juilliard Repertory Project, some programs of the Contemporary Music Project, and the Manhattanville Music Curriculum Program.

The International Education Act of 1966

The International Education Act of 1966 (P.L. 89–698) provided grants to institutions of higher education to establish and operate centers for research and training in international studies. Shortly thereafter, several colleges and universities founded institutes for comparative music education.

The Education Professions Development Act of 1967

Another piece of legislation important for music education, the Education Professions Development Act (EPDA) of 1967 (P.L. 90-35), amended and extended Title V of the Higher Education Act of 1965. The EPDA was intended to improve the quality of teaching and to help overcome the shortage of adequately trained teachers by implementing training and retraining programs. The act had the effect, among other things, of attracting top quality people capable of improving education during short- and long-term assignments in the profession. Through the Teacher Retraining Authorization of the EPDA, the Interdisciplinary Model Programs in the Arts for Children and Teachers (IMPACT) was established in 1970. The concept of IMPACT was in keeping with the third paragraph of the Tanglewood Declaration:

The arts afford a continuity with the aesthetic tradition in man's history. Music and other fine arts, largely non-verbal in nature, reach close to the social, psychological, and physiological roots of man in his search for identity and self-realization.[9]

Four arts education associations—MENC, the National Art Education Association, the American Theater Association and the Dance Division of the American Association for Health, Physical Education, and Recreation—established a plan of operation for IMPACT. Other organizations joined after IMPACT was founded. The USOE Arts and Humanities Program committed part of its Artists-in-Schools Program to the five sites in which IMPACT operated. The John D. Rockefeller III (JDR 3) Fund Arts Education program supported a program for IMPACT personnel during its first year, provided coordination services, and sponsored a tour of the IMPACT schools for the executive secretaries and presidents of the four arts education associations.

The purpose of the project was to demonstrate that school activities in the arts can transform the traditional curriculum into one that (1) emphasizes the integration of the arts into the mainstream of human experience; (2) aids students in becoming sensitive to the qualitative aspects of their own experiences as sources for artistic ideas; (3) explores the similarities and differences in the ways that professionals in the arts develop their ideas; and (4) challenges students to make effective use of their creative resources.[10] Five broad objectives were specified:

1. To reconstruct the educational program and administrative climate of the school in an effort to achieve parity between the arts and other instructional areas and between the affective and cognitive learnings provided in the total school program

2. To develop educational programs of high artistic quality in each art area, that is, the visual arts, music, dance, and drama, in each of the participating schools

3. To conduct in-service programs, including summer institutes, workshops, demonstrations, and other similar activities, for teachers, administrators, and other school personnel so they can implement programs exemplifying high aesthetic and artistic quality in their own schools

4. To develop ways of integrating the arts into all aspects of the school curriculum as a means of enhancing and improving the quality and quantity of aesthetic education offered in the school, and as a principal means for expanding the base for affective learning experiences in the total school program

5. To invite a number of outstanding artists, performers, and educators into the school system to enhance the quality of the arts experiences of children.[11]

IMPACT was implemented in five locations ranging from single schools to a consortium of three school districts. When IMPACT ended in 1972, it was considered to have been successful in terms of its own goals. Teachers who were not arts specialists became more confident of their abilities to use the arts in teaching, and children had the opportunity to learn in an aesthetic environment. Test results indicate that students who participated in IMPACT programs were significantly above grade level in reading and other skills several years after their arts experiences. They also showed that students developed self-esteem through their arts experiences and that their attitudes toward school improved.

The Public Broadcasting Act of 1967

The Public Broadcasting Act of 1967 (P.L. 90–129) created a corporation for public broadcasting responsible for funding noncommercial radio and television stations, program production groups, educational television networks, and construction of educational radio and television facilities.

The National Foundation on the Arts and the Humanities

In 1965 the passage of P.L. 89–209 created the National Foundation on the Arts and the Humanities as an independent federal agency in the executive branch of the government. Congress declared:

The practice of art and the study of the humanities requires constant dedication and devotion and . . . while no government can call a great artist or scholar into existence, it is necessary and appropriate for the Federal Government to help create and sustain not only a climate encouraging freedom of thought, imagination, and inquiry, but also the material conditions facilitating the release of this creative talent.[12]

The National Endowment for the Arts (NEA) and the National Endowment for the Humanities (NEH) are components of the National Foundation on the Arts and the Humanities. They are advised by the National Council on the Arts and the National Council on the Humanities. Also in the structure of the foundations is the Federal Council on the Arts and the Humanities, consisting of twelve agency heads and two members of Congress who are concerned with the arts and humanities.[13]

The NEA has provided funds for music education activities that have affected students all over the country. The most visible NEA program concerned with music education is Artists-in-Schools. It provides funds for artists to work in schools, allowing students to participate in the arts with professionals. Thousands of schools and over one million students are involved. When criticism has arisen over its involvement in arts education, NEA has often referred to the Artists-in-Schools program as its major educational activity. Arts educators, however, traditionally distinguish between educational activities in which children create art and those for which they serve as audiences. Although the arts education community appreciates the Artists-in Schools program, many consider it to be more of an employment program for professional artists than an educational program for students. As was stated earlier, there is a possibility of NEA becoming more involved in arts education in the future. NEA provides grants for eight categories of arts—theatre, visual arts, literature, dance, music, general arts, architecture and design, and education and public media. Grants are awarded for creation of new works and for production and performance of art works.

The National Endowment for the Humanities sponsors other kinds of activities that also involve the arts.

According to the Act which established the Endowment, the humanities include, but are not limited to, the following fields: history, philosophy, languages, linguistics, literature, archeology, jurisprudence, history and criticism of the arts, ethics, comparative religion, and those aspects of the social sciences employing historical or philosophical approaches. . . .

Because man's experience has been principally preserved through books, art works, and other cultural objects, the humanities are often defined in terms of specific academic disciplines. However, the concerns of the humanities extend, through the classroom, the library, and the media, to encompass a host of social, ethical, and cultural questions which all human beings confront throughout the course of their lives.[14]

The National Alliance for Arts Education

The National Alliance for Arts Education (AAE) was established in 1973 by the John F. Kennedy Center for the Performing Arts and the USOE, in cooperation with MENC, the National Art Education Association, the American Theatre Association, and the National Dance Association. The Alliance for Arts Education was created in response to the congressional mandate that the Kennedy Center, as a national symbol of excellence in the arts, become a vehicle and focal point for strengthening the arts in education at all levels (see Figure 4.1).

The purposes of AAE are to give young people access to the Kennedy Center as performers and as audience members, to make the Center's performances and services available to people all over the country, and to help the Center become a vehicle for strengthening the arts in education at the national, state and local levels. AAE sponsors many activities that focus attention on music education and provide opportunities for young people to perform. AAE has sponsored showcase series in which the best student work in music, drama, and other arts has been presented by the various states in the Kennedy Center.

Another way in which the alliance carries out the congressional mandate is by encouraging representative leaders in the arts in each state to establish individual state Alliance for Arts Education Committees. Virtually all of the states belong to the Alliance for Arts Education. The broad goal of the state committees is to promote arts education within each state in order to make the arts an integral part of public elementary and secondary education. The specific goals of each state vary. For example, the Constitution of the Maryland Alliance for Arts Education states:

The basic purpose of the Maryland Alliance for Arts Education . . . shall be to encourage and strengthen the arts in all educational processes in the state. This shall be done by: (1) organizing, unifying and promulgating an alliance of organizations supportive of the arts in the State of Maryland; (2) facilitating coordination and cooperation among appropriate state groups and agencies; (3) cooperating with appropriate agencies of the Federal Government, particularly the John F. Kennedy Center for the Performing Arts and the United States Department of Education in order to encourage their national aims and purposes and promote the cause of arts education throughout the United States.[15]

Many hopeful signs have appeared for future support of arts education at the federal level. One such sign is the establishment of the Congressional Arts Caucus, which is meant to provide both symbolic and legislative recognition of the arts by many members of Congress. In 1983 the leader of the Congressional Arts Caucus, Representative Thomas Downey (N.Y.), and Representative James Jeffords (Vt.) introduced a resolution in the U. S. House of Representatives that

FIGURE 4.1 AAE Organizational Chart.

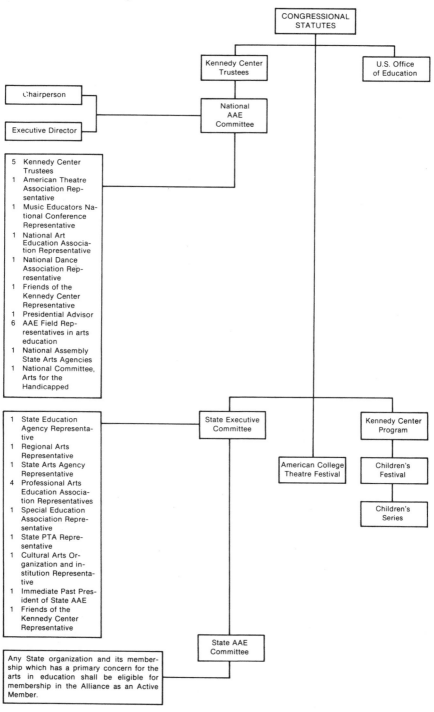

Note: Alliance for Arts Education, John F. Kennedy Center, Washington, D.C. 20566.

urged "all citizens to support efforts which strengthen artistic training and appreciation within our Nation's schools." Senator Edward Kennedy (Mass.) introduced a companion resolution in the Senate. It is hoped that passage of the resolutions "will stimulate a nationwide effort to promote and enhance the status of arts in education."[16]

SOME STATE ISSUES

Events in several states impacted on arts education as economic conditions led to "taxpayer revolts." The most well known of such events is the 1978 passage of "Proposition 13" in California. California is one of many states that permit laws to be passed by public referendum. Proposition 13, authored by Howard Jarvis and Paul Gann, tied government spending to economic growth. Taxes had imposed such a heavy burden on California residents that they welcomed the opportunity, in the form of Proposition 13, to vote for an initiative that promised economic relief. Proposition 13 reduced property taxes, but it also drastically reduced the financial resources available to the state, county, and local governments. As a result of Proposition 13, it became impossible to maintain previous levels of such government services as police and fire protection, street and highway maintenance, parks and recreation, libraries, and education. Public education in California had not been funded generously prior to 1978, and support for arts education had declined steadily for several years. The fiscal problem imposed in 1978 was felt in many school districts throughout the state. Arts education suffered, as did other curricular areas; teaching positions were eliminated, equipment could not be maintained and replaced as needed, and morale among educators plummeted.[17]

Proposition 13 was followed by similar initiatives in twenty-five other states. The most severe for educators was Proposition 2-½ in Massachusetts (1980). In 1979 Massachusetts was imposing a property tax on its homeowners at nearly twice the national average. Proposition 2-½ mandated that property taxes be limited to 2.5 percent of the assessed valuation of communities, and that increases be limited to 2.5 percent annually thereafter. Communities were no longer able to provide public services at the same level as before, and public works suffered. In the first year, 17,263 municipal employees were laid off across the state. The schools suffered even more than other public agencies because local school boards lost fiscal autonomy. They had previously been able to set their own budgets and impose the necessary tax levies to support their budgets, but Proposition 2-½ gave municipal governments control of school budgets. School employees were laid off in great numbers throughout the state.[18] At least 700 music teaching positions were eliminated, and in some communities, entire school music programs were lost. By the 1981–82 school year, more than one out of five music teaching positions were gone. By the second year of Proposition 2-½, more than 90 percent of the schools responding to a survey had made cuts in their music programs, and 70 percent of the departments had been forced to reduce or eliminate some programs in the music curriculum. Another problem was the scheduling conflicts that were created when course offerings in other subjects were also eliminated, making it difficult for many students to take music classes.[19] In addition, the position of Director of Music was eliminated in almost one out of every five school systems. In some cases music programs were put under the authority of supervisors of other subjects.[20] By the third year of operation under Proposition 2-½ (1983–84), the situation showed signs of stabilizing and in some cases, even improving. Although cuts in music programs continued, a number of school systems either reinstated previously eliminated areas of the music curriculum or expanded the program with new courses. While such actions did not balance out the hundreds of positions that were cut in 1981, there is cause for hope.[21]

Many states are prevented by the terms of their constitutions from creating laws by public referendum, but in some cases county or local initiatives are permitted. The Prince George's County, Maryland voters approved an initiative known as the "Tax Reform Initiative by Marylanders" (TRIM) in 1978. TRIM limited local revenues, which provide a major portion of the school budget, to the 1979 level of $144 million. The effect of TRIM was similar to those of Propositions 13 and 2-½. All public services, including education, were reduced. Numerous teaching positions were eliminated, and arts education programs suffered when entire programs were ended.[22]

Propositions 13 and 2-½, as well as those in many other states, created such broad and fundamental changes in the ways that state and local governments operated that their full effects are still not known. These effects are so sweeping and in many cases unforeseen that studies in California have been unable to determine the total impact of Proposition 13.[23] Public concern for the quality of education, however, led to the passage of the Hughes-Hart Educational Reform Act of 1983, which was probably the most massive piece of educational reform legislation ever created in the United States.[24] Its purpose is to restore the resources necessary for the schools to provide education of high quality.

RESPONSES TO ECONOMIC EXIGENCIES

Fund Raising

As the government's ability to support education has declined, school systems are turning ever increasingly to various alternatives for fund raising. One is to create partnerships with industry, which depends on American schools to provide both its future work force and its future customers. It is not unusual for school systems to receive support, either in the form of cash or equipment, from business, industry, foundations, and even individuals.

In California alone there are over 120 foundations that raise money for public schools. Although little of that money is used specifically for arts education, some is earmarked for it. In Piedmont, 70 percent of the parents donated $240 per child to the schools in 1983, for a total of $507,000. That money permitted the school system to continue offering music and art instruction. A San Francisco foundation raised over $600,000 in 1983 to fund an all-city student orchestra and to pay for other activities.[25]

Advocacy

Another form of response to economic exigency in the schools is advocacy. Advocacy is the means by which the needs of a specific cause (arts education, in this case) are made known to the legislators who create laws affecting the cause, the government administrators who make policies to implement the laws, public boards that control such functions as public education, and the electorate, which has ultimate control over public policy by means of the voting process. Advocacy is related to lobbying, but lobbying is a legally defined activity carried out by persons licensed to try to influence legislators for specific causes which they are paid to represent. Advocacy for arts education is usually carried out by arts educators and other interested citizens. It often takes the form of activities intended to enlighten the decision makers as to the importance of arts education, the effects of legislation and public policy on arts education, and what kinds of legislation and policy are needed to improve a particular situation.

Crisis intervention was an early example of advocacy. In 1972, the Superintendent of Schools in Chicago proposed the adoption of the next year's budget to the Board of Education. Because the necessary revenue was not available to maintain existing programs, the budget reflected a reduction of $98.5 million, which would have resulted in the elimination of the music, art, and physical education programs in the Chicago schools. When the media and the public learned of the proposed action, a strong advocacy campaign was begun. The Chicago Musicians Union, the area music dealers, the National Association of Music Merchants, the American Music Conference, the Chicago Orchestral Association, and *Down Beat* Magazine organized to fight the cuts. A budget of $24,000 was provided for the advocacy effort by segments of the music industry and some music teachers (only $11,000 was actually collected). A campaign called Save Our Music Education Citizens' Committee (SOME) was formed to carry out three objectives: (1) to restore music to the school budget at the level of 1 January 1972; (2) to persuade the Board that music was a necessary course of instruction for all public school students; and (3) to prepare a foundation for the improvement of the quality of music instruction in the Chicago schools. There was a strong media campaign to support the endangered programs, and a number of public figures advocated the maintenance of the programs. The House of Representatives of the State of Illinois adopted House Resolution No. 609, which stated:

This House was shocked to hear that the Chicago Board of Education has seen fit to do away with the Music, Art and Physical Education classes for elementary and secondary Chicago schools. . . . Be it resolved . . . that we do recommend that the Chicago Board of Education . . . do see fit to return to their budget the $3.7 million allocated for these very important educational classes. . . .

At the two day public hearing held by the Board of Education, 300 persons testified. Of these, 198 spoke specifically for music education. Benny Goodman provided testimony at the invitation of SOME, as did Charles Gary, Executive Secretary of MENC. A few days later, in order to dramatize the impact of the loss of the music program, more than 5,000 music students participated in a Parade of Silence, marching to the sound of muffled drums, carrying their instruments in cases, and wearing black armbands. The result of the well-planned and effective community effort was the restoration of the music program to the Chicago public schools. Although not every community action has been successful, the Chicago experience provides evidence that the public wants music in the schools, and that advocacy can be successful.[26]

Following the passage of Proposition 13, music education administrators in several parts of California joined together to strengthen the position of arts education in the state. They succeeded in having a fine arts requirement added to the secondary curriculum in many school districts and in persuading the University of California to recognize high school arts credits for admission. The music education administrators developed a five year legislative plan to address the needs of music and arts education in their state. An outline of the plan follows.

Goal I: California Music Educators Association (CMEA) shall establish as a high priority the expansion of legislative action.

- •Objective 1: Identify and develop strong community liaison relationships to support CMEA legislative action goals and objectives.
- •Objective 2: Involve the total CMEA membership in expanded legislature action.
- •Objective 3: Continue annual legislative conference.
- •Objective 4: Develop funding for legislative action, at the level of $5,000 annually.

Goal II: CMEA shall develop a unified voice for the arts at the state level.

- •Objective 1: Identify and establish a working coalition with arts advocacy groups.

Goal III: CMEA legislative action and advocacy efforts shall be focused on: (1) improvement of general funding for schools; (2) teacher preparation; (3) continuance of the state-funded Exemplary Arts Program; and, (4) mandates for the arts as an element of basic education.

- •Objective 1: Secure passage of legislation that will improve the general funding level for schools.
- •Objective 2: Prior to certification, all multiple-subject K–8 classroom teachers shall demonstrate proficiency in teaching of the visual and performing arts.
- •Objective 3: Continue the SB1735 (Senate Bill) Exemplary Arts Program
- •Objective 4: Achieve, through legislation, mandated programs in the visual and performing arts as elements of basic education.
- •Objective 5: Achieve, through resolution of the State Board of Education, the requirement for one year of instruction in visual and performing arts for high school graduation.

An example of strong support at the state level is the Texas State Board of Education, which adopted a position statement that reaffirmed "the importance of the fine arts in the basic curriculum" for all students. The board charged the state education agency to take an aggressive role "in communicating to the independent school districts, superintendents, principals and teachers, the advantages, benefits, and program for including fine arts in education offerings in the curriculum for all students."[27]

Another example of crisis intervention is provided by music educators in Memphis, Tennessee. In 1981 the city school system faced a $30 million deficit, and the entire elementary music program and orchestra program (elementary through high school) were threatened with elimination. The music education program was well known to the public and respected by it because of years of effective public relations. When the threat to the music program became known, numerous letters and telephone calls flooded the school board. The local media also supported the music program. The result was that 60 percent of the elementary music program was retained, as was all of the orchestra program. According to music consultant Tommie Pardue,

We have relied too long on the sounds of our students' music to carry our message. Take every opportunity to define the values of your program to parents, community, and administrators. Learn to speak in language that they understand. Give your public the tools to become strong music supporters. . . . The happy ending [is]. . . . during the fall of 1982 Memphis citizens voted to increase our local sales tax by three-fourths of a cent, providing $13 million for our school budget. For this school year sixteen elementary positions have been added to the system's music staff.[28]

NOTES

1. James Backas, "The Environment for Policy Development in Arts Education," *Proceedings of the 56th Annual Meeting* (Reston, Va.: National Association of Schools of Music, 1981), p. 5.
2. Joe N. Prince (Artists in Education Program, NEA) and Geoffrey Platt, Jr. (National Assembly of State Arts Agencies), memorandum to members of Alliance for Arts Education, 18 April 1984.
3. Reported in Anthony L. Barresi, "The Role of the Federal Government in Support of the Arts and Music Education," *Journal of Research in Music Education* 29, no. 4 (Winter 1981):253.
4. United States Office of Education, *The Elementary and Secondary Education Act of 1965: An Analysis* (Washington, D.C.: United States Office of Education, April 1965), quoted in William P. Lineberry, ed., *New Trends in Schools* (New York: H.W. Wilson, 1967), pp. 88–89.
5. Paul R. Lehman, "Federal Programs in Support of Music," *Music Educators Journal* 55, no. 1 (September 1968):53.
6. Lineberry, *New Trends in Schools*, pp. 93–94.
7. ESEA Title III Elementary Arts Teacher Training Project Statement of Goals, Montgomery County Public Schools, Rockville, Maryland, mimeographed.
8. John I. Goodlad et al., *The Changing School Curriculum* (New York: The Fund for the Advancement of Education, 1966), p. 84.
9. See chapter 3, "The Tanglewood Declaration."
10. David Boyle, ed., *Arts IMPACT: Curriculum for Change* (University Park, Pa.: Pennsylvania State University, 1973), p. 11.
11. Ibid., p. 3.

12. National Endowment for the Arts, *Guide to Programs* (Washington, D.C.: National Endowment for the Arts, 1975), p. 3.

13. Ibid.

14. National Endowment for the Humanities, *Program Announcements* (Washington, D.C.: National Endowment for the Humanities, 1976), pp. 1–2.

15. Constitution and Bylaws of the Maryland Alliance for Arts Education, mimeographed.

16. "Congressional Call for Arts in the Schools," *Music Educators Journal* 70, no. 8 (April 1984):11.

17. Rosemarie Cook, Music Consultant, Los Angeles County Public Schools, in interview with author, Downey, California, 11 January 1984.

18. Michael A. Hiltzik, "Proposition 13 Fever Became National Epidemic," *Los Angeles Times*, 6 June 1983, pp. 3, 14.

19. John J. Warrener, "The Effects of Proposition 2-½ on Music Education in Massachusetts," *Massachusetts Music Educator* 31, no. 3, (Spring 1983):8.

20. John J. Warrener, "The Effects of Proposition 2-½ on the Position of Music Supervisor in Massachusetts," *Massachusetts Music Educator* 31, no. 4 (Summer 1983):29.

21. John J. Warrener, letter to author, 1 May 1984.

22. "Worst of Both Worlds," *Baltimore Sun*, 17 February 1984, p. A10.

23. Terry Schwadron, "California's Fiscal Information Gap," *Los Angeles Times*, 10 July 1983, Part IV, p. 3.

24. "The Hughes-Hart Educational Reform Act of 1983: Summary of Implications." Los Angeles: Los Angeles County Board of Education, 1983, p. 1.

25. Elsa Walsh, "Schools Go Begging," *The Washington Post*, 7 November 1983, pp. A1, 24.

26. Charles Suber and Betty J. Stearns, "Music Alert: The Chicago Story" (Washington, D.C.: Music Educators National Conference, 1972).

27. Samuel D. Miller, "Music Education, Recent History, and Ideas," *Bulletin*, Council for Research in Music Education, no. 77, Winter 1984, p. 13.

28. Tommie Pardue, "Stay Public," *Music Educators Journal* 70, no. 5 (January 1984):27–28.

BIBLIOGRAPHY

Alliance for Arts Education. *Interchange*. Washington: D.C.: John F. Kennedy Center for the Performing Arts. Published bi-monthly. Official newspaper of the Alliance for Arts Education.

"Amount of Money Allotted to Each Discipline by State." *Bulletin*, Council for Research in Music Education, no. 58, Spring 1979, pp. 18–52.

Arts, Humanities, and Museum Services Act of 1979: Hearings before the Subcommittee on Education, Arts and Humanities of the Committee on Labor and Human Resources, United States Senate, Ninety-Sixth Congress, First Session on S. 1386 to Amend and Extend the National Foundation on the Arts and the Humanities Act of 1965, And for Other Purposes. Washington, D.C.: United States Government Printing Office, 1979.

Backas, James. "The Environment for Policy Development in Arts Education," *Proceedings of the 56th Annual Meeting*. Reston, Va.: National Association of Schools of Music, 1981, pp. 3–8.

Boyle, David, ed. *Arts IMPACT: Curriculum for Change*. University Park, Pa.: Pennsylvania State University, 1973.

Bulletin, Council for Research in Music Education, no. 43, Summer 1975. Special Issue: CEMREL Aesthetic Education Program.

Goekjian, Annie. "State Arts Agencies: An Overview." *Bulletin*, Council for Research in Music Education, no. 58, Spring 1979, pp. 1–8.

Goodlad, John I., Renata von Stoephasius and M. Francis Klein. *The Changing School Curriculum*. New York: Fund for the Advancement of Education, 1966.

Murray, Kate Rushford. "A Description of Various Projects of the State Arts Councils." *Bulletin*, Council for Research in Music Education, no. 58, Spring 1979, pp. 9–17.

National Endowment for the Arts. *Guide to Programs*. Washington, D.C.: National Endowment for the Arts, annual. Available from the Superintendent of Documents, U.S. Government Printing Office, Washington, D.C. 20402.

National Endowment for the Humanities. *Program Announcement*. Washington, D.C.: National Endowment for the Humanities, annual. Available from the Superintendent of Documents, U.S. Government Printing Office, Washington, D.C. 20402.

Lineberry, William P., ed. *New Trends in Schools*. New York: H. W. Wilson, 1967.

Miller, Samuel D. "Music Education, Recent History, and Ideas." *Bulletin*, Council for Research in Music Education, no. 77, Winter 1983, pp. 1–19.

Pardue, Tommie. "Stay Public." *Music Educators Journal* 70, no. 5 (January 1984):27–28.

Suber, Charles; and Betty J. Stearns. "Music Alert: The Chicago Story." Washington, D.C.: Music Educators National Conference, 1972.

Try A New Face! A Report on HEW-Supported Arts Projects in American Schools. Washington, D.C.: U.S. Department of Health, Education, and Welfare, 1979. U.S. Government Printing Office, Stock No. 017-080-01799-7.

Warrener, John J. "The Effects of Proposition 2-½ on Music Education in Massachusetts." *Massachusetts Music Educator* 31, no. 3 (Spring 1983):7–8.

———. "The Effects of Proposition 2-½ on the Position of Music Supervisor in Massachusetts." *Massachusetts Music Educators* 31, no. 4 (Summer 1983):28–29.

The Music Curriculum

Part II

5

Teaching Methods

A NEW APPROACH TO EDUCATION: CONCEPTUAL LEARNING

One of the most fundamental changes in education during the 1960s was in the way that psychologists and educators viewed the teaching/learning process. Prior to the 1960s, the process of education utilized various approaches to rote learning. Generally, children were expected to memorize specific information given to them by teachers and from books. It was assumed that children would develop understanding of a subject after having learned the appropriate facts about it. One of the significant early events in the history of the development of conceptual education was the Woods Hole Conference (chapter 1), which provided a stimulus for Jerome Bruner's book *The Process of Education*. That important book, only 97 pages in length, was a strong basis for curriculum development in all subject areas and helped to change the nature of instruction in American schools. *The Process of Education* discusses four important themes related to the teaching/learning process.

The first theme is the role of structure in learning and how it can be made central in teaching. Bruner asks the question, "What are the implications of emphasizing the structure of a subject, be it mathematics or history—emphasizing it in a way that seeks to give a student as quickly as possible a sense of the fundamental ideas of a discipline?"[1] The view is put forth that, in order to make exposure to a subject count in the lives of students, they must be given an understanding of the subject.

The teaching and learning of structure, rather than simply the mastery of facts and techniques, is at the center of the classic problem of transfer. . . . If earlier learning is to render later learning easier, it must do so by providing a general picture in terms of which the relations between things encountered earlier and later are made as clear as possible.[2]

The second theme concerns readiness for learning. Psychologists and educators had begun to suspect that children could begin to study difficult subjects at a younger age than had been realized. The discussion is introduced by the now-famous proposition, "The foundations of any subject may be taught to anybody at any age in some form." The acceptance of the proposition signified recognition of the fact that the schools wasted "precious years by postponing the teaching of many important subjects on the ground that they are too difficult." Bruner explains:

It is only when . . . basic ideas are put in formalized terms as equations or elaborated verbal concepts that they are out of reach of the young child, if he has not first understood them intuitively and had a chance to try them out on his own. The early teaching of science, mathematics, social studies, and literature should be designed to teach those subjects with scrupulous intellectual honesty, but with an emphasis upon the intuitive grasp of ideas and upon the use of these basic ideas. A curriculum as it develops should revisit these basic ideas repeatedly, building upon them until the student has grasped the full formal apparatus that goes with them.[3]

In the third theme intuition is involved:

The intellectual technique of arriving at plausible but tentative formulations without going through the analytic steps by which such formulations would be found valid or invalid conclusions. . . . The shrewd guess, the fertile hypothesis, the courageous leap to a tentative conclusion—these are the most valuable coin of the thinker at work, whatever his line of work.[4]

The desire to learn and how such desire may be stimulated are the concerns of the fourth theme:

Ideally, interest in the material to be learned is the best stimulus to learning, rather than such external goals as grades or later competitive advantage. While it is surely unrealistic to assume that the pressures of competition can be effectively eliminated or that it is wise to seek their elimination, it is nonetheless worth considering how interest in learning per se can be stimulated.[5]

The impact of Bruner's work (and that of many others who believed in conceptual learning) on curriculum development in the 1960s was profound. Music educators studied the implications of conceptual learning, developed new ideas about teaching and learning music, and gradually brought into being new practices and curricular materials. Russell Getz, president of MENC, stated:

One of the greatest changes for better music teaching was the gradual acceptance by general music teachers of the concept approach, as compared to previous efforts, which were often more concerned with associative properties of music. Instead of emphasizing story-telling through program music and correlating music with geography, social studies, mathematics, and science, the heart of music education has become the study of music itself, the components of pitch, duration, dynamics, and timbre, and the resultant concomitants such as melody, harmony, rhythm, instrumentation, style, and form.[6]

Another important book that described a conceptual approach to music education was published in 1967. *The Study of Music in the Elementary School—A Conceptual Approach*[7] provides a definition of "concept" upon which the rest of the book is predicated:

A concept is a relatively complete and meaningful idea in the mind of a person. It is an understanding of something. It is his own subjective product of his way of making meaning of things he has seen or otherwise perceived in his experiences. At its most abstract and complex level it is a synthesis of a number of conclusions he has drawn about his experience with particular things. A conceptual statement is a description of the properties of a process, structure, or quality, stated in a form which indicates what has to be demonstrated or portrayed so a learner can perceive the process, structure or quality for himself.[8]

The book also discusses the development of musical concepts:

[It] requires that children think musically. Since each child develops his own concepts individually, it is necessary for him to discover for himself what is in the music. If the teacher presents the child with a body of predetermined facts, there can be a gap between the lesson that is taught and the lesson that is learned. But when the child is making his own investigation of the music and when the processes of his investigation are consistent with the essential nature of the music, there will be no such gap. Too often information is simply poured into the minds of children, thereby depriving them of the exciting experience of discovering it for themselves.[9]

A major contribution of *The Study of Music* is its discussion of concepts about rhythm, melody, harmony, form in music, forms of music, tempo, dynamics, and tone color. It also relates the conceptual learning of music to the general music and instrumental music programs.

Performance in the General Music Class

One of the changes brought about by the conceptual education approach was a new emphasis on performance activities in general music classes. Singing has always been an important part of general music, and basic keyboard instruction has been an accepted practice for decades. During the 1960s and 1970s, however, there was a surge of interest among educators in instrumental performance by general music students because it was an excellent vehicle for conceptual learning. To learn to play classroom and/or social instruments, students must learn to read music and develop other conceptual knowledge of the subject.

One of the stimuli to classroom performance activities was the electronic revolution vis-à-vis instruments. Electronic keyboards made it possible for a group of students to learn to play the piano together because the keyboards cost less than pianos, were smaller and in some cases portable, and lent themselves to class instruction in ways that were not possible with traditional pianos (see Figure 5.1). At first considered to be just electric pianos, they have become complex instruments

FIGURE 5.1. Electronic Keyboard Laboratory.

Note. Photograph courtesy of Musitronic, Wenger Company.

capable of a variety of sounds and effects beyond those of the piano. They are used in music classes not only to teach students to play the piano, but to teach theory and harmony, and to provide ensemble experiences as well. The fact that an electronic keyboard laboratory permits each participant to play in a group or to communicate only with the teacher makes it possible for teachers to work with a large group of students while providing individual assistance in a single time period. The same is true of class guitar instruction. Although acoustic guitars are used in many school music programs, electronic guitar laboratories are often utilized in school general music programs. Another popular instrument for general music students is the recorder, which provides wind instrument experience. An instrumental medium that has gained considerable popularity in the schools since around 1970 is the handbell choir. Handbells are utilized in general music classes to teach musical concepts in a manner that permits students to perform aesthetically satisfying music. Handbell choirs also exist in high schools and have a status similar to that of other musical ensembles.[10]

Arts in Education

Another recent development is the trend toward what is known as arts in education, in which the arts are incorporated into the educational program of the school. Ronald Lee of Syracuse University states, "In such a program the arts most commonly include the visual arts, music, dance and movement, and the theater arts (e.g., drama, mime, puppetry). The arts can also include folk art, creative writing, architecture, costume and fashion design, crafts, poetry, film, television and radio, and photography."[11] Ideally, the arts in education program is an essential part of the curriculum in which the arts are integrated into the instruction received by every child. According to Lee, "In such a curriculum the arts are taught on the same level as and experienced together with disciplines such as English, mathematics, and foreign languages. They are not experienced as embellishments to the curriculum, nor are they isolated from the basic subject areas; they are part of the center or core of the educational program."[12] The Interrelated ARTS Program described in chapter 4 is an example of arts in education. Another example is found in the Pittsburgh, Pennsylvania, public schools. The Pittsburgh Comprehensive Arts Program

is primarily concerned with the development of *each* child's capacity and ability to perceive and respond to the expressive qualities of art. . . . Springing from the educational theories of Pestalozzi, Montessori, Dewey, Piaget, Bruner, and others, the Comprehensive Arts curriculum embraces the eclectic theory of intellectual development, suggesting that the learning process, when truly effective, involves the totality of the learner's personality. With the developing of aesthetic sensitivity as the goal, growth in the *affective* domain—the area of subjective attitudes such as feeling, taste, and valuing—is the primary concern.

Bruner felt that complex concepts could be understood by children at any stage of development if the fundamental structure was identified and organized properly: "In music, the basic elements are pitch, duration, dynamics, and timbre. In the visual arts, the elements are space, light/ color, line, and texture. In both cases, the resultant element is form. By developing curriculum approaches and materials based upon these elements, as well as those in dance, theatre arts, and media arts, at increasingly sophisticated levels of conceptualization, the desired spiral curriculum structure is realized."[13]

Approaches to the Music Curriculum

The various curricula described in this chapter incorporate conceptual learning materials, techniques, and practices. Obviously, not all of the curricula were conceived because of the work of American psychologists and educators. Indeed, in most cases the innovators who developed the methods were concerned almost entirely with helping children to learn music and worked from the basis of the music rather than from psychological theory. Several methods were imported from other countries. These systems met the needs of American music education and were recognized in this country as appropriate for the time and worthy of respect because they were (and still are) highly effective. Some of the topics in this chapter, such as the Manhattanville Music Curriculum Project and the work of Dr. Edwin Gordon and of Madeline Carabo-Cone, reflect contemporary American thought on the subject. They deserve recognition for their contributions not only to music education, but to general education in the United States. Comprehensive musicianship (chapter 7) is also based on principles of conceptual learning.

THE DALCROZE METHOD

Emile Jaques-Dalcroze (1865–1950) studied at the Conservatoire of Music in Geneva, in Paris under Leo Delibes and in Vienna under Bruckner and Fuchs. In 1892 he was appointed Professor of Harmony at the Geneva Conservatoire. Dalcroze realized early in his teaching career that the training of musicians was based on incorrect principles. It emphasized the training of individual faculties in order to develop excellence in technique. There was little regard, however, for musical expression. The education of musicians almost entirely neglected the development of the ability to express oneself musically.

The students were taught to play instruments, to sing songs, but without any thought of such work becoming a means of self-expression, and so it was found that pupils, technically far advanced, after many years of study were unable to deal with the simplest problems in rhythm and that their sense for pitch, relative or absolute, was most defective; that, while able to read accurately or to play pieces memorized, they had not the slightest power of giving musical expression to their simplest thoughts or feelings, in fact were like people who possess the vocabulary of a language and are able to read what others have written, yet are unable to put their own simple thoughts and impressions into words.[14]

In the view of Dalcroze, technique was only a means to art. The goal of music education should not be to train performers on their particular instruments or singers in vocal technique, but to develop the musical faculties. The musicality of the individual should be the basis for specialized musical study.

Dalcroze believed that it was necessary to make students aware of musicality through tone and rhythm. Because tonal sense could only be developed through the ear, he emphasized vocal exercises and singing. He found that students sang more musically when they beat time themselves, and so wrote "gesture songs." Gesture songs combined music with movement. At that time other educators discouraged the use of movement to music. Dalcroze not only encouraged it, but made the coordination of movement and music the basis of his method.

At first Dalcroze employed only the arm movements used by conductors. The next step was to develop a series of arm movements to express various meters from 2 to 12 beats per bar. The arm movements included such meters as 5/4, 7/4, 9/4, and 11/4. He also devised movements of the body and legs to correspond to various note values from whole notes to 12-beat notes. Although his students were very supportive of his work, the conservatory was not, and he had to form a voluntary experimental class that met after hours and away from the conservatory.

In 1905 his method was demonstrated at the Solothurn Music Festival and was warmly received. Until this time, the method was intended for the early education of musicians, but it became apparent that Dalcroze's work was also suitable for the musical education of children. He studied psychology with the help of his friend, psychologist Claparede, who recognized the potential of the method in teaching children. In Dalcroze's words,

It is true that I first devised my method as a musician for musicians. But the further I carried my experiments, the more I noticed that, while a method intended to develop the sense for rhythm, and indeed based on such development, is of great importance in the education of a musician, its chief value lies in the fact that it trains the powers of apperception and of expression in the individual and renders easier the externalization of natural emotions. Experience teaches me that a man is not ready for the specialized study of an art until his character is formed, and his powers of expression developed.[15]

In 1906 Dalcroze presented his first training course for teachers. The course was repeated several times until 1909, when the first diploma was granted. He considered it necessary to grant diplomas to his students because his method was used in other parts of the world by people whom he did not train, and who he felt were not equal to the standards of his own students. The method was introduced in the United States about 1915, although not in its authentic form. The techniques were adapted, and many teachers were influenced by derivations of the method. Charles Hoffer wrote:

The use of "walking" and "running" as designations for quarter and eighth notes is one common example in the elementary schools. By the 1930s a number of college music schools or physical education departments were requiring courses in *eurhythmics*, the term often used for Dalcroze-like instruction. The interest in it seemed to level off at that point and then decline. A modest renewal of interest in it has taken place since 1970. About twenty colleges offer some instruction in the approach, with four of them giving a Dalcroze certificate.[16]

The Method

EURHYTHMICS

Although eurhythmics is commonly thought to be the Dalcroze method, that is only one of its three aspects. The other two are ear training (solfège) and improvisation. Eurhythmics consists of exercises for the physical response to music. Students are helped to become sensitive to rhythm by responding with their entire bodies. Musical concepts are internalized by means of rhythmic movement. According to Dalcroze,

It is my object, after endeavoring to train the pupil's ear, to awaken in him, by means of special gymnastics, the sense of his personal body-rhythm, and to induce him to give metrical order to the spontaneous manifestations of his physical nature. Sound rhythms had to be stepped, or obtained by gestures; it was also necessary to find a system of notation capable of measuring the slightest nuances of duration, so as to respond to both the demands of the music and to the bodily needs of the individual.[17]

Students move freely to music in eurhythmics classes. The teacher (sometimes students) improvises at the piano. The students walk, run, and skip, creating individual movements expressive of the music they hear. Every person interprets what he or she hears differently, and so the movements of each student express individual interpretation and are therefore individualistic. Students develop movements that range from simple physical responses to complex combinations in which the arms conduct the meter, while the feet move in syncopated patterns and the head nods on certain beats. The following exercises were adapted by Jo Pennington in the book *The Importance of Being Rhythmic: A Study of the Principles of Dalcroze Eurhythmics Applied to General Education and to the Arts of Music, Dancing, and Acting*, which is based on Dalcroze's book *Rhythm, Music and Education*.

Exercise 1. Following the Music, Expressing Tempo and Tone Quality. The teacher at the piano improvises music to which the pupils march (usually in a circle) beating the time with their arms (3/4, 5/8, 12/8, etc.) as an orchestra leader conducts, and stepping with their feet the note values (that is, quarter notes are indicated by normal steps, eighth notes by running steps, half notes by a step and a bend of the leg, a dotted eighth and a sixteenth by a skip, etc.).

The teacher varies the expression of the playing, now increasing or decreasing the intensity of tone, now playing more slowly or more quickly; and the pupils "follow the music" literally, reproducing in their movements the exact pattern and structure of her improvisation. . . .

Exercise 4. Note Values, Syncopation. In the exercise to demonstrate note values, the pupils march one step for each beat while the teacher plays quarter notes; two for each beat in eighth notes; three for triplets, etc. The values of whole and half notes are also represented, the half note by a step and a bend, and the whole note by a step followed by three or more movements of the leg without stepping. Exercises in syncopation require more training. The teacher plays an even tempo—say quarter notes in four-four time. The pupils at a command walk in syncopation for one measure or more—stepping either just before or just after the beat . . . anticipating the beat or retarding it. As their *feet* take steps just *off the beat*, their *arms* must continue to beat the time regularly, each movement being made *on the beat*. This exercise then is one in concentration, mental and physical control (coordination) and in the understanding of the musical principles of polyrhythm and syncopation. . . .

Exercise 7. "Realization" of Rhythms. As explained in the program, to "realize" in the Dalcroze sense means to express in bodily movements all the elements of the music save sound. In this exercise the teacher plays a series of measures and the pupils, after listening to them, realize in their movements the rhythm which they have heard—expressing the note values, the meter, the shading, the quickness or slowness—they reproduce the rhythm in movement as definitely as though it were written in ordinary musical notation. In fact that is usually the next step in the exercise. This exercise combines several important elements of Dalcroze eurhythmics: ear training; the musical analysis of rhythm; memory and concentration; and the physical response necessary to the execution of the rhythm in movement. . . .

Exercise 9. Independence of Control. This exercise is one in polyrhythm, the pupil expressing several rhythms at the same time. He may perhaps beat three-four time with the left arm and four-four with the right at the same time walking twelve-eight with the feet. There are many variations of this though in the beginning pupils find it sufficiently difficult to beat two with one arm and three with the other, especially since each arm must "remember" so to speak, the accent which falls on the first beat of its own measure. Another form of this exercise is to have the pupils march one measure while beating time for another; as three with the arms and four with the feet. These are worked out mathematically at first but soon the pupils learn to keep in their muscular and mental consciousnesses the pulse of the two rhythms simultaneously.

Exercise 10. Rhythmic Counterpoint. Rhythmic counterpoint is an exercise in the appreciation of unplayed beats. The teacher improvises a short theme, let us say simply two half notes and a quarter in five-four time. The pupil, instead of stepping on the first, third and fifth beats of the measure, will do the counterpoint by stepping on the *second* and *fourth*. Or, if told to do the counterpoint in eighth notes, he will fill in every unplayed eighth note beat. This is an exercise in inhibition and in the accurate analysis of time values. A more complicated form of exercise is the realization of theme and counterpoint simultaneously. For example, the pupils may learn a simple melody for a theme and then proceed to sing this melody while executing a rhythmic counterpoint, as a sort of accompaniment, with steps, or with gestures. This is a very interesting exercise to watch for first one hears the note played by the teacher and following it the steps taken by the pupils to fill in the measure, the whole making a sound pattern as well as a rhythmic pattern.[18]

EAR TRAINING, OR SOLFÈGE

Dalcroze believed that the study of solfège helped students develop their abilities to listen, hear, and remember. The first exercises are in the key of C; they help the student develop a tonal memory for C. Various hearing and singing exercises are mastered, after which the student goes on to other keys. The purpose of ear training is to develop what Dalcroze called "inner hearing."

Solfège sessions are a part of each Dalcroze class. Students sing intervals and songs with syllables, and improvise vocally. In learning pitch relationships, students may sing one or more measures aloud, then one or more measures silently. Or, when ending one song and beginning another, students may sing the final pitch of the first song, then the beginning pitch of the second, naming the interval between them. The piano is used to test accuracy of the interval. Many times during a solfège session, students are asked to sing the syllable do, which in the European fixed-do system is always C. Students are expected to work toward acquisition of absolute pitch.[19]

IMPROVISATION

Improvisation is usually done at the piano, although other instruments can be utilized instead. The purpose is to help students develop the same freedom at the piano that they have in their bodily responses to music. They are given exercises in extemporaneous playing in given tempi.

For example, as children are moving freely to music improvised by the teacher, one child may be asked to move toward the piano, improvise a "flute part" in the high register or a "drum part" in the lower as the teacher continues his playing in the middle register, all without interruption of the pulse or the movement activity of the rest of the class.[20]

Dalcroze made much use of improvisation in his theoretical harmony classes. He would have students improvise melodies or melodic fragments as part of their development of comprehension of intervals. Improvisation also helped them become familiar with harmony. Improvisation with other instruments and voice is done in similar fashion.

The Use of Eurhythmics in Special Education

Dalcroze recognized the value of his method to students with special needs. He himself taught students who had exceptional ability and those who had physical handicaps, especially the blind. He taught blind students in Barcelona, using special exercises to develop consciousness of space of objects that could not be seen. He included several exercises for blind students in his book *Eurhythmics, Art and Education*, some of which follow:

Exercises for Developing the Sense of Space and the Muscular Sense. Two rows of pupils facing each other. Each pupil in the first row, with outstretched arms, touches the palm of the hand of a pupil in row 2. One step backwards, then again one step forward, clapping the hand that has been released. . . . Then two steps, three steps, eight steps, twelve steps. . . .

Exercises for Developing Tactile Sensibility and Muscular Consciousness. Realize on the arms of a sighted pupil the *crescendos* and (decrescendos) of muscular innervation, in their relation to fullness of gesture—then execute these dynamic nuances oneself. Control is easy to establish if, in moving his arms, the pupil can place the end of his finger on different steps of a ladder or on pegs planted in the wall and serving as guide-marks.

Exercises for Developing the Auditory Faculties in their Relation to Space and the Muscular Sense. The pupils, standing anywhere in the room, guide themselves by the voice of the master. He moves about, uttering a sound or beating a drum from time to time; they walk in the direction of the sound. . . . The master plays the piano, the pupils, attracted by the sound, make their way towards the piano, to right or left, pass round it, retreat from it during the decrescendo, etc.[21]

THE ORFF APPROACH

Carl Orff's approach to music education for children developed out of his own radical musico-theatrical style of composition. His eclectic interest in folksong, nineteenth century popular song, dance and theatre music, and the most accessible elements of medieval, Baroque, and Renaissance music led to his comprehensive theory of music pedagogy. It is an experiential method based on rhythm and improvisation, building on what children find natural, such as rhythms of strolling, skipping, running, swaying, and stomping, and the universal children's chant on the minor third.

In Munich during the early years of his career, Orff (1895–1982) was influenced by the dance-movement ("eurhythmics") theories of Emile Jaques-Dalcroze. In 1924, Orff and the dancer Dorothea Gunther founded the Gunther Schule, an innovative ensemble of dancers and musicians that developed and trained teachers in new forms of movement and rhythm. Many of the students at the Gunther Schule were preparing to be physical education teachers. Orff's goal was to develop creativity in his students by means of Dalcroze's principles. Improvisation was a major part of the program of the Gunther Schule.

With the help of Curt Sachs and Karl Maendler, Orff developed an instrumental ensemble at the Gunther Schule, which Orff described as follows:

In due course the Gunther school boasted an ensemble of dancers with an orchestra of their own. Music and choreography were supervised by Gunild Keetman and Maja Lex, respectively. Dancers and players were interchangeable. Suitable instruments (flutes, cymbals, drums, etc.) were integrated into the dance itself. The diverse and varied instruments employed included recorders, xylophones, and metallophones of all ranges, glockenspiels, kettledrums, small drums, tomtoms, gongs, various kinds of cymbols, triangles, tune bells; and sometimes also fiddles, gambas, spinettinos, and portatives.[22]

The ensemble traveled throughout Germany, playing for educational conferences and teachers' meetings, and generating interest in the work of the Gunther Schule. A plan to test the Orff–Gunther approach on a large scale in German schools was interrupted by World War II.

During the war, the Gunther Schule was completely destroyed. After the war, a Bavarian radio official discovered an out-of-print recording from the Gunther Schule. His interest in the record led to the gradual rekindling of national interest in Orff's work. When Orff reflected on the method that he had developed prior to the war, he began to think that rhythm education might be more effective if begun in early childhood rather than in adulthood. He explored this new idea and concluded that elemental, i.e., primeval, basic, music—music evolving from speech, movement, and dance—could become the basis of early childhood music education. With his lifelong associate, Gunild Keetman, he began to test his ideas in nursery schools and kindergartens.

A radio broadcast series in 1948, in which children performed elemental music on a small complex of Orff instruments, encouraged widespread interest in music that had appeal to great numbers of children. Help was received from Klauss Becker, who attempted to reconstruct the Orff instruments. In 1949 Becker opened a workshop, Studio 49, where he built and improved the instruments (see Figure 5.2).

Between 1950 and 1954, Orff published his five volume *Music for Children*, a compilation and complete reworking of his prewar work. The method, called *Schulwerk*, attracted international interest. Orff's books were translated into eighteen languages, and the exercises were adapted to the native rhythms and music of the countries that imported his techniques. The American (actually Canadian) adaptation by Doreen Hall and Arnold Walter consists of five volumes and a teacher's edition. It corresponds to the original *Schulwerk* in progression of subject matter, but the material itself has been selected and/or written especially for English-speaking children.

Orff's work as a composer was greatly influenced by his teaching. He felt that rhythm was not only the fundamental element, but was actually the basis of melody, contrary to the then-current concept of

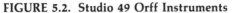

FIGURE 5.2. Studio 49 Orff Instruments

Note. Photograph courtesy of Magnamusic-Baton, St. Louis, Mo. 63132.

melody as the basis of rhythm. He felt that rhythm should evolve from dance movement, that melody should evolve from speech rhythms, and that sonority should evolve from layers of rhythms. Orff's own music is straightforward and insistent. Harmony is subordinate to the autonomous interaction of melody, rhythm, and sonority, as in folk songs. His attempt to infuse the musical theatre with pure musical/ visual forms culminated in *Carmina Burana* (1936), a scenic/oratorio named after the thirteenth-century manuscript collection of Latin folk poems at Benediktbevern in southwest Germany. It is his most successful composition and is performed frequently.

The Approach

Orff believed that music education should be patterned on the evolutionary stages of mankind. Children must relive the historical development of music in order to develop musicality within themselves. Orff used the word *elemental* to refer both to the music of early man and to the music of young children. The music of young children is unsophisticated and unrefined but natural and capable of development. Improvisation, an important part of elemental music, must be intro- duced at the child's level before it can be developed into a mature form. To Orff, this meant beginning with rhythm and allowing other musical elements to grow out of it. He devised simple rhythms and chants to serve as the basis for sequential developmental activities. Speech patterns familiar to children become their first musical materials. The patterns come from chants, games, and the vocal sounds that are already part of the child's vocabulary. The patterns are chanted, clapped, danced, and sung. Bergethon and Boardman wrote:

The essence of Orff's instructional plan is to help children build a vocabulary of rhythmic, melodic, and harmonic patterns that they can use in creating their own music. This they acquire through a progressive sequence of performance activities: speaking, moving, singing, and playing.[23]

Orff's emphasis on rhythm suggested to him the need for percussion instruments in music education. Working with instrument makers, he developed an ensemble of percussion and stringed instruments that included xylophones (soprano, alto, and bass), glockenspiels (soprano and alto), metallophones (soprano, alto, and bass), drums, cymbals, woodblocks, rattles, viola da gambas, and lutes. The instruments are designed to create the proper instrumental timbre for the music contained in the *Schulwerk*. Although they can be played with no training, children are encouraged to develop sufficient technique to play them correctly so they can be used expressively. The *Schulwerk* includes many exercises and ensemble arrangements for such usage.

Children are encouraged to imitate and improvise vocally and instrumentally. They create their own music both from inner feelings and in imitation of the sounds of their environment. They learn to become sensitive to sounds and to use them as sources for the development of other sounds. Rhythm serves as sources for imitation, answers to contrasting rhythms, and melodic invention.

Rhythm patterns, melodies, and ostinato figures are tried out and played on the instruments played earlier. These instruments are anything but toys. They are carefully selected and contrasted, they are in fact replicas of medieval ensembles, as meaningful to children now as they were to grown-up people in those days. They are difficult enough to be a challenge to a child yet simple enough to make improvisation possible. . . . And that is what Orff wants more than anything else—*to enable children to improvise, to invent their own rhythms, melodies, and accompanying figures.*[24]

Early experiences are informal and are often based on children's games. They are enjoyable for children and build a solid musical foundation. The children are encouraged to evaluate their music and to improve it in terms of sequence, structure, and other musical aspects. They are also encouraged to notate the music, inventing their own notational systems under the guidance of the teacher. Music is not separated from movement because for children both are part of the same thing—a mode of expression.

The first melody encountered by children in the Orff approach is the falling minor third (See also the following section on Kodály). Feeling is developed for tempo, direction, meter, and dynamics by chanting names of classmates and familiar words.

This, along with other simple intervals, grows almost imperceptibly out of rhythm. Other intervals and rhythmic patterns are added gradually. Once the children learn the pentatonic scale, they sing a repertory of pentatonic tunes. Orff considered it important to limit children to the pentatonic scale in the early stages of instruction because it is easier for them to be creative in this mode. If a seven note scale were used, the children might imitate music they already know, rather than creating their own music. Creativity, especially at the early stages, is all-important.[25]

The first lessons on harmony involve drones of open fifths, which Orff called *Borduns*. Borduns are effective when played against pentatonic melodies and are conducive to improvisation. They also lend themselves to ostinati. More sophisticated harmony evolves from the melodic movement of Borduns.

When rhythm and melody have become part of the children's vocabulary, studies in form and improvisation are introduced. Alternations between chorus and soloist provide the necessary contrast to delineate form. Canons are also used abundantly.

The *Schulwerk* provides music that is used for basic studies. It is organized as follows:

Volume I. Pentatonic Nursery Rhymes and Songs
Volume II. Major: Bordun (the fourth and seventh scale degrees are introduced)
Volume III. Major: Triads (tonic and supertonic, tonic and submediant)
Volume IV. Minor: Bordun (Aeolian, Dorian, and Phrygian modes)
Volume V. Minor: Triads (first and seventh triads, first and third triads, and other degrees)

The strength of Orff's *Schulwerk* is its appeal to children. It involves the children in creative activities that include singing, playing, and moving in ways that are natural to them. Adult concepts of music are not imposed on children; rather, musical concepts grow out of children's involvement with the creation and performance of music.

Most children welcome the opportunity to participate in music–rhythm–movement activities, and the fact that their own impulses have such importance further enhances the value and appeal of participation.

The *Schulwerk* approach recognizes children's speech as the basis for musical development. They learn musical concepts from the texture, dynamics, pitch patterns, and rhythms of speech. Children are guided, rather than taught, and their musical knowledge grows from their experiences.

Children are encouraged to combine movement with speech and vocal sounds and to express what they feel and hear—first individually, then, when ready, as a group. The children begin with imitation and repetition and go on to improvisation. Improvisation of sound and movement lead to concepts of form. Children analyze what they do in order to repeat and vary their creations.

Playing the Orff instruments extends the media of expression available to children. Kinesthetic activity is transferred from the body to a family of melodic and percussive instruments. Not only do the instruments provide opportunities for movement, but they offer the chance for improvisation of melodies, ostinati, drones, and Borduns, all of which extend beyond the range of the voice.

The value of the sensory approach to all learning has been recognized by many educators throughout history, and has been verified by contemporary research. Orff's *Schulwerk* allows children to grow artistically in ways that are most meaningful for them.

Orff-Schulwerk in the United States

The Orff approach is used in private and public schools in many parts of the United States. The American Orff-Schulwerk Association, founded in 1963 at Ball State University in Muncie, Indiana, promotes the dissemination of information about the Schulwerk and its uses in the United States through its official publication, the *Orff Echo*, and through scores of Orff-Schulwerk workshops offered each year.

The First International Symposium on Orff-Schulwerk that took place in May 1967 in Bellflower, California, was the first Orff-Schulwerk international meeting to be held in the United States. The symposium was a one week report and demonstration Title III federal project involving six school districts in California. The California Orff-Schulwerk Institute was one result of the Bellflower Project. The Institute provides courses and workshops in Orff-Schulwerk and publishes *The Circle*, a quarterly journal.

THE KODÁLY METHOD

Kodály believed that Hungarian music education should be designed to teach the spirit of singing to everyone, to educate all to be musically literate, to bring music into every day for use in homes and in leisure activities, and to educate concert audiences. He was concerned with the creative, humanizing enrichment of life through music and regarded the goal of music literacy for everyone as the first step toward his ideal.[26]

In addition to his goal of universal music literacy, Zoltán Kodály (1882–1967), a fervent nationalist, realized the need to build a national music culture. He brought about the means to develop individual musicality and a national music culture through his approach to teaching music in the schools, using nationalistic and folk songs for musical material.

Kodály was born on 15 December 1882 in Kecskemet, Hungary. His parents were amateur musicians. As a child, he learned the piano and violin, sang in a cathedral choir, and often visited the music library of the cathedral to study the scores of the masters. He became a composer after studying composition at the Budapest Academy of Music. Kodály had a strong interest in the nationalistic music of Hungary and after much study of that music realized that not enough was known about what made it distinctly and uniquely Hungarian (Magyar). Because of this, the published folk music was often poorly edited and arranged out of its true character. From 1906 to 1908, Kodály, with his lifelong friend Béla Bartók, wandered the country collecting native folk songs. Through their efforts, a body of authentic literature was assembled which they felt could serve as the basis for development of Hungarian nationalistic pride and self-knowledge. Much of the music was used by Kodály in helping children develop musicality.

Kodály was concerned that twentieth century Hungary was not as musical as it had been in the nineteenth century, when music was a part of many activities of everyday life. Society had lost its ability to stimulate musicality in individuals, and Kodály felt that the schools must assume that function. He created his pedagogical system in order to help the schools reawaken the musicality of the Hungarian people.

The Method

The Kodály method is a developmental curriculum that includes reading and writing music, ear training, rhythmic movement, singing, and listening. Rhythmic awareness and feeling are developed in children by means of movement and rhythm games that help them recognize and feel the basic beat and rhythm patterns aurally and visually. Simple rhythms are notated by means of line notation, and the names "ta" and "ti" are assigned to quarter and eighth notes so they can be sung in rhythm.

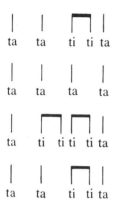

Children clap the rhythms, sing them, and move to them. Rhythms are derived from children's song literature and speech patterns. Improvisation is also a part of rhythm education. Children are given the opportunity to respond to rhythm phrases with their own improvised phrases. Thus feeling for meter, pulse, accent, and balance is developed. As rhythm experiences become more complex, students develop both increasingly acute sensitivity to rhythm and beat and skill in rhythm reading. The early training in rhythm is not an end in itself; students are eventually able to read and perform the rhythms of folk and art music.

Rhythm is not taught as a separate entity but in conjunction with melody. The sequence of melodic experiences is as structured and logical as that of the rhythmic experiences. Kodály recognized that children do not sing half steps in tune. He felt that if young children did not develop good intonation habits and skills they would not be able to improve them later. Rather than encourage faulty intonation, he based the literature of his approach on pentatonic songs and exercises. The scale built on *do, re, mi, sol,* and *la* contains no half steps. Children are capable of mastering, both musically and intellectually, a body of music literature built on that scale.

The pentatonic scale is the foundation of early Kodály training because it is the basis of much Hungarian folk music. The songs and modes of Hungary, however, are not appropriate material for American music education, and there were problems at first in the adaptation of the system for American usage. Americans have now begun to approach the Kodály method in earnest, and the problem has been overcome to the point where there is adequate song material to supply the needs of the curriculum. Much of the material is from the folk song repertory of our country, some from classical music literature, and some from the folk repertories of other countries, including Hungary. Researchers and educators are continually finding music that is meaningful to specific ethnic groups in the United States and that will be suitable for use in the Kodály curriculum.

The most natural interval for children to sing, and one that they sing as part of play, is the descending minor third (see example, p. 121).

When children make up songs, taunt each other, or chant sing-song ditties, it is usually on this interval. The next tone to be added during the course of the curriculum is the fifth degree of the pentatonic scale, which adds the intervals of the major second and perfect fourth to the children's musical vocabulary. This, too, is part of the natural melodic language of young children. Probably every young child has sung the following melody:

The Kodály method builds from the natural ability of children to use melody toward helping them develop intellectual awareness of what they are already able to do. As children develop musically and intellectually, the melodic vocabulary is expanded to include the other two notes of the pentatonic scale and the octave of the tonic.

When the pentatonic scale has been learned and exercises have been mastered, children have acquired a vocabulary of intervals that they are able to sing in tune, sight-read, and understand. When whole steps and perfect intervals are mastered, children are ready to conquer half steps. The fourth and seventh degrees are added, thus completing the major scale.

Upon mastering the tones of the major scale and all of the intervals contained in it, accidentals are introduced. This leads to the next logical step—minor and modal scales. There are two important aspects of this learning experience: (1) rhythmic and melodic experiences are usually combined—they are separate on occasion, but students do not lose sight of their relationship; (2) movable *do* is used from the beginning so that children develop the capability to feel at ease in any key.

Another important aspect of the Kodály method is kinetic development. Rhythm activities have been mentioned, but melodic development also utilizes kinetic activity in the form of hand signals. This feature of the curriculum was invented by the Englishman John Curwen around the middle of the nineteenth century; Kodály adapted it for children learning music by the use of his method (see Figure 5.3).

The use of hand signals helps children develop cognitive knowledge of notation because they are able to "read" music by translating it into body motion. They take dictation with hand signals, sight-read, and perform duets and part songs. Learning to sight-read by means of a medium other than the voice increases reading skills greatly. Hand signals are used rhythmically as well as melodically so that melody and rhythm do not become separated from each other in the minds of children.

Instruments

Students can learn to play instruments if they wish, but not until they have mastered the use of the voice. They are ready to address themselves to the technical problems of an instrument when their own musical competency allows them to play instruments with good tone and intonation, and in a musical manner. The use of the recorder is encouraged; students also play other wind and string instruments.

Results of the Kodály Method

Students who complete several years of the Kodály curriculum are able to sight-read with ease much of the folk song and art music literature. They can do so by means of melodic syllables, rhythmic syllables, and hand signals. They are able to analyze form and harmony. More important, most are able to perform the music in an aesthetically satisfying manner. Persons who can do this are musically educated, and music can be an integral part of their lives.

The Kodály Method in the United States

Kodály's work has been adapted for use in the United States by several educators, including Tibor Bachmann, Lois Choksy, Mary Helen Richards, and Denise Bacon.

Dr. Tibor Bachmann is a native of Hungary, where he taught the Kodály method in a Hungarian state teachers college. He came to the

FIGURE 5.3 Kodály Hand Signals

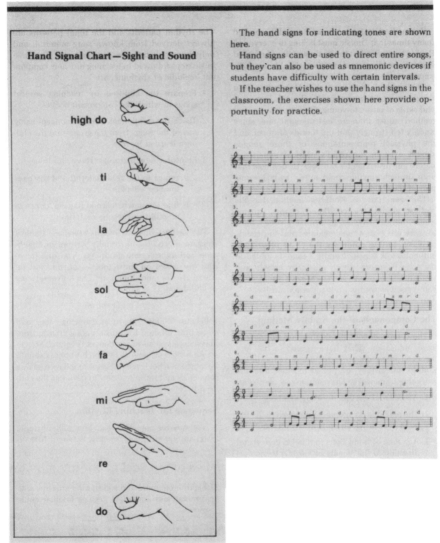

The hand signs for indicating tones are shown here.

Hand signs can be used to direct entire songs, but they can also be used as mnemonic devices if students have difficulty with certain intervals.

If the teacher wishes to use the hand signs in the classroom, the exercises shown here provide opportunity for practice.

Source: *The Spectrum of Music*, Grade 6, Teacher's Annotated Edition, by Mary Val Marsh, Carroll Rinehart and Edith Savage, Macmillan Publishing Company, Inc. Copyright © 1983 and reprinted with the permission of Macmillan Publishing Company, Inc.

United States in 1956 and became a naturalized citizen. Bachmann's approach to the Kodály method is presented in the series *Reading and Writing Music*.[27] His text contains few familiar songs because Bachmann believes that, if children are to learn to read music, it must be done with unfamiliar musical material. The child's introduction to notation is by means of a one-line staff, and additional lines are introduced as they become necessary. Rhythm is stressed from the beginning; sections on rhythm are designed to add emphasis by allowing the student to study and use rhythm apart from melody. Kodály's rhythm syllables are used, as well as the *sol-fa* syllables and hand signals for pitch designation. Bachmann incorporates tone games to encourage individual response in matching tones in order to help children develop musical hearing; dictation is utilized to develop tonal memory. Music writing is stressed because, according to Bachmann, students will be better able to handle music reading if they are familiar with music writing; children are made aware at an early stage that the music they write can be performed by themselves and others. Bachmann uses the movable *do* clef in order to spare children the necessity of learning key signatures before they are ready. Tone blending and intonation are developed in two-part singing exercises. After the G clef is introduced, key signatures are used to designate the location of *do*, and accidentals are introduced. Students study and analyze authentic Hungarian and American folk music in order to develop perception of the elements and structure of music.

Lois Choksy studied the Kodály method under Katinka Daniel, a student of Kodály. Choksy travelled to Hungary in 1968 and attended the Danube Bend Summer University at Estergon. She returned to Hungary in 1970 to study music education at the Franz Liszt Academy.

THE KODÁLY METHOD OF MUSIC INSTRUCTION

What the Kodály Method Is

Zoltán Kodály said many times that "music must belong to everyone." By this he meant that the competencies of musical hearing, reading, and writing should be known skills to all people. The method that bears his name is a child developmental sequence for teaching music concepts and skills to young children. It is a vocal method rather than an instrumental one, since Kodály felt strongly that the sounds of music and the physical representations of those sounds should exist in the child's musical vocabulary before any instrument is touched. He believed that only through singing could music truly become a part of the child.

The materials of the method for the earliest grades are childhood chants, singing games, nursery rhymes, and nursery songs. Most of these are three- or four-note tunes and so provide an easy starting point. As the children progress, authentic folk music, usually pentatonic, is added to their song repertory. Later, composed music is used, but it is always art music, music of known and recognized composers such as Mozart and Beethoven. Contemporary music is used also.

The Components of the Kodály Method

The components of the method are not new to music education. They have existed in bits and pieces in many countries for many years. In the Kodály system they are pulled together into one workable framework. The components consist of:

1. A system of rhythm duration symbols.

2. The movable *do* system, in which *do* is the home tone in major modes and *la* the home tone in minor modes.

3. A series of hand signs that aid in the development of tonal relationships.

During the first year of study, children develop a concept of in-tune singing, feeling the beat and accent in duple meter. They also learn to identify rhythmic patterns of familiar songs and to step and clap the rhythm and beat. In addition, they develop concepts of high and low, loud and soft, and fast and slow. Choksy, like Kodály, prefers to avoid half steps because of children's intonation problems, but does permit them to be used when necessary. She utilizes the same rhythmic syllables and hand signals as those used by Kodály. Choksy agrees with the current practice in the official Hungarian curriculum that restricts children in the second year of study to the keys of C, F, and G. The rationale is that children need to develop a strong feeling of key center, and familiarity with these keys will help them in future instrumental music study. Also, accidentals are avoided in the pentatonic scales in the keys of C, F, and G.

In a later stage of study, children are introduced to triple meter, the dotted half note, the anacrusis, syncopation, and 16th note patterns. The extended pentaton is also introduced. At that point *fa* and *ti* are formally introduced, and much study is devoted to the concept of major and minor keys and key signatures. Dotted rhythms are continued. Triplets and other meters are learned, and modal melodies are introduced. Choksy identifies four sources of difficulty in adapting the Kodály method for American education: (1) the nature of American culture, (2) school organization and teaching practices, (3) teacher training, and (4) materials.[28]

Mary Helen Richards received her Bachelor of Music Education degree from the University of Nebraska. She studied choral repertoire at Stanford University and Smith College, and later studied in Hungary with Kodály.

The Richards curriculum progresses by units, from simple to complex. It begins with music reading in the first year and continues with the building of musical knowledge and skills gradually through six levels. Her system is built on a sound rhythmic foundation. It is taught with rhythm syllables by means of physical movement. The pentatonic scale is taught with hand signals on a movable *do*. The basic instrument is the voice; two-voice singing parts are considered the perfect tool for developing good intonation. For the most part, pentatonic songs are used, including American pioneer songs, mountaineer songs, spirituals, and various ethnic songs. Singing begins with the natural chants of children; the intervals of these chants are the basis of the approach to melody.

The Richards approach emphasizes music reading and intervallic recognition in conjunction with the recognition of rhythmic syllables. Key signatures, clefs, and accidentals are not introduced until necessary to continue progress. Review is continued throughout the process of music learning, and each element of music is coordinated with the other elements. Experience charts, used to present concepts to an entire class, help to develop group musical response. The charts regulate the procedures to be followed by the teacher and serve as guides for the presentation of musical ideas. Charts on the first level take the class through four tones of the pentatonic scale. The fifth tone and the octave are introduced by means of the charts in the second year. By the end of the third year, the complete diatonic scale and complex rhythm patterns have been learned. Continual emphasis is placed on reading and singing because Richards considers these activities inseparable. Music writing is less important than in the Bachmann approach.[29]

Denise Bacon was director of the Dana School of Music in Wellesley, Massachusetts, when she traveled to Europe in 1967 to study the Orff and Kodály methods. She realized the potential of the Kodály curriculum and returned to Hungary several times to become more thoroughly acquainted with it. In 1969 the Ford Foundation granted $184,000 for the planning and development of the Kodály Musical Training Institute (KMTI), originally located in Wellesley. Denise Bacon was the first director of education at the Institute. KMTI is now located at the Hartt College of Music in Hartford, Connecticut. Bacon has founded another center for Kodály studies—the Kodály Center of America (KCA), located in Boston.

A number of institutions have established Kodály teacher education programs. There are programs at Silver Lake College, Alverno College, Holy Name College, and the University of Calgary. Several universities offer master's degree programs in music education with a concentration in Kodály taken at some of the above schools. Extensive summer offerings in the Kodály method are available at such schools as West

Chester University, Towson State University, Wisconsin Conservatory of Music, the Peabody Conservatory of Music, Westminster Choir College, and Michigan State University, among others.

The Organization of American Kodály Educators (OAKE) was formed in March 1974 for the purpose of supporting Kodály education in the United States and to act as a catalyst for its growth and development. Its official journal is *The Kodály Envoy*. In 1984 OAKE became an affiliated organization of MENC.

ORFF AND KODÁLY COMBINED

For several years during the 1960s, the names Orff and Kodály signified something new and exciting to American music teachers. For three reasons, however, the two approaches were often confused:

1. The Orff and Kodály approaches arrived on the American music education scene very close in time to each other.
2. Often, both were spoken of and written about by the same people in attempts to introduce them to American music educators.
3. There was a general lack of knowledge of the philosophy and methodology of each approach.

It was not unusual to hear the two names used interchangeably, as though Orff and Kodály were two aspects of one method. The confusion was compounded by the earlier tendency of American music educators to try to combine the approaches. These attempts were premature because the rank-and-file music teachers knew too little about them. Since that time, both methods have been clarified in publications, in the development of new materials, and in teacher training. Now that sufficient time has passed to permit teachers to know both as separate and distinct approaches, educators are finding effective ways of either merging the two or combining aspects of each.

Denise Bacon discussed the two approaches upon her return from her 1967 trip to Europe to study Orff and Kodály education. She stated that although educators try to combine the approaches, such was not the intent of Orff or Kodály, although they held great professional and personal respect for each other. In fact, the Orff Institute at that time used elements of the Kodály method, and Hungarian teacher-training institutes used Orff instruments.

The most fundamental difference between the two methods has been defined by their creators. Kodály conceived of his curriculum as a definite method, to be developed in a systematic, predetermined manner. Orff, on the other hand, did not see his approach as constituting a method, and did not want it to become structured; it can be used successfully even if modified and adapted for local conditions and musical traditions. An early attempt to combine the two approaches was evaluated by Denise Bacon:

I still believe they should be used in the same curriculum, but whether fused as a teaching procedure I cannot say yet. . . . My class is now doing Kodály one day a week and Orff one day a week. Kodály can exist independently without the Orff, but I do not believe the Orff will accomplish the objectives as well without the Kodály. At this moment, I tend to think the two should be used in parallel fashion rather than fused, and that the Kodály should precede the Orff and the instruments should not be used as accompaniment to singing until children have acquired some musical skills.[30]

Arnold Walter, president of the Inter-American Music Council, expresses strong opposition to the combination of the two methods:

The only question that concerns us here is whether it [Kodály] should be combined with basic Orff training. I am inclined to say that it should not. The Orff approach is the nearest thing to incidental learning a school can provide. It stresses impulse, fantasy, improvisation—characteristics that have nothing to do with the deciphering of printed scores, however valuable that may be in itself. The Schulwerk does not attempt to teach all about music. On the contrary, it leaves a great deal out. It limits itself to laying a firm foundation for studies yet to come, be they vocal, instrumental, theoretical, or historical. It is based on the premise that children can assimilate music in exactly the same way that they learn to speak. If that premise is false, the Schulwerk has obviously little value. If the premise is correct, we ought to be consistent, we ought to keep the pedagogical framework intact.[31]

The two approaches, however different in concept and execution, have proven adaptable to combination. The Orff encourages and stimulates authentic musical feeling in children through an evolutionary, musical creative process. Part of music's appeal, though, is intellectual, and the Kodaly method is capable of satisfying this need. Both aim for and achieve musicality and intellectual satisfaction, but these goals are achieved in radically different ways. It is possible that each method can enhance the other to allow children to learn music even more creatively and intellectually.

Grace Nash expressed the need for both Orff and Kodály, in combination with Laban's theory of motion in exploration of space, time and weight, developed on the principles of Dalcroze. She states that

placed in the center of the curriculum, this [Orff-Kodály-Laban] program could help children express their verbal experiences in sound, movement, color (nonverbal media) and similarly nonverbal experiences can be translated into articulate and beautiful language. The five senses, movement, color, and feeling would be combined with language and sound. Every child would be shown how to sing and control pitch knowledgeably. Their songs, poetry, and dances would be self-accompanied on precision-tuned easy-to-play instruments (classroom instruments), an ensemble of beauty and excellence of aesthetic proportion—student inspired and achieved.[32]

Nash discusses the dehumanizing environment brought on by contemporary society. There is an ever-increasing need to develop human sensitivity and awareness of the individual in a mechanized society. As people move further from nature they have fewer opportunities for play and fantasy, and less chance to develop those human attributes that can help people achieve stability and satisfaction.[33]

There are several similarities between the Orff and Kodály approaches that make it possible to combine them:

1. Bodily movement is an integral part of both methods, the Orff for creating music, the Kodály as an aid to learning music reading.

2. Both teach melody using the same intervals and begin with a pentatonic scale as the basis of the early body of literature. The Orff uses the pentatonic so that children's creativity will not be endangered by imitation of familiar music built on the seven-note scale. The Kodály uses the pentatonic because children have difficulty singing half steps in tune and should not be confronted with that interval until they are capable of producing it correctly.

3. Both stress the development of a musical vocabulary—the Kodály by assigning verbal and hand-signal symbols to melody and rhythm, the Orff a musical, nonintellectual use of movement.

4. Both rely on rhythmic and melodic improvisation, the Orff for the development of musical feeling and creativity and the Kodály for musical feeling and the development of music reading skills.

5. Both are used with groups of children, rather than individuals, and in many ways depend on the interaction of groups of children for the development of concepts.

6. Both begin with the child as the source of music, rather than by externally imposing music on the child.

Another reason for combining both approaches is that there is no uniform curriculum for music or any other subject in the United States. Often, the decisions concerning curriculum are made by individual teachers. Most elementary general music teachers meet their classes on a regular, but infrequent basis, and not under the best of conditions. Facilities and equipment are often less than adequate. Given these conditions, most American music teachers are not in a position to adopt new programs. They must instead adapt those parts of methods that they feel will best serve their individual purposes, a practice that does not always produce the best results. But conscientious and knowledgeable teachers have made effective use of certain elements of Orff and Kodály. They have combined those elements with traditional approaches and enriched their programs. If teachers must choose the elements they need to use, it is likely that they will select from both the Orff and Kodály approaches. This practice will probably strengthen the elementary general music program in the United States.

THE MANHATTANVILLE MUSIC CURRICULUM PROGRAM

We must stop pretending that we have the sacrosanct perspective and the duty to inflict it, in *our* terms, on captive students. Real education is not a study about things; it is experience *inside* things. If music is an expressive medium, learning involves expressing. If it is a creative art, learning means creating. If music has meaning, personal judgments are fundamental to the learning process. If music is a communicative art, the educational process must involve students in communication. Facts may be taught, but meaning is discovered. There is nothing antecedent to discovering meaning.[34]

This statement is the basic premise of the Manhattanville Music Curriculum Program (MMCP). The MMCP, funded by a grant from the U. S. Office of Education, was named for Manhattanville College of the Sacred Heart in Purchase, New York, where it originated. Its objectives were to develop a music curriculum and related materials for a sequential music learning program for the primary grades through high school.

The project produced the *synthesis*, a comprehensive curriculum for grades three through twelve, *interaction*, an early-childhood curriculum, and three feasibility studies: The Electronic Keyboard Laboratory, The Science-Music Program, and the Instrumental Program. In addition, twenty-three workshops for music educators were sponsored by institutions of higher learning for teacher re-education. The program has given music education an alternative to traditional practices and techniques.[35]

In all phases of operation and in the curriculums which were produced, the project has presented alternatives to the status quo. . . . From the ground up, in rationales, objectives, musical perspectives, structure of concepts, learning processes, educational expectations, even in consideration of what a music class is, the MMCP curricula have been grounded in the logic of a viable art and contemporary educational ideas.[36]

Exploratory Study

The MMCP began in 1965 with an exploratory study of ninety-two innovative and experimental music programs in thirty-six states; fifteen of the programs, located in several parts of the country and unrelated to each other, were studied in depth. Each experiment/innovation emphasized at least one element in the following four categories: content, strategy of learning, use of media, and performance and literature. Several conclusions were drawn from the study of the programs and six common factors were discovered:

1. Each program had clearly defined objectives.
2. The students' frame of reference was a basic concern in planning instruction.
3. The relationship of skill and cognitive growth was a primary factor in program development.
4. Teachers assumed the role of resource persons and guided students rather than imposed knowledge on them.
5. Development of skills and cognitive learning depended on the individual student's ability to accept responsibility; students were given the opportunity to learn by trial and error and by hunch.
6. The teachers had active musical lives outside of their schools.[37]

The Project

MMCP was a three-phase program. Phase One (1966) dealt with perspectives of student learning potentials, problems of curriculum reform, and classroom procedures. Phase Two (1967) dealt with the refinement and synthesis of information gained in the first exploratory period and the organization of information into a feasible curriculum. Phase Three (1968) consisted of the refinement and field testing of all curriculum items, the initial investigation of a separate curriculum for early childhood, the preparation and testing of plans for teacher retraining, and the development of an assessment instrument that reflected the program objectives.

PHASE ONE

Phase One was a period of reflection and introspection in which the validity of traditional music education values and practices were questioned. A need for innovative procedures was established on the basis of insights gained about the nature of students' personal involvement in music. A contradiction was found between the classroom style of the teacher and the learning style of the student. In considering the unconventional classroom the MMCP Project Director, Ronald B. Thomas, stated that "a basic core of concepts and related factors of skill development, environment, process, and objectives were shaped from the observed logic and enthusiasm of students in the experimental classrooms."[38]

PHASE TWO

The work of refining and synthesizing the data produced in Phase One was approached with the conviction that, to be successful, the curriculum had to consist of more than information and concepts. It would have to be an integrated plan designed to meet the needs of the students, the subject matter, and the educational objectives. Before such a task could be begun it was necessary to define the fundamental characteristics of music. The identification of the characteristics served as the basis of musical and educational decisions throughout the writing of the curriculum.

The results of Phase One made it clear that students did not hear music the way that teachers thought they did, and did not understand what teachers thought they should about music. That which was of concern to teachers was often of no interest to students. Students perceived music in a way valid for themselves, regardless of the teacher's values. Their perceptions were based on their own interests, observations, and ideas of form and structure. Hearing processes were also considered. It was known that students' attitudes and manners of perception were influenced by the type of learning situation in which they experienced music.

The spiral curriculum took shape during Phase Two. The term *spiral* refers to a sequence of concepts in the curriculum, each of which is presented several times at various stages of development. Every successive presentation of a concept is at a higher, more refined level. The results of Phase Two were tested in selected classrooms called experimental stations.

PHASE THREE

The first objective of Phase Three, the refinement of the curriculum, was carried on in a manner similar to the previous year. In Phase Three, however, the work was conducted in larger field centers rather than in experimental stations, where plans were given their initial trials.

During Phase Three the spiral curriculum proved to be unsuitable for very young children, so a precycle program for kindergarten through grade two was developed. With the cooperation of the Central Atlantic Regional Educational Laboratory, the program was explored and tested, as the spiral curriculum had been during the previous two years.

Teacher in-service programs began receiving consideration during Phase Three. Four issues were considered:

1. Teachers did not know enough about music to work with students creatively.
2. Teachers found it difficult to consider goals other than skill achievement and performance.
3. Many teachers were method oriented and found it difficult to work in a new framework.
4. Many teachers had not personally experienced creative accomplishment and were therefore not secure in an atmosphere of creativity.

Assessment materials and instruments were surveyed, but none were found to be capable of measuring the effectiveness of the MMCP. During the third phase an assessment model was created, but because of time limitation, not tested.

The Products of MMCP

The United States Office of Education granted funds for the MMCP to execute four specific contractual obligations: (1) a curriculum guide and related material for a sequential music program; (2) a meaningful sequence of basic musical concepts in terms of the students' understanding; (3) a spiral curriculum that would help to unify the philosophies and directions of all aspects and levels of the music curriculum; and (4) a curriculum for teachers to increase their ability to work with the MMCP.

CURRICULUM GUIDES

Synthesis

The MMCP *synthesis* was the major curriculum produced by the project. A compilation of the work done in the project, it offers a functional and operational plan. It provides for learning experiences to grow from the students' perspective rather than the teacher's, and includes suitable materials. The *synthesis* is a flexible guide rather than a tightly structured syllabus.

Interaction

The goal of *interaction* is the musical experience. Children become involved as creative and active musicians; they are required to make judgments, discover new ideas, sounds, and meanings. Sensitivity to the elements, materials, and expressive possibilities of music are inherent goals of the children's experiences. Formal musical concepts are not presented in a planned approach; they are approached informally by experiencing five phases: free exploration, guided exploration, exploratory improvisation, planned improvisation, and reinforcement.

Electronic Keyboard Laboratory

Questions that arose concerning the relationship of skill and concept were answered in a feasibility study of the electronic keyboard. The report on the electronic keyboard laboratory dealt with operational procedures and the relationship of the keyboard experiences to the other MMCP curricula. The structure is related to both the *interaction* and *synthesis* and follows the developmental plan of musical exploration. This curriculum is more tightly structured than the *interaction* and *synthesis* because of the need for children's dexterity development while learning to play keyboard instruments.

Science–Music Laboratory

This program is a synthesis of music and scientific learning experiences based on electronic music. Science and music are integrated by the use of technological musical equipment and the awareness that there is a strong relationship between the two fields.

Instrumental Program

The instrumental program is a creative and aural approach to instrumental development. Tape models replace lesson books and students create their own pieces instead of studying exercises. The structure of the instrumental program is similar to that of the other curricula.

Teacher Re-education Plan

The teacher re-education program requires sixty to ninety hours of instruction and experience in the MMCP. Teachers learn to understand the musical and educational ideas of the various MMCP curricula. It is used in conjunction with the *synthesis* and provides experiences for teachers parallel to the ones in the *synthesis*.

The College Curriculum Study

The MMCP includes the area of teacher training, which was completed several years after the other curricula. It is designed to develop a different perspective on the purpose, procedures, and results of college education for music education majors.

The Application of MMCP

MMCP first encourages children to listen to the sounds of their world and to create sounds by clapping, stamping, tapping, snapping, scraping, whistling, moaning, and so on. Working in groups, children put together sounds to form compositions, which are analyzed and discussed by the students and teacher (guide), and suggestions and trials are made for alterations and/or improvements. As concepts such as form, balance, and contrast develop, the combinations of sounds become more refined and begin to reflect aesthetic feeling in their planning and execution. As children develop sensitivity, they begin to use more musical sounds that involve melody and rhythm. They are also encouraged to develop their own notational systems, which increase in refinement along with the musical compositions. Eventually, this creative approach can lead children through several stages of exploration and creativity until they develop the ability aesthetically to perceive, perform, and create music.

Music, as defined by Ronald Thomas, has three purposes: it is a vehicle for communication, it is an art that interprets one's environment, and it is a means of creative fulfillment. Children, to be able to utilize music for these purposes, must develop certain skills that allow them to use their cognitive knowledge of music. They must be able to hear music the way the composer does—to perceive music without having first to interpret it cognitively. Children must be able to think in the medium of music, to conceptualize and recognize musical structure, and to comprehend the language of musical sounds.[39] Students need to study music in an unfragmented manner to experience all aspects of music. Students in the MMCP compose, perform, conduct, listen, and evaluate. The purpose of such a comprehensive approach is to stimulate the development of sensitivity to musical meaning, to allow the student to get beyond the mechanics of music. As Thomas states, "He does not simply stand back and observe it with reverence—he uses it as a means of creating, exploring, and in his own way, achieving."[40]

The music lab is recommended as the best environment for MMCP activities, because in a special setting a variety of activities can take place. In the lab, students are involved in the total musical process— composing, performing, conducting, listening, enjoying, sharing, and reacting. The lab experiences recommended by Thomas include seven types of activities: MMCP strategies (composing, performing, evaluating, conducting, listening), student recitals, listening to recordings, research and oral reports, guest recitals, skill development, and singing

FIGURE 5.4. MMCP Curriculum Concept Spiral

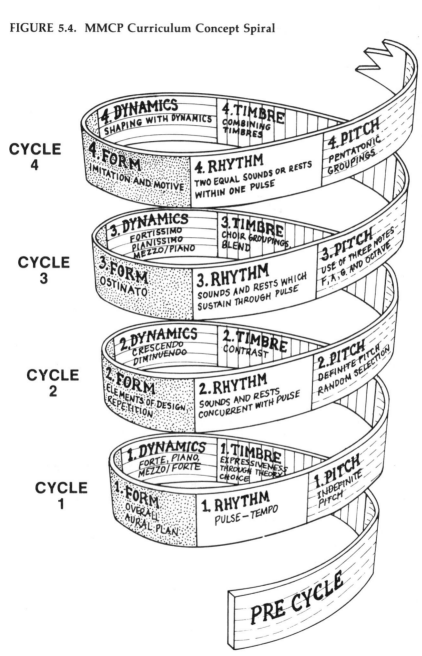

Note. Ronald B. Thomas, *MMCP Final Report*, Part 1, Abstract (United States Office of Education, ED 045 865, August 1970). pp. 39–49.

for enjoyment. Students participate in each as they wish. Most are individual or small-group activities. Students plan their own lab time, and the teacher plans his or her schedule to meet individual needs. These diversified activities, which often take place simultaneously, require a large open room with areas set aside for different purposes, such as listening, recitals, and composing.

Much learning occurs in the context of problem-solving situations. Each successive problem grows out of another and contains a factor that requires new judgment or synthesis of facts. The teacher is guided by the spiral curriculum in devising learning strategies (see Figure 5.4). Strategies are designed so that success is assured; if a student fails to find a solution, the problem is presented differently, allowing him or her a different approach to, or perception of, the problem.

CYCLE 1

Timbre

The quality or color of sound, the timbre, is a major factor in the expressiveness of music. The timbre may be shrill, intense, dulcet, silvery, nasal, smooth, bright, or dull. Choosing the timbre that best expresses what the composer has in mind is one of many decisions which he must make when creating music.

Dynamics

The degree of loudness or softness, the volume or the dynamics of the sound, also must be determined by the composer. Music may be loud, *forte* (f), soft, *piano* (p), or medium-loud, *mezzo-forte* (mf). The volume of the music or any one part of the music will affect the total expressive result.

Pitch

The comparative highness or lowness of sounds is also determined by the composer. Initially, his choices will deal with sounds of indefinite pitch such as those produced by a triangle, a cymbal, a drum, etc. In such cases, highness or lowness often depends on preceding and/or following sounds. (A cymbal sounds low after a triangle but high after a large drum.)

Form

The plan, the shape, the order, the form of a piece of music is another determination made by the composer. Form refers to the aural design, the way the sounds are put together. The composer's plan or form is based on his expressive intent.

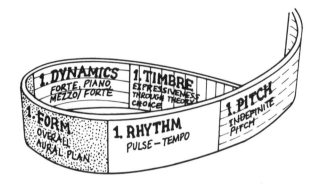

Rhythm

Tempo is that characteristic of music that makes it appear to go fast or slow. The pulse is the underlying beat (sometimes not heard but only sensed) that may help to create a feeling of motion in music. These items are the choice of the composer.

CYCLE 1 SKILLS

Aural

Identify the general and comparative pitch characteristics of sounds of indefinite pitch (differences between drum sounds, cluster sounds, sounds made by objects, etc.).

Identify various timbres used in the classroom and the instruments used to produce them.

Identify volume differences in student compositions and in illustrative recordings.

Identify pulse and changes in tempo.

Recognize simple sequences.

Dexterous

In performing:
  Produce sounds (vocal or instrumental) at the instant they are demanded and control the ending of the sound.
  Produce the desired tone quality (vocal and instrumental).
  Produce sounds of three volume levels (f, p, mf) when allowed by the nature of the instrument.
  Maintain the tempo when necessary.

In conducting:
  Indicate precisely when to begin and when to end.
  Indicate pulse, where appropriate (not meter).

Indicate desired volume.

Indicate general character of music (solemn, spirited, etc.)

Translative

Devise graphic symbols, charts, or designs of musical ideas that allow for retention and reproduction. Such visual translations should represent the overall plan, include distinguishing signs for different instruments or timbres, and relative durational factors. Volume should be indicated by the standard symbols: f, p, mf. Words designating the character of the music, such as quietly, forcefully, smoothly, or happily, should also be used.

Vocabulary

Timbre	Form	Indefinite pitch	Volume
Dynamics	Tempo	Aural	Improvise
Forte	Pulse	Devised notation	Composer
Piano	Pitch	Cluster	Conductor
Mezzo-forte			Performer

TEACHING STRATEGY 5.1 —

Cycle 1 Sample Strategy

THE QUALITY OR COLOR OF SOUND, THE TIMBRE, IS A MAJOR FACTOR IN THE EXPRESSIVENESS OF MUSIC

- Each student selects an item or object in the room with which he can produce a sound. Preferably, the item or object will be something other than a musical instrument.

- After sufficient time has been allowed for students to experiment with sounds or selected objects, each student may perform his sound at the location of the item in the room.

- Focus on "listening" to the distinctive qualities of sounds performed. Encourage students to explore other sound possibilities with the item of their choice.

- Discuss any points of interest raised by the students. Extend the discussion by including the following questions:

  How many different kinds of sounds were discovered?
  Could the sounds be put into categories of description, i.e., shrill, dull, bright, intense, etc.?
  After categories of sound have been established, experiment with combinations of sounds.

- Is there any difference between sounds performed singly and sounds performed in combination?

- In listening to the recorded examples focus on the use of timbre.

Teaching Strategy 5.1 (cont.)

- How many different kinds of sounds were used?

- Could we put any of the sounds in this composition into the categories we established earlier, i.e., bright, dull, shrill, etc.?

- Were there any new categories of sounds? Could we duplicate these?

ASSIGNMENT

Each student should bring one small object from home on which he can produce three distinctly different sounds. The object may be a brush, a bottle, a trinket or anything made of wood, metal, plastic, etc.

  Suggested Listening Examples:
"Steel Drums," Wond Steel Band; Folk 8367
"Prelude and Fugue for Percussion," Wuorinen, Charles; GC 4004
"Ballet Mechanique," Antheil, George; Urania (5) 134

THE PLAN, THE SHAPE, THE ORDER OF A PIECE OF MUSIC IS DETERMINED BY THE COMPOSER

- Each student may perform his three sounds at his own desk. Focus on "listening" to distinctive qualities of sounds performed.

- Encourage students to focus attention on other exploratory possibilities by investigating the sound-producing materials with greater depth.

  Can you produce a sound on your object that is bright, dull, shrill, intense etc.? How is this done?

- Discuss any points of interest relative to the activity.

- Extend the discussion by focusing on the following questions:

  Why is silence in the room necessary for performance to be effective?
  How did sounds vary or seem similar?
  Which objects produced the brightest, dullest, most shrill, most intense sounds?
  What makes a sound dull, bright, intense, etc.?

- Divide the class into groups of 5 or 6 students. A conductor–composer should be selected by each group. He will determine the order of sounds and the overall plan of the improvisation. Conducting signals should be devised and practiced in each group so that directions will be clear.

- Allow approximately 10 minutes for planning and rehearsal. At the end of the designated time each group will perform.

- Tape all improvisations for playback and evaluation. Discussion should focus around the following questions:

  Did the improvisation have a good plan? Did the music hold together?
    What was the most satisfying factor in this piece?
    How would you change the improvisation?
    What are some of the conductor's concerns?

- In listening to the recorded examples, focus attention to the overall shape or plan of the music. In listening to a single example two or three times, students may map out a shape or a plan that represents the composition. These plans can be compared and used for repeated listenings.

Teaching Strategy 5.1 (cont.)

Suggested Listening Examples:
"Construction in Metal," Cage, John; KO8P-1498
"Poéme Electronique," Varise, Edgar; Col. ML5478; MS6146

THE DEGREE OF LOUDNESS OR SOFTNESS, THE VOLUME OR THE DYNAMICS OF THE SOUND, WILL AFFECT THE TOTAL EXPRESSIVE RESULT

- Using the entire class as performers on object instruments, volunteer students will conduct an exploratory improvisation to investigate the effects of: sounds used singly, sounds used in combination, and dynamics. It is suggested that before the improvisation the volunteer conductors choose 3 or 4 students who will play singly when directed. Conducting cues for entrances and exits should also be established.

- Tape the exploratory improvisations for immediate playback and evaluation. Discuss all perceptions verbalized by the students. Extend the discussion by including the following questions:

How did volume or dynamics affect the total result?
Can all the object instruments be heard at an equal level of volume when performed in a group?

- Groups consisting of 4 or 5 students will plan an improvisation. Focus attention to the quality of sounds used singly, the quality of sounds used in combination, and the expressive use of volume. Consideration for the overall shape of the piece should also be a concern.

- Following a short planning and practicing period (about 10 minutes), each group will perform the improvisation for the class.

- Tape the improvisations for immediate playback and evaluation. Discuss students' comments as they relate to the improvisations. Extend the discussion by focusing attention on the following questions:

What degree of loudness or softness was used most frequently by the performing groups?
Did the improvisations have an overall shape or design?

- Summarize the discussion by introducing forte (f), piano (p), and mezzo-forte (mf). In listening to the recorded examples, ask students to identify the dynamic level used most frequently by the composer.

- Did you get any musical ideas from this composition that you might be able to use?

Suggested Listening Examples:
"Parade," Gould, Morton; Columbia CL 1533
"Te Deum, Judex Crederis," Berlioz, Hector; Columbia ML 4897
"Prélude á i'Aprés-midi d'un faune," Debussy, Claude; London LS 503

THE PULSE IS THE UNDERLYING BEAT THAT MAY HELP TO CREATE A FEELING OF MOTION IN MUSIC

- Allow 30 seconds for each class member to think of an unusual vocal sound. The sound can be made with the throat, voice, lips, breath or tongue.

- Each student may perform his/her sound for the class. Focus "listening" on the distinctive qualities of the vocal sounds performed.

Teaching Strategy 5.1 (cont.)

- Discuss any points of interest raised by the students. Extend the discussion by including some of the following questions:

  Did anyone perform his/her sound long enough to communicate a feeling of motion?
  How would you describe the motion?

- Divide the class into groups consisting of 4 or 5 students. One person in each of the groups should be a conductor. Each group will concentrate on producing their individual sounds to the motion of an item of their choice or one that has been suggested to them, i.e., the steady motion of a carpenter hammering a nail, the steady motion of a worm crawling, the steady motion of a person jogging, the steady motion of a horse galloping, etc.

- Allow approximately 10 minutes for groups to plan and practice their improvisations. At the end of the designated time each group will perform.

- Tape each improvisation for immediate playback and analysis. Discuss any comments made by the students. Extend the discussion by including the following questions:

  How would you describe the motion, slow, medium, or fast?
  Did it have a steady beat or pulse?

- Summarize the discussion by introducing tempo as the characteristic that refers to the speed of music and pulse which is the underlying beat (sometimes not heard but only sensed).

- In listening to the recorded examples, focus attention on the use of tempo.

  How would you describe the tempo, slow, medium, or fast?
  Did the pulse or underlying beat change before the end of the composition? What was the effect?

  Suggested Listening Examples:
  "Flight of the Bumblebee," Rimski-Korsakov, Nicolai; Epic LC 3759
  "String Quartet No. 79, Op. 76, No. 5, Haydn, Joseph; Turnabout TV 34012S

CYCLE 2

Timbre

Sounds of different quality may be used effectively to create a feeling of contrast in music. These sounds may occur at the same time. Often, the differing timbres result in clarity for each of them. (When sleigh bells sound with timpani, each is heard clearly and distinctly.) A change of timbre, one sound color followed by a contrasting tone quality, gives variety to a piece of music (sleigh bells and timpani followed by slide whistles and wood blocks). Also, one part of a composition may display one timbre while another section may employ a contrasting timbre.

Dynamics

Gradual changes from one level of loudness or softness to another often contribute to the expressiveness of a piece of music. *Crescendo*, growing louder, and *diminuendo*, growing softer, can create a sense of climax or anticlimax, of increasing excitement or approaching calm. The rate of such changes may vary, some requiring a relatively long and some a relatively short period of time.

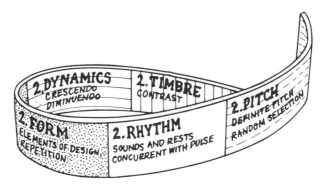

Form

The reuse of musical material is basic to musical structure. Repetition of single sounds, small groups of sounds, longer musical statements, or whole sections of music has been the practice of most composers. However it is used, repetition serves as a unifying factor in a piece of music.

Pitch

If the pitch of a sound can be identified and can be reproduced by another sound source, it is called definite pitch. There are many gradations of definite pitch between high and low. Any definite pitch may be combined with, or may precede or follow, other definite pitches or sounds of indefinite pitch.

Rhythm

If a piece of music has a regularly recurring pulse, some sounds and some silences may begin with a pulse and end with the next pulse. Several such sounds or rests may follow each other. Any desired sequence of sounds and silences is, in fact, possible.

CYCLE 2 SKILLS

Aural

Identify the general relationships of a wide variety of pitched sounds. Recognize contrast in timbre.

Identify gradual volume changes.

Develop memory of simple linear groupings.

Identify simple repetitions.

Identify pulse as it continues through rests.

Dexterous

In performing:
Produce notes and rests that have a one-pulse duration.

Repeat simple musical ideas used previously.

Control instrument or voice in gradual volume change.

Assume correct posture for performance and develop correct techniques for holding instruments, sticks, and beaters.

In conducting:
Indicate crescendos and diminuendos.

Cue in performers.

Indicate changes in mood.

Indicate changes in tempo.

Translative

Prepare musical scores that indicate functions and responsibilities of separate parts. This requires a separate horizontal line for each part.

Use quarter notes and quarter rests where appropriate (not the five-line staff).

Use <> for crescendo and diminuendo, a double bar ‖ for the ending, and repeat signs :‖ for repeats.

Vocabulary

Contrast	Definite pitch	Mood	Double bar
Crescendo	Rest	Score	Repeat sign
Diminuendo	Concurrent	Quarter note	Linear grouping
Repetition	Cue	Quarter rest	

Composition in the music lab is done individually and in groups. Improvisation is included with composition in order to stimulate awareness of compositional style and creativity. Everything composed by students is performed, either in the lab or in recitals, for friends, teachers, or parents. Each performance is followed by a critical evaluative session.

Strategies are included in the MMCP *synthesis* for each cycle of the spiral curriculum. The strategies are in the form of behavioral objectives, and state the prerequisites necessary for a student to progress to the next cycle. The *synthesis* includes sample strategies, indexes of cycles and concepts, and categorized discography.

The MMCP *interaction*, written for children from kindergarten through second grade, focuses on musical sound and involves little notational activity. *Interaction* is based on the premise that all children enter school with a significant musical background, upon which new concepts can be developed. *Interaction* does not have to be presented by a music specialist—it is designed to be used by classroom teachers. It is a process of musical exploration in five developmental phases: free exploration, guided exploration, exploratory improvisation, planned improvisation, and reapplication. Each phase includes sample encounters, principal ideas, objectives for students, procedures for the teacher, and evaluative criteria.

The goals of *interaction* are that the child (1) is involved as a creative, active musician; (2) learns through experience not only to discriminate but also to perceive the manner in which sounds are arranged, is able to critically determine whether the arrangements of sounds are used effectively, and is encouraged to consider alternative arrangements of the sounds; (3) participates in the discovery of the basic concepts of sound manipulation and organization; (4) gains the simple skills that allow for a musical realization of his musical ideas; and (5) develops those attitudes toward music that assure that the educational experiences have intrinsic meaning and are personally rewarding.[41] The objectives of *interaction* are outlined below.

Skill objectives:
1. To explore a wide variety of sound sources to discover a wide variety of sounds.
2. To explore a wide variety of ways of producing sounds on the sound sources provided.

Cognitive objectives:
1. To develop awareness of a great variety of sounds by identifying sounds in the auditory environment and sounds deliberately produced by the child and others.
2. To perceive the differences and similarities in sounds and to identify them operationally in ways that relate to personal experiences and by describing their physical characteristics.
3. To identify a wide variety of sound sources in the environment.

Attitudinal objectives:
1. To engage freely in exploratory activities initiated by self and teacher.
2. To share discoveries of new sounds and sound-producing techniques with the class.
3. To develop an openness to experience, to generate an excitement for discovery.[42]

TEACHING STRATEGY 5.2—

Cycle 2 Sample Strategy

SOUNDS OF DIFFERENT QUALITY MAY BE USED EFFECTIVELY TO CREATE A FEELING OF CONTRAST IN MUSIC

- Each group will create a composition that is intended to convey two distinct feelings. Students may decide the feelings they will express or use the following suggestion:
- Describe the feeling of walking through jello and the contrasting feeling of speeding along a raceway.
- Divide the class into groups of 4 or 5 students. Each group will work independently in a different area of the room. Students may either select instruments first or feeling first, whichever appears to them to be the most practical.
- Each group should plan to make some written plan for their composition. Any kind of written plan is acceptable as long as the performers can understand it.
- After sufficient time has been allowed for students to plan and practice their compositions, each group will perform for the class.
- Tape all compositions for immediate playback and evaluation.

Focus questions and comments on the following:
How were the two feelings achieved?
How did the quality of sound differ when the feeling changed?
What new musical factors were used?
How would you change the composition?

- In listening to recorded examples focus attention to the way in which sounds of different quality are used to create a feeling of contrast in music.
- Discussion should include other musical factors as they relate to contrasting feelings, i.e., use of dynamics, tempo, etc.

Suggested Listening Examples:
"Contrasts," Raaijmakers, Dick; Epic LC 3759
"Contrasts for Violin, Clarinet, and Piano," Bartók, Béla; Bartók Records

WHEN A PIECE OF MUSIC HAS A REGULARLY RECURRING PULSE, SOME SOUNDS AND SOME SILENCES MAY BEGIN WITH A PULSE AND END WITH THE NEXT PULSE

- Using the entire class as vocal performers, volunteer students will conduct an improvisation that makes use of sounds in combination, sounds heard singly, and brief periods of silence.

Teaching Strategy 5.2 (cont.)

- Each composer–conductor will select three sounds that can be made with the throat, voice, lips, breath or tongue. Each of the three sounds will be performed by a group of students. The class can be divided into three equal groups each with an assigned vocal sound. Before beginning the composer–conductor will relate his cueing signals to the class.

- Following the improvisations, discuss any analytical, judicial, or creative perceptions made by the students. Discussion may be extended with the following questions:

  Did you feel a steady pulse throughout the improvisation?
  What was the distribution of sounds heard singly, sounds heard in combination, and silences?

- Divide the class into groups of 4 or 5 students. Each group will choose a conductor.

- The students will plan a short piece of music that will be approximately 30 to 40 seconds in length. (This could be done as homework.)

- This piece will have a regularly recurring pulse with some sounds heard singly, some sounds heard in combination, and brief periods of silence. Students may want to devise a plan to assist them in recalling their ideas at performance.

- Tape all performances for playback and analysis. Discuss the improvisations beginning with student comments. Extend the discussion by including some of the following questions:

  Was a steady pulse present throughout the improvisation?
  Was there variety in the length of sounds used?
  To what extent was silence effective?
  What made some pieces particularly exciting or interesting?

- In listening to the recorded examples, focus attention on the use of sounds over a regularly recurring pulse. Ensuing discussion could include the following:

  What new musical factors did you hear?
  How was silence used effectively?
  How would you identify the tempo of this composition?

  Suggested Listening Examples:
  "Pictures At An Exhibition," "The Market Place," "Catacombs," Moussorgsky, Modest; Columbia ML 4700
  Piano Quartet, Op. 25, Rondo alla Zingarese, Brahms, Johannes; Turnabout TV 34037S

MMCP in Practice

The MMCP is used in some schools, but the most common usage is in the adaptation of its concepts and strategies for use in traditional music programs. Its special requirements for successful implementation have often caused it to be less effective than it might be under more ideal circumstances. One of the requirements is that the teacher must be thoroughly prepared to work within a framework far removed from traditional music programs. It is also necessary to educate administrators, fellow teachers, and parents not to expect music instruction to "justify itself" by means of traditional performances. The sounds that emanate from the music room do not always sound like music; in fact, unless passers-by understand what is going on, it is likely that they will sometimes interpret the sounds as noises. The initiated are aware that the catalogue of sounds is part of the creative process.

Finally, the MMCP takes place in an informal and relaxed atmosphere. There are no rows of desks facing the front of the room. Students arrange themselves to fit specific situations, so a traditional classroom is unsuitable. An open room with movable furniture is desirable; it should contain various kinds of musical instruments, recording and playback tape equipment, and phonographs; synthesizers can also be used. The MMCP can be fairly expensive compared to traditional programs. In some school systems in which creativity is viewed as an essential part of education, however, the cost of the MMCP is not a factor. The informal, self-motivated approach of the MMCP corresponds closely to the philosophical basis of open education.

TEACHING MUSIC THROUGH MUSIC LEARNING THEORY: THE CONTRIBUTION OF EDWIN E. GORDON
By John M. Holahan

Most music educators agree that a major purpose of music teaching is to enable students to appreciate music. Moreover, there is a consensus that it is the music educator's responsibility to provide the appropriate readiness for students to experience music appreciation. Traditional music education practice has been justified by the belief that appreciation is a function of aesthetic response, without need for further explanation, i.e., music for music's sake. Without abandoning the purpose of attaining music appreciation, music learning theory is intended to explain the music learning process. In terms of music learning theory, one develops true appreciation for music by understanding music. To understand music, one must experience and learn music as sound, not as metaphors, descriptions, or as analogies to other art forms. For the teacher who has an awareness of the music learning process, teaching becomes a matter of providing students with what they need to know and are capable of learning, rather than merely presenting opportunities for aesthetic response without the sequential development of music understanding and music learning.

Music learning theory is a comprehensive model of the music-learning process based on available evidence from research in the psychology of music and related disciplines. As a model, music learning theory is intended to explain how one learns when one learns music skill and music content. Music skills include listening, performing, reading, writing, creating, and improvising. Music contents are the musical materials that are used when one is engaged in a music skill. Major, minor, Dorian, and Lydian tonalities are examples of classifications for tonal music content. Duple and triple meters are examples of classifications for rhythm content. Because a music skill cannot be learned without a music content, an important function of music learning theory is to provide a framework to include both. Thus the many levels of skill and many levels of tonal content can be brought together in the form of sequential objectives for tonal learning, and the many levels of skill and the many levels of rhythm content can be brought together in the form of sequential objectives for rhythm learning.

Method and Technique

Music learning theory should not be interpreted as being either a method or merely a set of techniques, although both method and technique are related to music learning theory. A method specifies one sequence of objectives for learning. Music learning theory defines a domain of possible sequences of objectives for learning. Therefore, music learning theory encompasses many possible methods. A teaching technique describes how a specific objective is to be taught. Music learning theory defines as appropriate those techniques that make learning most efficient and that do not disrupt the sequential learning process.

"Audiation"

Before the skill-learning hierarchy is described, one fundamental concept must be understood. The most crucial aspect of music learning cannot be observed directly. When students engage in meaningful music learning, they are also engaged in *audiation*. The coined verb "to audiate" means to hear music in the mind. Audiation is different from aural perception because the source of aural perception is sound from the external world, whereas the source of audiation is the mind. Audiation can take place through re-creation or representation, without aural perception taking place concurrently. Music-learning theory is designed to encourage students to audiate, first with the aid of aural perception, and ultimately without the aid of aural perception.

Skill Learning Sequence

The first principle of skill learning sequence is that some music skills should be learned before others. Lowell Mason may be considered a skill learning theorist because he urged that music "sound" should be taught before music "symbol," that is, listening and singing should be taught before reading. For the same reason, Kodály may be considered a skill learning theorist. Mason and Kodály created two-step skill-learning theories. Music learning theory expands the two-step learning theory into a theory that includes eight levels of skill in two basic categories: discrimination and inference.

DISCRIMINATION

Discrimination learning takes place when students perform a music task to correspond to the teacher's performed example. To learn by discrimination is to learn by rote. Inference learning takes place when students perform music tasks that they have not learned by rote. To learn by inference is to think for oneself. Discrimination learning precedes inference learning because one must be given the materials to think with before thinking for oneself can take place. There are five levels of discrimination learning. They are listed below and will be explained in the stepwise order in which music learning theory indicates that they should be learned.

- aural/oral
- verbal association
- partial synthesis
- symbolic association
- composite synthesis

Aural/Oral

The first level of discrimination learning is aural/oral. For students to engage in successful learning at the aural/oral level, they must have a wide variety of experience singing with, and moving to, many rote songs and other music. Through experience with rote songs, students eventually are able to audiate a pitch center tonally and to audiate a steady beat rhythmically. Prior to the aural/oral level, students experience music holistically. At the aural/oral level, students learn to hear (aural) and to perform (oral) tonal patterns sung or rhythm patterns chanted by the teacher with a neutral syllable. Tonal patterns and rhythm patterns are the crucial "parts" that make up the whole that is experienced as music. Thus students' attention is drawn away from the complex whole of music and is drawn toward the parts of music. Tonal patterns are taught void of rhythm, and rhythm patterns are taught void of melody. Teaching patterns in this way enables the students to attend to tonal elements or rhythm elements without confusion. By learning at the aural/oral level, students can again experience rote songs and other music holistically, but with new insight and greater precision.

Tonal patterns and rhythm patterns are to music what words are to language. In language, the more words children have in their language vocabulary, the better able they are to comprehend the conversations they hear. As in language, the more tonal patterns and rhythm patterns children have in their music vocabulary, the better able they are to comprehend the music they hear. When students can sing tonal patterns with good intonation or chant rhythm patterns with a consistent tempo, they are ready to engage in the second level of discrimination learning: verbal association.

Verbal Association

At the verbal association level of learning, the teacher sings with syllable-name tonal patterns or chants with syllable-name rhythm patterns that were made familiar at the aural/oral level. Students reproduce the tonal patterns or rhythm patterns in an echo response. Tonal patterns are sung with movable *do* tonal syllables and rhythm patterns are chanted with syllables that give rhythm patterns internal logic. Moreover, at the verbal association level, students learn "proper" names for categories of tonal patterns and rhythm patterns. Words such as major, minor, Dorian tonic, dominant, and subdominant are associated with tonal patterns in the appropriate category. Words such as duple, triple, macrobeat, microbeat, division, and elongation are associated with rhythm patterns in the appropriate category. Verbal associations serve two purposes. First, they provide a means for students to organize the patterns they hear and audiate. Second, they provide a precise vocabulary for teacher and students to use when communicating about music not only as it is heard and audiated but also as it is read or written. When students can sing tonal patterns with tonal syllables or chant rhythm patterns with rhythm syllables, they are ready to learn at the partial synthesis level.

Partial Synthesis

At partial synthesis, familiar tonal patterns or familiar rhythm patterns are grouped into tonal phrases or rhythm phrases. Students are taught to recognize the tonality that a group of tonal patterns suggests or the meter a group of rhythm patterns suggests. In language, the young child hears groups of words and interprets them as being sentences. In music, students hear groups of patterns and interpret them as being in tonalities or meters. Thus, partial synthesis enables students to comprehend the syntax of music. When students can recognize the tonalities or meters suggested by groups of familiar patterns, they are ready to learn to read and write music.

Symbolic Association

At symbolic association, the teacher shows students familiar tonal patterns or rhythm patterns in music notation. The teacher points to the notation of each pattern and performs the pattern with its verbal association. Students respond by performing the patterns they see. Because students have already developed audiation skill and verbal association skill, learning to read familiar tonal patterns or rhythm patterns is a relatively simple matter of associating symbols with what they have already audiated. Moreover, because of partial synthesis, students comprehend the notation they see.

Students also learn to write at the symbolic association level. Learning to write familiar tonal patterns or rhythm patterns provides another means for students to communicate the music they hear and audiate. Learning to write also improves students' reading skills.

Composite Synthesis

Soon after students can read and write individual familiar tonal patterns and rhythm patterns, they are ready to read and write familiar tonal phrases and rhythm phrases in the last level of discrimination learning: composite synthesis. In composite synthesis, students comprehend the sight of music notation in terms of tonality and meter, just as they learned to comprehend the sound of music at partial synthesis. In Kodály's words, students "hear with their eyes" and "see with their ears."

INFERENCE

The principle underlying all levels of discrimination learning is that the tonal pattern or rhythm patterns made familiar at the aural/oral level of learning are brought to each higher level of discrimination learning. In inference learning, tonal patterns and rhythm patterns that are unfamiliar to students are incorporated into the learning process.

Three levels of inference learning remain to be explained. The three levels are listed below and will be discussed in the stepwise order in which they should be learned.

- generalization
- creativity/improvisation
- theoretical understanding

Generalization

Although students think for themselves when they make inferences, teachers must guide students in inferential thinking. Of the three levels of inference learning, generalization is most common and most basic. Students generalize when they identify correctly some aspect of unfamiliar music. They accomplish that by comparing unfamiliar music with music that they have learned by rote. Students can generalize aurally/orally, verbally, or symbolically. Students generalize aurally/orally by comparing sets of tonal patterns or rhythm patterns, some of which are unfamiliar, and judging whether patterns are the same or different. Students generalize verbally by identifying syllable names or proper names for unfamiliar tonal patterns or rhythm patterns. Students generalize symbolically by reading or writing unfamiliar tonal patterns or rhythm patterns. *Generalization symbolic* reading is commonly referred to as sight-reading and *generalization symbolic* writing is commonly called dictation.

Creativity/Improvisation

The next level of inference learning is creativity/improvisation. Creativity/improvisation can be learned aurally/orally or symbolically. Students are asked to perform, aurally/orally, tonal patterns and rhythm patterns different from, but related to, those tonal patterns and rhythm patterns performed by the teacher. Symbolically, students read or write created or composed tonal patterns and rhythm patterns. With appropriate musical readiness, students can engage in unbounded creativity and improvisation.

Theoretical Understanding

The final level of inference learning is theoretical understanding. It is last for two significant reasons. First, genuine theoretical understanding includes conjectures about why music is what it is. Students need never concern themselves with why music is what it is until they comprehend what it is. When audiation skill and knowledge of music are solidified, students can then engage in theoretical speculation on the foundation of their own knowledge and can make inferences about the theoretical conjectures of others. Second, the common application of music theory— the names of the lines and spaces of the staff, so-called key signatures and meter signatures, the mathematics of time values of notes, and so on—is not necessary for any of the previous levels of the music learning process, especially music reading and writing. Moreover, when such information is introduced into the learning process, the development of skill learning and, more important, of audiation becomes limited. In language, no one is presumptuous enough to teach children the theory of the alphabet, parts of speech, or syntax before they can speak the language with great fluency. Similarly, music learning theory mandates that students learn to "speak the language of music," in terms of audiation and performance, with great fluency before they learn the technical details of music notation theory.

SPIRALING

The eight levels of skill learning sequence have been summarized in hierarchical stepwise order. Research evidence and teaching practice, however, indicate that students profit from engaging in limited inferential activities when they are learning at discrimination levels. Because inference learning is dependent on discrimination learning, music learning theory provides for temporary skips in the stepwise discrimination learning process to specific levels of inference learning. Spirals, which are temporary skips, accomplish two things. First, they give students an opportunity to experience inference learning in small segments throughout the learning process, which motivates them to continue discrimination learning. Second, and perhaps more important, spiraling to an inference level of learning does not teach much of the inference level, but solidifies the discrimination levels on which the inference learning is based. For example, soon after learning tonal patterns at the aural/oral level, a spiral to the creativity/improvisation level with those patterns can take place. When students engage in creativity/improvisation they learn little about creativity/improvisation. They learn, however, a great deal about the tonal patterns that they used in the inference activity.

By combining discrimination and inference learning in a sequential learning process, students can learn about all music skills in an orderly fashion. By following the principles of skill learning sequence, the teacher is assured that students are ready to learn each successive skill learning objective. To know the sequence of skill learning, however, does not account for the complete learning process. What about music content? Should students learn major tonal patterns before minor tonal patterns? Should they be taught major and minor concurrently? What about rhythm patterns? Should duple meter be taught before, after, or concurrently with triple meter? Those questions are matters of content learning and are answered by content-learning sequence.

Content Learning Sequence

Like skill learning sequence, the first principle of content learning sequence is that some levels of music content should be learned before others. Kodály and Orff may be considered tonal content learning theorists because they believed that students should learn to sing pentatonic music before they learn to sing diatonic music. Any approach to music instruction that specifies a sequence for learning music content is a content learning theory.

The second principle of the content learning sequence is that, when students learn tonal content or rhythm content, they learn to perform and audiate tonal patterns and rhythm patterns. Students learn tonal patterns to develop a sense of tonality. Students have acquired a sense of tonality when, for example, they can recognize a music excerpt as being in major, minor, or Lydian tonality. Likewise, students learn rhythm patterns to develop a sense of meter. Students have acquired a sense of meter when, for example, they can recognize a music excerpt as being in duple or triple meter.

In music learning theory, there are two separate content learning sequences: tonal and rhythm. Brief outlines of the tonal content sequence and the rhythm content sequence are presented below.

Tonal Content Learning Sequence

READINESS FOR LEARNING TONAL CONTENT

Before students are asked to perform and audiate tonal patterns, they are first given many opportunities to sing and to listen to music. Informal exposure to music is particularly important for young children. Researchers interested in the music development of young children have observed that they learn music in much the same way that they learn to speak a language. Young children's first attempts at singing melodies are barely recognizable to an adult. Such seemingly incoherent "music babble" is similar to the language babble of infants. Although little is known about young children's "music babble," it seems reasonable to suggest that the "babble stage" may be the most important phase of music development. Observational evidence indicates that exposure to rote songs enables "babbling" young children to develop a sense of pitch center. A sense of pitch can be detected when the children's performance of a rote song is characterized by the prominence of one pitch to which other pitches are contrasted. Soon after children have developed a sense of pitch center, their song performances are characterized by diatonic intervals in relation to a pitch center. Students are ready to learn tonal patterns when their sense of pitch center has solidified and they can sing rote songs in major and minor tonalities with relatively good intonation.

LEVELS OF TONAL CONTENT

At the first level of tonal content learning sequence, students learn to perform and to audiate tonal patterns in major and minor tonalities. Two tonalities are taught concurrently because students learn one tonality by comparing it to another. After students have learned tonal patterns in major and minor tonalities, they are ready to learn rote songs and tonal patterns in Dorian, Mixolydian, Phrygian, Lydian, and Aeolian tonalities. When students develop a sense of tonality for more than one tonality, the teacher may introduce multitonal and multikeyal content. For multitonal and multikeyal content, students learn to audiate and to recognize tonal patterns that incorporate changes of tonality or key, such as modulations, in combinations of familiar tonalities. When students become familiar with multitonal and multikeyal content, they acquire the readiness for polytonal and polykeyal content. For polytonal content, students learn to perform and to audiate tonal patterns in two or more parts and in two or more simultaneously sounding tonalities or keys. Polytonal and polykeyal content differs from multitonal and multikeyal content in that multitonal and multikeyal content includes one part or one melody, whereas polytonal and polykeyal content includes two or more simultaneously sounding parts or melodies. The final classification of tonal content is harmonic tonal content. Students learn to perform and to audiate tonal patterns, in two or more simultaneously sounding parts, that create harmonic progressions within any familiar tonality. Thus tonal content learning sequence progresses from (1) tonalities in one part, to (2) changes in tonality or key in one part, then to (3) two or more tonalities or keys in two or more parts, and finally to (4) harmonic progressions in two or more parts.

Tonal Content Learning Sequence

Step	Content Category	Description
1	Major and Minor Mixolydian and Dorian Lydian and Phrygian Aeolian	Tonal patterns performed in one voice part.
2	Multitonal/Multikeyal	Modulations in one part.
3	Polytonal/Polykeyal	Multitonal content in two or more parts.
4	Harmonic	Harmonic progressions in two or more parts.

Rhythm Content Learning Sequence

READINESS FOR LEARNING RHYTHM CONTENT

Before students are asked to perform and to audiate rhythm patterns, they are first given many opportunities to move rhythmically in response to rote songs and other music. Informal exposure to rhythmic movement is particularly important for young children. Young children's first attempts at rhythmic movement seem uncoordinated to an adult. Such "rhythm babble" seems to be crucial to the development of a good sense of rhythm. Observational evidence indicates that informal exposure to rhythmic movement enables young children to develop a sense of steady beat. A sense of steady beat can be detected when the children's rhythmic movement is characterized by recurring movements that are not typically repeated in a consistent tempo. Soon after children have developed a sense of steady beat, their rhythm performance is characterized by consistency of tempo. Children are ready to learn to perform and to audiate rhythm pattens when their sense of steady beat has solidified and they can move with a consistent tempo to music in duple and triple meters.

DEFINITION OF RHYTHM

An important component of music learning theory is its definition of rhythm. Rhythm consists of three elements: macrobeats, microbeats and melodic rhythm. Although this is an oversimplification, macrobeats are pairs of beats to which one may walk or march. Microbeats are divisions of macrobeats. When macrobeats of equal length are divided in twos, duple meter is the result. When macrobeats of equal length are divided in threes, triple meter is the result. Melodic rhythm is the rhythm of the text or melody of a piece of music.

LEVELS OF RHYTHM CONTENT

At the first level of rhythm content learning sequence, students learn to perform and to audiate rhythm patterns in duple and triple meters. Two meters are taught concurrently because students learn one meter by comparing it to another. After students have learned rhythm patterns in duple and triple meters, they are ready to move to and perform rhythm patterns that combine duple meter and triple meter in alternation. Duple, triple, and combined meters are considered to be "usual" meters in contrast to the next level of rhythm content: unusual meter. When students can audiate and perform patterns in combined meter, they are ready to move to and perform rhythm patterns in unusual meter. Unusual meter consists of macrobeats of unequal lengths. Music written in 5/8 or 7/8, for example, is typically in unusual meter.

When students can perform and audiate rhythm patterns in usual and unusual meters, they can be introduced to rhythm patterns that include changes of meter or tempo, or changes in both meter and tempo. When students can perform and audiate multimetric and multitemporal rhythm patterns, they can be taught to perform and audiate rhythm patterns in two or more parts. Students first learn rhythm patterns with all parts in the same meter or tempo (monometric or monotemporal), then with parts in different tempos or meters (polymetric or polytemporal). Thus the rhythm content-learning sequence progresses from (1) rhythm patterns in usual meters, to (2) unusual meters in one part, to (3) changes of meter or tempo in one part, then to (4) two or more parts in the same meter or tempo, and finally to (5) two or more parts in different meters or tempos.

Rhythm Content Learning Sequence

Step	Content Classification	Description
1	Usual Duple and Triple Usual Combined	Rhythm patterns performed in one part.
2	Unusual Meter	
3	Multimetric/Multitemporal	Changes of tempo or meter in one part.
4	Monometric/Monotemporal	Rhythm patterns performed in two or more parts.
5	Polymetric/Polytemporal	

Combined Skill- and Content Learning Sequences

With an understanding of skill learning sequence, tonal content learning sequence, and rhythm content learning sequence, the development of specific sequential curricular objectives for tonal learning and rhythm learning can be understood. Music learning theory provides rules that describe the step-by-step process of creating sequential objectives. Simply stated, for any level of content, learning begins at the aural/oral level of skill and continues through the skill learning sequence with or without appropriate spirals to inference skill levels. Because students often study more than one level of tonal content or more than one level of rhythm content concurrently, it becomes increasingly complex for the teacher to monitor the sequential learning process. Nonetheless, the internal logic of skill- and content learning sequences makes the creation of sequential objectives for tonal learning and rhythm learning possible. The process is simplified because tonal content learning sequence is separate from rhythm content learning sequence. There is no need to coordinate specific objectives for tonal learning with specific objectives for rhythm learning, although neither type of music content should be emphasized in the instructional process at the expense of the other.

Teaching to Individual Musical Differences

Music learning theory is unique because the measurement and evaluation of students' music aptitudes and music achievement is an integral component of the instruction process. When the teacher has constructed sets of sequential objectives for tonal learning and rhythm learning, a method of instruction has been developed. Before instruction begins, however, the teacher needs to be aware of students' individual musical differences. With knowledge of students' levels of music aptitudes and music achievement, the teacher can adapt instruction based on skill- and content learning sequences to the students' musical needs.

The importance of music aptitude tests cannot be overstated. One important use for a valid music aptitude test is for identifying students' potential to learn music. Care must be taken to select an aptitude test that is appropriate for the students' age and level of previous musical experience. In contrast, a measure of music achievement can be used by the teacher to determine the specific tonal objective or specific rhythm objective that is appropriate for students to achieve.

Knowledge of students' tonal aptitudes and rhythm aptitudes is particularly valuable for teaching to students' individual musical differences. For example, students who possess high levels of tonal aptitude but who do not demonstrate a high level of tonal achievement can be identified and guided in the learning process to achieve in accordance with their potential. Likewise, students who possess average or low levels of tonal aptitude can be taught to achieve to the extent their aptitudes will allow, without the frustration of attempting to learn at too high a level.

The teacher appropriately adapts instruction to the aptitudes of students by introducing the content associated with a specific objective in increasing levels of difficulty. To achieve a specific objective for tonal learning or rhythm learning, the teacher presents the appropriate tonal pattern or rhythm pattern content in three phases. In the first phase, all students learn patterns that are easy to audiate. In the second phase, the teacher adapts instruction by introducing patterns that are moderately difficult to audiate to students with average and high levels of aptitude. In the third and final phase of teaching to the objective, the teacher introduces patterns that are difficult to audiate to students with high levels of aptitude, while continuing to teach moderately difficult and easy patterns to students with average and low levels of aptitude. It should be understood that the distinctions between low, average, and high aptitude and easy, moderate, and difficult patterns serve only as a guide. In practice, some students will demonstrate deviation from expected achievement. Such deviation occurs because of errors of measurement associated with aptitude and achievement tests, and because of human error. The teacher must be sensitive to the responses of students and should assist students to make the most of their music aptitudes and music experiences.

DEVELOPMENTAL MUSIC APTITUDE

Evidence from recent research indicates that teaching to the individual differences of students in kindergarten and primary grades has a profound impact on the students' music achievement and developmental music aptitudes. Until recently, it was believed that a child's music aptitudes were fixed innate traits. With the creation of valid music aptitude tests for children in kindergarten and primary grades, research evidence suggests that informal exposure to, and instruction in, music can affect the child's levels of music aptitudes. If the young child's musical environment is rich, then the child will retain the potential with which he was born. Unfortunately, if the young child's musical environment is impoverished, then the child will tend to lose the potential with which he was born. At approximately age 9, the child's music aptitudes stabilize, probably for life. The young child is said to be in the developmental aptitude stage, whereas the child 9 years of age and older is said to be in the stabilized aptitude stage. Thus, for students to make the most of their musical potential, appropriate music instruction beginning in kinder-garten, if not before, is of great importance. Observational research evidence suggests that informal exposure to music during the child's music babble stage, throughout infancy and early childhood, may be crucial for the development of the young child's musical potential.

The Application of Music Learning Theory to Elementary General Music

It is generally accepted that music instruction should include a wide variety of music experiences. Accordingly, the achievement of specific sequential objectives for tonal learning and rhythm learning must be applied to a wide variety of music-making activities. Edwin Gordon and David Woods have collaborated in designing a general music series that is based on music learning theory and includes a multitude of music experiences. *Jump Right In: The Music Curriculum*[43] is designed for use by general music teachers from preschool through high school levels, and can be adapted for use in the instruction of beginning and intermediate vocal and instrumental ensembles.

The series materials are in two parts: Learning Sequence Activities and Classroom Activities. Learning Sequence Activities include the materials necessary for teaching sequential objectives for tonal learning and rhythm learning based on music learning theory. Learning Sequence Activities comprise five to ten minutes of the general music class period. Classroom Activities include activities and teaching techniques for use in general music classes. Classroom Activities comprise the remainder of the general music class period. A more detailed description of the two parts of *Jump Right In* is given below.

LEARNING SEQUENCE ACTIVITIES

Learning Sequence Activities include fifty-three tonal units and fifty-three rhythm units. Each unit represents one specific sequential objective. A specific sequential objective is the combination of one level of skill learning with one level of content learning. Tonal units are separate from rhythm units because skill learning sequence is combined with tonal content learning sequence apart from the rhythm content learning sequence, and vice-versa.

Jump Right In is unique because the materials used by the teacher are separate from the materials used by students. For example, students do not see music notation in their materials until they have achieved the necessary readiness for symbolic association. The teacher's materials include two register books: one is for tonal learning and the other for rhythm learning. Space is provided on the achievement record sheet for the teacher to record each student's achievement for a specific sequential objective. Students' names can be written in the achievement record sheet in accordance with their tonal aptitude levels or rhythm aptitude levels. As can be seen in Teaching Strategy 5.3, the achievement of a specific sequential objective is defined more specifically in sections, for example, A and B. Space is provided within each section to record the achievement of an objective with patterns of three levels of difficulty: (E)asy, (M)oderate, and (D)ifficult. Students with high levels of aptitude are expected to learn to perform tonal patterns or rhythm patterns that are easy, moderate, and difficult to audiate, whereas students with low levels of aptitude are expected to perform tonal patterns or rhythm patterns that are easy to audiate. The shaded portion within each section is designed to be a reminder to the teacher that different levels of achievement should be expected for students with different levels of aptitude.

In addition to achievement record sheets, the register books include teaching/evaluation guides for each section of each unit. As can be seen in Teaching Strategy 5.3, the teaching/evaluation guide begins with a statement of the specific sequential objective of the unit. Then the level of skill learning and the level of content learning are identified. The teacher introduces the five criteria to students in the order in which they are listed in each section in the teaching/evaluation guide.

Emphasis is given to the measurement and evaluation of performances by individual students. Students learn to perform and to audiate tonal patterns and rhythm patterns in ensemble and individually. When the teacher is ready to evaluate students' progress, credit for the achievement of a criterion is awarded when the student can perform the criterion in a solo response.

TEACHING STRATEGY 5.3—TONAL UNIT 1: TEACHING/EVALUATION GUIDE

Sequential Objective: Perform tonic and dominant patterns in major and minor tonalities which were taught by rote.

AURAL/ORAL   TONIC AND DOMINANT
                                              IN MAJOR AND MINOR

Section A

The student echoes using a neutral syllable or hums

1. only the first tone of one familiar tonic or dominant pattern in major tonality sung in entirety by the teacher with a neutral syllable,
2. only the resting tone associated with two or more familiar tonic patterns in major tonality in familiar or unfamiliar order sung in entirety by the teacher with a neutral syllable,
3. one familiar tonic pattern in major tonality sung by the teacher with a neutral syllable,
4. one familiar dominant pattern in major tonality sung by the teacher with a neutral syllable,
5. one familiar tonic pattern and one familiar dominant pattern in major tonality in familiar or unfamiliar order sung by the teacher with a neutral syllable.

Section B

The student echoes using a neutral syllable or hums

1. only the first tone of one familiar tonic or dominant pattern in minor tonality sung in entirety by the teacher with a neutral syllable,
2. only the resting tone associated with two or more familiar tonic patterns in minor tonality in familiar or unfamiliar order sung in entirety by the teacher with a neutral syllable,
3. one familiar tonic pattern in minor tonality sung by the teacher with a neutral syllable,
4. one familiar dominant pattern in minor tonality sung by the teacher with a neutral syllable,
5. one familiar tonic pattern and one familiar dominant pattern in minor tonality in familiar or unfamiliar order sung by the teacher with a neutral syllable.

Note: Reprinted by permission of G.I.A. Publications.

Achievement Record Sheet

Class List	Section A			Section B		
High Aptitude	E	M	D	E	M	D
Average Aptitude	E	M	D	E	M	D
Low Aptitude	E	M	D	E	M	D

The 4-x-6-inch tonal pattern card used in conjunction with section A of tonal unit 1 is presented in Teaching Strategy 5.4. In this illustration, there are patterns notated across the top of the card. Those patterns are performed by the teacher and echoed by the students in ensemble. The "class patterns" are used to establish and maintain tonality, and to provide a context for individual students to engage in solo responses. There are numbered lines of patterns below the first line of patterns. The number of each line corresponds to the criterion in the teaching/evaluation guide. Those patterns are performed by individual students in solo responses. The letter M at the beginning of each line of patterns stands for major tonality and the letters E, M, and D above each line stand for easy, moderate, and difficult patterns. The tonal pattern card can be attached to the tonal register above the achievement record sheet, thus making evaluation of student progress relatively simple.

The teaching/evaluation guide for sections A and B of rhythm unit 3 is presented in Teaching Strategy 5.5. The teaching/evaluation guide for rhythm unit 3 is used in the same manner as the teaching/evaluation guide for tonal unit 1. Sections A and B of rhythm unit 3 are sequentially ordered. Section A should be completed with easy, moderate, and difficult patterns before section B is taught. The five criteria of section A are evaluated first with easy rhythm patterns, then with moderately difficult rhythm patterns, and finally with difficult rhythm patterns.

TEACHING STRATEGY 5.4—TONAL UNIT 1, SECTION A

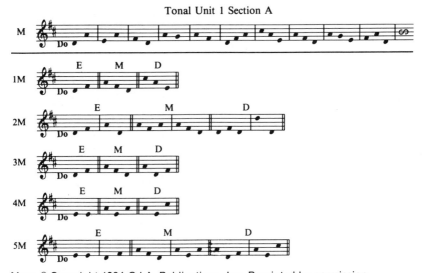

Tonal Unit 1 Section A

Note. © Copyright 1984 G.I.A. Publications, Inc. Reprinted by permission.

TEACHING STRATEGY 5.5—RHYTHM UNIT 3: TEACHING/EVALUATION GUIDE

Sequential Objective: Perform macro and micro beat and division and elongation patterns in usual duple and usual triple meters which were taught by rote.

AURAL/ORAL   MACRO AND MICRO BEATS AND
                              DIVISIONS AND ELONGATIONS
                              IN USUAL DUPLE
                              AND USUAL TRIPLE

Section A

The student echoes using a neutral syllable in the following familiar or unfamiliar order

1. one familiar macro and micro beat pattern and one familiar division and elongation pattern in usual duple meter chanted by the teacher with a neutral syllable.
2. one familiar division and elongation pattern and one familiar macro and micro beat pattern in usual duple meter chanted by the teacher with a neutral syllable,

The student echoes using a neutral syllable
3. two familiar division and elongation patterns in usual duple meter chanted by the teacher with a neutral syllable,
4. two familiar macro and micro beat patterns and one familiar division and elongation pattern in usual duple meter chanted by the teacher with a neutral syllable.
5. one familiar macro and micro beat pattern and two familiar division and elongation patterns in usual duple meter chanted by the teacher with a neutral syllable.

Section B

The student echoes using a neutral syllable in the following familiar or unfamiliar order

1. one familiar macro and micro beat pattern and one familiar division and elongation pattern in usual triple meter chanted by the teacher with a neutral syllable.
2. one familiar division and elongation pattern and one familiar macro and micro beat pattern in usual triple meter chanted by the teacher with a neutral syllable.

The student echoes using a neutral syllable
3. two familiar division and elongation patterns in usual triple meter chanted by the teacher with a neutral syllable.
4. two familiar macro and micro beat patterns and one familiar division and elongation pattern in usual triple meter chanted by the teacher with a neutral syllable.
5. one familiar macro and micro beat pattern and two familiar division and elongation patterns in usual triple meter chanted by the teacher with a neutral syllable.

Note: Reprinted by permission of G.I.A. Publications.

Following that procedure, instruction is adapted to students' individual differences.

The rhythm pattern card used by the teacher for section B of rhythm unit 3 can be seen in Teaching Strategy 5.6. Here, again, there are patterns notated across the top of the card. Those patterns are performed by the teacher and echoed by students in ensemble. Those "class patterns" are used to establish and maintain meter, and to provide a context for individual students to engage in solo responses. There are numbered lines of patterns below the first line of patterns. The number of each line corresponds to the criterion in the teaching/evaluation guide. Those patterns are performed by individual students in solo responses. The letter T at the beginning of each line of patterns stands for triple meter and the letters E, M, and D above each line stand for easy, moderate, and difficult patterns.

CLASSROOM ACTIVITIES

The majority of the Classroom Activities portion of *Jump Right In* consists of approximately 3,000 activities and techniques for music making in the general music classroom. The activities are printed on color-coded 4-x-6-inch file cards. Classroom Activities are based on Orff, Kodály, Dalcroze, Laban, Manhattanville, and CMP. "Core" activities are those that can be used in typical classroom situations. An important supplement to the

TEACHING STRATEGY 5.6—RHYTHM UNIT 3, Section A

Note. © Copyright 1984 G.I.A. Publications, Inc. Reprinted by permission.

"core" activities are "component" activities designed for use with students with special needs. Other activity cards include suggestions for effective teaching, instrumental instruction, and activities for students to do outside the music classroom. All of the Classroom Activities are extensively cross-referenced and indexed. Each activity is coordinated with appropriate tonal units and appropriate rhythm units of the Learning Sequence Activities.

ADDITIONAL MATERIALS INCLUDED IN *JUMP RIGHT IN*

Jump Right In also includes a bound song collection. The collection includes more than 600 traditional songs, art songs, non-Western songs, and composed songs. Each song is indexed according to range, tonality, and meter, and each song is cross-referenced by holiday, special occasion, and season.

Activity books are provided for use by students in school as well as at home. The activities are coordinated with Learning Sequence Activities and Classroom Activities. They include materials for music reading and writing; special projects; and instructions for playing guitar, autoharp, and other instruments.

A *Teacher's Manual* is provided in *Jump Right In*. The manual includes a complete description of the organization and content of *Jump Right In* and instructions for coordination of Learning Sequence Activities and Classroom Activities. Edwin Gordon's *Learning Sequences in Music: Skill, Content, and Patterns*[44] is also included as part of *Jump Right In*. That text provides an extensive description and detailed explanation of music learning theory. *Tonal and Rhythm Pattern Audiation Cassettes*,[45] also by Gordon, are available for teachers to develop their audiation skills.

The Future of Music Learning Theory

THEORETICAL ADVANCEMENTS

Three aspects of current research contributing to music learning theory are: (1) an understanding of the young child's music development during the "music babble" stage, (2) a description and explanation of the nature of developmental and stabilized music aptitudes, and (3) a description and explanation of the nature of the audiation process. As research evidence from the psychology of music and related disciplines accumulates, and researchers gain more insight into the music learning process, music learning theory undoubtedly will become more precise.

INSTRUCTIONAL MATERIALS

At the time of this writing, Edwin Gordon and Richard Grunow are collaborating to create materials for use in beginning instrumental music instruction. The instrumental series will be designed for use by students of band instruments. The materials in the instrumental series will be based on music learning theory and they will be coordinated with many of the materials in *Jump Right In.*

THE CARABO-CONE METHOD

By Madeleine Carabo-Cone

A Sensory-Motor Approach to Music Learning

For preschool and primary grade children, a sensory-motor approach provides both musical foundation and intellectual stimulation for academic achievement. Exemplifying the observations of psychologists Piaget and Bruner, Carabo-Cone methodology is based on the belief that structured cognitive learning can be introduced to preschool children if integrated into their actions and environment at an early age. Piaget and others have demonstrated that the learning and thinking of young children are linked to the concrete, the seeable, and the touchable. There is hardly a better way to present a concrete representation of an abstract idea than through visual and tactile experience that is reinforced and coordinated with the auditory and the kinesthetic. Among children, as among all people, there are individual differences; some learn more easily through seeing, others through hearing, and still others through touch and movement. These differences should be met by a multiple sensory approach that will increase chances for successful teaching.

The grand staff (and its notation) becomes an environment into which the children are "born." Using their instinctive learning powers, they form all concepts in relation to themselves, acting dynamically inside the framework of a gigantic music staff whose image they encounter everywhere—on the floor, wall, table, keyboard, and clothing. Structurally correlated, this multiplicity of almost similar images (horizontal, large, vertical, small, etc.) provides built-in practice for discovering relationships, and acts as a mental gymnasium for developing perceptions. These, incorporated into actions, are strengthened by continual physical contact with simple learning materials, mostly of paper and tape, many of which are made by the children themselves, who, through continual interaction with the environment, becomes its "partners." This produces constant feedback from the physical to the mental. Since the learning environment is absorbed naturally, children of various backgrounds are on an equal footing, for only natural, innate resources count, not verbalization skills. The exterior world, represented by this structured environment, is assimilated through identification with self, through dramatization; it becomes the child's interior world—within his mind.

Through personal experience, all children come to grips with the concepts represented by the words "above," "below," "in," "on," "in between," "nearest," "higher," "lower," and the like, as well as by syllables and by mathematical concepts of sequence and equality. Understanding facilitates recognition and comparison, lengthens the attention span, strengthens the visual focus, and intensifies concentration. The giant music staff functions as a gymnasium for developing perceptive skills and basic concepts that are essential not only for music learning, but for general academic school work. Notes are not named with the alphabet. The learning area is limited to ten black lines and their adjacent white spaces and to the stark simplicity of the straight "sticks" and "circles" (notes) that are the components of simple musical note values. According to Piaget, even infants can discriminate between sticks and circles. Yet it is the lightning-quick recognition of these stick and circle elements in alphabet letters that is the basis of reading. With the isolation of these primitive components, the stage is set for learning in depth.

Because abstract ideas are transformed into "held-in-the-hand" objects made of paper, tape, and other familiar kindergarten materials, these learning tools are so simple as to be self-teaching. Thus, the regular kindergarten or nursery teacher can learn along with the children, whom they lead in delightful gamelike activities. Identification with self, dramatization, and muscular coordination are dominating factors. All the children are gradually drawn out. Their self-images develop as they become the central core of each new concept and identify themselves as separate elements in the learning material. No fear of failure restrains the children, whose physical, psychological, and potential intellectual powers are totally involved in "becoming" various musical elements. For example, a child becomes a "landmark line." The human eye needs to fix on landmarks for security, for focus, and for general perception. Thus it is important to find the natural distinguishing characteristics that set one symbol apart from other symbols. In the grand staff, there are three landmark lines: one line passes between the two dots of the bass clef; one passes through the center of the round part of the treble clef; and one line (middle C) is invisible when not in active use as a sound. In addition, the top and bottom lines of each staff remain as instinctively perceived landmarks.

At all stages these focal points of reference serve as visual supports. Many of the first "identification activities" are centered on the landmark lines. For example, some children become the bass F-line. They stand on it while others toss paper discs or beanbags toward their feet. The same procedure is used with the other landmark lines. The throwing is always done after a measured rhythmic signal, thus incorporating a rhythmic element. Then, while listening and humming its sound, the children walk along each landmark line, always beginning from the clefs to reinforce left-to-right reading habits. Before starting to walk on the F-line, they hop on the two bass-clef dots on both sides of it. Before starting on the G-line, the children trace the round part of the treble clef with their feet. These sensory-motor techniques intensify focus.

The child can then "become" a staff. On his or her body the child feels five lines of bass or treble at feet, knees, waist, shoulders, and head, each responding to a specific sound with corresponding movement. Spaces are interpreted by thrusting arms out into the space between neighboring "body lines." Each space is defined as a location between its two neighboring lines, thus accelerating mental and visual focus and also intensifying the concept of neighboring tones. The C-line (middle C) is acted out by drawing an imaginary line in the air. The child's own body is the chief learning aid, reinforcing ear training and reading.

The child's hand also becomes a staff. In more advanced classes, the five fingers of the right hand become the five staff lines of the treble clef, which is used when singing. With the index finger of the free hand, the child acts out the notes of a song, stroking the staff-line fingers and poking into the spaces between them. This literal representation of the musical score is the basis of the Carabo-Cone system of hand symbols. It has several advantages:

1. Immediacy—the basic idea is readily grasped and quickly learned.
2. Continuity—the same staff-reading techniques are used in the body staff, the grand staff box (which uses velvet ribbon for lines), and all other representations of the grand staff.
3. Reading and writing aid—it is a literal translation of the printed music staff and is therefore unified with the reading and writing process; one's own hand is an ever-present learning device.
4. Keyboard application—placing the hand on the keyboard, each staff-line finger can play its own corresponding piano key without change of hand position.

Rather than being arbitrarily devised to represent a tone in the diatonic scale, without relationship to reading, writing, or instrumental playing, these hand symbols can represent notes in any scale, even in atonal music, and portray the notes on their location in the staff so precisely that they are not merely symbols, but the score itself.

The child "becomes" a musical instrument by stretching five black tapes across the feet, knees, and so on, of the "music staff children." Singing songs written at first on lines only, the staff children wiggle their corresponding part while the other children move the corresponding tapes as if they were strings on musical instruments. The child "becomes" a specific line or space through his or her identification sound or location; this makes the children aware of their relationship to those of their classmates. Developing a sense of order is an important element in structured thought. One of the most basic activities, choosing a staff-line identity, involves the child in concepts of order. Whereas the grand staff has been experienced before in its totality, when children select a "staff-line stick," they confront the staff line taken out of context. In order for it to take on meaning for them again, they must mentally fit it back into the total structure. Having chosen their sticks, the children must arrange themselves in a sequence, from highest to lowest, or vice versa, as they go to the wall chart to write their notes. As they discuss who is highest or lowest, they are involved with the concepts of number and sequence.

After the experience of arranging themselves in a sequence, the children are ready for a new plan. The teacher seizes some moment when the children are dispersed on the floor staff, says, "Stay as you are!" and asks, "Who is closest to the clefs?" The order in which each child writes the note will be determined by the child's distance from the clefs. The element of chance sets up a new laboratory experiment each time, providing a new opportunity to study new intervals and/or new melodies.

The child "becomes" part of a song by creating original themes out of musical identity. Thus, the concepts of intervals, neighboring tones, and rhythmic variety are developed creatively. Then each child becomes a note in different themes from musical literature. A typical example is the first theme in the last movement of Brahms's *First Symphony*:

The child representing the first note in the theme stands nearest to the clef on the floor; each successive "note child" in the song takes his or her place on the floor staff, each standing on large, cut-out paper notes (see Figure 5.5). (Sometimes the children construct the notes from cookies

FIGURE 5.5 The Carabo-Cone Methodology: Correlation of a Structured Learning Environment (Endorsed by Jean Piaget)

1. Song	5. Keyboard Guide	9. Table Staff
2. Identification Cards	6. Staff-line Sticks	10. Grand Staff Music Box
3. Piano	7. Floor Staff	11. Cut-out Notes
4. Piano Rack Chart	8. Wall Chart	12. Note Hats

All writing surfaces are covered with clear plastic. Writing in grease pencil can be rubbed off easily.

Note. Copyright © 1957, 1969 by Madeleine Carabo-Cone; used by permission.
SOURCE: *Music Teacher* 50; no. 4 (April 1971): 10 (London: Evans Brothers Limited).

carefully placed on the table staff.) Then, in the proper order, the children write their notes on the wall staff. As the group sings the theme, all the children in turn, like a struck piano key or a finger going down on a string, squat down for their notes' required duration. Each theme can be acted out in many different ways.

Children "become" a time value and a rhythm pattern by walking and talking to articulate specific durations—prolonging steps and singing syllables—while their arms swing to the beat. They see their duration demonstrated spatially as they move onto sheets of bright paper, each representing a beat. Mr. Half Note, for instance, moves into a two-room "apartment," constructed from two sheets of paper, each representing one beat. The child squats like a struck piano key for a specific duration while acting out a pattern or theme (see Figure 5.6).

In order to convey the pendulum or pulsation concept of rhythm, the children begin with relaxed, swinging movements of arms and body. The children first learn to feel the beat or pulsation (combined with articulation of their one-syllable nicknames) in a special handshake ritual with their teacher; they then bend from left to right at the waist, imitating a pendulum with torsos. Having learned to feel the pulsations with their bodies, they add the dimension of duration through spatial demonstration and verbalization. In the "time-value coordination marches," they act out all the primary time values through coordinated leg movements, arm swings, and vocal articulations. They gradually progress to the more complex small-muscle movements that merge into a complete unit of simultaneous coordinations. Different parts of the body perform various interpretations of pulse and duration (see Figure 5.7).

FIGURE 5.6 Constant physical contact with the materials reinforces concepts, helping the child to be his own teacher.

Note. Copyright © 1965 by M. Carabo-Cone. Reprinted by permission.

FIGURE 5.7 The Bass Clef Team lie down on the lines they "own." The Treble Clef team lie on their field or playground. If the child at the piano plays a first line in the treble, the treble team wiggle their feet. For a second line, they shake their knees; the sound of the third line calls for patting the "tummy," fourth line, tickling the neck and top line, brushing the hair. Bass Clef Team responds similarly to the sound of their lines.

Note. Copyright © 1965 by M. Carabo-Cone. Reprinted by permission.

SUZUKI TALENT EDUCATION

All human beings are born with great potentialities, and each individual has within himself, the capacity for developing to a very high level. Although some individuals display a remarkable ability during their lifetime, we are not primarily concerned here with these extraordinary cases. There are many others, born with a high potential, who, through unfavorable conditions, fail in some way to develop their original power, so that their lives end at a comparatively low level. . . .

. . . Talent Education has realized that all children in the world show their splendid capacities by speaking and understanding their mother language, thus displaying the original power of the human mind. Is it not probable that this mother language method holds the key to human development?[46]

Dr. Shinichi Suzuki developed his philosophy of education while searching for a way to help post-World War II Japanese children develop to their full potential in a nation devastated by the war.

Theory of Talent Education

Suzuki was born in 1898 into a musical family in Japan. His father owned the first violin factory in Japan. Suzuki often played there as a boy; he later worked there and learned about violin design and construction. His musical training began in Japan and later included eight years of study with Karl Klinger in Berlin. His experiments in teaching led to the development of his method. In Matsumoto, Suzuki had adopted a young orphan boy, to whom he began to teach the violin. Violins were scarce in postwar Japan, so that when Suzuki began to work with several other children, they had to share one instrument. His success led to the procurement of more instruments and more students; within a few years his method became the object of serious interest to parents and teachers. The method, called *Talent Education*, is built on a solid philosophical foundation developed from Suzuki's theory of education. He called his method the "mother-tongue method." It is based on what psychologists refer to as psycholinguistic development. Suzuki realized the potential of young children to learn much more than they are normally taught; he came to this realization by the awareness of how easily and naturally children learn that which most adults learn only with great difficulty— their own mother tongue. Young children become expert in their own language no matter how difficult and complicated it may be. If children have the ability to master something as challenging as a language, Suzuki felt, that ability must also allow them to master many other kinds of knowledge and skills if presented to children in the same manner as their mother-tongue—by observation, imitation, repetition, and gradually developing intellectual awareness.

The Method

The Suzuki Talent Education method is predicated on the belief that people are products of their environment. The environmental conditions necessary to promote good learning by children are well defined and strictly adhered to by teachers of the method, although they are based on the informal process of learning the mother tongue. Each aspect of the method is related to one or more steps in the process of developing language communications skills.

Talent education begins during infancy, when recorded music is played frequently enough to make it part of the child's environment. Children do not play the violin until age 3, when they are physically capable of manipulating it and have its sound in minds. They learn the violin by rote, as they do language. Listening is an important part of the process; they listen to their teacher and more advanced students play.

The development of technique precedes music reading. The students must memorize all of the music that they learn. Actual note reading begins as an association process in which the students match what they are playing to the printed note. There is no emphasis on sight reading because all reading development is approached through the material that the student has already memorized. The musical materials are well defined; all talent education students progress through the same sequence of songs, exercises, and literature. New technical skills are introduced as they become necessary to perform the music being studied. The students are not expected to master skills that have no immediate application.

Talent education lessons are private and geared to individual needs. Length is determined by the attention span of the student. Parents are deeply involved in the process and learn along with the child. At least one of the parents attends lessons and helps with daily practice. Parental involvement is important not only for technical development, but also to provide the child with a feeling of the value of violin study.

In order to help the children relate as much as possible to the instrument, the physical environment is arranged so that the students are not distracted or tempted to develop poor playing habits. Much of the paraphernalia that is part of traditional violin lessons is not present. Chairs, music stands, music, and other unnecessary devices (cleaning cloths, tuning instruments) are left out of sight and mind during the lesson. Another reason for not using a chair is that young violinists are more likely to develop good posture and position if they stand rather than sit. Standing also allows for more freedom and flexibility of movement. Talent education instruction includes cello study; cello players, of course, sit when they play.

Teaching is by rote so that the child's attention is focused on the instrument and so that the development of technique is not diverted by the problem of learning to read music. The first several volumes of the literature are accompanied by recordings; the most advanced music is heard on commerical recordings by concert artists. The recordings serve as models and are often as important as the teaching in developing good tone and musicality. Rote teaching is more successful when the child has a mental image of what he is striving for.

Rote teaching continues for two years, longer if necessary. The length of time depends upon the age of the students and their rates of progress. Even after reading has begun, rote teaching continues so that technical development continues. An important aspect of the method is that lessons are private, not in groups, although this is an area in which adjustments have been made for the American adaptation of the method;

in the U.S., group instruction techniques are often used. Reading skills are usually developed best in ensemble situations where the many demands of interaction require printed music to hold the group together; this is another reason for rote teaching during private lessons. The large (sometimes huge) groups of children playing together in Suzuki festivals do not reflect class size.

Suzuki's concept of repetition is manifested throughout the child's career as a student. When new music is learned and new skills developed, previously learned music is not abandoned. It remains in the repertory of music that grows increasingly difficult, and continues to be played even when the most difficult music has been mastered. Suzuki festivals in which older students participate often include, in addition to standard violin and cello literature, such pieces as "Twinkle, Twinkle Little Star," the first piece learned by talent education students.

Suzuki believes that it is of utmost importance for children to play with good tone and intonation from the very beginning. The usual scratching and screeching sounds are avoided by allowing beginners to use only the upper half of the bow; it is the lower half of the bow that causes the offensive sounds often associated with beginning string students. A simplified bow hand grip is sometimes used for students whose hands are not large enough to grip the bow in the traditional manner. The problem of intonation is addressed by placing pieces of tape on the fingerboard to mark the exact location of finger placement. Equally important, students have already heard enough music performed in tune to be aware of what good intonation is.

The large Suzuki festivals held in Japan and in many parts of the United States represent the work of many teachers who wish to provide a musical outlet for their students. Since all Suzuki students play a common repertoire, there is no problem of several teachers having to agree on the same music. The problems are logistical rather than musical. Some festivals include thousands of children who represent every level of advancement. Usually the most advanced play first. When they have completed their high-level music, a slightly less advanced group joins them and the two combined groups play the next lower level of music. When the next group arrives, it joins the others and they all play together the music of the least advanced students. In this way, the number of performers continually increases as the level of difficulty of music decreases. When the youngest students join in, the entire assembly plays the beginners' literature, including "Twinkle, Twinkle Little Star."

The Suzuki festivals provide public showcases for students, for whose talents and skills they are especially created and designed, just as school concerts are structured for the special skills of those performing groups. The festivals also serve as public relations devices; as such, they seldom fail to convince audience members who are unfamiliar with talent education of the value of the method.

Talent Education in the United States

The American introduction to talent education occurred in 1958 when, at a meeting of the American String Teachers Association at Oberlin College, a film of 750 Japanese children playing the Bach *Concerto for Two Violins* was shown. Teachers at the meeting were so impressed that they decided to send a representative to Japan to observe the method in use. Communication was established with Suzuki, who extended an invitation, and John Kendall made the trip in 1959. He made another trip to Japan in 1962 to continue his study of the method.

In 1964 Suzuki and a group of ten children, ranging in age from 5½ to 14, travelled to the United States and performed at the MENC convention in Philadelphia, among other places. The excellence of the group's performance and the demonstration of the method were a revelation to the American teachers. The impact on the group is reflected in a statement made by an American string teacher, who noted that 4- and 5-year-old Japanese children were playing music of professional caliber, while American children usually did not begin to study the violin until age 9 or 10.

Talent education activity began to develop in the United States from the time of the 1964 convention. Because of the differences between American and Japanese societies and education, the method could not be implemented in the United States exactly as Suzuki developed it in his country. Several American string educators, including John Kendall, Paul Rolland, and Tibor Zelig, have developed solutions to problems that arose in adapting the method and have themselves developed successful Suzuki programs and published articles and materials on the subject.

One reason for the differences between the American and Japanese versions of the method is that it is difficult for American teachers to find students of preschool age. Most formal education situations for preschool children are not geared for the utilization of talent education. Until recently, the American public has not recognized the possibility of intense instruction for children of preschool age. Attitudes have changed since talent education has become better known, and private talent education schools have been established. However, the Suzuki method is utilized in public school systems that do not have 3-year-old students. Also, regardless of the age of beginners, many parents do not have time to participate in lessons because in American society it is not unusual for both parents to work. In some cases, programs function with limited parental involvement.

Many Suzuki programs in the United States use class, rather than private, lessons. Athough difficulties arise, this often proves advantageous because a spirit of cooperation is established among the children, who help each other during the lessons.

Suzuki talent education has proved beyond doubt that young children are capable of developing the necessary skill to perform difficult, but authentic, string literature. It is controversial, though, because many talent education students do not learn to read music proficiently, nor do they become effective orchestra members. Talent education advocates answer that their students do learn to read music if they are taught properly, and that it is not the purpose of talent education to train orchestra members. This controversy has prevented a greater proliferation of talent education programs in public schools. Despite the criticisms, talent education is most successful in terms of its own purposes, and the movement continues to grow.

COMPREHENSIVE MUSICIANSHIP

Comprehensive musicianship is the term used to describe the interdisciplinary study of music. In traditional music courses, especially at the high school and college levels, the various aspects of the subject are usually studied as separate and distinct areas of music. History and theory, for example, are taught as separate and unrelated courses, often by different people who make little attempt to relate the two subjects. This is even more true of applied music, in which students do not learn the relationship between the music literature studied and the well-defined historical and stylistic periods and theoretical systems from which the literature came. Students learn music without knowing the history and theory that shaped it. Their fragmented view of music prevents them from developing insights necessary for true musical understanding.

History of Comprehensive Musicianship

The problem of fragmented and incomplete musical knowledge is probably as old as the study of music. Not until the establishment of the Contemporary Music Project did a distinguished group of musicians and music educators formally recognize the problem and make a systematic effort to overcome it. In April 1965, at Northwestern University in Evanston, Illinois the Contemporary Music Project sponsored the four-day "Seminar on Comprehensive Musicianship—the Foundation for College Education in Music." The participants—scholars, educators, theorists, composers, historians, and performers—examined the content and orientation of basic college music courses in history and theory.

Background information was provided to the seminar participants in five papers delivered by experts. The papers were "The Role of Programmed Instruction in the Development of Musical Skills" by James Carlsen, "The Role of the Study of Music Theory in the Development of Musical Understanding" by Allen Forte, "Philosophy of Music Education" by Charles Leonhard, "The Role of Music History and Literature in the Development of Musical Understanding" by William Mitchell, and "Current Trends in Curriculum and Instruction" by Ole Sand. For purposes of discussion, the topic of comprehensive musicianship was divided into two aspects—concepts and skills—and all related music courses were grouped into three categories—composition, analysis, and history. This allowed the participants to consider the relationship between concepts and skills in one or more areas, and to examine any single area within the total curriculum.

Three discussion groups were formed, each of which made recommendations at the end of the seminar. The groups addressed the following topics: "Compositional Processes and Writing Skills," "Musical Analysis and Aural Skills," and "History and Literature and Performing Skills." The specific recommendations of each group were focused on the comprehensive study of each area. Several recommendations were common to all three groups. They summarized the recommendations of the seminar for comprehensive music study in college music programs as follows:

1. The content and orientation of musicianship training should serve all music degree students regardless of their eventual specialization.
2. Comprehensive musicianship training incorporates conceptual knowledge with technical skills to develop the capacity to experience fully and the ability to communicate the content of a musical work.
3. The courses in musicianship training should be designed to synthesize knowledge acquired in all other musical studies.
4. All musicianship studies should relate contemporary thought and practices with those of former times.
5. Musicianship courses should be considered as evolving and open-ended disciplines. The student must be given the means to seek and deal with materials outside and beyond his formal education in music.
6. The relevance of musicianship training to professional studies should be made clear to the student. The clarity of purpose may be achieved if musicianship training is based on the student's own musical development and expressive needs.
7. Courses constituting comprehensive musicianship training are directly related to each other. The study of any specific subject matter need not be confined to a given course but approached in several ways in other complementary disciplines.[47]

The Northwestern University Seminar resulted in six Institutes for Music in Contemporary Education (IMCE), which were held at thirty-six educational institutions. The purpose of the institutes was to implement comprehensive musicianship as formulated at the Northwestern Seminar. The IMCE courses were discussed at a four-day symposium held at Arlie House in Warrenton, Virginia, in May 1967. The purpose of the symposium was to devise a means of evaluating the IMCE courses. An assessment was agreed upon that was in keeping with the theory of comprehensive musicianship, but that would allow for local differences in the various IMCE courses. Four areas were included in the assessment—descriptive competence, performing competence, creative competence, and attitude. The following outline describes the assessment.

A. *Descriptive Competence:* The student is expected to listen to specific musical examples from various periods including the contemporary and describe:

1.   The musical elements relevant to structure
2.   The formal elements relevant to the example
3.   The relation of musical and formal elements to the expressive character of the example, including the role of extra-musical elements, and
4.   The relation of musical, formal, and expressive elements to the stylistic factors in the example

B. *Performing Competence:* The student is expected to demonstrate his:

1.   Literacy in conventional notation and terminology, and other systems of notation
2.   Ability to study and perform a solo work and an ensemble work
3.   Ability to evaluate performance, including his own, with respect to technical accuracy and interpretation
4.   Ability to coach and instruct in a variety of situations, and,
5.   Knowledge of musical repertoire in general and program-building in his own field of specialization

C. *Creative Compentence:* The student is expected to demonstrate his ability to:

1.   Write examples illustrating a variety of melodic and rhythmic constructions, and harmonic and contrapuntal procedures
2.   Write examples illustrating the characteristics of various styles
3.   Adapt and rearrange music from the original medium to a different medium
4.   Improvise in a given style or in his personal idiom, and
5.   Compose an original work for available performing resources

D. *Attitude:* The student is asked to indicate on a questionnaire the degree of importance he attaches to thirty specified activities and experiences outside his class work. His instructor is asked to fill out a separate questionnaire in which he assesses the student's attitude toward specified classroom activities.[48]

The assessment was intended for students in their second year of music study at the college level.

Uses of Comprehensive Musicianship

Since the Northwestern University Seminar, the realization of comprehensive musicianship has been gradual. Relatively few colleges have instituted comprehensive musicianship programs. Those that have usually combine the study of performance, theory, and history. The concept has had more impact in the elementary and secondary schools, especially in relation to performing ensembles. More and more directors of bands, orchestras, and choruses are adopting comprehensive musicianship ideas and practices. The reason for this, as stated in the Yale Seminar discussion of performance in public school music programs, is that performance-oriented music programs, excellent though they may be, often do little to increase the musicality and musical appreciation of the individual musician. In the past, performance itself was considered sufficient justification for school performance organizations because communities could hear the excellent results. Educators, however, have questioned the value of such activity if the individual student learns so little. Music teachers have also questioned the basic philosophy of various school performance organizations. They have decided that individual growth and development are more important than collective results, which provide questionable benefits for the individuals involved. In other words, performance is not an end in itself—it is a means to an end.

Traditionally, American school performance ensembles have no formal curriculum. The music played by a group has usually served as the curriculum. If a high school band prepares twenty-five pieces during one school year, then the curriculum for one particular student might be the second clarinet parts of those twenty-five pieces. Although many directors have always been concerned about learning, in most performance ensemble programs, if the second clarinetist learns anything about music history, style, theory, and analysis, the development of such knowledge is purely incidental. The deficiency of this kind of curriculum was summarized by R. Jack Mercer:

There are few band curricula that take the student through the basics of music theory and history. Instead, scores are selected to meet the requirements of the next performance, and the curriculum is the score. Consequently, the content of the course of study is fortuitous, depending almost entirely upon whether it is football season or concert season. . . . The goal of musical training is to present a polished musical performance.[49]

The musical score, then, is the curriculum in traditional programs, but individual students do not obtain the kind of broad musical experience that prepares them to become musical adults. The performance ensemble is expected to give concerts, to enter contests and festivals, and to play at certain other functions such as ceremonies, parades, and assemblies. The ensemble is functional and ceremonial; it serves as a public relations unit of the educational system and provides an enjoyable activity for its members. This is music making but not necessarily music education. Charles Benner summarizes the problem:

It can be inferred that performing group participation has little effect on musical behavior other than the acquisition of performance skills, unless there is a planned effort by the teacher to enrich the performing experience with additional kinds of musical understanding.[50]

The problem is well-recognized, and many directors make serious and sincere efforts to overcome it. The solution lies in the music performed; used properly, it can be the basis for learning about music. Joseph Labuta offers a definition of musicianship as it applies to student performers in a comprehensive sense: "the term musicianship is often used when referring to comprehensive musical attributes and abilities of performers. It is theory applied to practice; it is knowledge and skill applied to practical music making."[51]

Books and articles have been published to help directors use the music as the basis for broader musical learning, and musical materials that include analytical, theoretical, and historical information that can be used for a comprehensive approach have become available. In *Blueprint for Band*, Robert Garofalo identifies the director's responsibilities in a comprehensive musicianship situation:

To organize a viable program of studies that correlates instrumental music performance with the study of music structure and style, and encompasses a diversity of musical behaviors—performing, listening, analyzing, composing, conducting, arranging; and . . . to establish a stimulating musical environment in which students are continuously brought into contact with the "creative musical experience" either directly or indirectly.[52]

Garofalo's approach takes into account understanding, knowledge, and skills. He suggests that rehearsals be planned to meet specific objectives that are developed around each musical composition. The composition is not only played, but studied as well.[53] He provides an outline (see Outline 5.1) of the areas in which objectives might be developed.

This approach requires a different kind of long- and short-term preparation by the director. Long-term goals must be set, and each rehearsal is actually a combination of rehearsal, class, and laboratory (see Figure 5.8). It necessitates outside work by individual students in excess of regular practicing, as well as additional equipment and facilities. The director, students, parents, and administrators must understand that the performance ensemble can serve a valuable educational function for its individual members, but that the addition of these activities prevents the ensemble from fulfilling all of its traditional functions, at least in terms of numbers of performances. This means that is does not always fulfill traditional expectations. Garofalo writes:

It must be clearly understood that the proposed curriculum is not antiperformance. The band must continue to work toward achieving the

```
┌─────────────────────────────────────────────────────────────┐
│              OUTLINE 5.1——BLUEPRINT FOR BAND                  │
│                                                               │
│                                                               │
│                   OUTLINE OF OBJECTIVES                       │
│   I.  Understanding of the structural elements of music       │
│       A. Pitch                                                │
│          1. Melody (horizontally organized pitches)           │
│          2. Harmony (vertically organized pitches)            │
│       B. Duration (rhythm)                                    │
│       C. Timbre (individual or combined tone colors—          │
│              bandstration)                                    │
│       D. Intensity (dynamics)                                 │
│       E. Texture (homophonic, polyphonic, and so on)          │
│       F. Design (form)                                        │
│       G. Compositional techniques and considerations          │
│          1. Melodic (thematic) transformation                 │
│          2. Harmonic transformation (such as modulation)      │
│          3. Rhythmic transformation                           │
│          4. Unity and variety (contrast)                      │
│          5. Dissonance and consonance (tension and relaxation)│
│                                                               │
│  II.  Knowledge of music as a creative art form of man in a   │
│       historical context                                      │
│       A. Historical background information about a            │
│              composition                                      │
│       B. Biographical information about the composer          │
│       C. Stylistic and performance practices of the           │
│              historical period that the composition represents│
│                                                               │
│ III.  Skills                                                  │
│       A. Aural skills (ear-oriented)                          │
│          1. Identification and discriminataion as concerns    │
│              the structural elements of music (see under      │
│              I, A to E)                                        │
│             a. Pitches (including intonation)                 │
│             b. Durations (including ensemble—that is,         │
│                   rhythmic precision)                         │
│             c. Timbres (including tone quality and blend)      │
│             d. Intensities (including balance)                │
│             e. Textures                                       │
│          2. Recognition tasks associated with extended        │
│              listening (see under I, F and G)                 │
│       B. Dexterous skills (hand-oriented)                     │
│          1. Instrumental                                      │
│          2. Conducting                                        │
│          3  Vocal (optional)                                  │
│       C. Translative skills (eye-oriented)                    │
│          1. Music reading                                     │
│             a. Individual parts                               │
│             b. Multiple parts (score reading)                 │
│          2. Sight reading                                     │
│   Reprinted by permission of J. Weston Walch, Publisher, Box  │
│   658, Portland, Maine 04104.                                 │
└─────────────────────────────────────────────────────────────┘
```

Note. Revised edition. Copyright © 1983, Meredith Music Publications. Reprinted by permission.

Figure 5.8. The Rehearsal—A Laboratory Experience in Applied Music Understanding

Blueprint of Objectives

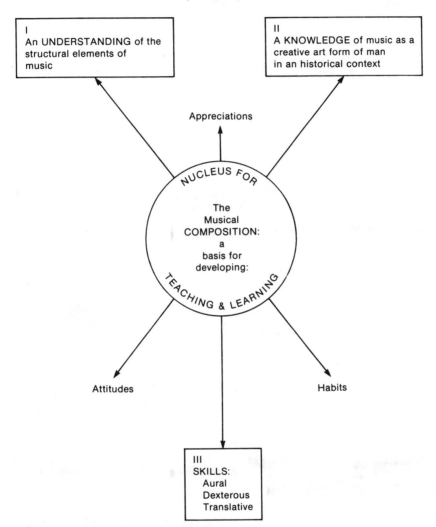

Note. Revised edition. Copyright © 1983, Meredith Music Publications. Reprinted by permission.

highest level of performance it is capable of attaining. Performance standards must not be slighted in any way. Indeed, a high level of performance is a necessary condition for any comprehensive musicianship curriculum of this type. Furthermore, evidence has shown that when students are taught both concepts and skills through the performance repertoire, they perform as well or better because they understand the music they are playing.[54]

The comprehensive musicianship approach has also been explored in relation to general music. General music, by its very nature, comes closer to providing broad musical knowledge for students than do performance ensembles. Often, however, the experiences that children have in general music classes are too narrow to permit them to develop musical concepts and knowledge that can be transferred to various styles of music. One weakness is that children do not have in-depth performance experiences that validate the conceptual knowledge developed in class. Also, the curriculum is often based on the unit approach, which usually addresses such nonmusical topics as the westward movement in the United States, Broadway shows, or lives of composers. It is really a humanities approach that explores the historical and sociological aspects of music without delving very deeply into the music itself. It, too, is changing, and many current general music materials are more concerned with music than with extramusical topics. One such text is *Comprehensive Musicianship through Classroom Music*, published in 1974.[55] It is the result of the Hawaii Music Curriculum Program, which began in 1968 under the sponsorship of the Hawaii Curriculum Center in Honolulu. Its purpose was "to create a logical, continuous educational program ensuring the competent guidance of the music education of all children in the state's public schools and to test and assemble the materials needed by schools to realize this problem."[56] It was possible to develop a state-wide curriculum for the public schools of Hawaii because of that state's unique educational structure. There are no local school systems—only a statewide educational system.

According to the Hawaii Music Curriculum Program, the term "comprehensive" means that students will be involved with music in school in the same ways in which people are involved with music in the outside world, that is, as composers, performers, listeners, and scholars. Because the school should be a microcosm of the outside world, students should become competent in the four activities.

The curriculum is based on seven basic concepts—tone, rhythm, melody, harmony, form, tonality, and texture—that are presented in the form of a spiral curriculum. All other musical concepts can be classified under one or more of the basic seven. A taxonomy of musical concepts was derived that progressed from the general to the specific, and from the simple to the complex. For example, the concept of rhythm is developed early in a child's life. Throughout the curriculum the child deals with rhythm in an increasingly complex and sophisticated progression. A chronology of concepts and teaching was then planned.

The taxonomy of concepts was translated into a curriculum by means of a five part division that covers the entire K–12 music experience. It is an ungraded curriculum that represents "levels of sophistication" rather than formal school grade levels. It is intended to serve as a guide for students who progress through the curriculum at individual rates of progress. The divisions, called "zones," are as follows:

Zone I: General music, consisting of singing; playing on rudimental instruments such as recorder, autoharp, bells, and the usual trappings of the traditional elementary music class; listening, composing, discussing, and a rudimentary kind of research; introduction to the graphic representation of musical sounds.

Zone II: Essentially a continuation of Zone I, but with greater emphasis on performance with rudimentary instruments; introduction to reading and writing of standard musical notation.

Zone III: Introduction to performance on various traditional instruments and singing as a technique; vocal, brass, woodwind, percussion, and string categories during the first third of the zone; selection of "major" instrument concentration (including vocal) during final two-thirds of zone; continuation of activities of previous two zones

Zone IV: Formation of ensemble groups that permit playing for special interest combinations; continuation of listening, composing, analyzing work along with ensemble performance

Zone V: Continuation of ensembles, addition (for those who so elect) of music theory, and/or music literature courses (grades 9–10); participation in a music ensemble as prerequisite for election of theory course, and/or advanced music literature course.[57]

See figure 5.9 for grade level equivalents of zones and kinds of musical activities in each zone. Every area of instruction is divided into three parts—objectives, learning activities, and evaluative procedures. The objectives are stated in behavioral terms; the learning activities involve students with music as composers, performers, listeners, and scholars. The evaluative procedures are of several kinds; some require "high level cognitive behavior such as analysis, synthesis, and evaluation."[58]

Thomson states that, despite the traditional appearance of the curriculum, "the separate classes comprising the zones—including band, chorus, and orchestra—are to be regarded not *as ends in themselves, but rather as contexts for learning musical concepts.*[59]

Summary

Comprehensive musicianship has undergone considerable development since the Northwestern University Seminar. It began as a concept for educating college music students, but its influence has shifted to elementary and secondary education. If students approach music as a discipline and learn to be performers, listeners, composers, and scholars, then music in the schools involves more than entertainment, public relations, and fun. The problem is that it adds another dimension to the activities of performing ensembles, which are already tightly scheduled. School ensembles are expected to perform and to perform well, and those

FIGURE 5.9. The Hawaii Music Curriculum Project
Teaching Media Charted Relative to Instructional Zones

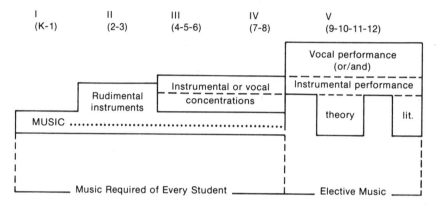

ZONES OF INSTRUCTION (with grade approximations)

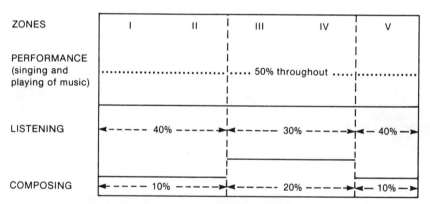

Note. Reprinted by permission of Curriculum Research and Development Group, College of Education, University of Hawaii.

people who make budgetary and curricular decisions that affect music programs are usually most impressed by performance. They may also be impressed by what students gain from the study of music, but all too often, performance is the most significant factor in maintaining public support for music programs.

Many ensemble directors have implemented comprehensive musicianship practices and find that their students learn more about music and have better attitudes toward music and performance than do students in traditional programs. Those directors, however, must work very hard to prepare for comprehensive teaching and to evaluate their programs.

They must also be willing to de-emphasize somewhat the performance aspect of their programs. To do so requires them to be music teachers rather than directors, a role that demands a different expenditure of time, effort, and resources than that of the traditional ensemble director. These two problems, then, must be overcome if comprehensive musicianship is to be implemented. Education authorities must be convinced of the value of music study through performance, and teachers must have the knowledge, ability, resources, and positive attitude to develop comprehensive musicianship programs.

NOTES

1. Jerome S. Bruner *The Process of Education* (Cambridge, Mass.: Harvard University Press, 1960), p. 3.
2. Ibid., p. 12.
3. Ibid., p. 12.
4. Ibid., pp. 13, 14.
5. Ibid., pp. 14, 15.
6. Russell P. Getz, "Music Education in Tomorrow's Schools: A Practical Approach," in *The Future of Musical Education in America* (Rochester, N.Y.: Eastman School of Music Press, 1984), pp. 24, 25.
7. Charles L. Gary, ed., *The Study of Music in the Elementary School—A Conceptual Approach* (Washington, D.C.: Music Educators National Conference, 1967).
8. Asahel D. Woodruff, unpublished paper; quoted in Gary, *The Study of Music in the Elementary School*, p. 2.
9. Ibid., p. 3
10. James L. Fisher, "Handbells in the Schools," Schulmerich Carillons, Inc.
11. Ronald Lee, "Arts in Education: A Curricular Approach to Explore" (Paper presented at National In-service Conference, Music Educators National Conference, Chicago, March 1984).
12. Ibid.
13. Terrell Stackpole, "Overview of the Comprehensive Arts Education Program," Division of Arts Education, Pittsburgh, Pa., Public Schools, July 1984.
14. M. E. Sadler, in Emile Jaques-Dalcroze. *The Eurhythmics* (Boston: Small Maynard and Company, 1915), p. 32.
15. Ibid., p. 35.
16. Charles R. Hoffer. *Introduction to Music Education* (Belmont, Calif.: Wadsworth, 1983), p. 123.
17. Emile Jaques-Dalcroze, "Teaching Music Through Feeling," *Etude* 39, (June 1921): 368.
18. Jo Pennington, *The Importance of Being Rhythmic: A Study of the Principles of Dalcroze Eurhythmics Applied to General Education and to the Arts of Music, Dancing, and Acting* (New York: G. P. Putnam's Sons, 1925), pp. 26–27.
19. Beth Landis and Polly Carder, *The Eclectic Curriculum in American Music Education: Contributions of Dalcroze, Kodály, and Orff* (Washington, D.C.: Music Educators National Conference, 1972), p. 23.
20. Ibid., pp. 26–27.
21. Emile Jaques-Dalcroze. *Eurhythmics, Art and Education*, trans. Frederick Rothwell, ed. Cynthia Cox (New York: B. Blom, 1972) pp. 145–68.

22. Landis and Carder, *The Eclectic Curriculum*, p. 156

23. Bjonar Bergethon and Eunice Boardman, *Musical Growth in the Elementary School*, 4th ed. (New York: Holt, Rinehart and Winston, 1979), p. 231.

24. Arnold Walter, "Carl Orff's 'Music for Children,' *The Instrumentalist* 13, no. 5 (January 1959):39. Used by permission.

25. Arnold Walter, Introduction to *Music for Children* by Carl Orff and Gunild Keetman, trans. and adapted by Arnold Walter and Doreen Hall, 5 vols. (Mainz: B. Schott's Sohne, 1955), vol. 1.

26. Loraine Edwards, "The Great Animating Stream of Music," *Music Educators Journal* 57, no. 6 (February 1971):38–39. Reprinted by permission of Music Educators National Conference.

27. Tibor Bachmann, *Reading and Writing Music* (Elizabethtown, Pa.: Continental Press, 1968).

28. Lois Choksy, *The Kodály Method* (Englewood Cliffs, N.J.: Prentice-Hall, 1974).

29. Mary Helen Richards, *Threshold to Music* (Belmont, Calif: Fearon Publishers, 1964).

30. Denise Bacon, "Kodály and Orff: Report from Europe," *Music Educators Journal* 55, no. 88 (April 1969):55–56. Reprinted by permission of Music Educators National Conference.

31. Arnold Walter, "The Orff-Schulwerk in American Education" (Muncie, Ind.: American Orff-Schulwerk Association, 1969); copyright © 1969. Used by permission.

32. Grace C. Nash, "Media for Human Development," in *The Eclectic Curriculum in American Music Education* (Washington, D.C.: Music Educators National Conference, 1972), p. 173. Reprinted by permission of Music Educators National Conference.

33. Ibid., pp. 173–74.

34. Ronald B. Thomas, "Rethinking the Curriculum," *Music Educators Journal* 56, no. 6 (February 1970):70.

35. Ronald B. Thomas, *MMCP Final Report*, part 1, Abstract (Washington, D.C.: U.S. Office of Education ED 045 865, August 1970), p. vii. Reprinted by permission.

36. Ibid., p. vii.

37. Ronald B. Thomas, "Learning Music Unconventionally—Manhattanville Music Curriculum Program," *Music Educators Journal* 54, no. 9 (May 1968):64. Reprinted by permission.

38. Thomas, *MMCP Final Report*, p. 2.

39. Ronald B. Thomas, *MMCP Synthesis* (Bardonia, N.Y.: Media Materials, 1970), p. 4.

40. Ibid., p. 6.

41. Ronald B. Thomas, *Manhattanville Music Curriculum Program: Final Report*, "MMCP Interaction) (Washington, D.C.: United States Office of Education, 1970), pp. 7–8.

42. Ibid., pp. 11–12.

43. Edwin E. Gordon and David Woods, *Jump Right In: The Music Curriculum* (Chicago: G.I.A. Publications, 1984).

44. Edwin E. Gordon, *Learning Sequences in Music: Skill, Content, and Patterns* (Chicago: G.I.A. Publications, 1984).

45. Edwin E. Gordon, *Tonal and Rhythm Pattern Audiation Cassettes* (Chicago: G.I.A. Publications, 1983).

46. John D. Kendall, *Talent Education and Suzuki*, quoting from a speech by Shinichi Suzuki, given at the National Festival, Tokyo, 1958 (Washington, D.C.: Music Educators National Conference, 1966), p. 9. Reprinted by permission of Music Educators National Conference.

47. *Comprehensive Musicianship The Foundation for College Education in Music* (Washington, D.C.: Music Educators National Conference, 1965), p. 21. Reprinted by permission of Music Educators National Conference.
48. "Evaluative Criteria for Music in Education," *Music Educators Journal* 54, no. 7 (March 1968):66–67. Reprinted by permission of Music Educators National Conference.
49. R. Jack Mercer, "Is the Curriculum the Score—or More?" *Music Educators Journal* 58, no. 6 (February 1972):51–53. Reprinted by permission of Music Educators National Conference.
50. Charles H. Benner, *Teaching Performing Groups* (Washington, D.C.: Music Educators National Conference, 1972), p. 10.
51. Joseph A. Labuta, *Teaching Musicianship in the High School Band* (West Nyack, N.Y.: Parker, 1972), p. 7.
52. Robert J. Garofalo, "Blueprint for Band," *Music Educators Journal* 60, no. 3 (November 1973):39–42.
53. Robert J. Garofalo, *Blueprint for Band* (Fort Lauderdale, Fla.: Meredith Music Publications, 1983)p. 98.
54. Ibid., p. 98.
55. William Thomson, *Comprehensive Musicianship through Classroom Music* (Belmont, Calif.: Addison-Wesley, 1974.
56. William Thomson, "Music Rides a Wave of Reform in Hawaii," *Music Educators Journal* 56, no. 9 (May 1970):73.
57. William Thomson, *The Hawaii Music Curriculum Project: The Project Design* (Honolulu: College of Education, University of Hawaii), p. 14. Used by permission.
58. Allen W. Flock, "The Comprehensive Music Program," *PMEA News* (Pennsylvania Music Educators Association) 40, no. 4 (May 1976):47.
59. Ibid., p. 47.

BIBLIOGRAPHY

Conceptual Learning

Bruner, Jerome S. *The Process of Education.* Cambridge Mass.: Harvard University Press, 1960.
Gary, Charles L., ed. *The Study of Music in the Elementary School—A Conceptual Approach.* Washington, D.C.: Music Educators National Conference, 1967.

The Dalcroze Method

Books

Brown, Margaret; and Betty K. Sommer. *Movement Education: Its Evolution and A Modern Approach.* Reading, Mass.: Addison-Wesley, 1969.
Driver, Ann. *Music and Movement.* London: Oxford University Press, 1936.
———. *A Pathway to Dalcroze Eurhythmics.* London: Thomas Nelson and Sons, 1963.
Findlay, Elsa. *Rhythm and Movement: Applications of Dalcroze Eurhythmics.* Evanston, Ill.: Summy-Birchard, 1971.
Hoffer, Charles R. *Introduction to Music Education.* Belmont, Calif.: Wadsworth, 1983.
Jaques-Dalcroze, Emile. *The Eurhythmics.* Boston: Small Maynard and Company, 1915.
———. *Rhthmic Movement.* 2 vols. London: Novello and Co., Ltd., 1920–21.

------. *Rhythm, Music and Education,* Translated by Harold F. Rubenstein. Abridged reprint edition. London: The Riverside Press, Ltd., 1967.

Landis, Beth; and Polly Carder. *The Eclectic Curriculum in American Music Education: Contributions of Dalcroze, Kodály, and Orff.* Washington, D.C.: Music Educators National Conference, 1972.

Periodicals

Aranoff, Frances W. "Games Teachers Play: Dalcroze Eurhythmics." *Music Educators Journal* 57 (Feb. 1971):28–32.

Boepple, Paul. "The Study of Rhythm." *Yearbook of the Music Supervisors National Conference,* 1931, pp. 192–94.

Brody, Viola A. "The Role of Body-Awareness in the Emergence of Musical Ability." *Journal of Research in Music Education* 1 (Spring 1953):17.

Gehrkens, Karl W. "A Page or Two of Opinions." *Educational Music Magazine* 29 (Sept–Oct. 1949):11–13.

------. "Trends in Music Education." *Yearbook of the Music Supervisors National Conference,* 1932, pp. 258–62.

Grentzer, Rose Marie. "Eurhythmics in the Elementary School Program," *Etude* 62 (Jan. 1944):22.

Hall, Lucy Duncan. "The Value of Eurhythmics in Education." *Yearbook of the Music Educators National Conference,* 1936, pp. 150–53.

Naumberg M. "The Dalcroze Idea: What Eurhythmics Is and What It Means," *Outlook* 106 (17 Jan. 1914):127–31.

Scholl, Sharon. "Music for Dancers," *Music Educators Journal* 52 (Feb.–March 1966):99–102.

The Orff Approach

Books

Glasgow, Robert B.; and Dale Hamreus. "Study to Determine the Feasibility of Adapting the Carl Orff Approach to Elementary Schools in America." Monmouth, Oregon: Oregon College of Education. ERIC document no.ED 020 804.

Landis, Beth; and Polly Carder. *The Eclectic Curriculum in American Music Education.* Washington, D.C.: Music Educators National Conference, 1972.

Olson, Rees Garn. "A Comparison of Two Pedagogical Approaches Adapted to the Acquisition of Melodic Sensitivity in Sixth Grade Children: The Orff Method and the Traditional Method." Ph.D. dissertation, Indiana University, 1967.

Thomas, Werner. *Carl Orff: A Report in Words and Pictures.* Mainz: B. Schott's Sohne, 1955.

Periodicals

Breuer, Robert. "The Magic World of Carl Orff." *Music Journal,* March 1957, p. 56.

Flagg, Marion. "The Orff System in Today's World." *Music Educators Journal* 53 (December 1966):30.

Hamm, Ruth Pollock. "The Challenge of the Orff Approach for Elementary Music Education." *Musart,* April–May 1970, p. 16.

------. "Orff Defended." *Music Educators Journal* 50 (April–May 1964):90–92.

Keller, Wilhelm. "What Is the Orff-Schulwerk—and What It Is Not." *Musart,* April–May 1970, p. 50.

Klie, Ursula. "Principles of Movement in the Orff-Schulwerk. *Musart,* April–May 1970, pp. 42–43.

Nash, Grace C. "Orff," *The Instrumentalist*, Oct. 1965, p. 47.
———. "The Orff-Schulwerk in the Classroom," *Music Educators Journal* 50 (April–May 1964):92.
Nichols, Elizabeth. "Adapting Orff to the Music Series," *The Orff Echo*, Feb. 1970, p. 2.
Olson, Rees Garn. "Orff-Schulwerk . . . Innovation at Bellflower," *The Instructor*, May 1967, p. 76.
Ponath, Louise; and Carol Bitcon. "A Behavioral Analysis of Orff-Schulwerk." *Journal of Music Therapy*, Summer 1972, pp. 56–63.
Siemens, Margaret. "A Comparison of Orff and Traditional Instruction Methods in Music." *Journal of Research in Music Education*, Fall 1969, p. 272.

Methods

Birkenshaw, Lois. *Music for Fun, Music for Learning*. Toronto: Holt, Rinehart and Winston of Canada, Ltd., 1977.
Bitcom, Carol. *Alike and Different*. Santa Ana, Calif.: Rosha Press, n.d.
Keetman, Gunild. *Elementaria*. St. Louis: Magnamusic-Baton, n.d.
Nash, Grace C.; Geraldine W. Jones; Barbara A. Potter; and Patsy S. Smith. *Do It My Way: The Child's Way of Learning*. Sherman Oaks, Calif.: Alfred Publishing Co., 1977.
Orff, Carl; and Gunild Keetman. *Orff-Schulwerk*, 5 vols. Mainz: B. Schott's Sohne, 1955.
Wampler, Martha, ed. *Design for Creativity*. ESEA Title III Project. Bellflower, Calif.: Bellflower Unified School District, 1968.
Wuytack, Joseph. *Musica Viva*. St. Louis: Magnamusic-Baton.

The Kodály Method

Bachmann, Tibor. *Reading and Writing Music*. Elizabethtown, Pa.: The Continental Press, 1968.
———. *Growing with Music*. Elizabethtown, Pa.: The Continental Press, 1968.
———. *Songs to Read*. Elizabethtown, Pa.: The Continental Press, 1970.
Choksy, Lois, "Kodály in and out of Context." *Music Educators Journal* 55 (April 1969):57–59.
———. *The Kodály Context*. Englewood Cliffs, N.J.: Prentice-Hall, 1981.
———. *The Kodály Method*. Englewood Cliffs, N.J.: Prentice-Hall, 1974.
Daniel, Katinka. "The Kodály Method." *Clavier* 7 (Sept. 1968):20–21.
Darazs, Arpad; and Stephen Jay. *Sight and Sound*. New York: Boosey and Hawkes, 1965.
Edwards, Loraine. "Hungary's Musical Powerline to the Young—The Great Animating Stream of Music," *Music Educators Journal* 57 (Feb. 1971):38–40.
Eosze, L. *Zoltan Kodály: His Life and Work*. Translated by Istvan Farkas and Gyula Gulyas. Boston: Crescendo, 1962.
Erdei, Peter; and Katalin Komlos, eds. *150 American Folk Songs to Sing, Read, and Play*. New York: Boosey and Hawkes, 1974.
Kodály Curriculum Guide for Silver Burdett Music. Morristown, N.J.: Silver Burdett Company, 1983. Grades 1–3, Harold L. Caldwell; Grades 3–5, Peter R. Allen; Grade 6, Sr. Lorna Zemke.
Kodály, Zoltán. "Folk Song in Pedagogy." *Music Educators Journal* 53 (March 1962):59.
———. *The Kodály Method Applied to the Teaching of Instruments*. Wellesley, Mass.: Kodály Musical Training Institute, 1974.
Teaching Music at Beginning Levels Through the Kodály Concept. 3 vols. Wellesley, Mass.: Kodály Musical Training Institute, 1973.

Kraus, Egon. "Zoltán Kodály's Legacy to Music Education." *International Music Educator* 16 (September 1967): 513–32.

Landis, Beth; and Polly Carder. *The Eclectic Curriculum in American Music Education.* Washington, D.C.: Music Educators National Conference, 1972.

Lewis, Aden. *Listen, Look and Sing.* Morristown, N.J.: General Learning Corporation, 1971.

McLaughlin, Elizabeth. "The Significance of the Kodály Conception in America." *Musart* 23 (Jan. 1971):8–9.

Richards, Mary Helen. "The Kodály System in the Elementary Schools." *Bulletin,* Council for Research in Music Education no. 8, Fall 1966, pp. 44–48.

———. *Threshold to Music.* Belmont, Calif: Fearon Publishers, 1964.

Szonyi, Erzsebet. *Kodály's Principles in Practice.* New York: Boosey and Hawkes, 1973.

———. *Musical Reading and Writing.* London: Boosey and Hawkes, 1974. Teacher's manual. 2 vols.

———. *The Child in Depth.* Portola Valley, Calif.: Mary Helen Richards, 1966.

———. *Teaching Music through Songs.* Palo Alto, Calif.: Fearon Publishers, 1966.

———. *Threshold to Music.* Belmont, Calif.: Fearon Publishers, 1964.

Orff and Kodály Combined

Bacon, Denise. "On Using Orff with Kodály." *Musart,* April–May 1969.

———. "Kodály and Orff—Report from Europe," *Music Educators Journal* 55 (April 1969):53.

Bergethon, Bjonar; and Eunice Boardman. "Ancillary Procedures for Teaching Music." *Musical Growth in the Elementary School,* 4th ed. N.Y.: Holt, Rinehart and Winston, 1979, pp. 228–36.

Landis, Beth; and Polly Carder. *The Eclectic Curriculum in American Music Education.* Washington, D.C.: Music Educators National Conference, 1974.

Nash, Grace C. "Kodály and Orff." *Clavier* 7 (Sept. 1968):23–25.

Wheeler, Lawrence; and Lois Raebeck. *New Approaches to Music in the Elementary School.* Dubuque, Iowa: William C. Brown, 1974.

———. *Orff and Kodály Adapted for the Elementary School.* Dubuque, Iowa: William C. Brown, 1978.

The Manhattanville Music Curriculum Program

Fisher, Renee. "Learning Music Unconventionally—Manhattanville Music Curriculum Program," *Music Educators Journal* 54 (May 1968):61–64.

Gibbs, Robert. "Effects of the Manhattanville Music Curriculum Program in the Musical Achievement and Attitude of Jefferson County, Colorado, Public Schools Students." Ph.D. diss., University of Colorado, 1972.

Thomas, Ronald B. "Rethinking the Curriculum," *Music Educators Journal* 56 (Feb. 1970):68–70.

———. "Objectives of the MMCP Curriculum." In *Instructional Objectives in Music: Resources for Planning Instruction and Evaluating Achievement.* Edited by J. David Boyle. Vienna, Va.: Music Educators National Conference, 1974, pp. 100–110.

———. *Manhattanville Music Curriculum Program: Final Report.* Washington, D.C.: U.S. Office of Education, Bureau of Research, August 1970. ERIC document ED 045 865.

———. "Sound of a Revolution." *Catholic School Journal,* April 1970, pp. 14–18.

———. *A Study of New Concepts, Procedures, and Achievements in Music Learning as Developed in Selected Music Programs.* Washington, D.C.: U.S. Office of Education, Bureau of Research (Project no. V-008), 1966.

Teaching Music Through Learning Theory

Music-Learning Theory

Gordon, Edwin. *Learning Sequences in Music: Skill, Content, and Patterns.* Chicago: G.I.A. Publications, 1984.

General Sources Related to Music Learning Theory

Bruner, Jerome S. *The Process of Education.* Cambridge: Harvard University Press, 1960.

Gagne, Robert. *The Conditions of Learning.* New York: Holt, Rinehart, and Winston, 1977.

Gordon, Edwin. *The Psychology of Music Teaching.* Englewood Cliffs: Prentice-Hall, 1971.

Moorhead, Gladys Evelyn; and Donald Pond. *Music of Young Children.* Santa Barbara, Calif.: Pillsbury Foundation for Advancement of Music Education, 1977.

Smith, Frank. *Understanding Reading* New York: Holt, Rinehart, and Winston, 1975.

Research Related to Music-Learning Theory

DeYarman, Robert. "An Experimental Analysis of the Development of Rhythmic and Tonal Capabilities of Kindergarten and First Grade Children." *Experimental Research in the Psychology of Music: Studies in the Psychology of Music* 8 (1972):1–44.

Dittemore, Edgar E. "An Investigation of Some Musical Capabilities of Elementary School Children." *Experimental Research in the Psychology of Music: Studies in the Psychology of Music* 6 (1970):1–44.

Gordon, Edwin. "Toward the Development of a Taxonomy of Tonal Patterns and Rhythm Patterns: Evidence of Difficulty Level and Growth Rate." *Experimental Research in the Psychology of Music: Studies in the Psychology of Music* 9 (1974):39–232.

Gordon, Edwin. *Tonal and Rhythm Patterns: An Objective Analysis.* Albany: State University of New York Press, 1976.

Gordon, Edwin. *A Factor Analytic Description of Tonal and Rhythm Patterns and Objective Evidence of Pattern Difficulty Level and Growth Rate.* Chicago: G.I.A. Publications, 1978.

Kesson, William; Janice Levine; and Kenneth A. Wendrich. "The Imitation of Pitch in Infants." *Infant Behavior and Development* 2 (1979):93–99.

MacKnight, Carol B. "The Effects of Tonal Pattern Training on the Performance Achievement of Beginning Wind Instrumentalists." *Experimental Research in the Psychology of Music: Studies in the Psychology of Music* 10 (1975):53–76.

Miller, Philip. "An Experimental Analysis of the Development of Tonal Capabilities of First Grade Children." *Experimental Research in the Psychology of Music: Studies in the Psychology of Music* 10 (1975):77–97.

Music Aptitude Tests

Gordon, Edwin. *Musical Aptitude Profile.* Boston: Houghton Mifflin, 1965.

Gordon, Edwin. *Primary Measures of Music Audiation.* Chicago: G.I.A. Publications, 1979.

Gordon, Edwin. *Intermediate Measures of Music Audiation.* Chicago: G.I.A. Publications, 1982.

Research Related to Music Aptitude Tests

Flohr, John W. "Short-term Music Instruction and Young Children's Developmental Music Aptitude." *Journal of Research in Music Education* 24 (1981):219–23.

Gordon, Edwin. *A Three-Year Longitudinal Predictive Validity Study of the Musical Aptitude Profile.* Iowa City: The University of Iowa Press, 1967.

Gordon, Edwin. "The Contribution of Each Musical Aptitude Profile Subtest to the Overall Validity of the Battery." *Council for Research in Music Education* 12 (1967):32–36.

Gordon, Edwin. "Fourth- and Fifth-Year Results of a Longitudinal Study of the Musical Achievement of Culturally-Disadvantaged Students." *Experimental Research in the Psychology of Music: Studies in the Psychology of Music* 10 (1975):24–52.

Gordon, Edwin. "Developmental Music Aptitudes as Measured by the Primary Measures of Music Audiation." *Psychology of Music* 7 (1979):42–49.

Gordon, Edwin. "Developmental Music Aptitudes Among Inner-City Primary Children." *Council for Research in Music Education* 63 (1980):25–30.

Gordon, Edwin. "The Assessment of Music Aptitudes of Very Young Children." *The Gifted Child Quarterly* 24 (1980):25–30.

Gordon, Edwin. *The Manifestation of Developmental Music Aptitude in the Audiation of "Same" and "Different" as Sound in Music.* Chicago: G.I.A. Publications, 1981.

Holahan, John Michael. *The Effects of Four Conditions of "Same" and "Different" Instruction on the Developmental Music Aptitudes of Kindergarten Children Receiving Tonal Pattern Training.* Ph.D. Diss., Temple University, Philadelphia, Pa., 1983.

Holahan, John M.; and Selma W. Thomson. "An Investigation of the Suitability of the Primary Measures of Music Audiation for Use in England." *Psychology of Music* 9 (1981):63–68.

Jordon-DeCarbo, Joyce. "Same/Different Discrimination Techniques, Readiness Training, Pattern Treatment, and Sex on Aural Discrimination and Singing Ability of Tonal Patterns by Kindergarteners." *Journal of Research in Music Education* 30 (1982):237–46.

Shuter-Dyson, Rosamund, and Clive Gabriel. *The Psychology of Musical Ability.* London: Methuen, 1981.

The Carabo-Cone Method

Carabo-Cone, Madeleine. *Sensory-Motor Approach to Music Learning.* New York: MCA Music, 1965.

———. "A Game's Eye View into the World of Music." *Clavier,* Jan. 1969, pp. 40–43.

———. "Notes for Disadvantaged Preschool Children." *Music Journal,* 969 Annual, pp. 30–31.

———. "A Sensory-Motor Approach to Primary Music Learning." *Music Teacher,* April 1971, pp. 9–10.

———. "Learning How to Learn: A Sensory-Motor Approach." *Music Journal,* Jan. 1973, pp. 16–17.

Suzuki Talent Education

Books

Berardocco, Diana B. "A Study of the Philosophy and Method of Shinichi Suzuki." Master's thesis, The Catholic University of America, 1974. Includes an extensive bibliography.

Cook, Clifford A. *Suzuki Education in Action.* New York: Exposition Press, 1970. A concise history of the Suzuki method and its use in the United States.

Kendall, John D. *Talent Education and Suzuki: What the American Music Educators Should Know About Shinichi Suzuki.* Washington, D.C.: Music Educators National Conference, 1966.

——. *Suzuki Violin Method in American Education*. Washington, D.C.: Music Educators National Conference, 1973. An overview of the philosophy, history, methodology, and materials of the Suzuki method.

Mills, Elizabeth; and Therese Cecile Murphy, eds. *The Suzuki Concept*. Berkeley, Calif.: Diablo Press, 1973.

Suzuki, Shinichi. *Nurtured by Love*. Translated by Waltraud Suzuki. New York: Exposition Press, 1969. Suzuki's description of his method, including historical and philosophical background.

Wickes, Linda. *The Genius of Simplicity*. Princeton, N.J.: Summy-Birchard Music 1982.

Periodicals

Brunson, Theodore. "A Visit with Doctor Suzuki." *Music Educators Journal* 55 (May 1969):54–56.

"Fiddling Legions." *Newsweek*, 23 March 1964, p. 73.

Garofalo, Robert. "The Suzuki Method at the Campus School." *Musart*, Feb.–March 1971, p. 13.

Garson, Alfred. "Learning with Suzuki: Seven Questions Answered." *Music Educators Journal* 56 (Feb. 1970):64.

Gerard, Sister Jane Elizabeth, C.S.J. "Some Thoughts on Suzuki." *American String Teacher*, Summer 1966, p. 3.

Kendall, John. "A Report on Japan's Phenomenal Violinists," *Violins and Violinists*, Nov.–Dec. 1959, pp. 241–44.

——. "The Resurgent String Program in America." *Music Educators Journal* 50 (Sept.–Oct. 1963):45–48, 51. Also published in *Perspectives in Music Education: Source Book III*. Washington, D.C.: Music Educators National Conference, 1966, pp. 394–401.

Kesler, Marilyn. "Cello Instruction for Four and Five Year Olds." *American String Teacher*, Winter 1967, pp. 38–39.

Publisher's Newsletter. Published periodically. Princeton, N.J.: Summy-Birchard Music.

Shultz, Carl. "Shinichi Suzuki: The Genius of His Teaching." *American String Teacher*, Summer 1964, p. 9.

Suzuki World: The Magazine of Talent Education. Published bi-monthly. P.O. Box 466, Athens, Ohio.

Wassell, Albert. "Suzuki Answers Questions." *The Instrumentalist*, March 1964, pp. 68–69.

——. "Visit with Shinichi Suzuki in Japan." *American String Teacher*, Summer 1964, p. 9.

Zelig, Tibor. "A Direct Approach to Preschool Violin Teaching in California." *The Strad*, Jan. 1966, p. 310.

Methods

An Introduction to the Suzuki Method. Princeton, N.J.: Suzuki Method International, 1984.

Kendall, John D. *Listen and Play*. 3 vols. Evanston, Ill.: Summy-Birchard, 1965. Includes accompaniment books and recordings.

Sato Cello School. The Suzuki Method. Evanston, Ill.: Summy-Birchard, 1971. For cello, with English text.

Suzuki, Shinichi, *Suzuki Violin School: Suzuki Method*. 10 vols. Tokyo: Zen-on Music, 1955. Available from Summy-Birchard Company.

Zahtilla, Paul. *Suzuki in the String Class*. Evanston, Ill.: Summy-Birchard, 1971.

Comprehensive Musicianship

Benner, Charles H. *Teaching Performing Groups.* Washington, D.C.: Music Educators National Conference, 1972.

Boyle, David J. *Instructional Objectives in Music.* Vienna, Va.: Music Educators National Conference, 1974.

Comprehensive Musicianship: The Foundation for College Education in Music. Washington, D.C.: Music Educators National Conference, 1965.

Garofalo, Robert J. *Blueprint for Band.* Fort Lauderdale, Fla.: Meredith Music Publications, 1983.

————. *Rehearsal Handbook for Band and Orchestra Students.* Fort Lauderdale, Fla.: Meredith Music Publications, 1983.

Labuta, Joseph A. *Teaching Musicianship in the High School Band.* West Nyack, N.Y.: Parker, 1972.

Texter, Merry. *Musicianship in the Beginning Instrumental Class.* Washington, D.C.: Music Educators National Conference, 1973.

Thomson, William. *Comprehensive Musicianship through Classroom Music.* Belmont, Calif.: Addison-Wesley, 1974.

————. *The Hawaii Music Curriculum Project: The Project Design.* Honolulu: College of Education, University of Hawaii.

6

Materials and Tools of Music Education

POPULAR MUSIC

1926

I share the view that jazz is the most distinctive contribution America has
made to the world-literature of music. What we now need is proper guidance
of the jazz germ. There are two kinds of germs in the physical world—those
that kill and those that preserve human life. Jazz germs are of the same
nature. It is for the open-minded American musicians and musical educators
to discover, preserve, and develop the worthy elements of jazz. Jazz as an
end in itself, except for dancing and the like, is to be deplored. Jazz as an
idiom for something worthwhile, as a stepping-stone to something better
than we now recognize, is, as Shakespeare put it, "a consummation devoutly
to be wished."[1]

1967

Music of all periods, styles, forms, and cultures belongs in the curriculum.
The musical repertory should be expanded to involve music of our time in its
rich variety, including currently popular teenage music and avant-garde
music, American folk music, and the music of other cultures.[2]

Popular music includes jazz, rock, soul, country, Broadway and
others. This genre of music has only recently found a welcome place
in American music education. Popular music has been called "youth
music" in the past. It was a designation coined by MENC for use in the
November 1969 issue of the *Music Educators Journal*, which was dedicated to
the philosophical and practical aspects of popular music in American
education. Prior to that time, popular music had found little acceptance
by most music educators.

For many years a peripheral part of the music curriculum has been
what was originally called the "dance orchestra," later called the "jazz
band," and then the "jazz lab band." Peter Dykema and Karl Gehrkens

wrote extensively and negatively about jazz (or swing, or dance music) in *The Teaching and Administration of High School Music,* an influential book published in 1941. In a chapter dealing with the dance orchestra, they complained that it had more than gained a foothold in school music programs, and that it was too late to eliminate it. They admonished music teachers to be aware that dance orchestras were likely to damage students' playing habits and to corrupt their musical tastes. In a chapter entitled "The High School Pupil," Dykema and Gehrkens stated:

Swing music—which is merely a highly emotionalized style of playing jazz, and to which we are in no sense objecting to as a legitimate type of human experience—is primarily physical. It induces violent physical movement—note the *jitterbug*. It is "fleshly" in its entire conception. It does not lead toward the spiritual. It is "good fun" at the time, but it does not yield abiding satisfaction. To use such music in the school as a substitute for serious music is to cheat youth of a highly important experience which has the possibility of assisting in the development of spiritual resources.[3]

Speaking as representatives of the music education profession, Dykema and Gehrkens warned of the dangers of using jazz as part of the school music program, whether as a performance or listening activity. Discussions of jazz and popular music in articles (see especially the *Music Educators Journal*) and books throughout the 1940 and 1950s usually argued for the avoidance of such music, even though jazz and other popular music had been gaining ground steadily in the schools since the mid-1930s.

It became common during the 1950s for general music teachers to include units on jazz and Broadway music. No special importance was given to the music, and it was not presented as an aesthetic experience. Usually, it was just a unit of study for general music classes.

As late as 1963 the participants in the Yale Seminar recommended that stage bands be included in school music programs because they would draw into music programs students who then might be attracted to ensembles that played more serious music. Some educators felt that the stage band had developed and grown in American education with little justification and planning, and that the true need for such an organization in the curriculum had not been established. These people feared that by bowing to the pressure to include popular art forms in the curriculum, the schools would certainly leave themselves open for well-deserved criticism. In 1966 William Sur and Charles Schuller stated:

The question of whether the dance band should be part of the school instrumental program is debatable. There seems to be general agreement that if it is offered it should be reserved for senior high school and should be considered a noncredit music activity.[4]

Speaking for those teachers who had accepted wholeheartedly the use of jazz and popular music as a subject of study and performance, Walter

Anslinger defended the stage band on grounds of student interest, the development of good technique and playing habits, and as a suitable aesthetic experience. Anslinger did not accept the use of rock and roll, however. Thus continued the tradition of nonacceptance of popular music in music education by identifying a kind of music that appeals strongly to youth, but which has no place in the schools because it "is nothing more than hillbilly set to jungle rhythms."[5]

The changes in American society in the 1960s persuaded many educators that the popular arts had a definite place in American education. The years of violence and protest during the sixties resulted in the recognition of many basic rights for several groups of American citizens, including students. The results of the confrontational tactics used by young people were increased permissiveness toward the younger generation and acceptance of its taste in clothing, music, and other aspects of lifestyle. Such acceptance greatly changed the general academic atmosphere of music as well as of other programs. For example, minicourses in many areas of interest were introduced. In general, individuals became increasingly aware of individual personal value in relation to school and society. The word "relevant" took on new importance, especially in reference to school curricula. Colleges that may or may not have recognized the popular arts began to develop major programs in jazz. Secondary schools that had previously offered elective courses only in music appreciation began to offer courses in jazz, rock, and other areas of music.

The music education revolution of the late 1960s received a strong boost from the MENC when the Tanglewood Symposium adopted a comprehensive viewpoint toward music:

Man reaches for one music, then another, then another throughout life. But youth will say, "The music today is completely different." And so music will be, as long as people are different, and as long as there is another day. . . . If we respect the human being or the human element in music, we will respect man's right to his own taste and his equal right and privilege to change it.[1]

The symposium recognized that there are many kinds of music and that different kinds of music have different functions and relative degrees of aesthetic values. But the determination of relative aesthetic value requires judgments that, by their subjective nature, are bound to cause disagreement. The question is raised, therefore, of whether it is possible and appropriate to assign a hierarchy to various kinds of music. The symposium did not answer the question directly, but by implication stated that any music that has meaning to some people should be respected: "The music repertory should be expanded to involve music of our time in its rich variety, including currently popular teenage music."

The National Association of Jazz Educators

For many years, jazz was an integral part of the entertainment industry, and provided employment for great numbers of professional musicians who played in clubs, recorded, worked for the broadcast industry, and found other outlets for their music. During the 1940s, the character of jazz evolved from popular entertainment to intellectual gratification. As jazz developed into "bebop" it became more subjective; it gradually lost much of its popular appeal and began to develop into a connoisseur art. This was due partly to the new type of improvisation, and partly to the fact that popular songs were no longer used as the basic ingredient. The new type of jazz utilized a different melodic, harmonic, and rhythmic basis than popular music. Jazz branched off from the field of popular music; in doing so, it lost a large part of its audience. From the early 1950s to the present, there have been big band revivals, many "nostalgia" records and concerts, re-releases of old recordings, and, since the 1960s, a strong jazz festival movement. None of these has managed to return jazz to its old place as a major musical force in American society. No longer do great numbers of musicians earn their living by playing jazz. There are relatively few jazz clubs now in the big cities; the professional jazz festivals have, for the most part, ceased and been replaced by college festivals; jazz record sales have been at a low level for years; there are few jazz radio programs; and jazz has undergone several evolutionary changes in attempts to merge it once again with various popular forms, such as jazz-rock. As jazz subordinates itself to other musical forms, it seems to become weaker as an art and a profession. The terms applied to the merger of jazz with other kinds of music are "eclectic jazz" and "fusion," but eclecticism may well represent a dilution rather than a new style. According to William Anderson,

Cultural phenomena, like biological entities, go through the cycle of birth, generation, and death, and there seems no reason to make of jazz an exception. Born in humble circumstances, it made its way, through the most natural kind of growth, out of the saloon, across the tracks, into the concert hall, and finally, in its maturity, into the classrooms of our universities. That history, moreover, continues to determine its audience. . . . Young converts . . . will more than likely be of the intellectual sort and small in number, those capable of recapitulating and digesting this fascinating—and lovable—history for themselves. Jazz may therefore be around for some years to come, but it will not again, I think, regain the spotlight. That is reserved for whatever comes after rock.[7]

Jazz has been given a new lease on life in American schools and colleges. Many college teacher education programs emphasize jazz; an increasingly large number of stage and jazz lab bands are coming into existence; and many jazz festivals are held on campuses in all parts of the country. The public schools have become as strongly committed to jazz as have the colleges. Jazz is included in the curriculum as a subject of serious study because of its aesthetic, sociological, and historical importance, and is now a respected performance medium for school musicians.

When the MENC bestowed its blessing on jazz and other popular musics in the curriculum, the way was opened for the full development of stage bands. In 1968 the National Association of Jazz Educators (NAJE), which had been in the planning stage for two years, was formed and accepted as an associated organization of MENC. Involved in the founding of NAJE were such people as Stan Kenton, Louis Wersen, John Roberts, and Charles Gary, all of whom, having participated in the Tanglewood Symposium, saw NAJE as a means of implementing the philosophy developed there. Because the purpose of NAJE was "to further the understanding and appreciation of jazz and popular music, and to promote its artistic performance,"[8] the affiliation of the two organizations at that particular time seems to have been inevitable. The specific objectives of NAJE, as stated by M. E. Hall, president of the organization, were:

1. To foster and promote the understanding and appreciation of jazz and popular music and its artistic performance.
2. To lend assistance and guidance in the organization and development of jazz and popular music curricula in schools and colleges to include stage bands and ensembles of all types.
3. To foster the application of jazz principles to music materials and methods at all levels.
4. To foster and encourage the development and adoption of curricula that will explore contemporary composition, arranging, and improvisation.
5. To disseminate educational and professional news of interest to music educators.
6. To assist in the organization of clinics, festivals, and symposia at local, state, regional, and national levels.
7. To cooperate with all organizations dedicated to the development of musical culture in America.[9]

Since its founding, NAJE has helped to promote jazz-oriented curricula by encouraging students to perform, compose, arrange, and improvise jazz. The activities of the organization affect all levels of education, from elementary through graduate school. The materials distributed by NAJE include lists of stage band literature, choral literature, string literature, listening materials, and materials for general music classes. Units of NAJE have been organized in a majority of states, and many colleges and universities have student chapters. Its official publication, *The NAJE Educator*, includes philosophical and practical articles about all aspects of jazz education. The many advertisements of materials, supplies and equipment in the publication indicate strong backing of jazz education by the music industry.

The third national convention of NAJE was held in January 1976 at California State University at Northridge. Three trends became evident at the convention.

1. Competition is declining at stage band festivals, but the quality of the band is increasing. There is also an increase in the variety of styles of bands at both high schools and colleges.
2. There is a renewed emphasis òn combos in school jazz programs.
3. There is a renewed effort to involve more blacks in jazz programs, and more attention given to the compositions of black composers in order to preserve the jazz heritage.[10]

The Youth Music Institute

The Youth Music Institute was held at the University of Wisconsin in Madison from 7 July to 1 August 1969 for the purpose of bringing together rock-oriented young people and music teachers to communicate about rock music and music education. During the two years following the Tanglewood Symposium, rock music had not become an integral part of the curriculum in most music programs. The institute was organized by Emmett Sarig, a participant in the Tanglewood Symposium, and was sponsored by MENC, the U.S. Office of Education, and the Extension Music Department of the University of Wisconsin.

Few music educators had the background or experience to deal with rock in their classrooms; most had negative attitudes toward it. The institute provided the opportunity for young people to perform for, guide, instruct, and converse with music educators about rock. Eighteen youth music groups and thirty-one music educators representing school systems from all over the United States were invited to participate in the institutes. Guidance counselors from participating school systems also attended the institute. Professional rock artists and groups performed and joined in the discussions.

Each youth music group attended the institute for one week. Performance was an important part of the experience. Even more important were the discussions, which allowed the students the opportunity to talk about the music creation process as they saw it and to share their views on rock music and music education. There was also a project teaching staff that included anthropologists, sociologists, and psychologists.

Small groups were formed for workshops or panels to discuss specific issues. Some of the issues were "Should Youth Music Be Included in the Curriculum," "How to Close the Communication Gap," "Youth Music and Its Role in the Music Education Program," and "Is the Music Educator's Assistance with Youth Music Desired or Necessary?" The educators found the experience enlightening. They became more open-minded about rock music and more sensitive to the musical taste of young people. Many of the young participants, who had had negative experiences with music education in their schools, were reluctant at first to communicate verbally with music educators, who they felt were not receptive to their music and attitudes. Many students also feared that if rock music were to become part of the school curriculum it would become too academic. For the most part, however, the exchange was healthy and profitable. Students made their needs known to teachers, and the prejudices of many educators against youth music were dispelled, or at least lessened.

A three-day symposium was held from 23 to 25 July 1969 to analyze the progress of the institute and to extend its effects to a larger population of educators. Over 200 music educators, administrators, critics, and journalists attended. The participants, like the participants in the institute, heard young people and professional rock musicians perform and share their views with the group. The message of the symposium was clear: music educators must keep up with the times by becoming enlightened, knowledgeable, and skilled in the type of music with which many of their students identify.

The Wisconsin Youth Music Institute also made many music educators realize the extent of fragmentation in what had come to be called "youth music." Many educators have questioned whether there really is such a music. Each type of youth music has its own fans, who often exclude other types of music from their lives. Jazz and rock fans ignore each other's music, as do devotees of blues, soul, and the various branches of rock. It is not enough that music educators become knowledgeable about these forms; they must decide what kind of popular music best serves their own students. Teachers must also try to expand their students' interests by exposing them to more than one kind of music.

The Uses of Popular Music in Music Education

American music educators use popular music in varying degrees. Some teachers are reluctant to teach students music with which they are saturated outside of school. Other teachers, accepting popular music without reservation, have taken the attitude that students must be approached through their own interests. They feel that if their students' knowledge and appreciation of a certain kind of music can be deepened and expanded, then it is not necessary to introduce other kinds of music into the curriculum. Most teachers stand between the two extremes. They recognize popular music as one of many kinds of music that should be included in their programs. When general music teachers teach listening skills by means of popular as well as classical music of different periods and styles, it is treated simply as one kind of music, with no value judgments offered. This attitude is reflected in the multitude of materials that publishers have made available. Elementary graded music series commonly contain popular music, and the accompanying records include representative jazz, rock, and soul music, as well as the traditional variety of folk music, classical music, and children's songs. Many elementary and secondary level books and audiovisual materials published recently teach music concepts and skills through popular music and introduce students to its historical and sociological implications.

School instrumental music has also been greatly affected by popular music. Many instrumental training materials now include at least some rock and/or jazz. Rock and jazz compositions and arrangements for school bands, orchestras, and choruses are abundant. Marching bands have been more affected by popular music than have other musical ensembles. On football fields or in parades, it is now more common to hear marching bands play various kinds of popular music than marches. Marching band directors can purchase a seemingly infinite number of popular arrangements, some of which incude complete half-time shows.

Many colleges offer courses in jazz history, and courses in other forms of popular music are not unusual. Students often elect such courses in place of traditional "music appreciation" classes. Because music education majors must be prepared to deal with youth music after graduation, music education curricula often include courses in jazz and rock history, improvisation, and in performing instruments peculiar to popular music, especially the guitar.

The impact of popular music in American education is reflected in the growth of stage bands. Until the late 1950s, the repertoire of school dance bands consisted of commercial stock arrangements. After that time, there were enough school dance or stage bands in existence to make it profitable for publishers to distribute arrangements and new music composed specifically for school groups. Such music has increased in quality and quantity to the point where it is used not only by student musicians but also by commercial bands. A huge repertoire of music for different ages and levels of ability has been amassed for stage bands.

Most high schools, many middle schools, and even elementary schools have stage bands, many of which include smaller specialty units that play dixieland, blues, ragtime, or various kinds of rock. The growth of the stage band at the college level has been a major factor in the development of the jazz major, which is offered by many institutions of higher education. College jazz lab bands often rival professional groups in quality. In fact, it is not unusual for college jazz lab bands to record commercially. Jazz has become so popular at some colleges that the jazz major program sometimes attracts more students than do other music programs.

Conclusion

The rapid growth of popular music in American education has been phenomenal. The stage band movement achieved maturity within ten years. Many different materials of high quality are available for all aspects of popular music education. Although popular music has not been accepted philosophically by all music educators, its place in music education appears to be assured. A balance should be achieved between popular music and traditional music in all of its rich and varied forms. David McAllister speaks for concerned music educators who, while they accept popular music, feel that young people should also become familiar with the artistic achievements of other times and places:

We affirm that it is our duty to seek true musical communication with the great masses of our population. While we continue to develop and make available, to all who are interested, the great musics of the middle class and aristocracy, we must also learn the language of the great musical arts which we have labeled "base" because they are popular. . . . When we have learned that any musical expression is "music," we hope to be able to reduce the class barriers in our schools and our concert halls. The resulting enrichment of our music will, we hope, give it a new vitality at all levels, and provide a united voice that can speak, without sham, of our democratic ideals.[11]

TECHNOLOGY AND MUSIC EDUCATION

Technology has developed to the point that the current generation of music students considers it a normal part of their lives. Yet it was as recently as the 1950s that synthesizers began to come to the attention of the public and electric guitars were considered advanced technology in the field of musical performance. Now we are accustomed to a seemingly infinite variety of electronically generated musical sounds, and many students utilize them as casually in their music making as students used traditional instruments less than a generation earlier. Technology has affected music education not only in sound production and manipulation, but through the use of computers as well. Computers are used routinely for instructional purposes, as components of electronic music equipment, and for data storage and retrieval for scholars and researchers.

Electronic Music

Music of all periods, styles, forms, and cultures belongs in the curriculum. The musical repertory should be expanded to involve music of our time in its rich variety, including . . . avant-garde music.[12]

Electronic music consists of sounds that are generated, modified, and controlled by electronic means. Musique concrete is a kind of electronic music that utilizes both natural and electronic sounds that are electronically processed and manually spliced.

Electronic music became viable in the 1950s with the development of the Columbia-Princeton Music Center in New York City. The composers Vladimir Ussachevsky, Otto Luening, and Milton Babbit established the center, which provided leadership in the development of electronic music. It was followed by the University of Illinois electronic music center, and then by electronic music studios at numerous other colleges and universities. Because of the cost, large bulk, and complexity of the equipment, and the strange sounds that it produced, electronic music was considered esoteric and not of great interest to most musicians or to the public. By the late 1960s, however, conditions were beginning to change. Lower cost portable synthesizers were becoming available and people were gradually becoming accustomed to electronic sounds, which were used not only in laboratories, but also in media commercials and movies. Some composers of electronic music realized familiar traditional music entirely with the electronic medium, and some original music was composed that suited the taste of a fairly large segment of the public.

Electronic Music in the Schools

In the late 1960s electronic music slowly began to find its way into school music education programs. Opportunities for teacher preparation were inadequate at that time. Only a few colleges offered courses in electronic music, and they dealt with composition, theory, and the techniques of musique concrete. Music education courses in electronic music, if any, were limited to a few summer workshops. Also, the cost of setting up an electronic music studio was prohibitive. Because of these problems, many music educators took a "wait and see" attitude. At first electronic music was treated as music literature. It was studied as a new form of music, but without the capability of producing it in the schools. A significant breakthrough came in 1967 when the Pilot Electronic Project (PEP) was established in eighteen schools in Connecticut by the State Department of Education. Funds were provided by Title III of the Elementary and Secondary Education Act. The purpose of the project was to provide a medium of creativity for students. With the assistance of consultants, including Ussachevsky and Babbit, curricula were established. Students learned musical concepts by experimenting with and creating electronic music. They also developed original notational systems to score their music.

At about the same time that Project PEP was operating, synthesizers suitable for schools were being invented. In fact, the ElectroComp 200 was developed in response to the needs of the Connecticut schools. By the end of the 1960s it was possible to purchase synthesizers that were portable and usable by students for around $1,000. During the 1970s many schools around the country set up electronic music studios, some with minimal basic equipment and others with complex collections of sophisticated synthesizers, other sound manipulation devices, and elaborate playback equipment.

During the past few years, rapid technological advances have brought about new types of synthesizers that are extremely portable, more versatile, and less expensive than ever before. The new low-priced synthesizers, like personal computers, are considered consumer items. They can be purchased in department stores as well as in music stores. Because synthesizers are so improved and are readily available, they are having a great effect on the concepts and methods of producing electronic music. Practitioners are moving away from tape splicing techniques and toward live performance techniques. The trend in music education is also in that direction. Many colleges, including the Berklee College of Music, North Texas State University, the University of Colorado at Denver and others now emphasize performance. In an ever-increasing number of schools, synthesizers are used for performance purposes to accompany stage bands, to accompany instrumentalists and singers, and even in synthesizer ensembles.[13]

The problems of electronic music in education are being solved as teachers and students become more knowledgeable about synthesizers and electronic music and find ways to include the medium in the music curriculum. Some teachers choose to use synthesizers to teach form and analysis, theory, acoustics, and keyboard techniques, without exploring the innovative electronic music aspects of the instrument.

Computers in Music Education

Computers are used in many ways in education. One of the most important uses in the schools is known as Computer Assisted-Instruction (CAI). In music, as in other areas of education, CAI is used to present material to students in a manner that requires students to interact with the computer. In other words, a body of material is presented, and the student must select the appropriate response in order to progress to new material, or to review material not yet learned. In most cases, microcomputers (the same ones purchased for home use) are utilized, and the software consists of floppy discs.

A great deal of software is available for CAI, and teachers who wish to use it must keep themselves aware of what is on the market and how well the various programs meet their needs. The major problem is that software is developed for a large potential market, and often does not

FIGURE 6.1. Composer Don Muro performing his "Badlands Overture" for synthesizer and band with P.M.E.A. Region III Festival Concert Band.

Note. Photo courtesy Don Muro.

closely match the needs of a particular class. Also, although some of the software is of good quality, much is not. As in selecting textbooks or music, teachers must be wary of software that is irrelevant, trite, uninteresting, improperly sequenced, or inaccurate. Many teachers with special needs learn programming in order to be able to develop their own software.

An example of CAI is the GUIDO (Graded Units for Interactive Dictation Operations) system, developed at the University of Delaware. It is used to help students develop aural skills and is effective with groups that have wide learning differences. GUIDO is a series of programs that helps increase aural abilities in intervals, melodies, chord qualities, harmonies, and rhythms. In the display in figure 6.2, the student hears an interval played electronically. It is one of the intervals displayed in the boxes at the top of the screen. The student touches the box that he or she thinks displays the correct interval. The program keeps track of the number of correct and incorrect answers, and keeps the student informed of how many more correct answers are necessary to complete the learning unit. The boxes in the middle of the screen control the way in

FIGURE 6.2. Micro GUIDO Ear-Training System, The MicroGUIDO Music Learning Station.

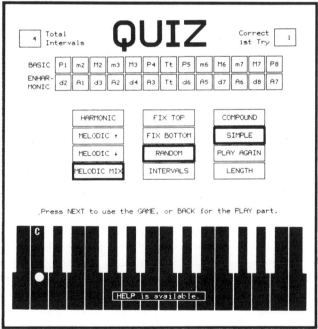

Note: © 1977 by the University of Delaware. Reprinted by permission.

which dictation is given. They can be preset by the teacher, or the student can set them as desired. The column on the left allows the intervals to be played melodically, harmonically, and melodically up or down. The middle column provides the option of fixing the top or bottom notes of the interval, or to have them selected randomly. The third column lets the student select simple or compound intervals, to repeat the interval, and to control the amount of time the interval is heard. The keyboard at the bottom is used by the student to fix the top or bottom note of the interval.[14]

Another system for aural training in MEDICI (MElodic DIctation Computerized Instruction), which is used at Florida State University School of Music.

> While using the MEDICI program, the student jots down the melody on manuscript paper while he is listening to it being played by the Gooch Synthetic Woodwind. Then an interactive music editing system is used to enter the student's version of the melody into computer memory, so that it can be judged as to accuracy. This interactive music editor is quite elaborate, because students learning melodic dictation skills make unforeseeable mistakes. The computer must be able to accept student responses which may only slightly resemble the actual melody. The MEDICI editor permits the student to notate music on the terminal screen almost as freely as it can be notated on manuscript paper.[15]

CAI is used in a similar manner with elementary and secondary students to develop aural skills and to study musical form, theory, and history. The Verona Middle School Instrumental Music Department in Verona, Wisconsin has a CAI Music Lab that covers music literacy, comprehensive musicianship, and composition. The software falls into five categories: (1) drill and practice, in which the student is presented material for which there is only one answer; (2) tutorial, which presents new material at the proper pace for individual students, and including drill and practice activities; (3) simulation, in which the computer performs the student's composition; (4) games, which are utilized for some drill and practice; and (5) computer-managed instruction, which permits the teacher to perform routine tasks, including administrative work, quickly and efficiently.[16]

The National Consortium for Computer-Based Music Instruction (NCCBMI) was founded in 1973 "to provide a forum for the exchange of ideas among developers and users of computer-based systems for music instruction; second, to establish and maintain a library of music courseware; third, to reduce redundant effort among courseware and hardware developers; and fourth, to provide consultation for new users of computer-based music instruction."[17] NCCBMI publishes an annual directory of music courseware.

Fred Hofstetter lists five capabilities of CAI for providing effective instruction: (1) it is a means of individualizing instruction because students progress through programs at their own rates; (2) it emphasizes "the intrinsic joy of learning and deemphasizes competition with peers as a motivating force"; (3) it encourages "students to tailor learning experiences to meet their own objectives"; (4) it gives immediate feedback, requiring each student to partake in a dialogue with the computer; (5) it saves time because the level of instruction is adjusted for each student.[18]

Computers and Information Processing in Music Education

An aspect of computer usage that is of great importance to music education researchers is information processing, which includes collection, storage, retrieval, and dissemination. Vast amounts of information are available via computer networks by computer retrieval organizations that organize information data files. Specific search systems are used to retrieve information from the data files. Lockheed and SDC are examples of companies that offer search systems that can retrieve information from such files as ERIC (chapter 4), CIJE, RIE, PA, DAI, and others. The Lockheed system, for example, is called DIALOG. Through it, a large variety and number of data files are available.

Of special interest to music educators is CIJE (Current Index of Journals in Education), a part of ERIC, which contains the indices of *Music Educators Journal* and the *Journal of Research in Music Education*. JRME is also indexed in PA (Psychological Abstracts). RIE (Resources in Education), also a subsection of ERIC, provides information on government grants in music. Dissertations in music are indexed in DATRIX, which is operated by University Microfilms, the publisher of most doctoral dissertations in the United States.[19]

NOTES

1. Edwin J. Stringham, "Jazz—An Educational Problem," *The Musical Quarterly* 12, no. 2 (April 1926):190–95.
2. The Tanglewood Declaration, article 2.
3. Peter W. Dykema and Karl W. Gehrkens, *The Teaching and Administration of High School Music* (Boston: C. C. Birchard, 1941), p. 455.
4. William R. Sur and Charles F. Schuller, *Music Education for Teen-Agers* (New York: Harper and Row, 1966), p. 147.
5. Walter Anslinger, "The Stage Band: A Defense and an Answer," *Perspectives in Music Education* (Washington, D.C.: Music Educators National Conference, 1966), pp. 533–35.
6. Robert A. Choate, ed., *Documentary Report of the Tanglewood Symposium* (Washington, D.C.: Music Educators National Conference, 1968), p. 122. Reprinted by permission of Music Educators National Conference.
7. William Anderson, "A Reprise for Jazz," *Stereo Review* 33, no. 1 (July 1974):6.

Copyright © 1974, Ziff-Davis Publishing Company. Reprinted by permission of *Stereo Review Magazine*.

8. John T. Roberts, "MENC's Associated Organizations: NAJE," *Music Educators Journal* 55, no. 7 (March 1969):44–46. Reprinted by permission of Music Educators National Conference.

9. M.E. Hall, "How We Hope to Foster Jazz," *Music Educators Journal* 55, no. 7 (March 1969):44–46. Reprinted by permission of Music Educators National Conference.

10. Allen Scott, "NAJE Convention: Casualty Rates," *Radio Free Jazz* no. 3 (March 1976):9.

11. David McAllister, "Curriculum Must Assume a Place at the Center of Music," in *Documentary Report of the Tanglewood Symposium*, p. 138.

12. The Tanglewood Declaration, article 2.

13. Don Muro, interview with author, 17 January 1984.

14. Fred T. Hofstetter. "Computer-Based Aural Training: The GUIDO System." *Journal of Computer-Based Instruction* 7, no. 3 (February 1981):84–92.

15. Steven R. Newcomb, Bradley K. Weage, and Peter Spencer, "MEDICI" Tutorial in Melodic Dictation," *Journal of Computer-Based Instruction* 7, no. 3 (February 1981):63–69.

16. Brian Moore, "A CAI Music Lab in the Middle School," *Dialogue in Instrumental Music Education* 7, no. 1 (Spring 1983):19–23.

17. NCCBMI, application for membership.

18. Fred T. Hofstetter, "Microelectronics and Music Education," *Music Educators Journal* 65, no. 8, (April 1979):39–45.

19. David B. Williams, remarks on information data files, *Report of The Third Annual Loyola Symposium*, New Orleans, 13–15 February 1980, pp. 1, 2.

BIBLIOGRAPHY

Arenson, Michael, ed. *Courseware Directory*. National Consortium for Computer-Based Music Instruction. Published annually.

Bonner, Paul. "The Sound of Software." *Personal Computing* 8, no. 6 (June 1984):94–102.

Dialogue in Instrumental Music Education, vol. 7, no. 1, Spring 1983. Contains several articles on technoloy in music education.

Eddins, John M., ed. *Journal of Computer-Based Instruction*, vol. 7, no. 3, February 1981. Special Issue: "The Yearbook of Computer-Based Music Instruction."

Hofstetter, Fred T. "Computer-Based Recognition of Perceptual Patterns in Chord Quality Dictation Exercises." *Journal of Research in Music Education*, vol. 28, no. 3, Fall 1980.

———. *"Evaluation of a Competency-Based Approach to Teaching Aural Interval Identification."* *Journal of Research in Music Education*, vol. 27, no. 4, Winter 1979.

———. "Microelectronics and Music Education." *Music Educators Journal* 65, no. 8 (April 1979):39–45.

Swanzy, David; and William English, eds. *The Collection, Organization, and Dissemination of Information on Music*. Report of the Third Annual Loyola Symposium. New Orleans: School of Music, Loyola University, 1980.

Williams, David Brian; and I. Sue Beasley. "Computer Information Search and Retrieval: A Guide for the Music Educator." *Bulletin of the Council for Research in Music Education*, no. 51, Summer 1977, pp. 23–40.

Areas of Concern for Music Education

Part III

7
Music Education for Specialized Needs

MUSIC IN URBAN EDUCATION

The music education profession must contribute its skills, proficiencies, and insights toward assisting in the solution of urgent social problems as in the "inner city" or other areas with culturally deprived individuals.[1]

At one time, urban school music programs were leaders in excellence and innovative practices. During the last few decades, however, many factors have come to bear on urban education, and the quality of both general education and music education has suffered. Although some individual urban music education programs function well and provide excellent music education for children, they do so because of the superlative efforts of individual teachers and administrators. Yet there are reasons for hope, namely, in the 1980s movement toward excellence in education, which has begun to impact on the quality of education in urban schools.

The Social Revolution and Education

Education in the United States was as deeply affected by the social revolution of the 1960s as was any other aspect of American life. Until that time, it was generally agreed that the educational needs of middle class white children in suburbs and small communities were representative of the needs of all American children, and were therefore the proper basis for educational decision making. American education had still not completely shed the influence of the early twentieth-century "melting pot" idea. It propounded that people of all ethnic backgrounds, upon experiencing life in America and undergoing American education, would be assimilated into American society, and that all persons, regardless of ethnic or racial heritage, would share American ideals, hopes, standards, and wealth. Although this was a popular American notion for many years, little real effort was made to apply it to the minority population that was not of European descent. Blacks and other minority groups were forced to accept a low social status in American society. Many minorities do not consider social status to be inherently important, especially those who formed their own social groups within the large population, as did blacks, Hispanics, and Asians. By living in ghettos within the cities, they could live in their own societies in an atmosphere of familiarity and acceptance. They created social orders within their own societies. But not all aspects of their lives could be governed by themselves. They were often employed in the white community, where their social status limited the types of jobs available to them to low-paying, unchallenging, and usually menial labor. To be sure, many minority-group members rose above their social status to attain success in almost all areas of American life, but the majority has not yet achieved that level.

One important area of American life over which minority groups had little or no control in the past was education. Having little political influence, they had to accept the American educational system because it offered one of the few possible means of rising above poverty to a better life, if only to a few fortunate people. Education, however, was usually designed to meet the needs of children of a different social status, who could reasonably aspire to rewarding, satisfying, and comfortable lives. It was controlled by boards of education that perpetuated the middle-class philosophy of education upon which school systems functioned. The "separate but equal" system of school segregation that predominated in some parts of the country until the 1950s was a method of educating minority children to their previously established social level (although it should be noted that many segregated schools that served minority students were of equal or higher quality than those whose students were white). That many minority children grew up to achieve the American dream is a tribute to their own determination and to the people who helped and supported them. It was not until 1954 that American schools were legally desegregated, but even then, social influences in urban areas frequently perpetuated the separation of races in school systems.

Despite the problems of urban education, expenditures for education during the 1950s were about the same in the large cities as in their suburbs. By 1962 the cities were spending an average of $145 less per pupil than their suburbs. This state of affairs reflected the growing disparity between the economic situation of the cities and the suburbs. To make matters worse, the formulas used to determine the amount of state aid for education favored the suburbs, which at that time received an average of $40 more per pupil than the cities.[2]

In his analysis of school desegregation, Robert Havighurst defines three phases of education integration.[3] The first, from 1954 to 1958, consisted of the response to the 1954 Supreme Court decision (*Brown vs. Board of Education of Topeka, Kansas*) that upheld the legality of school integration. During this period, numbers of blacks migrated to cities, a phenomenon that made the implementation of desegregation not only practical, but fairly smooth. During the years 1958 to 1963, a period of concern and controversy, school segregation actually increased, primarily because of the temporary 1958 economic depression. The extent of de facto segregation was exposed, and the reasons for it made apparent. It was caused by residential patterns within ethnic ghettos and the economic conditions of the ghetto residents. Court decisions upheld the legality of de facto segregation if it resulted from residential patterns, but not if it were caused by school attendance areas deliberately drawn to segregate schools.

It was during this time that blacks were beginning to assert their independence from the traditionally segregated societal system. Martin Luther King, Jr., led the nonviolent resistance movement against segregation practices during this period.

Havighurst identifies the period from 1963 to 1966 as that of black revolution. During that period, school integration and other racial problems came to a head. The March on Washington occurred in August 1963; in this huge protest against traditional racial policies and practices, King and thousands of blacks were joined by many white leaders who sympathized with the civil rights movement. The Civil Rights Act of 1964 prohibited many specific aspects of racial discrimination, and the Voting Rights Act of 1965 increased black political power, especially in the South. During this time, boards of education were beginning to take active measures against school segregation.

Martin Luther King, Jr. had been able to contain the black revolution and maintain its nonviolent nature, but after his assassination in 1968, black urban populations exploded in bursts of violence. The force of the violence made all Americans aware of the depth of frustration and resentment in many black people. Since then, the courts and school authorities have tried to hasten the implementation of school desegregation, and gains have been made toward racial equity in all areas of life, including employment and housing.

School Decentralization

Another aspect of change in urban (and many suburban) school systems is decentralization of decision making authority and administration. Decentralization is the process whereby policy making authority is transferred from a central office to local areas within the city. The policy areas affected are usually personnel, curriculum, and budget. There are over 16,000 separate school districts in the United States, each operating with some degree of autonomy, supposedly in accordance with local needs and desires. Many boards of education are elected, and so reflect the educational wishes of communities, but in large cities most people are not able to make direct contact with the individuals who make decisions, as is also true in other areas of government. In response to the need for more localized control over public institutions, a new participatory ethic developed among minority group citizens, who in the past had been excluded from meaningful participation in school and other governmental affairs. The federal government encouraged local participation in policy making by funding such programs as the Model Cities Program and Title III of the Elementary and Secondary Education Act of 1965. These programs promoted and supported local participation. New leadership developed on the neighborhood level and was often tested and proven in connection with local schools. The development of lower level leadership led to various degrees of decentralization in several cities, which has since been expanded to give more people greater control over schools.

There are two general types of decentralization—community control and delegation of administrative control to lower levels. In the latter, authority is transferred to various field units, but selection of field-unit administrators and important policy decisions remain in the control of the central office. Community control places policy and personnel decisions in the hands of community boards or neighborhood associations. Legislative and administrative control is held by local communities within cities. Some large cities, such as New York and Detroit, have several boards of education that legislate and govern the administration of the schools in particular sections of cities. Other cities, such as Washington, D.C., and Chicago, retain a strong central bureaucracy that delegates authority to local administrative offices.

The effect of decentralization on urban music programs has been somewhat negative. Those cities that had strong music programs before decentralization usually had a music supervisory and administrative staff to develop and maintain effective music programs in all parts of the city. In those school systems that retained a central bureaucracy after decentralization, the supervisory personnel were usually reclassified as consultants who had no actual authority. Their services are utilized for several traditional supervisory functions, but they have no control over the music program other than through persuasion. Therefore, there is a wide range of quality in the music programs of different schools within cities; standards are often dependent on community-level administrators who may or may not be supportive of music education. Moreover, those school systems that are under community control have unevenly developed music programs. Some localized boards of education retain one or more music supervisors and administrators who support and guide the music program, but many have no specialized music support service at all. Music education depends on the ability of music teachers to develop and maintain individual school programs on their own. As a result, some of these school systems have no music program.

Authority is also delegated in other ways. For example, task forces are sometimes appointed to provide policy making guidance for local boards of education, or neighborhood councils are utilized to provide local input. Thus, policy makers sometimes act on advice from laymen who are not capable of evaluating the total educational program. For that reason, decisions concerning music teachers, curricula, and music budgets do not always encourage the development of well-conceived music programs. Many different philosophies of education are brought to bear in making decisions about the music program, and often the prevailing philosophy does not support music programs aimed at the development of aesthetic responsiveness.

Preparing Music Educators for Inner City Teaching

The success of any educational program depends more on the quality of teaching than any other single factor. It has not been until recently that teacher education institutions have attempted seriously to deal specifically with urban, or inner city, teacher preparation. In general, inner city students are educationally disadvantaged and often are not motivated toward education. Until schools began to turn away from traditional middle class values and to base programs on community needs, the problem was practically impossible to overcome. Minority control of schools has given urban populations more control over their own destinies.

Students who are not motivated to learn must be treated differently from those who are so motivated. Inability to deal with such students has resulted in many schools becoming custodial, rather than educational, in nature. Teacher preparation programs must include consideration of the problems of inner city children. Robert Strom wrote in 1965:

Many opportunities for teaching and guidance are forfeited because [teachers] lack understanding regarding the customs, mores, and values that govern behavior; the mechanism through which slum children can most be influenced; the structure and operation of powerful peer groups; [and] the indigenous system of incentives that affect motivation and discipline. . . . Although most prospective teachers need and desire training in these areas, seldom do college counseling, curriculum, and scheduling encourage it.[4]

The problem still exists but is being addressed in teacher education programs. Agencies that accredit such programs now require evidence of multicultural education in teacher preparation curricula.

It is generally accepted that the arts can stimulate student motivation for learning. According to James Standifer, "Aesthetic education could not only help provide blacks with a much needed sense of pride in themselves but also serve to increase man's understanding of man."[5]

The Tanglewood Symposium Committee on Critical Issues discussed the lack of relevant preparation of music teachers in inner city areas. Recommendations were made for improvement of teacher preparation programs. The January 1970 issue of *Music Educators Journal* was devoted to the topic of music in urban education. One of the major problems discussed was that of inadequate teacher preparation.

Many of the music teachers interviewed recalled the disillusionment they suffered during their first years of teaching when they found that what they were taught in college could not be used. They explained how they were forced to discard teaching techniques, concepts of curriculum and course content, educational philosophy, methods and materials that had been recommended to them as workable. Many felt that their college education was not only inadequate, but that it did them a disservice by actually leading them in the wrong direction.[6]

Minority Group Heritages

The nature of American society has been such that nonwhite heritages were sublimated for generations. It was widely accepted that they were less worthy of attention than European heritages. This is ironic, because American society has been deeply influenced by the black heritage. Popular music, dance, speech, and other aspects of American life have been shaped, to a great degree, by Afro-American influences. In Leonard Goines' words, "From the day of the white minstrels to the present day rock musicians, white artists and business men have assimilated and incorporated black elements into their musical offerings. All of today's popular music, in fact, is based on various blends of blues and gospel forms."[7]

Members of every ethnic group have kept their heritages alive, but often only within their own communities. Jazz, which grew from the black heritage and is universally acknowledged to be a major contribution to American culture, is a notable exception. Centuries of slavery and years of lower class citizenship had repressed American Black culture in many ways. When the slaves were brought here from Africa, they were forced to leave behind much of their heritage and to adapt quickly to white traditions and customs.

Only religion (and magic) and the arts were not completely submerged by Euro-American concepts. Music, dance, religion, do not have *artifacts* as their end products, so they were saved. These nonmaterial aspects of the African's culture were almost impossible to eradicate. And these are the most apparent legacies of the African past, even to the contemporary black Americans.[8]

Tenaciously, and often secretly, the black heritage remained alive in music, art, dance, and other aspects of life. In the 1960s, it was still alive and vital and had earned the respect of the general population.

Minority leaders realized that if equality was to be a realistic goal for their people, then self-knowledge and pride must be instilled in them, for people who have low self-esteem cannot feel equal with those who do not. Self-knowledge and pride come from an awareness of one's past and of the accomplishments and cultural achievements of one's race. If minorities could come to know their roots and traditions, they could move forward on their own terms, rather than trying to adapt to the Western heritage. Hence, the rationale for the self-knowledge movement—"Black is Beautiful." Its goal was to instill awareness of self in order to develop pride and confidence, thus making upward social movement possible.

Self-awareness and pride also became goals for minority education. In effect, this was a major shift in educational emphasis. The education of minorities had previously focused primarily on vocational education with varying degrees of emphasis on intellectual development. In 1968, Shirley Schell wrote:

The emphasis of integration should have been to provide the black student with a better opportunity to discover himself and realize his own potential. Perhaps the white child should have understood that integration would have some advantages for him, too—opportunities to know people different from himself, to learn from them and to share his own experiences.[9]

The new focus after the social revolution was on the sociological aspects of education because it was hoped that minorities would realize that social equality was not only possible, but inevitable.

Civilizations are known, to a great extent, by their arts. The black race in America had maintained its culture by means of the arts, especially music. This was an effective tool with which blacks could develop self-awareness. Self-discovery is also an important goal in music education. Ellsworth Janifer elaborated on this theme:

If the "lost" musical heritage of black Americans is to be reclaimed and made to be a meaningful, relevant force in their lives an intensive program of re-education must be launched in which all the lies, myths, distortions, and propaganda of the past will be exposed and revealed for what they are. The only way that this can be done effectively is to revise completely existing curricula in music education for black students so that they will focus around the black musical experience, for as Terry Francois points out, "The first responsibility of any individual is to find out *who* he is, *and then* accept himself for *what* he is."[10]

Before the social revolution, music in urban schools had not been appreciably different from experiences in other kinds of school systems. It consisted of the same performing and general music experiences that constituted most music programs, and it utilized the same materials.

Although this is still true of many urban music programs, in the late 1960s and early 1970s greater emphasis began to be put on music that reflected minority cultures. In effect, music was taught for the attainment of a sociological goal—the awakening of self-awareness and development of self-pride through music. The aesthetic aspect of music was not ignored because music that is sociologically and historically significant must have meaningful aesthetic content.

The social revolution awakened the same openly professed desire for awareness and pride in all minority groups. Assertive ethnicity urged the direction of American society away from the melting pot ideal toward a society composed of distinct ethnic groups, each preserving its own customs, traditions, and in many cases, language. In virtually all ethnic groups, traditional music is preserved.

The Tanglewood Symposium, which took place during this social revolution, signified the recognition of societal change by music educators. Although the symposium reaffirmed old beliefs and goals in the Tanglewood Declaration, several of the recommendations leading to the declaration signified that music educators were ready to use whatever tools were necessary to keep music programs relevant and viable. One of the most important statements of the symposium was the following:

There are different kinds of music existing side by side with relative degrees of aesthetic values. Separate musics have separated functions; and the functions are multiplying. There are happenings all around us, on the street corners, in churches, events both political and social. They pose the problem of value judgments, not only of the quality of the music, but quality within the function of the musics [as well]. Can we and should we assign a hierarchy to various musics?[11]

Wiley Housewright went a step further when he said:

There is much to be gained from the study of any musical creation. Rock, soul, blues, folk, and jazz cannot be ignored. To delimit concert halls, schools, and colleges to a steady diet of the "masters" is as absurd as permitting only Euripides, Shakespeare, and Molière to be performed in the theater. Music education must encompass all music. If student musical attitudes are to be affected by music education, the music teacher's openness to new music serves as a necessary model. The Music Educators National Conference through its Tanglewood Declaration not only accepts rock and other present-day music as legitimate, but sanctions its use in education.[12]

Music teachers had used ethnic, pop, and rock music as teaching materials before the Tanglewood Symposium, but those kinds of music were not openly accepted by the profession. The statements quoted above reflect the changing attitude of music educators about the use of various kinds of music in music education programs. To raise the question of whether a hierarchy could and should be assigned to various kinds of music was a major step for the tradition-bound profession. That these kinds of music came to be considered valid for use in school music programs was not so much because of the statement made during the symposium, but because of the self-awareness movement. The symposium participants recognized that such musics would be coming into common usage and that they could serve aesthetic purposes for those people who identified more with ethnic or popular music than with Western art music.

The literature of many urban music programs changed in the late 1960s to ethnic, pop, and jazz. The shift from Western art music was helpful to people who wished to learn more about themselves, at least in those situations in which there was a teacher who knew something of the history of a particular kind of ethnic music, and of its evolution to contemporary popular music forms. The teacher of ethnic or any other kind of music must be able to analyze, perform, and possibly create in the style of the music. Unfortunately, this was not always so, and students who were exposed to African music, for example, without being given the information and tools to understand the music, found themselves no better able to comprehend it than they could Western art music that was presented without proper instruction. In such cases the use of ethnic music was often self-defeating.

Pop and jazz are related by evolution to ethnic music, and young people have a strong affinity for such music. One effect of the social revolution was the recognition of the rights of young people regarding such things as dress, music, and general lifestyle. The use of music that held strong interest for young people therefore served two groups of people—the young and those who viewed pop and jazz as extensions of ethnic music (thereby serving a sociological purpose). Like the teachers who attempted to use ethnic music without sufficient knowledge and skill, many teachers found that they did not know enough about current pop and jazz to use them effectively in their teaching.

The problem of insufficient self-knowledge was faced on a national scale when black studies programs were instituted in colleges and universities in the late 1960s. The programs, often initiated as the result of student demonstrations and protests against traditional emphasis on the Western heritage, offered courses in black history and culture. The programs were popular and often effective, but unfortunately did not have much influence on music teacher education programs. The people who learned about black history and culture were often not the ones who would teach them to children. Only after college music departments began to offer courses in jazz, then courses in various aspects of popular and ethnic music, did they begin to incorporate this music literature into music education methods courses. Students preparing to teach music in urban schools began to have opportunities to learn the music and skills that would be relevant to their particular teaching situations. Teacher preparation programs that included types of music new to school curricula became common by the early 1970s.

During the process of change, however, the quality of urban education did not improve. Student achievement in reading, mathematics, and other skills continued to decline. School dropout and crime rates increased, and there was no improvement in student motivation. The violent phase of the social revolution was followed by a time of permissiveness in which students found greater freedom in the schools. Although it was equally true of suburban schools in many cases, discipline became virtually impossible to maintain in many urban schools. Teachers and administrators were faced with a dilemma: enforcing strict discipline caused student dropout rates to increase, but relaxing discipline caused achievement rates to decline. The introduction of student bills of rights, often agreed upon by boards of education, further reduced the schools' ability to maintain discipline. It was not until the early 1980s that most superintendents began to support school principals who insist on strong disciplinary codes. Such principals have brought about dramatic change in their schools in many cases.

In such difficult situations it is especially important to educate students by offering them what they consider not only important, but also relevant. For this reason, education in the arts has met with more success than many other subject areas. The worsening conditions of large cities and urban education frustrates many people concerned with education, including teachers, administrators, parents and students. Music has often been a bright spot in urban education because the school music program can reflect the musical life of minority groups to whom music making is a natural part of life.

Pop and ethnic music are now commonly found in elementary basal series, general music texts, and in the literature of all school performance ensembles. More urban music teachers have learned to use music for affective development as well as for social purposes. Many teachers recognize the need for all kinds of music and have become expert enough to teach history, traditions, and customs through various kinds of music, and to influence aesthetic development in children.

Virtually all kinds of ethnic music are now used in school programs. Schools that are heavily populated by particular ethnic groups are likely to use the music of those people in their music programs. Publishers are making available more literature of various ethnic groups, and it is becoming more common for students to write and arrange their own music, much of which reflects an urban viewpoint. It is not unusual to find in urban schools African, Hispanic, and other ethnic instrumental and vocal ensembles. Western art music still forms the basis for some urban music programs, but it is no longer viewed as the only "correct" kind of music for school use. The various music classes and performance ensembles make effective use of Western art music, and excellent bands, orchestras, and choruses perform the standard repertory in many urban schools. Traditional Western musical ensembles have declined, however, partly as a result of the cultural change and partly because of inadequate school budgets. Bennett Reimer has stated:

It is of little help and can even be harmful to make broad generalizations about what specific music will provide the best balance for every case. Teachers must be sensitive to the possible. They cannot assume, on the basis of the skin color of their students, that only a particular kind of music will be accepted. They also cannot cram unaccepted music down unwilling throats. . . . If a situation rules out anything perceived as even remotely "white," the teacher must accept that fact. He must work with music that can be taught and help the children share deeply in the musical values of that music. Music education must not assume that its only rightful materials is Western art music, and that without that literature music education cannot exist. . . .

Further, music associated with one group can be shared and should be shared by other groups, for the widening of the repertoire of culturally connected musical flavors is one of the most pleasant and satisfying of musical adventures. . . . Only the most provincial would assume that no one can or should share the musical benefits of a group other than the one to which he happens to belong.[13]

A problem that has developed is that popular music is sometimes the only music used in some music education programs. This is something of a reaction to the overuse of art music in previous years. Popular music is so accessible to children through recordings and the media that some children become immersed in it. It is the only music they want to hear in school, and some teachers are pleased to oblige them. They are more disc jockeys than teachers, and although they please many of their students, they entertain, rather than educate them. This practice gives students no more than what they have outside of school, where they listen to and participate in the same music in the same way as in school. The problem is especially acute now that popular music is recognized as important and valid for educational use. Fortunately, most teachers avoid this practice and base their programs on a variety of music, all of which are used to further students' conceptual and aesthetic development. Their students develop a broader perspective of music, and are in a position to learn to understand, respect, and possibly enjoy several kinds of music.

Music in Urban Schools: Conclusion

The problems of urban education are myriad, but conditions appear to be improving. The transfer of authority to more localized levels and the recognition of the need to develop curriculum according to local needs provide hopeful signs for improvement, as does the movement toward excellence in education of the early 1980s. The economic depression of the mid-1970s deprived music programs of teachers, facilities, equipment, and materials. Student motivation, lack of relevant teacher preparation, inadequate financial support, and other problems have created a difficult situation, but music teachers are nonetheless meeting with success in many schools. Teachers are helped by the fact that music education is desired by most communities. As long as students, parents, and other community members are aware of the necessity of music in the schools, it will survive. There is hope that it will gain strength and flourish.

MUSIC IN SPECIAL EDUCATION

Programs of teacher education must be expanded and improved to provide music teachers who are specially equipped . . to work with the very young, with adults, with the disadvantaged, and with the emotionally disturbed.[14]

The term *special education* refers to all or part of the process of educating exceptional children that is different from the process of educating normal children. Exceptional children are those whose abilities, because of physical, mental, or emotional abnormalities, deviate sufficiently from those of normal children to require special and/or modified educational experiences. Many special institutions exist to help exceptional children overcome their problems and to educate them. The focus of this chapter, however, is on special education for exceptional children in the regular music classroom and by the regular music teacher.

The foundation of a philosophy of special education was laid at about the same time that contemporary philosophical foundations were being developed in other subject areas. Dr. Leonard Mayo said in 1954:

Above all, we believe in the exceptional child himself; in his capacity for development so frequently retarded by the limits of present knowledge; in his right to a full life too often denied him through lack of imagination and ingenuity on the part of his elders; in his passion for freedom and independence that can be his only when those who guide and teach him have learned the lessons of humility, and in whom there resides an effective confluence of the trained mind and the warm heart.[15]

Children classified as exceptional include the mentally retarded, the intellectually gifted, the emotionally disturbed, the physically handicapped, and individuals who for reasons unknown achieve less than might reasonably be expected of normal children.

Exceptional children have the same needs for love, respect, encouragement, and friendship as do normal children. The classroom or music teacher who does not recognize that fact and who emphasizes only their condition, denies exceptional children recognition of what they are. The needs of exceptional children must be addressed, as must the unique needs of any child.

Arguments have continued for years about whether exceptional children should be mainstreamed (educated in regular classrooms) or put in special schools staffed and equipped to handle specific problems. Some exceptional children, such as the uneducable, cannot function in the regular classroom and need very special attention. The controversy over placement of other exceptional children in regular classrooms has been resolved—it is now a common practice mandated by law. Interaction with normal children is thought to be beneficial for special students; it helps them adjust to the conditions of the world outside of school. They are challenged by working with normal children and often achieve far beyond what they would have in a closed, protected environment. Because of their special problems, they often need additional help from specialists outside of the classroom; thus, not all of their time is spent in the "normal" situation. Special help may be in the form of remedial reading, speech therapy, counseling and various kinds of adjustment, remedial or therapeutic assistance for physically handicapped children. Included in the category of special help are enrichment activities for gifted children whose abilities allow them to achieve far more than normal children, and who do not find sufficient challenge in normal classroom activities.

A Legal Basis for Special Education—P.L. 94-142

The Education for All Handicapped Children Act (P.L. 94-142) was passed in November 1975. The bill stated:

It is the purpose of the Act to assure that all handicapped children have available to them, within the time periods specified in section 612 (2) (B), a free appropriate public education which emphasizes special education and related services designed to meet their unique needs, to assure that the rights of handicapped children and their parents or guardians are protected, to assist States and localities to provide for the education of all handicapped children, and to assess and assure the effectiveness of efforts to educate handicapped children.

Before the passage of P.L. 94-142, millions of handicapped children had either limited access to educational opportunities or, in some cases, none at all. Since 1975 such children have had a legal right to free public education with full educational opportunities. All of the states have complied with the law to various extents. It has been difficult to find qualified personnel, develop appropriate facilities, and fund such an expansion of public education. A great deal of progress has been made, and school systems continually work toward the goal of providing the best opportunities for handicapped children in public schools. There is still much to be done in music programs. Sona Nocera writes:

Of interest to music educators is the estimate that only about two million handicapped children (out of eight million) are currently receiving *any kind of arts education*. Certainly this situation will need to be rectified if schools are to comply with providing appropriate educational experiences and full educational opportunities for the handicapped as well as the nonhandicapped. Since music education programs are a part of the curriculum for nonhandicapped in virtually all parts of the United States, failure to provide a music education for handicapped children would clearly be discriminatory.[16]

Music and Special Education

Although P.L. 94–142 does not mandate mainstreaming, its language clearly implies that handicapped children must receive educational opportunities as nearly normal as possible. Therefore, the usual interpretation of the law results in the practice of mainstreaming whenever possible. Nocera points out that mainstreaming can benefit normal children as well as those who are handicapped:

It is important for us as educators to understand that P.L. 94–142 is a human rights issue and that we arrived at mainstreaming for social rather than educational reasons. Indeed, there is no research that proves mainstreaming to be a *superior educational* approach for children with learning difficulties. Mainstreaming came about on the heels of the civil rights legislation of the 1960s and the public demand for equal opportunities for all. No one can argue the potential social value to society as a whole when average children grow up working and playing with children who are different. Perhaps the greatest fruits of current mainstreaming efforts will be that the next generation of adults will not have the stereotyped ideas regarding handicapped individuals that are held by much of the adult population today.[17]

INDIVIDUALIZED INSTRUCTION FOR HANDICAPPED CHILDREN

P.L. 94–142 specifies that handicapped children be provided individualized services, part of which is a written individualized education program (IEP). The act states:

A written statement for each handicapped child developed in any meeting by a representative of the local educational agency or an intermediate educational unit who shall be qualified to provide, or supervise the provision of, specially designed instruction to meet the unique needs of handicapped children, the teacher, the parents or guardians of such child, and whenever appropriate, such child, which statement shall include (A) a statement of the present levels of educational performance of such child, (B) a statement of annual goals including short-term instructional objectives, (C) a statement of the specific educational services to be provided to such child, and the extent to which such child will be able to participate in regular educational programs, (D) the projected date for initiation and anticipated duration of such services and appropriate objective criteria and evaluation procedures and schedules for determining, on at least an annual basis, whether instructional objectives are being achieved.

FIGURE 7.1. Music Education Assessment Sheet

Music Education Assessment Sheet

2 = regular music class placement
1 = would progress best in resource or special room setting
0 = cannot perform the task at present

		ALONE	WITH OTHERS	WITH MUSICAL ACCOMPANIMENT	Scores
Singing	Familiar Song				
	Harmony Part				
	Sight-reads				
Playing Instruments	Rhythm Instr.				
	Chordal-fretted				
	Melodic-percussive				
Rhythmic Response	To Words				
	To Beat in Music				
	To Subdivision of Beat				
Describing Music	Same vs. Different				
	Loud vs. Quiet				
	Fast vs. Slow by Bodily Movement				
Creative Response/ Expression	Bodily				
	Vocal				
	Instrumental				
	Graphic				

TOTAL _____

Related Services:
1. Adapted Musical Instruments _____
2. Transportation _____
3. Hearing or Visual Aids _____
4. Other _____
Statement of Present Level of Performance in Music: _____

Note. From Richard M. Graham and Alice Beer, *Teaching Music to the Exceptional Child: A Handbook for Mainstreaming*, p. 20. Copyright © 1980 by Prentice-Hall. Reprinted by permission.

FIGURE 7.2. Individualized Education Program

Individualized Education Program

STUDENT'S NAME (FIRST, LAST) Johnny Smith		DATE OF BIRTH September 24, 1972	PUPIL ID 8-11-01	
SCHOOL George Washington Elem. School	DISTRICT IV	IEP REVIEW DATE Sept. 2, 1979	TODAY'S DATE Sept. 2, 1978	
TEACHER(S) Ms. R. Jones; Ms. E. Kimbrough (Music)			GRADE/PROGRAM	
PRIMARY ASSIGNMENT(S)			STARTING DATE	EXPECTED DURATION OF SERVICE
Regular Class, First Grade				
Special Education (Reading, Arithmetic)				
Music (Special Education)				
SERVICES				
Wheelchair, Transportation				
REASON FOR ASSIGNMENT(S): Assessment revealed poor reading and inability to handle basic number concepts. Music assessment shows minimal ability to sustain a singing voice and very poor rhythmic abilities.				
ADMINISTRATOR/SUPERVISOR RESPONSIBLE FOR PROGRAM (NAME AND TITLE) Mr. V. Smith, Principal				
ADDRESS George Washington Elementary School. 2nd and Cherry			PHONE 765-4321	

THE FOLLOWING PERSONS HAVE PARTICIPATED IN THE EDUCATIONAL PROGRAM PLANNING CONFERENCE

SCHOOL DISTRICT REPRESENTATIVE (NAME AND TITLE) Mr. V. Smith, Principal	
TEACHER(S) Mrs. R. Jones, 1st grade; Ms. E. Kimbrough, Music Consultant	
OTHERS Mr. A. Wright, Educational Psychometrist	
STUDENT Johnny Smith	PARENT Ms. Elizabeth Smith

PARENT RESPONSE: I ☐ DO   *APPROVE OF THE INDIVIDUALIZED EDUCATION PROGRAM*
               ☐ DO NOT   *WHICH IS RECOMMENDED.*

_____   _____

       Signature of Parent   *Date*

Once you indicate approval, the program will be implemented.

If you disapprove of the educational placement or program recommended for the student, you may request a hearing to resolve any differences by checking the space provided for disapproval and signing your name. To request a hearing, you must send your request within 20 days of the date of the program planning conference. You must send in your request within 10 days if you received it by mail.

If you indicate disapproval, the program will not be implemented. No change in assignment will occur until the decision of the hearing officer is received. Please review the notice which was previously sent to you. It contains an outline of hearing procedures.

If you do not respond within 20 days of the program planning conference, it will indicate that you approve of the educational placement and program that was discussed at the conference and any revisions which are attached. No response also indicates that you waive the right to a hearing at this time.

Note. From Richard M. Graham and Alice Beer, *Teaching Music to the Exceptional Child: A Handbook for Mainstreaming,* p. 33. Copyright © 1980 by Prentice-Hall. Reprinted by permission.

FIGURE 7.3. Educational Levels & Objectives

EDUCATONAL LEVELS & OBJECTIVES

SCHOOL George Washington Elem **STUDENT'S NAME** Johnny Smith

ASSESSMENT PROCEDURES	CURRICULAR AREA	DESCRIPTION OF PRESENT EDUCATIONAL LEVELS	DATE	PROGRAM PLANNER
Music assessment instrument	Music	Strength: Imitates short vocal sounds, shows an interest in music. Needs: To develop better rhythmic response: unable to tap feet to music. To sing phrases.	9/10	Ms. E. Kimbrough
Reading: Peabody Individual Assessment Test	Reading	Strengths: Recognizes letters, has good visual memory. Needs: To work on letter sounds, blending		Ms. R. Jones
PT/OT/functional evaluation and Denver PT test	Gross Motor Skills	Leg turns inward, awkward ambulation, poor balance, arm strength is weak		Mr. T. Walls

INSTRUCTIONAL AREA — **ANNUAL GOALS** — **PROGRAM PLANNER**

INSTRUCTIONAL AREA	ANNUAL GOALS	PROGRAM PLANNER
Music	Will respond to music by tapping the feet / and imitate short phrases	Ms. E. Kimbrough
Reading	Will improve letter sounds and blending to a criterion of at least 55%	Ms. R. Jones
Physical Education	Will show substantial growth in arm strength	Mr. T. Walls

SHORT TERM OBJECTIVES	ASSESSMENT PROCEDURES	PRE TEST DATE	PRE TEST SCORE	POST TEST DATE	POST TEST SCORE
Will tap feet at the sound of a drum.	Will tap feet with the drum beat as teacher plays 16 measures of four four meter with 80% accuracy.				
Will imitate short vocal sounds in a song.	Will imitate short vocal sounds in two of three consecutive sessions.				
Will sound 5 letters correctly.					
Will increase strength in arms.					

Note. From Richard M. Graham and Alice Beer, *Teaching Music to the Exceptional Child: A Handbook for Mainstreaming*, p. 34. Copyright © 1980 by Prentice-Hall. Reprinted by permission.

Obviously, mainstreaming must be planned carefully and effectively by teachers who understand the needs of each handicapped child and who knows what services the school is capable of providing. Beer and Graham suggest the use of the *Music Assessment Sheet* to establish the musical needs of handicapped children, and provide examples of IEPs for their musical education.

The Special Student

The various categories of special students who are often placed in the regular classroom for at least part of the school day are (1) the neurologically handicapped, the most likely of whom to be found in the classroom are the mentally retarded, the minimally dysfunctioning, the speech handicapped, the autistic, the psychologically disturbed, and the perceptually insufficient; (2) the physically handicapped; (3) the emotionally disturbed; and (4) the gifted.

NEUROLOGICALLY HANDICAPPED CHILDREN

According to Welsbacher, neurologically handicapped children behave in ways that are exaggerations of normal behaviors. It is the degree of exaggeration that makes their behavior other than normal. Such exaggerated behavior often prevents the child from responding to stimuli normally, and from learning in classroom situations as other children do. Neurologically handicapped children often exhibit behavioral signs that the teacher can use to devise effective teaching strategies. One such behavioral sign is rigidity, or lack of ability to accept change. The child desires order, and if objects are placed where they are not normally located, or if schedules deviate from the normal, such change represents disorder. The needs of this kind of child might include repetitive singing of the same music, performed in the same way each time. Another behavior is hyperirritable attention, which is manifested in what appears to be lack of attention. Some children may, for example, be unable to sort out and classify the sounds they hear, and may only hear certain sounds on a recording. Emotional lability, another behavioral sign, affects the child's emotional response to music and to other stimuli. This behavior may cause the child to react differently from other children to a particular stimulus, and the inappropriate response is difficult for others to understand. Initiatory delay causes the child to respond to stimuli after an abnormally long delay. Children who exhibit this behavior sometimes appear not to respond to music, but do so after a few seconds, minutes, hours, or even days have elapsed. Children who have the behavioral problem of abstracting difficulties are unable to perceive relationships and transfer knowledge to various situations. Speech, writing, and musical notation are often beyond the grasp of such children because of lack of understanding of symbols like a word, which represents a particular entity, or a printed musical note, which represents a sound.

All of these behaviors present challenges to the music teacher, who must not only teach musical concepts, but must often try to discover how music can help children improve their behaviors. To make the matter more difficult, the degree of the behaviors vary. They may be quite intense at one time and seem to disappear a few minutes later. Such behavior is similar to normal patterns, but to an exaggerated degree. Newell Kephart explains:

To most teachers, as well as parents, the slow learner is a complete enigma. One day he learns the classroom material to perfection; the next he seems to have forgotten every bit of it. In one activity he excels over all the other children; in the next he performs like a two-year-old. His behavior is unpredictable and almost violent in its intensity. . . .

Too often these aberrant performances are attributed to willful misbehavior, stupidity, or lack of interest. Actually, in many cases, the child's problems are not his fault. His central nervous system is treating these items in a different way. . . .

The teacher of the slow learner needs two basic competencies; a rationale which permits consistent interpretation of the child's learning behavior and a repertory of techniques by which information can be presented in myriad ways.[19]

Another complicating factor is that such children may or may not have normal intelligence. Neurologically handicapped children are of all intelligence levels. They may have other physical handicaps, they may be emotionally disturbed, and they may be gifted. What makes this complicated is that the teacher is faced with handicapped children of different learning abilities. Obviously, the teacher must analyze the place of every child in the class and devise unique remedial and learning activities for each.

Like other children, the neurologically handicapped child usually responds well kinesthetically to music. Some can respond only on this level, while others are capable of all the activities in which other children participate. Kinesthetic response strongly suggests a heavy reliance on rhythm for music activities. Rhythm seems to be perceivable by all children. It is a part of common body movements and functions (walking, running, dancing, speech), and it is used to diagnose and remedy problems.

Children who do not move easily or gracefully can be helped with the use of rhythm activities. Rhythmic speech helps some children to memorize material that makes no impression if presented unrhythmically. This activity can lead to poetry, which opens many new possibilities for mental and physical development, and which can be used effectively with music by most children. Many children with learning problems are able to analyze rhythm and understand the relationship between beat, meter, and tempo after developing kinesthetic abilities in response to music. Melody, timbre, and dynamics are often most successfully presented in conjunction with, or in response to, rhythm. This was recognized by Carl Orff, who based his approach to music for children on rhythm.

MENTALLY RETARDED CHILDREN

There are many degrees of mental retardation. For educational and training purposes, three categories of retardation are recognized— educable mentally retarded, trainable mentally retarded, and dependent mentally retarded. It is unusual to find other than educable mentally retarded children in regular classrooms, and it is with that category that this section deals.

Two important goals for which teachers of the mentally retarded strive are the promotion of social development and the development of the ability to communicate, especially by speech. Mentally retarded children have the same social needs as normal children, but have difficulty relating to people. Musical activities allow them to be contributing group members in an enjoyable experience. Musical games and other activities are especially important to these children, because play, an integral part of all children's lives, is a major vehicle for learning. Rhythm and movement games that require these children to follow instructions are more likely to be successful than drills and exercises, which are of little benefit to most retarded children.

Retarded children are usually not very imaginative and have difficulty dealing with the abstract. Both areas can be improved if the teacher is cognizant of the students' needs and is willing to promote activities that will stimulate them. Games involving music and other arts, especially drama, are helpful. Rhythm and movement games help them develop their large muscles and to motivate them to be imaginative. Melodic activities encourage socialization and the use of imagination, as well as musical growth. Retarded children who are given the opportunity to join normal children in a music class often experience personal growth, which adds much pleasure to their lives and helps them to function more effectively.

Music experiences that introduce concepts and vocabulary can help retarded children communicate more effectively and become more aware of their environment. Music and speech are closely related, and properly guided music activities help prepare children for the abstract symbolism of language. In some cases it is even possible to place educable mentally retarded children in performance ensembles. It is unusual for retarded children to perform as well as normal children on musical instruments, but ·many have developed sufficient skill to participate. Unfortunately, their participation sometimes lowers the performance standards of the ensemble. This is a serious problem for those ensembles that are strongly oriented toward performance. The teacher and students must evaluate the purpose of the group in making decisions about accepting special students who cannot meet the established standards of the group. Decisions for and against membership of special students have been made in various schools. The choice between the highest possible musical standards and personal growth and satisfaction for the special student can be difficult to make.

EMOTIONALLY DISTURBED CHILDREN

Less is known about emotionally disturbed children than about other exceptional children. In fact, so little is understood about their problems that it is possible for a teacher to harm an emotionally disturbed child while trying to help. In some cases it is difficult to distinguish between the emotionally disturbed child and the mentally retarded child. Frequent and specialized testing is required to learn exactly what condition exists. Teachers who deal with emotionally disturbed children as they would retarded children might produce an adverse effect. Severely disturbed children are often physically aggressive and are not usually found in the regular classroom. Although music experiences can be beneficial for them, it is usually the music therapist, rather than the music teacher, who works with emotionally disturbed children.

PHYSICALLY HANDICAPPED CHILDREN

Despite the severity of the handicaps of some physically handicapped children, classroom and music teachers often find it easier to work with them than with disturbed or retarded children. The problems of physically handicapped children are easy to identify, and decisions concerning the best place for them to be educated have usually been made by experts before they enter regular classrooms. Physically handicapped children often benefit more by being placed in a regular classroom if the nature of their disabilities does not prevent them from functioning effectively. They should have the same educational experiences as other children because they will eventually assume places in the normal world. Many physically handicapped children also have emotional problems, and need more teacher and peer support and encouragement than other children. Fortunately, the physically handicapped child is usually treated compassionately in the classroom, more so than other types of special students whose behavior problems may be disruptive.

　　Physically handicapped children include individuals who are completely or partially blind or deaf, who are mute, and who cannot function normally because of other physical impairments. Handicapped children often enjoy music and the other arts, and gain much from participating in them. The arts offer handicapped children experiences that are not only aesthetic but often therapeutic as well.

Schools such as the California School for the Deaf at Riverside, the Metropolitan School for the Deaf in Toronto, and the New York State School for the Blind at Batavia have developed music programs that prove the value of music education for blind and deaf children. That the blind enjoy and participate in music is well known; indeed, the number of excellent blind professional musicians in our society is evidence that sight is not a prerequisite for musical participation on a high level. Deaf children lack the one sensory ability by which most people perceive music. Because of the nature of sound, however, people can also perceive vibrations through sense of touch. The sensation of rhythm is not affected by lack of hearing, and so it is possible for deaf children in a normal classroom to enjoy music without actually "hearing" it. Fahey and Birkenshaw describe how the deaf experience music.

Those of use who work with the deaf have seen the face of a tiny child light up when he places his hands on a piano or organ and feels the vibrations of music or feels and hears amplified music on records. We have seen deaf children enjoying rhythm bands, and reciting words to music, deaf teenagers enjoying square dancing and social dancing, and deaf adults gathered around a piano singing songs.[20]

Because the deaf do not hear themselves speak, they have difficulty in developing clear and accurate pronunciation. One of the important goals of music education for deaf children is clear speech. Rhythm, movement, and vibratory perception activities all incorporate the use of speech. A. van Uden states:

Deaf children have a great and basic need for a total rhythmic education from childhood, the method of which must use sound perception to its full extent. . . . It may be clear, too, that music and dance continuously train the auditory-vibratory senso-motoric functions as such. They train the memory for such sequences and their "praxias" [the practice of an art, as opposed to theory] so indirectly the basic functions of speech and language [are developed]. . . . An intense training in rhythm of the whole body, of breathing and speech, integrated with sound perception auditory remnants and vibration/feeling, is a must in schools for the deaf.[21]

Blind students are capable of most activities in which sighted students participate. Many develop acute powers of perception and can focus their attention very intensely in order to compensate for lack of sight. Because of this, they can be successful in the study of voice or an instrument and can participate in musical ensembles, including band, orchestra and chorus.

Blind students who read braille can learn to read braille music, which uses the same system of raised dots to form symbols as does literary braille. Various agencies and publishers provide materials for the blind that can be used by the music teacher. *The New Braille Musician, Young Keyboard Junior, Overtones, Music Journal, the Musical Quarterly,* and *High Fidelity,* for example, are available in braille or on magnetic tape. The American Printing House for the Blind in Louisville, Kentucky, and the Division for the Blind and Physically Handicapped of the Library of Congress provide braille music and books. Mu Phi Epsilon sponsors a project in which music is taped at slow speeds so blind people can learn the music by ear. The tapes are distributed by the Library of Congress. The Sigma Alpha Iota project for partially sighted musicians provides music printed in large print. It is also distributed by the Library of Congress.[22]

Children whose disabilities prevent them from normal usage of their bodies are often able to participate in many normal music activities. Activities that require physical movement (rhythm and movement games, for example) can often be modified to permit handicapped children to participate from their chairs. The music teacher must be willing and able to devise changes in activities, create special activities, and alter materials that allow physically handicapped children to participate and gain musical and therapeutic benefits from the music program.

GIFTED CHILDREN

A category of exceptional children that in the past has received relatively little attention in public education is the gifted. Although more attention has been given to their problems in recent years, they are often left to move ahead of their classmates on their own, without the extra stimulation they might need for motivation. This can be devastating for a child of superior intellect or talent. The gifted child who becomes bored with school work may actually do poorly, earn criticism, and develop a negative attitude toward school and learning, resulting in a frustrated, unhappy individual and a waste of valuable human resources.

Giftedness in children does not necessarily imply a superior intelligence quotient (although children with an IQ above 115 are usually considered gifted). It can also mean superior talent in one or more areas, such as music or mathematics. Some gifted children have the ability to excel in everything they do; others excel in only one thing. Strang describes giftedness as follows:

Giftedness is many-sided, many patterned. Among the intellectually gifted we find persons talented in many different fields. Different pattens of personality have been noted among children with different kinds of talent— scientific, artistic, musical, leadership ability. Giftedness may take many forms depending upon the particular circumstances.

Gifted children are far from being a homogeneous group; there are wide individual differences among children designated as gifted.[23]

Music can be especially stimulating for gifted children, regardless of the area of giftedness, because they sometimes respond more deeply to aesthetic stimuli than do other children. Many gifted children also have the ability to analyze, create, and perform music. Their study of music can be somewhat deeper than that of normal children; in some cases it must be deeper if they are to gain satisfaction from it. The music teacher must recognize the abilities and interests of gifted children, plan carefully for their musical experiences, and demand more of them. When gifted students are placed in a normal music class the teacher must provide enrichment activities over and above those offered to normal students. It is for this kind of situation that individualized instruction is especially valuable. Most of the teacher's time needs to be spent with the majority of students, but some should be reserved for guiding gifted children in individualized activities. The teacher should be aware of what resources are available (library facilities, learning activity packets, audiovisual hardware and software, community resources) and make the best possible use of them for gifted students.

Students gifted in music present other kinds of problems and responsibilities for the music teacher. Musical giftedness can take different forms. A musically gifted child might excel in several aspects of music, or might be an excellent composer, but be unable to develop performance skills.

Many more opportunities have been made available for gifted children recently than in the past. Partly because of the influence of P.L. 94–142, and partly because boards of education have recognized their moral obligation to such children, special high schools have been established in many cities, in some cases by states, to provide a higher level of education and training for the gifted. Many high schools that specialize in the arts now exist in the United States. At the elementary level, magnet schools have been established in many communities to provide special opportunities for students gifted in one or more areas, including the arts. Some states also provide summer study and performance opportunities for gifted children.

MUSIC IN OPEN EDUCATION

The arts play a radically different role in the open classroom than the traditional school. Painting, sculpture, music dance, crafts—these are not frills to be indulged in if time is left over from the real business of education; they are the real business of education as much as reading, writing, math, or science. For the arts are the language of a whole range of human experience; to neglect them is to neglect ourselves and to deny children the full development that education should provide.[24]

TEACHING STRATEGY 7.1 IMPROVEMENT OF MOTOR COORDINATION

Harriet Heltman

Goal: To Improve Motor Coordination
Handicap: Emotionally Disturbed
Level: primary, intermediate

Objective	Learning Experience	Resource
To improve motor coordination skills.	As the children begin to know the words and tune of this song, set up a marching situation: follow the leader, with the children taking turns being the leader.	"Marching to Pretoria," *Making Music Your Own*, p. 116.
To improve motor coordination of the total body.	As the children learn the words of the song, have all do the actions the words indicate. Develop right and left concept.	"Busy," *Making Music Your Own* (Kindergarten), p. 129.
To develop keen awareness of all parts of the body.	For total body awareness: the children stand in a circle, a single line, or a double line facing each other. Sing words and do actions indicated to the tune of "Merrily We Roll Along": Touch your toes and then your knees, And let your hands go clap. Touch the floor and stand up tall, And let your feet go stamp. Lift your foot and kick the ball, And let your hands go clap. Hug yourself and turn around, And let your feet go stamp. Lift your knee up in the air, And let your hands go clap. Stand on tiptoe and turn around, And let your feet go stamp. Point your toe and take a bow, And let your hands go clap. Bend your body down and up, And let your feet go stamp. Rock your shoulders side to side, And let your hands go clap.	"Merrily We Roll Along" (traditional), *Teaching Music Creatively*, p. 168.

Note. From Richard M. Graham, *Music for the Exceptional Child* (Reston, Va.: Music Educators National Conference, 1975), pp. 224, 225.

TEACHING STRATEGY 7.2—REINFORCEMENT OF SELECTED DIRECTIONALITY CONCEPTS

Frances A. Jones

Goal: Reinforcement of Selected Directionality Concepts Leading into Dancing Activities
Handicap: Trainable and Educable Mentally Retarded

Objective	Learning Experience	Resource
Student demonstrates understanding and identification of right and left.	Color code hand with color tape so that child will have a color to see and match. Sing songs with right and left hand directions.	Color tape. "Hokey Pokey" and "Looby Lou"
Student demonstrates the ability to understand directions of stop and go.	Have children play games of stop and go. Children march, clap, play instruments. When music stops, children also stop. Integrate traditional colors of green and red in traffic directions. Without verbal cues, teacher holds green or red cards to give directions.	Chairs and piano or record player for playing Musical Chairs. Red and green construction paper.
Student demonstrates understanding of in and out.	Play circle games. To step out, go away from the circle. To step in, come back to the circle.	"Go In and Out the Window" and "Bluebird Through My Window."

Goal: Awareness of Environmental Sounds and Improvement of Auditory Perception
Handicap: Trainable Mentally Retarded

Child explores his body as an instrument of sound.	Activities of whistling, clapping, stamping, humming, singing, popping fingers, blowing.	"If You're Happy and You Know It," This Is Music (Book Two). Kazoo.
Child demonstrates ability to recognize environmental sounds.	Children listen and imitate sounds of whistles (trains, boats), sirens, horns, thunder, wind, and so forth.	Tape recorded sounds, sound effect records, pictures of objects. "Cloudburst" from Grand Canyon Suite.
Child demonstrates recognition of animal sounds.	Children will sing songs that imitate sounds of animals.	"Old MacDonald" and "Barnyard Song," This is Music (Book Two).
Child demonstrates recognition of instrument sounds.	Teacher plays various instruments and has students recognize them aurally.	"Listen," Music Activities for Retarded Children.

Teaching Strategy 7.3 (cont.)

Goal: Altering of Selected Inappropriate Behavior
Handicap: Educable and Trainable Mentally Retarded

Inappropriate Behavior	Technique of Modification
High distractibility	Focus attention on one object by removing other stimuli in room to which child is attracted. Designate areas of space in the room to be used in activities. Reward child's adherence to limits and attention to activity with tangible reinforcers or verbal praise.
Aggressive, self-directed behavior	Stop the activity until child is able to decrease inappropriate behavior. Do not always reinforce behavior with negative verbal feedback. Wait until child has resumed appropriate behavior and give positive verbal feedback. Therapist ignores child's inappropriate behavior by turning head away from child or lowering head to avoid looking at child.
Short attention span	Change activities frequently. Vary teaching methods. Use visual, kinesthetic, and tactual approaches. Reward students who complete entire activity.
Hyperactivity	Match the child's mood in a music activity. Music that is fast, having strong accents, and loud, or music activities that allow active body movement may match a child's hyperactive state. This is called iso-moodic principle. After child's attention is received, the level of music and/or activity is gradually lowered, thus lowering child's hyperactivity.

Note. From Richard M. Graham, *Music for the Exceptional Child* (Reston, Va.: Music Educators National Conference, 1975), pp. 228, 229.

The Development of Open Education

The idea of open education was born in the progressive education movement that began in the 1890s. John Dewey's philosophy and educational theories helped to shape this movement. After the publication of his book *Schools of To-Morrow* (1915), he was recognized as a spokesman for the movement.

The Progressive Education Association was founded in 1919 in Washington, D.C. Although Dewey's name was closely connected to it, he disassociated himself from it in 1928 because its practices did not reflect his philosophy. He felt that the progressive classroom was artificial, not modelled on real life. The association had a history of dissension, which began after Dewey's disavowal of its principles. In 1955 the Progressive Education Association ceased to exist.

Progressive educators considered the child's natural way of learning

TEACHING STRATEGY 7.3—LESSON PLAN
SPECIAL EDUCATION

Lesson Plan   **Date** _____

WHO   Class (describe: visually impaired, hearing impaired, moderately retarded, mainstreamed. This requires deline-
ating individual disabilities within the group.)

_____

_____

WHY   Objectives:

_____

_____

_____

WHAT   Activity: _____ Source: _____

_____

_____

_____

HOW   Methodology: (Include materials needed, room preparation,
as presentation format.) _____

_____

_____

_____

OUTCOMES   Evaluation: _____

_____

_____

_____

INDIVIDUAL STRATEGIES OR ASSIGNMENTS

Name	**Action**
Example: Billy B.	Ignore covering face with hands;
	praise him whenever he is sitting
	with his face uncovered—"How
	glad I am to see your face—
	you're so handsome."
Sarah J.	Be sure to keep promise of
	beginning class with "Hey, Liley."

Note. From Kay W. Hardesty, *Music for Special Education* (Morristown, N.J.: Silver Burdett
Company, 1979). © 1979 Silver Burdett Company. Reprinted by permission.

to be the best way for the child to learn. Dewey recognized that the child's world was defined by his own limited experiences, and that education came from individual growth through children's life experiences. Dewey considered the formal atmosphere of traditional education to be stifling to mental growth. For that reason, the style of progressive education was informal. Rather than impose knowledge from an external source (the teacher) on the children, it should be developed intrinsically, through experience. This changed the status of the children from passive observers to active participants in their own education. In several ways the progressive classroom was a microcosm of American society, because learning grew from experiences that were the experiences of real life. Learning took place in an atmosphere of reality; therefore, the social interaction of children was authentic, rather than artificial, as experienced in the formal classroom environment. The schools reflected real life, rather than sheltering children from it in a fabricated situation. Dewey's criticism of traditional education is a plea for a more experiential approach:

[The child's world] has the unity and completeness of his own life. He goes to school, and various studies divide and fractionalize the world for him. . . . Facts are torn away from their original place in experience and are arranged with reference to some general principle. . . . The adult mind is so familiar with the notion of logically ordered facts that it does not recognize . . . the amount of separating and reformulating which the facts of direct experience have to undergo before they can appear as a "study," or branch of learning.[25]

Dewey realized that children develop new knowledge through their own experiences and observations, and by trial and error. So did Maria Montessori, whose work contributed to the development of progressive education. From 1910 on she emphasized individualized learning and the importance of an environment that would stimulate the child. The Montessori method is based on biological principles of growth and development, which correlate at various stages with educational activities. Montessori realized that children need a natural environment in which to learn, and that the typical home and school environments are not conducive to learning. Since children in a natural environment are free to learn, Montessori created a natural environment for children (a paradoxical situation perhaps, but the best way of providing the ideal environment, short of utilizing nature itself, as Rousseau proposed in *Emile*). E. M. Standing defines it as "a method based on the principles of freedom in a prepared environment."[26] The fundamental principle of Montessori education is that the child is different from the adult because "the child is in a state of continuous and intense transformation of both body and mind, whereas the adult has reached the norm of the species."[27] This developmental principle indicates that the child's world is different from the adult world; therefore, children's response to this world and their method of learning are different from adult response. The adult works toward an external goal—to accomplish a specific task or to achieve a goal, but the child's work is internally oriented and is not meant to have any effect on the physical world. Young children live in an eternal present, and do not conceive of the future and the changes that it will bring. Indeed, they do not even conceive of change being brought about by their actions. It is very common for children to complete a task and then repeat it many times over. This is because children are oriented to the task itself, rather than to its completion, which would serve to produce some kind of change. Because children's work is inner-directed, their real education actually is, in a sense, actually self-education. The teacher must avoid giving unnecessary help to the child because that interferes with self-education, which comes about through trial and error and all other kinds of experience with the physical world. Montessori states that, "The child must do his own work or die." According to Montessori, children work spontaneously. If a child does not, the teacher has presented the subject incorrectly. All normal children are self-motivated to work if they are not bored by, or uncomprehending of, what they are trying to learn. The natural environment provides the correct stimuli for children.

Progressive education had a profound effect on British education. In 1931 the Consultative Committee, chaired by Sir Henry Hadow, published *The Primary School*, a report that emphasized the importance of participation and experience in learning, as opposed to the acquisition and retention of facts. Traditional education was considered to be too abstract for truly effective education.

The concepts of open education were furthered in many writings published during the 1930s. Dewey, still very active, published his definitive work *Experience and Education* in 1938. He stated that learning must grow out of immediate experience, and that experience must awaken a desire in the child to learn more, which in turn would lead him to grasp new ideas. The progression from experience to extended interest to new ideas to new experiences is a self-expanding cycle. It helps one to develop learning patterns that extend throughout one's lifetime.

The English Education Act of 1944, which required that children be educated according to their "age, ability, and aptitude," and which created new educational opportunities for poor children, stimulated experimental programs in the late 1940s and 1950s. Educators continued to publish works about open education, and by the 1960s the philosophy of open education, which had been developed in two decades of writings, was beginning to be implemented in experimental centers and public schools in England and the United States.

In 1963 the English Central Advisory Council for Education, chaired by Lady Bridget Plowden, was charged with the task of evaluating the Hadow report's emphasis on individual progress in education. The comprehensive two-volume report *Children and Their Primary Schools*, completed in 1967, is commonly referred to as the Plowden Report. It examined, analyzed, and made innovative recommendations for the entire British educational system. The Plowden Report is considered to be the bible of the open education movement. An excerpt from the report gives its rationale:

Individual differences [among] children of the same age are so great that any class, however homogeneous it seems, must always be treated as a body of children needing individual and different attention. Until a child is ready to take a particular step forward, it is a waste of time to try to teach him to take it. . . . Since a child grows up emotionally, physically, and intellectually at different rates, his teachers need to know and take into account his developmental age in all these respects.[28]

Much of the progress made in the open education movement since the release of the Plowden Report has been based on the report itself. Since that time, many open education centers have been founded in the United States; it has become the style of education for a large proportion of British primary schools. Despite its relationship and strong resemblance to American progressive education, open education differs in one important aspect—the role of the teacher. In open education, the teacher's role is strongly defined; it is, in fact, central to the success of open education. The progressive education teacher's role was more laissez-faire, and children were expected to figure out their own way with less guidance than is offered in the open classroom. The open teacher, much more so than the progressive teacher, defines the curriculum and gives direction to learning, although the children are often unaware of this role.

A Description of Open Education

Open education is a process that differs in attitude and practice from traditional American education. It is finding acceptance in many places in the United States. Of all new aspects of American education, it is the least susceptible to precise definition. Indeed, as Roland Barth points out,

Open education does not exist. It does not lie somewhere out there—like a planet in the solar system—awaiting discovery and description. Attempts to more carefully refine and define its essence are not resulting in a clearer and wider concept. To the contrary, those who are most carefully and persistently trying to capture the essential nature of open education are, by doing so, *creating* it. For this reason, there is and will always be disagreement about what open education is.[29]

Various terms relating to open education overlap; the terms "open education," "open classroom," and "informal education" are usually considered to be interchangeable. Some educators prefer to use no term to identify their style of education, because a term becomes a label for a specific practice. Specification can lead to standardization, something that is against the philosophy of open education. It is a style of education that grows from the attitudes of educators toward children, and different attitudes produce different styles. By its very nature it cannot be confined to a specific style, curriculum, or set of experiences.

The attitudes of open education teachers toward children are different from the traditional teacher perspective. In traditional education, children are expected to conform to well-defined and enforced patterns of behavior and learning. The subject matter to be learned is decided upon by adults who base their decisions on their own education and experience. When the body of knowledge to be learned is decided upon, the method of teaching it is determined. This is the prerogative of school administrators, school board members, and people involved with teacher education programs at the higher education level. Professors of education often have a voice in decisions about teaching methods, and they are the individuals responsible for preparing teachers to do the job in the way that administrators and school board members consider to be proper and effective. Children are expected to do their part in the educational process, at times by sitting quietly and listening to what they are told, and at other times by participating in activities that their teachers plan and structure for them. Most decisions about their education are made for them, and there is little flexibility in the education process. Assessment of children's success in learning is done by means of tests. Children who achieve the highest scores are assumed to have learned the most. This process has been used in American education since its beginning, with certain notable exceptions.

Change in education comes slowly, and some aspects of traditional education are still based on the same philosophical and psychological concepts that were in use at the turn of the twentieth century. Traditional education is obviously effective for many students, but it is most effective for the best students. The others are required to struggle on with decreasing interest and motivation. Their potentials are often unrecognized and undeveloped, and when they finish their formal education—if ever—they are often excluded from occupations and professions in which they might have been successful and satisfied. The fact that they did not do well scholastically does not necessarily mean that they are incapable of success in a particular field of employment; scholastic success, however, is often the entrance requirement for such employment. The result—personal unhappiness and wasted human resources—is a national problem caused to some extent by an educational system that is unable to cope with students who do not perform near the norm in a traditional classroom environment.

Open education turns the process around and starts with the child as the basic source of knowledge. Each child is seen as an individual with unique strengths, weaknesses, needs, interests, and desires. Respect for the individual child is the foundation of open education. The same might be said for the various types of individualized instruction that are in use in American schools now, except that in most cases individualized instruction is not based on discovery that stems from the child's interest. Furthermore, current concepts of individualized instruction do not take the child's goals into account. Most individualized instruction requires the child to achieve someone else's goals. Many materials and techniques of individualized instruction are used in open education, but usually in a different context than in the traditional classroom.

Open education is based on principles of growth and development, which must be respected by people responsible for the educational process. The same principles are well known to American educators, and experiences in traditional schools are often planned with them in mind. Because of the nature of traditional education, however, only the most committed and creative teachers can actually plan their teaching on those principles, which are that (1) children have individual rates of learning; (2) children learn in different ways; (3) children learn from both individual and group experiences; (4) children learn best when they are actively involved; and (5) children's interests are varied and transitory.[30] Silberman states that

it is not enough merely to respect childhood; it is necessary to respect children as well, which means respecting students' individuality, their interests, their needs, their strengths, their weaknesses. This means valuing individual differences instead of seeing them as a problem. It means accepting the legitimacy of individual students' individual interests—understanding that students do have interests, indeed whole agendas, of their own that are legitimate and worth recognizing. And this, in turn, means letting students' learning, at least part of the time, proceed from their interests; it means giving them freedom to explore and supporting them in their explorations.[31]

The implications of Silberman's statement are many and deep. Obviously, teachers who are completely oriented to traditional education cannot support children's interests to the degree necessary for open education. The open education curriculum is based solidly on the individual child's interest. This does not mean that children learn only what they want to learn. Open educators must be extremely perceptive about where children's interests can lead them and skillful in guiding children from one point to the next by helping to unfold new areas of interest. For example, young children are attracted to musical instruments on which they can produce a variety of sounds and rhythms. Their natural interest will usually motivate them to select such instruments and play with them. It is the teacher's responsibility to allow the children to play until that precise time when interest begins to wane. Then the children might be asked to make a different variety of sounds; compose a walking, jumping, or sleeping song; figure out what makes the sound in the instrument, or why it makes high and low sounds or soft and loud sounds. If asked correctly and at the right time, these questions can lead children to discover musical concepts as well as facts about acoustics and other areas of physics. They can also lead to a child's participation in a group musical activity that will develop other musical concepts and possibly lead to new knowledge about the child's relationship with his or her peers. If children seem interested in the physics of the instrument, they may go on to examine more sophisticated instruments to learn about instrument construction, tonal properties of stretched strings, other sound producers such as the human voice and various sources of *musique concrète*, or explore any other avenue that is opened by their interest.

Sister M. Tobias Hagan points out that a common misconception about the open education curriculum is that it lacks structure. However, as Hagan also states, structure in open education is defined by the child's abilities.

The establishment of clear learning goals is very important. Otherwise, learning may be so haphazard that it is virtually useless. However, the goals must be open-ended, not projecting beyond what a student is actually able to do nor limiting him in his learning progress.[32]

In this kind of situation the teacher must be willing to trust children's willingness to work. This is difficult for traditional teachers, who feel that the teacher must provide the motivation. Work based on interest is similar to play, and play is usually its own motivation. That children work without extrinsic motivation is continually demonstrated in open schools, where students frequently arrive early, leave late, and find each day productive and exciting. Teachers who respect the individuality of each student work to help children develop their knowledge and skills in ways that are related to each student's individuality. The basic assumption is that the child learns best if learning develops from interest and takes place in a congenial and stimulating atmosphere.

From what has been said thus far about open education, one might think that the subject matter of education is decided upon casually and spontaneously. This is not so. The teacher's role includes decision making about subject matter. The approach to subject matter, however, varies from child to child. One way or another, the teacher helps the children develop an interest to the point where the children are led to something unexplored by them, which will of course lead them to do something else. The approach to education is informal, that is, without the formal structure of traditional education that relies on lesson plans, planned activities, evaluation of learning and teaching, and the assumption that all children can learn the same thing in the same way at the same time. In open education, learning happens naturally, as children play. Critics of open education decry the use of play as the basis of learning, but, as

Silberman states, "Play *is* a child's work: the distinction between work and play, so central to formal schooling, is not one that children make until adults force it on them. . . . Play is one of the principal ways young children learn."[33] Play, however, is only the basis for learning. The teacher must guide the child from play as a random activity to that of a structured learning activity. The insight and skill necessary to do this makes the job of teaching in an open classroom extremely demanding.

Open education is integrated education, meaning that learning is integrated with life experiences, rather than apart from them. In traditional education it is customary to separate those facts about a subject which are to be taught from those which are not, and to present them in such a way that children often cannot integrate them with the subject itself. Traditional learning, as Marshall McLuhan shows, does not present information realistically.

There is a world of difference between the modern home environment of integrated electric information and the classroom. Today's television child is attuned to up-to-the-minute "adult" news—inflation, rioting, war, taxes, crime, bathing beauties—and is bewildered when he enters the nineteenth-century environment that still characterizes the educational establishment where information is scarce but ordered and structured by fragmented, classified patterns, subjects, and schedules.[34]

In the informal classroom, learning comes from experiencing the objects of real life, which are available and easily accessible to children in great variety and sufficient quantity. Children's interest in common wood blocks, for example, can be used to develop concepts of measurement of the square and cube, weight in relation to mass, and, if struck, sound in relation to its size, material, and density. The children are led to the discovery of these concepts by their interest in the blocks, rather than by a textbook or lecture/demonstration approach. Their active participation in the learning experience (the measurement of the block) helps them develop concepts that they would be unlikely to develop in a more passive educational environment.

Traditional educators argue that there is a common body of knowledge to be learned by all children and that their normal experiences do not always lead them to it. Advocates of open education point out that the pace at which human knowledge increases makes it virtually impossible for any individual to keep up with it, even in a narrow field of specialization. It is more important that children learn how to gain knowledge than to ingest information that they may or may not consider relevant. Relevancy is also taken into account by open classroom teachers, who maintain that teachers do not know what is relevant for children for the present, much less for the future. Relevancy grows from the individual's interests and experiences; those are the factors teachers should view as the basic tools of education. The tools are used to lead children to the development of common concepts about their environment; that different routes are taken to those concepts simply affirms the need for individualized instruction. Open educators also point out that the concept of a common body of necessary knowledge is a myth. No two people have the same knowledge, and even experts in various fields have knowledge gaps that affect neither their ability to function nor their professional reputations.

There are certain things that people must know and be able to do in order to be able to function effectively in society. People must be able to communicate, relate to others, develop critical judgment, and understand certain aspects of the physical world. These areas are addressed by open teachers, and sometimes by means of traditional approaches. In many situations, teachers resort to other than informal approaches to supplement the normal environment of the open classroom.

The physical facility itself stimulates children's interests. The open education classroom usually does not contain neat rows of desks and chairs facing the teacher's desk. Instead there is space for children to move around, to socialize, and to do things that require space. There are special areas for various interests. For example, there might be areas for math, science, reading, music, and art. Each area contains many items that children can use for play and to explore worlds that are new to them. The music center might contain various rhythm instruments, which are likely to be handmade by the children and teacher; simple melodic instruments, some of which might also be made by the children and teacher; books of and about music; materials that can be used to create sounds; pictures of instruments; recordings; playback equipment (equipped with earphones to avoid disturbing other children); and possibly tape recording equipment. Children are free to play with, examine, and use any or all of the items. They can wander from one interest area to another, and can involve themselves in group activities. They may do neither and choose to simply sit and contemplate. The important thing is for the teacher to know what the children are doing, to be available for help or suggestions, and to provide structure for the children's experiences.

Open education does not have to take place in a specific kind of room. The term "open" refers to the *style* of education rather than the physical surroundings. Many open or informal classrooms are in old buildings built for traditional learning. In many schools that do not have sufficiently large classrooms, hallways are used as extensions of the classrooms. Interest centers might be located there, for example. The most important physical characteristic of open classrooms is the utilization of space for different purposes. There is always something new for children to try or explore; there is room for group activities; and there are places where a child can go to be alone if he wishes.

The atmosphere of open classrooms is happy, vital, and interesting. It is not unusual for children to arrive early and stay late—they can pursue their interests in school more effectively than out of school. School is not seen as a place where one spends several hours each day out of touch with the real world. It is perceived, rather, as being integral to out-of-school life, when one also plays and explores interests. Play and interest exploration are one and the same to many open school children, and the desire to leave school and be released from its work is uncommon.

The Arts in Open Education

The arts hold an important place in the cultures of all people, and it is by their arts that they are remembered. The advancement of science in the twentieth century has created an even stronger need for art. Through science we learn the nature of the physical world in truths that provide a common basis of knowledge for all people. But human experience is an individual matter. Experience is a means by which we learn to interpret physical reality. The individual interpretation of experience is the basis of art. Regardless of the societies from which they emerged, successful artists are sensitive to relationships with the physical world, and are able to effectively communicate their insights through the medium of an art form.

Everyone, including children, utilizes art in this way. Art communicates experience. Children who create and sing a melody, paint a picture, dramatize an experience, or mold a figure from clay are communicating their unique interpretation of reality. As the children mature, more of their individual experiences will be communicated by means of language. Even then, however, language will not serve adequately to communicate feeling and emotion. The person who is able to utilize an art form in an uninhibited manner, and who is able to effectively perceive the activities of others, is able to communicate on a deeper level than is done by means of language, which is basically intellectual communication.

Because the child's interest is the basis of learning, music, painting, sculpture, drama, and movement are used to a greater extent in open classrooms than in traditional classrooms. Participation in the arts is play for children; for that reason, the arts are not considered to be of central importance in traditional education. In open education, the arts are integrated into ordinary life activities. Through the arts, children learn language skills and cognitive knowledge. For example, children's interest in drawing can be the basis for discussion about the drawings, for the development of interest in reading (and therefore the development of increased reading skills), and for the development of mathematical concepts and skills. Discussing their drawings may help the children discover principles of art by which they can evaluate and appreciate the art works of others. Their desire to improve their drawing ability may lead them to define relationships of size and distance, which is done by measuring, thus leading them into another area of knowledge.

Many art activities are done in groups, in which children learn that other people perceive, interpret, and express experiences differently. Knowledge and acceptance of this fact provides a healthy basis for developing relationships with other individuals and with various groups of people. Many kinds of learning take place in open classrooms, much of it growing from art experiences.

Art is created and perceived on many different levels. In Western societies, art created by recognized professional artists and exhibited or performed in concert halls, art galleries, and museums is considered to be the "best" art. This is not children's art, though, because in order to truly appreciate it, the perceiver must be experienced and sophisticated in aesthetics. Art in the open classroom is not always done to develop art techniques and sophistication, although these are often long-term goals. The immediate objective is for children to use their natural art abilities to express and communicate experience. If children are required to learn to read music before being encouraged to create it, they may never wish to create music or respond to it. On the other hand, music reading ability may develop from the children's need to be able to re-create their music or somebody else's music at a later time. Children who create successful pieces of music may also be encouraged to devise their own notational system so that the pieces can be reproduced later. The self-devised system may use written symbols, or perhaps colors or various shapes and sizes of building blocks, to represent specific sounds. Refinements of the notational system can lead the children to learn conventional notation, which skills can in turn lead to the study and understanding of art music.

Given the basic concepts of open education, one would rightly assume that there is no one best way to teach music. In schools with open classrooms, there is usually an interest center for music that houses paraphernalia for creating music, books about music, and listening equipment. Children use the center when they wish, often for purely musical purposes, sometimes to use the equipment for nonmusical projects. More than one music interest center is often found in open classrooms. Some may emphasize electronic music, music in the community, music and science, and *musique concrète*. The importance of the centers lies in the rich variety of musical experiences that are made available to children.

The purposes of music in open education are the same as they are in traditional education, but, like other disciplines, it is approached differently in open education. Music develops the children's aesthetic sensitivity; nurtures their awareness of its potential for expression and communication; and helps them to cultivate the skills and knowledge necessary to be able to create, respond to, and perform music. True to the philosophy of the integrated curriculum, music is not taught as a special subject apart from the rest of the curriculum, but in conjunction with, or along with, other subjects.

Team teaching is common in open schools. In team-teaching situations the music specialist functions as a member of the team. Part of the music specialist's job is to make the other teachers aware of the potentials of music in terms of aesthetics, communication, and its use in learning other subjects. The music teacher also plans effective strategies for individual and group learning. Of course scheduling is a problem for the music teacher because he is usually required to teach in several classrooms. Although the students may have access to the music areas at any time, the specialist's services are not always available. For this reason, team-planning meetings usually include discussion of strategies for music activities by the nonmusic teachers.

The time spent in each classroom by the music specialist is usually divided into periods of group activity—singing, compositional activities, discussion of music and performance, music reading—and individual instruction. This time is devoted to students who are gifted in music, who have learning problems, who are very interested in music, or who, having elected not to use any of their free time for music, receive special encouragement. All of these children benefit from individual time with the teacher. The various vocal and instrumental ensembles that are formed require scheduled rehearsal time of the teacher. Except in certain cases, a casual approach to scheduling ensemble rehearsals is not successful. In addition to classroom activities, musical experiences often include attendance at concerts outside of school and visits to such places as electronic music studios, recording studios, and university music departments.

Sister Hagan has identified four aspects of the teacher's function inherent in the teaching of music in an open situation.

1. The primary function of the teacher is to serve as a resource rather than as a transmitter of information, because true learning happens when the student encounters the subject matter without teacher mediation.

2. The teacher structures the learning environment, and so has control of it. Situations are set up for individuals and small groups, rather than for the entire group, although some situations involve the entire group.

3. The teacher must challenge the capable and interested students by allowing them independence in learning.

4. The uninterested student must also be challenged.[35]

The Manhattan Music Curriculum Program (MMCP) is especially well suited to the open classroom (see Chapter 5, The Manhattanville Music Curriculum Program). It is based on learning by discovery and creativity. Musical concepts grow out of experience, and lead to new discoveries. The spiral curriculum serves as a guide to the music specialist, who constantly attempts to open new areas of interest to students, and the *interaction* of MMCP can be used by nonspecialist teachers for children in grades K–2. Many open classroom music specialists use the MMCP, or parts of it, with positive results, and some music teacher education programs that prepare teachers for open education use the Manhattanville curriculum. According to Margaret Haynes, any successful method can be adapted for open classroom usage.

Any music teacher attempting to work in this new learning environment need not hesitate to start with what he already knows. Any well-developed program, including the approaches of the CMP, Manhattanville, Orff, or Kodály, could be adapted to the open classroom idea.[36]

Hertzberg and Stone list seven steps toward openness in music:

1. Treat music not as a "subject" but as a natural means of expression, as communication, and as an integral part of the school day.
2. Give children many opportunities to sing. Help children discover the world of music beyond the graded text.
3. Help children create music through a variety of explorations into sound.
4. Encourage those children who play instruments to share their interests with the class.
5. Help children to explore a variety of rhythms as a basic means of expression.
6. Help children to find listening enjoyment through a wide range of recordings.
7. Help children to express themselves through improvisation in movement.[37]

Hagan summarizes the concept of openness in open education by saying:

When a music teacher fully understands the new function of the teacher and the underlying structure of the subject, he has acquired the basic requisites for open teaching. The motivations, the activities, the environment, the specific musical encounters that he plans for the students will be extremely varied and actually can be whatever seems to fit the situation. The specific choices will be right because they emerge from an open mind that clearly understands the relation of the student to the subject matter, the teacher to the student, and the basic organization of the subject matter.[38]

NOTES

1. The Tanglewood Declaration, article 7
2. "The Widening Gap in Quality," *Carnegie Quarterly*, vol. 14, Fall 1966, quoted in *New Trends in the Schools*, ed. William P. Lineberry (New York: H.W. Wilson, 1967), p. 24.
3. Robert J. Havighurst, *Education in Metropolitan Areas* (Boston: Allyn and Bacon, 1966), pp. 169–76.

4. Robert D. Strom, *Teaching in the Slum School* (Columbus, Ohio: Charles E. Merrill, 1965), p. 33.
5. James A. Standifer, "Arts Education Deserves a Black Eye," *Music Educators Journal* 55, no. 5 (January 1969): 30.
6. "Overtones," *Music Educators Journal* 56, no. 5 (January 1970): 103–104. Reprinted by permission of Music Educators National Conference.
7. Leonard Goines, quoted in *Black Manifesto for Education,* ed. Jim Hoskins (New York: William Morrow, 1973), p. 151
8. Leroi Jones, *Blues People* (New York: William Morrow, 1963), p. 16.
9. Shirley H. Schell, "The Spirit of the Law," *Educational Leadership* 26, no. 2 (November 1968): 124.
10. Ellsworth Janifer, "The Role of Black Studies in Music Education: A Critical Analysis," *Black Manifesto for Education,* ed. Jim Hoskins (New York: William Morrow, 1973), p. 152.
11. Robert A. Choate, ed., *Documentary Report of the Tanglewood Symposium* (Washington, D.C.: Music Educators National Conference, 1968), p. 122. Reprinted by permission or Music Educators National Conference.
12. Wiley L. Housewright, "Youth Music in Education," *Music Educators Journal* 56, no. 3 (November 1969): 45. Reprinted by permission of Music Educators National Conference.
13. Bennett Reimer, "General Music for the Black Ghetto Child," *Facing the Music in Urban Education* (Washington, D.C.: Music Educators National Conference, 1972), p. 89. Reprinted by permission of Music Educators National Conference.
14. The Tanglewood Declaration, article 8
15. M. E. Frampton and Eleva D. Gall, *Special Education for the Exceptional Child* (Boston: Porter Sargent, 1955), p. xxvi.
16. Sona D. Nocera. *Reaching the Special Learner Through Music* (Morristown, N.J.: Silver Burdett Company, 1979), p. 4.
17. Ibid.
18. Betty T. Welsbacher, "More than a Package of Bizarre Behaviors," in *Music in Special Education* (Washington, D.C.: Music Educators National Conference, 1972), pp. 10–12.
19. Newell C. Kephart, *The Slow Learner in the Classroom,* 2nd ed. (Columbus, Ohio: Charles E. Merrill, 1971), pp. v–vi.
20. Joan Dahms Fahey and Lois Birkenshaw, "Bypassing the Ear: The Perception of Music and Feeling and the Touch," in *Music in Special Education* (Washington, D.C.: Music Educators National Conference, 1972), p. 31.
21. A. van Uden, *A World of Language for Deaf Children* (Rotterdam: Rotterdam University Press, 1970), p. 179, quoted in John Grayson, "A Playground of Musical Sculpture" *Music Educators Journal* 58, no. 8 (April 1972): 51.
22. Muriel K. Mooney, "Blind Children Need Training, Not Sympathy," *Music Educators Journal* 58, no. 8 (April 1972): 59.
23. Ruth Strang, "The Nature of Giftedness," *The Fifty-seventh Yearbook of the National Society for the Study of Education,* part II, Education for the Gifted, ed. Nelson B. Henry (Chicago: University of Chicago Press, 1958), p. 64.
24. Charles E. Silberman, *The Open Classroom Reader* (New York: Random House, 1973), p. 749.
25. John Dewey, *The Child and the Curriculum,* quoted in Silberman, *The Open Classroom Reader,* p. 522.
26. E. M. Standing, *The Montessori Revolution in Education* (New York: Schocken Books, 1966), p. 5.
27. Ibid., p. 8.

28. Department of Education and Science, *Children and Their Primary Schools* (London: Her Majesty's Stationery Office, 1967), pp. 25–26.

29. Roland S. Barth, "First We Start with Some Different Assumptions," *Music Educators Journal* 60, no. 8 (April 1974): 25. Reprinted by permission of Music Educators National Conference.

30. Alvin Hertzberg and Edward F. Stone, *Schools Are for Children* (New York: Schocken Books, 1971), pp. 13–15.

31. Silberman, *The Open Classroom Reader*, pp. xix–xx.

32. Sister M. Tobias Hagan, "How the Teacher Functions in an Open Classroom," *Music Educators Journal* 59, no. 3 (November 1972): 43–46. Reprinted by permission of Music Educators National Conference.

33. Silberman, *Crisis in the Classroom*, p. 237.

34. Marshall McLuhan and Quentin Fiore, *The Medium Is the Message* (New York: Bantam Books, 1967), p. 18.

35. Hagan, "How the Teacher Functions in an Open Classroom," pp. 44–45.

36. Margaret S. Haynes, "The Open Classroom—Its Structure and Rationale," *Music Educators Journal* 59, no. 3 (November 1972): 40–43. Reprinted by permission of Music Educators National Conference.

37. Hertzberg and Stone, *Schools Are for Children*, pp. 55–56. Reprinted by permission of Music Educators National Conference.

38. Hagan, "How the Teacher Functions in an Open Classroom," p. 46. Reprinted by permission of Music Educators National Conference.

BIBLIOGRAPHY

Music in Urban Schools

Choate, Robert A., ed. *Documentary Report of the Tanglewood Symposium*. Washington, D.C.: Music Educators National Conference, 1968.

———— *Facing the Music in Urban Education*. Washington, D.C.: Music Educators National Conference, 1970.

George, Luvenia A. *Teaching the Music of Six Different Cultures in the Modern Secondary School*. West Nyack, N.Y.: Parker Publishing Company, 1976.

Haskins, Jim, ed. *Black Manifesto for Education*. New York: William Morrow, 1973.

Havighurst, Robert J. *Education in Metropolitan Areas*. Boston: Allyn and Bacon, 1966. A historical analysis of the evolution of education in American cities.

Jones, Leroi. *Blues People: Negro Music in White America*. New York: William Morrow, 1963. A social history of black Americans and their music.

Lee, Ronald Thomas. "A study of Teacher Training Experiences for Prospective Inner-City Instrumental Music Teachers." Ph.D. diss. University of Michigan, 1970.

Murphy, Judith; and Ronald Gross, *The Arts and the Poor*. Washington, D.C.: United States Government Printing Office, 1968. An interpretative report of the Conference on the Role of the Arts in Meeting the Social and Educational Needs of the Disadvantaged, Gaithersburg, Maryland, 15–16 November 1966.

Music Educators National Conference. *Facing the Music in Urban Education*. Washington, D.C.: Music Educators National Conference, 1970. Articles on music in urban education originally published in the *Music Educators Journal*, vol. 56, no. 5, January 1970.

Roberts Joan I., ed. *School Children in Urban Slums*. New York: The Free Press, 1967.

Silberman, Charles E. *Crisis in Black and White.* New York: Vintage Books, 1964. An excellent description of urban conditions and causative factors, with insight into the historical basis of current racial problems.

Music in Special Education

Bradley, R.C. *The Education of Exceptional Children.* Wolfe City, Tex.: The University Press, 1970.

Cruickshank, William M. *Misfits in the Public Schools.* Syracuse, N.Y.: Syracuse University Press, 1969.

Cruickshank, William M.; and George Orville Johnson, eds. *Education of Exceptional Children and Youth.* 2nd ed. Englewood Cliffs, N.J.: Prentice-Hall, 1967.

Dunn, Lloyd, ed. *Exceptional Children in the Schools.* 2nd ed. New York: Holt, Rinehart and Winston, 1973.

Erickson, Marion J. *The Mentally Retarded Child in the Classroom.* New York: Macmillan, 1965.

Gaston, E. Thayer. *Music in Therapy.* New York: Macmillan, 1968.

Giangreco, C. Joseph; and R. Marianna. *Education of the Hearing Impaired.* Springfield, Ill.: C.C. Thomas, 1970.

Graham, Richard M. *Music for the Exceptional Child.* Reston, Va.: Music Educators National Conference, 1975.

Graham, Richard M.; and Alice S. Beer. *Teaching Music to the Exceptional Child.* Englewood Cliffs, N.J.: Prentice-Hall, 1980.

Hardesty, Kay W. *Music for Special Education.* Morristown, N.J.: Silver Burdett Company, 1979.

Havighurst, Robert J., ed. *Education for the Gifted.* National Society for the Study of Education, fifty-seventh yearbook, part 2. Chicago: University of Chicago Press, 1958.

Hewett, Frank M. *The Emotionally Disturbed Child in the Classroom.* Boston: Allyn and Bacon, 1968.

Kephart, Newell. *The Slow Learner in the Classroom.* 2nd ed. Columbus, Ohio: Charles E. Merrill, 1971.

Kirk, Samuel A. *Educating Exceptional Children.* 2nd ed. Boston: Houghton Mifflin, 1972.

McCaslin, Nellie. *Creative Dramatics in the Classroom.* 2nd ed. New York: David McKay, 1974.

Music Educators National Conference. *Music in Special Education.* Washington, D.C.: Music Educators National Conference, 1972. Published originally in the *Music Educators Journal,* vol. 58, no. 8, April 1972.

Nocera, Sona D. *Reaching the Special Learner Through Music.* Morristown, N.J.: Silver Burdett Company, 1979.

The Role of Music in the Special Education of Handicapped Children. Conference Proceedings. Albany, N.Y.: University of the State of New York/The State Education Department Division for Handicapped Children and the Division of the Humanities and the Arts, 1971.

Siegel, Ernest. *Special Education in the Regular Classroom.* New York: John Day, 1969.

Music in Open Education

Barth, Roland S. *Open Education and the American School.* New York: Schocken Books, 1974.

Barth, Roland S.; and Charles Rathbone. *A Bibliography of Open Education.* Newton, Mass.: Early Childhood Education Study, Education Development Center, 1971.

Dewey, John. *The Child and the Curriculum and the School and the Society* (1902). Chicago: University of Chicago Press, 1956.

Hadow, Sir Henry. *The Hadow Report: A Report of the Consultative Committee on the Primary School* (1931). London: Her Majesty's Stationery Office, 1962.

Hertzberg, Alvin; and Edward F. Stone. *Schools Are for Children: An American Approach to the Open Classroom.* New York: Schocken Books, 1971. An excellent description of the British system of open education.

Featherstone, Joseph. *Schools Where Children Learn.* New York: Liveright, 1971. A critical description of current British and American educational practices, including informal education. Included is a collection of essays from *The New Republic* on some exemplary reforms in American education.

Meske, Eunice Boardman; and Carroll Rinehart. *Individualized Instruction in Music.* Reston, Va.: Music Educators National Conference, 1975. An anthology of articles about music in open education.

Montessori, Maria. *The Discovery of the Child.* Translated by M. Joseph Costelloe, S.J. New York: Ballantine Books, 1972.

Music Educators Journal, vol. 58, November 1972. Contains several articles on individualized instruction and open education.

Music Educators Journal, vol. 60, April 1974. Subtitled "Music in Open Education." Contains excellent articles on theoretical and practical aspects of open education in music.

Plowden, Lady Bridget. *Children and Their Primary Schools: A Report of the Central Advisory Council for Education.* 2 vols. London: Her Majesty's Stationery Office, 1967. Can be purchased from Pendragon House, 259 East Bayshore, Palo Alto, California 94303. An important publication that analyzes open education in British schools and offers recommendations for the entire British educational system.

Silberman, Charles E. *Crisis in the Classroom: The Remaking of American Education.* New York: Random House, 1970. An examination and criticism of traditional American education. This book includes an excellent section on open education, and also a section on teacher education as an aspect of the education crisis.

——— ed. *The Open Classroom Reader.* New York: Random House, 1973. A collection of articles on open education that covers many aspects of the subject. The chapter "The Role of the Arts" is especially important. This book should be the first to be consulted by readers who are unfamiliar with open education.

Standing, E. M. *The Montessori Revolution in Education.* New York: Schocken Books, 1966. A description of the background, principles, and applications of the Montessori method. This is an excellent introduction to the subject.

8

Music Education in Colleges and Universities

THE EDUCATION OF MUSIC TEACHERS

Until the late 1960s, music teacher education was very much as it had been for a long time. It consisted primarily of traditional classroom courses in liberal arts, applied music, music theory, history, and literature, and music education method courses. Because of the new public interest in educational accountability, and of the general recognition that the teacher education system was in need of an overhaul, however, a new national movement began. The movement was called "Competency-Based Teacher Education" (CBTE). CBTE is also known as "Performance-Based Teacher Education" (PBTE). The movement toward CBTE in music education was as strong as in other education disciplines. In 1968 Wiley Housewright, president of MENC, appointed a Commission on Teacher Education to make recommendations for the improvement of the education of music teachers. Dennis Holt wrote, "It was the judgment of the Music Educators National Conference that many teacher education programs had been overtaken by obsolesence. Concern was expressed for developing mature teachers who could demonstrate identifiable competencies as musicians as well as educators. . . ."[1] In its report, the commission stated:

The development of music teacher competencies should result from the total program of the teacher training institution. The demonstration of competence, rather than the passing of a course, should be the deciding factor in certification. This means that proficiency tests, practical applications of historical, theoretical, and stylistic techniques, and advanced standing procedures should be enforced; and that an adequate means of final assessment should be developed and implemented.[2]

265

Music education majors in typical collegiate programs usually took courses for three years and spent much of the fourth year as student teachers. In many cases, the only other experiences that students had in school music programs was occasional observation periods. Because new teachers graduated from college with so little experience in the classroom, it was not unusual for them to be unprepared to handle their classes. The first year of teaching was often extremely difficult for new teachers and their students. Many were successful because they possessed natural talent for teaching and had strong support from their principal, supervisors, and colleagues. Another aspect of the same problem was that, because students did not gain actual teaching experience until the senior year, they were not sure if they would respond well to the teaching situation until then. Their teachers in the college classroom had had no opportunity to make judgments about their teaching effectiveness prior to student teaching, and so could not give effective advice about becoming teachers. Those who were not suited to the profession were well into the senior year before deciding that it would be better to seek another profession. That was often a personal tragedy for the student and a waste of university resources. For these reasons and others to be discussed later, it became imperative to change the character of teacher education programs. The result of the change was CBTE.

Competency-Based Teacher Education

Competency-Based Teacher Education (CBTE) is an individualized method of educating teachers that began to attract serious attention in the early 1970s. Although competency-based programs existed as early as the 1950s, the current system had its beginning in the social upheaval of the 1960s, which was partially responsible for the movement toward accountability in education. CBTE is a means by which the concept of accountability is extended from school teachers and administrators to the colleges and universities that prepare personnel to work in schools.

The sit-ins, campus riots, and other manifestations of dissatisfaction with the inequities of American society in the 1960s were aimed not only at the impersonal government "establishment," but also at the American system of higher education. The insensitivity of colleges and universities to members of minority groups was bitterly protested on campuses across the country. Teacher education programs had given little recognition to the specific professional needs of students who would become teachers of minority group children. Teacher education was, for the most part, based on the needs of the American middle class. The admission standards of teacher education programs often tended to exclude minority youth. The social, cultural, and educational requirements for entering students were sometimes unattainable by minority youth. In the field of music, the problem was manifested by lack of technical development in performance, undeveloped music reading skills, and inexperience with traditional Western art music. Urban school systems had unique social and cultural needs; because teacher education institutions had not adequately prepared teachers to meet those needs, the problems were perpetuated. The social revolution of the 1960s made the American education establishment aware of the necessity to recognize social and cultural heritage in educational planning. Eventually, music education leaders recognized the value and importance of jazz, popular music, and ethnic music in the curriculum.

Teachers themselves had had little part in the decision-making processes that affected education. As teacher associations and unions gained strength during the 1960s, the teachers demanded and won a more equitable share in the governance of education. This, too, was a factor in the development of CBTE.

Other factors that encouraged the development of CBTE had to do with recent developments in research and technology. The new technology of the sixties made possible new teaching techniques and expanded the scope of learners. Television and other media made possible an almost unlimited variety of vicarious experiences for each child, and individualized instruction offered children the opportunity to assimilate knowledge in ways better suited to the individual than to the class. The act of teaching itself became a subject of research and study, and was analyzed by its component parts; a new science of teacher education was thus established. As a result, there are new teacher evaluation tools that serve to identify behavioral models upon which teacher education concepts can be based.

Not the least of the major factors that brought about CBTE was the interest of the federal government in education. The government's financial support of educational research and curriculum development played a major part in bringing about a new mode of teacher education that has provided relevant education for preservice and in-service teachers, and has made such education available to all qualified students who desire it.

Characteristics of Competency-Based Teacher Education

Students in CBTE programs are expected to demonstrate teaching competencies as part of their program exit requirements. The demonstration of competencies replaces, to a degree, the traditional course examination concept. Competencies are stated in terms of behavioral objectives that make it possible to assess objectively the student's degree of success. Assessment criteria are based on the competencies to be demonstrated; these criteria determine the level of mastery and under what conditions it is expected and are revealed to the student in advance. Student assessment is based on performance, but takes into account the student's knowledge of the subject, ability to plan, analyze, interpret, and evaluate situations and behaviors.

In keeping with the philosophy of individualization, instruction is modularized. A module consists of a set of learning activities, including objectives, prerequisites, pre-assessment, instructional activities, post-assessment, and remediation. Modules, rather than traditional courses, are the basic unit of progress of the teacher education program. Being somewhat smaller in scope than the course, they allow for individualization in completion time, independent study, and alternative means of instruction. Modularization permits the students to develop individual competencies, although there is a danger that the development of an overall view, usually gained from the traditional course, will be sacrificed.

The learner, through constant feedback, is kept aware of how others react to his or her performance and so is able to continually evaluate work effectiveness. This factor also helps to personalize the program of each student. Because there are constant indications of what modifications are required, learning activities are often assigned on an individual basis.

The emphasis of CBTE programs is on exit, rather than entrance, requirements. Traditional requirements for matriculation are stressed less, and more importance is placed on the requirements of the program as the learner proceeds through it. The student is accountable for his or her own performance. The program is completed upon demonstration of the competencies that have been established as necessary for a particular teacher role or function.

CBTE is a field-centered approach. There is more emphasis on work involving real students in authentic teaching/learning situations than on the college classroom lecture/demonstration approach. Simulated situations are also used. The materials that students use, and the experiences they have, focus on concepts, skills, and knowledge that can best be gained in a specific instructional setting—usually an authentic classroom, but often a simulation. The instructional system is designed by both the students and the college faculty. Because the student is preparing to become a teacher, part of the learning experiences includes making personal decisions about his or her own education. This not only helps the student learn what is involved in educational decision making, but is also helpful in designing a program that is relevant to special skills and interests. As students develop an understanding of the teaching process and specific concepts involved in teaching, they proceed from mastery of specific techniques to combinations of techniques. This is called role integration and is usually not fully developed until the teacher is thoroughly experienced. For this reason, teacher education is not viewed by CBTE planners as only a preservice experience, but as a developmental process that extends throughout the career of the teacher.

Decision making for CBTE programs is usually shared by everyone involved with teacher education programs, including college faculty, students, school teachers, administrators, and sometimes community representatives. It is not unusual for consortia consisting of representatives of the above groups to be formed for the purpose of jointly developing CBTE programs.

Competency-Based Certification of Teachers

CBTE is intrinsically related to Competency-Based Certification (CBC), a procedure by which many state departments of education certify teachers. To a great extent, those states have abandoned the traditional certification procedures of evaluating courses and counting numbers of credit hours in favor of automatically granting certification to graduates of approved CBTE programs. Graduates of traditional programs are not certifiable in certain states unless they have had successful teaching experience elsewhere. In other states, certification regulations do not exclude graduates of traditional programs, but require that college programs in their own states be evaluated in the light of CBTE concepts. This practice has resulted in extensive modification of traditional teacher education programs.

CBTE and Music Education

The accrediting agency for collegiate music and music education programs is the National Association of Schools of Music (NASM). NASM recommendations are usually highly respected by member institutions and are implemented as thoroughly as possible. NASM published new curricular recommendations in its 1973 edition of *Proposed Revision of Standards for Baccalaureate Degrees and Recommendations for Graduate Study in Music*. Many of the recommendations are based on CBTE principles. Some of them are as follows.

1. The professional education component should be dealt with in a practical context, relating the learning of educational principles to the students day-by-day musical experiences. Students should be provided opportunities for various types of teaching and observation experiences throughout the period of undergraduate study.

2. Laboratory experiences that give the conducting student opportunities to apply rehearsal techniques and procedures are essential.

3. Laboratory experience in teaching beginning instrumental students—individually, in small groups, and in larger classes—is essential.

FIGURE 8.1. Conceptual Model of Competency-based Teacher Education

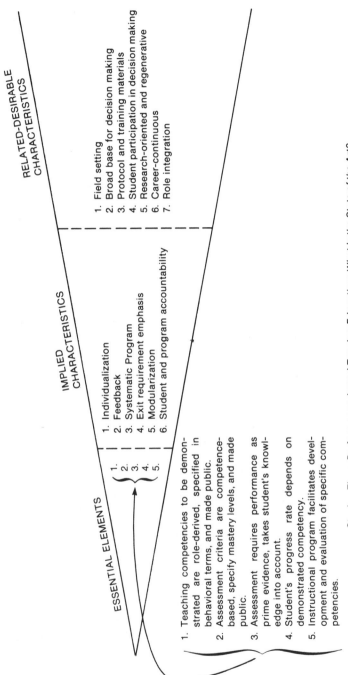

Stanley Elam, *Performance-based Teacher Education: What Is the State of the Art?*, PBTE Series no. 1 (Washington, D.C.: American Association of Colleges for Teacher Education, December 1971), p. 8. Reprinted with permission of the American Association of Colleges for Teacher Education.

FIGURE 8.2. A Systematic and Comprehensive Approach to Music Education

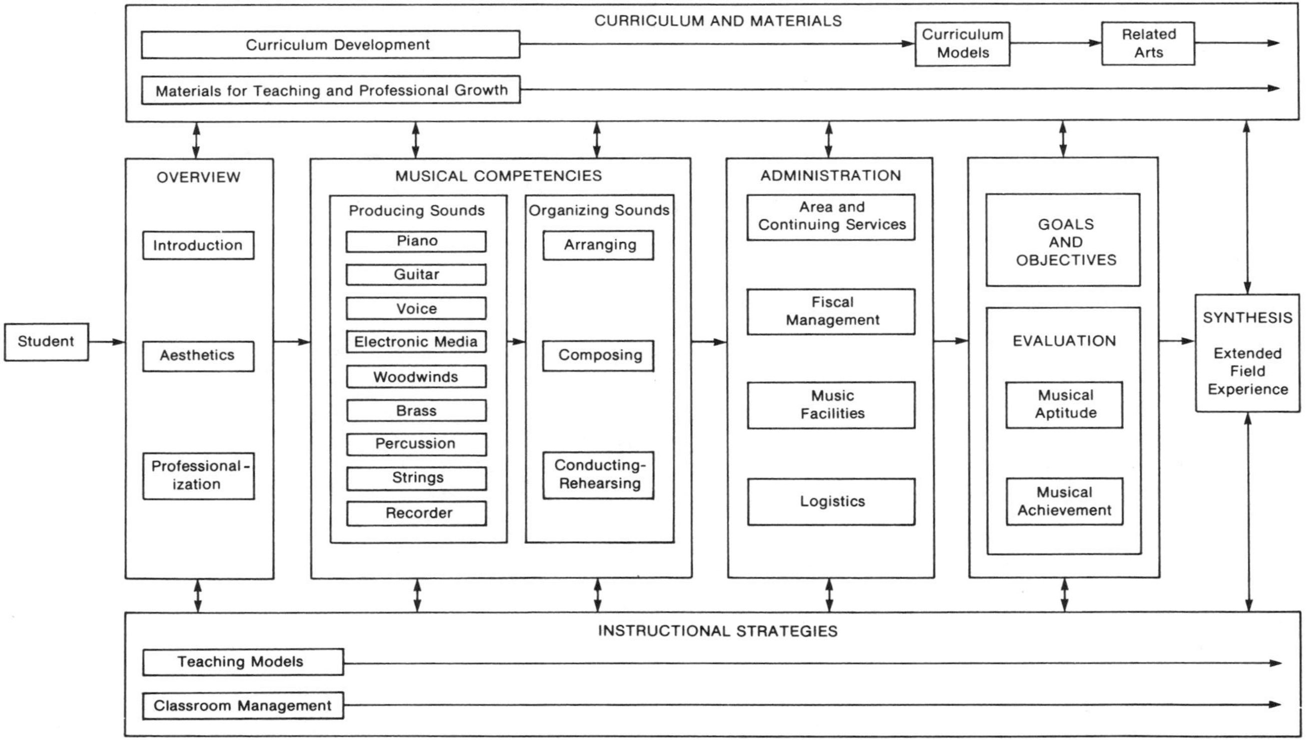

Ronald Lee and Paul E. Eickmann, © Center for Instructional Development, Syracuse University, Sept. 1973.

4. Institutions should encourage observation and teaching experiences prior to formal admission to the teacher education program; ideally, such opportunities should be provided in actual school situations. These activities, as well as continuing laboratory experiences, must be supervised by qualified music personnel from the institution and the cooperating schools.

MUSIC EDUCATION METHODS COURSES

Rather than offering the traditional courses in vocal, general, and instrumental methods, learning modules guide students through the necessary steps to learn how to teach music. The modules are based on predetermined competencies that successful teachers must achieve. Each module requires several activities of the learner, including research observation and practical application. Because the individuals help design their own programs, students may select different activities in order to achieve the same goal. As learning and skill development become more individualized, more variation must be introduced into modules in order to develop skills, abilities, and interests to their maximum. The activities specified in the module require learners to spend much time in actual school music programs and in simulated teaching situations, such as microteaching, where they observe, help teachers, and teach students prior to the actual student teaching, or internship, experience. By defining the separate competencies necessary for the teaching process, students are able to approach one problem at a time by observing successful teachers, developing skills in a particular area by practice and study, developing new methods of teaching, and by actual practice teaching. A possible danger in this mode of education is that the student will achieve many teaching competencies without developing either a broad view of the teaching process or the ability to integrate the competencies into a comprehensive teacher role. This danger is recognized by CBTE planners and practitioners, and conscious effort is made to avoid the problem.

The greatest problem of CBTE in music education is the identification of competencies that students are expected to achieve. The Commission on Teacher Education of MENC published a list of competencies recommended as the basis for granting certification to music teachers. They are as follows:

Personal Qualities

Music educators must:
1. Inspire others
2. Continue to learn in their own and in other fields
3. Relate to individuals and society

4. Relate to other disciplines and arts
5. Identify and evaluate new ideas
6. Use their imaginations
7. Understand the role of a teacher

Musical Competencies

All music educators must be able to:
1. Perform with musical understanding and technical proficiency
2. Play accompaniments
3. Sing
4. Conduct
5. Supervise and evaluate the performance of others
6. Organize sounds for personal expression
7. Demonstrate an understanding of the elements of music through original composition and improvisation in a variety of styles
8. Demonstrate the ability to identify and explain compositional choices of satisfactory and less satisfactory nature
9. Notate and arrange sounds for performance in school situations
10. Identify and explain compositional devices as they are employed in all musics
11. Discuss the affective results of compositional devices
12. Describe the means by which the sounds used in music are created

Professional Qualities

Music educators must be able to:
1. Express their philosophy of music and education
2. Demonstrate a familiarity with contemporary educational thought
3. Apply a broad knowledge of musical repertory to the learning problems of music students
4. Demonstrate, by example, the concept of a comprehensive musician dedicated to teaching[3]

Specific Applications of CBTE

To demonstrate how a module is developed and used in music education, let us isolate one important skill that successful junior high or middle school choral directors must master. They must be able to listen to student singers and then analyze, evaluate, predict, and place students in the proper section of the chorus. A teacher who is unable to do this successfully will have a poorly balanced chorus and the individual singers may well develop vocal problems and poor attitudes toward singing. When the competencies for testing voices have been identified and agreed upon by the class participants, various learning activities are decided upon to help the student develop the competency to test voices successfully. Before the unit, or module, is begun, students are informed of the assessment criteria that will indicate successful completion of the module; they know in advance exactly what level of performance will be expected and under what conditions. The requirement will probably include listening to a certain number of children sing during a specified time span, and making correct decisions about their placement in a chorus.

Part of the learners' assignment might include listening to individual singers and choruses for specific qualities that will affect a teacher's ability to make predictions about singers. Students will also be expected to read much of the literature available about the subject, explore sources of material for voice testing, view films and videotapes, and work with children in a school. When the various assignments have been completed, the students will demonstrate competence in the predetermined method. If successful in terms of the criteria set forth in the evaluation section of the module, they have then completed the module and proceed to the next, which incorporates the skills and knowledge derived from previous modules. If the students do not develop the necessary competence, it is necessary to receive advice and guidance regarding particular weaknesses in order to correct or improve them. Students view their own performances via videotape and receive critiques from the professor, classroom teachers, and fellow students. Remediation may include the assignment of more reading and/or observation. If the weakness is in the selection of material for voice testing, research may be required to find more suitable material. If the weakness is in the relationship with children, more time might be spent observing teachers and working with children. Feedback concerning progress is continual to maintain constant awareness of how the learners relate to students. When ready, the students again demonstrate the competency developed while working on the module and during the ensuing remediation period.

For another example, let us segregate a competence required of instrumental music teachers—the ability to teach children to develop a correct clarinet embouchure and produce a good tone. In order to teach clarinet embouchure successfully, one must know what constitutes a correct embouchure, must be able to produce a good tone, must be able to impart the necessary information and guide skill development, and must have the ability to motivate children to learn. This module would

FIGURE 8.3. Suggested Components of Behavioral Objectives in Music Education

Questions to be Answered in Writing Behavioral Objectives	Examples of Verbs Used in Writing Behavioral Objectives			Musical Concepts/ Techniques/ Instruments to be Mastered
	General Verbs	Musical Verbs		
Who?	verbalize	*General*	*Instrumental*	*Melodic Concepts*
By whom?	comment	crescendo	shake	contours
To whom?	express	decrescendo	strike	phrases
With whom?	relate	accelerate	pluck	pitch
	report	retard	rub	sequence
What?	repeat	listen	bow	
With what?	explain	conduct	scrape	*Melodic Instruments*
To what?	react	accompany	strum	bells
What will be heard?	decide	rehearse	stroke	recorder
What will be observed?	determine	play	play	piano
What will be produced?	select	sing	blow	
What will be judged?	review	phrase		*Rhythm Concepts*
	research	improvise	*Body Movement*	beat
How?	distinguish	perform	leap	meter
In what way?	differentiate	sight read	march	patterns
Aurally? Visually?	group	practice	step	duration
How many?	isolate	write	hop	
How much?	match	tape	dance	*Rhythm Instrument*
How little?	outline	participate	tiptoe	drum
How often?	compare	involve	slide	tambourin
How well?	combine	chord	roll	sticks
How long?	finalize	present	spin	
	explore	teach	circle	*Harmonic Concepts*
Who will do what?	research	organize	swing	interval
How?	consider	identify	bend	chords
Where?	discover	follow	skip	part singing
When?	question	interpret	sway	
	discuss	imitate	swoop	*Harmonic Instrument*
	investigate	compose	jump	piano
		create	somersault	guitar
		vary		autoharp
		alter	*Head*	
		dictate	blink	*Form*
		analyze	nod	types
		select	turn	cultural and historical
		recreate	shake	origins
		experiment	flop	listening
		discriminate		reading
		recognize	*Feet and Legs*	composing
		orchestrate	tap toes	
		score	mark time	*Other Concepts*
		notate	click heels	tempo
		choreograph	step high	mood
		dramatize		timbre
		illustrate	*Hands and Arms*	dynamics
		arrange	tap	tonalities
			catch	staff
		Vocal	snap	clef
		sing	clap	notation
		chant	shake	lines & spaces
		call	roll	signs
		yell	point	symbols
		hum	throw	key signatures
		sigh	catch	
		moan	give	
		whistle	reach	
		shriek	take	
			gather	
			conduct	
			cue	

Note. Clifford K. Madsen and Cornelia Yarbrough. *Competency-Based Music Education* (Englewood Cliffs, N.J.: Prentice-Hall, 1980), p. 83

probably be one of several in a unit on teaching the clarinet (or woodwind instruments). Previous modules, which are prerequisite, would have assured the student's competence in selecting reeds, assembling the instrument, and playing it (to a minimum level of performance). Before the learners actually teach embouchure, they are expected to read the appropriate literature, view films and videotapes, observe accomplished clarinetists to learn variations of correct embouchure, and observe young clarinetists to learn the sequence of steps necessary to develop their embouchures. Learners are also required to teach the skill in a simulated experience to college students. Finally, the learners work in a school, or learning center, where they help individual students and develop the confidence and ability to work effectively with young clarinetists. The final task is to instruct a group of children of predetermined age or grade level to develop a good clarinet embouchure. The children's competencies in satisfactory tone production serve as the determining factor in evaluating the college students' competence to teach this aspect of clarinet playing.

The same pattern is followed for the various methods courses. Students learn to teach instruments, voice, musical knowledge and concepts, and direct ensembles by developing a sequence of competencies that eventually evolve into the ability to guide children in musical learnings and skills. Rather than being isolated from real life experiences, students learn by actually participating. They develop specific competencies; the demonstration of the competencies replaces traditional examinations and quizzes that determine the success of students in conventional programs. Competency development also provides realistic and meaningful evaluative criteria for the potential employer who must evaluate the quality of the collegiate work of applicants for teaching positions.

If the program is accredited by a state department of education as a CBTE program, then the students are eligible for teaching certificates because the state has approved the competencies that have been developed and the methods by which they have been achieved.

ANOTHER VIEW OF CBTE

Many educators have expressed reservations about CBTE because some of its tenets and practices are based upon assumption, opinion, and casual observation. It is generally conceded that the system is imperfect, but many states have nevertheless expressed sufficient confidence in the program to base teacher certification requirements on it. Andrews identified four commonly held assumptions about CBTE that are in fact false:

1. A list exists which includes the basic competencies all teachers should possess and be able to demonstrate.

TEACHING STRATEGY 8.1—DAILY LESSON PLAN

when?   *who?*

20 minutes

Pinpoint: At the end of (class, lesson increment) the   class
will demonstrate acceptable   student
                group
                class

What?   *How?*

singing and stepping to   singing and stepping the
quarter and eighth notes   rhythm of the song, "Sewing
                            Needle" with 95% accuracy while
                            standing next to desks with eyes
                            closed

—————————————— by ——————————————

Examples: Examples:
Performance ability   Playing the entire piece
sight-singing   without stopping
    proficiency   Sight-reading 8 measures
research of the classical   with 80% accuracy
    period   Submitting a 20-page re-
                            port free from factual
                            error

Record: (See above format)
At the beginning of the   lesson   the
       class   demonstrated   approximately
20% accuracy in stepping quarter and eighth-note rhythm
combinations
by stepping the rhythm to the song, "Sewing Needle" at their
desks with their eyes closed.

Consequate: *Time allotted for lesson or lesson increment:*   20 minutes

     A. What you will do: Teach song—extrapolate combinations
        of   and   notes; have students imitate with steps,
        claps and words—play game with students in a chain,
        "sewing" each other—allow students to lead the needle
        while singing and stepping
     B. How the student will respond (anticipation of success and
        failures): Students will forget to step in rhythm in their
        enthusiasm for the game—will need to prompt for the first
        two or three leaders
     C. Audio-visual aids (use at least two per lesson):
        (1) small & large pictures of needles & thread
           corresponding to rhythm of song
        (2) Metallaphone to play ostinato

Evaluate: A. Students' successes and failures: approximately 30% of
        students were not able to transfer the idea of stepping in
        the game to stepping in place
     B. Teacher's successes and failures: Failed to teach for
        transfer from game to stepping in place—successful in
        teaching song and eliciting imitation from students

Note. Clifford K. Madsen and Cornelia Yarbrough. *Competency-Based Music Education* (Englewood Cliffs, N.J.: Prentice-Hall, 1980), p. 84.

TEACHING STRATEGY 8.2

Teacher Training Module for High School Music Theory I

OBJECTIVE

By the completion of this module the student will demonstrate the competency to teach high school students the basic elements of pitch and rhythm as described in the high school theory outline (see Theoretical Objectives).

PREREQUISITES

A. Completion of the module on instructional objectives
   1. Knowledge of rationale for and use of behavioral objectives
   2. Ability to develop and write all levels of behavioral objectives
   3. Ability to assess behavioral objectives

B. Completion of piano proficiency requirements
   1. Ability to play all major and minor scales (two octaves)
   2. Ability to sight-read piano music of the level of a Bach chorale
   3. Ability to play major, minor, augmented, and diminished triads in all inversions
   4. Ability to transpose a simple block chord melody to keys up to two sharps and two flats away from the key of the song, and to the related minor key
   5. Ability to harmonize a simple melody at the piano in suitable style

C. Completion of all previous modules

PRE-ASSESSMENT

A. The student must have achieved the objectives set forth in the high school theory course under pitch and rhythm (see Instructional Objectives).

B. The student will write lesson plans for three classes, specifying objectives, instructional activities, materials (including text, audiovisual media, and evaluation).

LEARNING ACTIVITIES

A. The student will evaluate each of the texts listed in the Bibliography for Teacher Training Module. Use the Text Evaluation form.

B. The student will compile a list of software that are useful for teaching pitch and rhythm, and evaluate each.

C. The student will observe the videotapes in the Learning Resource Center on the teaching of pitch and rhythm concepts to high school students. Evaluate in writing the following: teaching techniques, planning, use of audiovisual media, general effectiveness of the teacher.

D. The student will observe 5 consecutive high school theory classes, and write an evaluation of each.

E. The student will write lesson plans for objectives A1 and A2 (see Instructional Objectives), and have a conference with the professor to evaluate the lesson plans.

F. The student will teach the lessons as planned (see above), using microteaching techniques.

Teaching Strategy 8.2 (cont.)

POSTASSESSMENT

A. The student will write lesson plans for objectives A3, A4, B1, and B2 (see Instructional Objectives).

B. The student will present one of the above lessons in a simulated teaching situation.

C. The student will write a self-assessment of success in preparing and presenting this lesson, citing particular strengths and/or weaknesses in his teaching. Note evidence of improvement.

D. After discussing the self-assessment with the professor, the student is to write a summary of his performance and progress in this module, including suggestions of how improvement may be brought about in needed areas. The student is to have another conference with the professor to discuss the summary.

REMEDIATION

A. If the student did not complete this module successfully, he is to implement the suggested procedures for improvement or remediation.

B. The student will have a conference with the professor to discuss the remedial steps taken and evaluate his/her success in their implementation.

Theoretical Objectives for High School Music Theory I

Goal 1—By the completion of the semester the student will understand musical terms and symbols.
Goal 2—By the end of the semester the student will be able to perceive and demonstrate knowledge of the elements of music.

OBJECTIVES TO BE DEVISED FOR THE
FOLLOWING COURSE OUTLINE

A. Pitch
    1. Staff
    2. Clefs
    3. Notes—pitch
    4. Introduction to keyboard
    5. Whole and half steps
    6. C scale

B. Rhythm
    1. Pulse
    2. Grouping metrical divisions
    3. Quarter note
    4. Measure—bar
    5. Quarter rest
    6. Other note and rest values to the eighth
    7. Meter signatures (4/4, 2/4, 3/4)
    8. Dotted values—tied notes

Teaching Strategy 8.2 (cont.)

   C. Melody
- 1. Structure
- 2. Tempo
- 3. Simple composition
- 4. Dynamics
- 5. Different keys
  - a. Scales
  - b. Key signatures
- 6. Accidentals
- 7. Transposition
- 8. More complex rhythms
- 9. Minor keys
- 10. Intervals

   D. Harmony
- 1. Triads
  - a. Major
  - b. Minor
- 2. Tonic, subdominant, dominant
- 3. Harmonic symbols
- 4. Cadences
- 5. Harmonize simple melody
- 6. Inversions
- 7. Dominant seventh

Instructional Objectives for High School Music Theory I

A. Pitch
1. Given a grand staff, the student will write 10 given notes in their correct places in 90 seconds or less without error.
2. Given a grand staff with no more than 2 ledger lines above and below, the student will write 6 given notes in 60 seconds or less with 5/6 accuracy or better.
3. Given a grand staff with 15 written pitches, the student will play all of them correctly on the piano in 2 minutes or less.
4. Given a written 3-octave C-major scale, ascending and descending, the student will play that scale on the piano and, while playing, name the whole and half steps as they occur, without error, in 2 minutes or less.

B. Rhythm
1. Given 3 8-measure rhythm lines in 4/4, 3/4, 2/4, the student will write bars and accents over strong beats with 90% accuracy in 2 minutes or less.
2. Given 4 2-measure rhythm patterns played on the piano, the student will write the meter and write the rhythmic notation with 80% accuracy. Each pattern will be played 2 times.

C. Melody
1. Given a written melody of the difficulty and length of "Oh, Susanna!,"

Teaching Strategy 8.2 (cont.)

the student will bracket and indicate by letter the sections with 100% accuracy in 5 minutes or less. The student may play or sing the piece as an aid.

2. Given 4 2-measure rhythm patterns played on the piano, the "Oh, Susanna!," the student will bracket and indicate by letter the sections with 100% accuracy in 5 minutes; he may play or sing the piece as an aid.

3. The student will write a 4-phrase song indicating tempo. The structure will be based on repetition and complementary phrases.

4. Given the student's composition, he will write at least 2 sets of dynamics and will perform the piece vocally or instrumentally with 90% accuracy. The student may choose to perform publicly or privately.

5. Given the student's composition, he will transpose it into 2 different major keys, with key signatures, with 85% accuracy during one class period.

6. Given a written 16-measure melody, the student will circle and write the names of the accidentals with 100% accuracy in 2 minutes or less.

7. Given a short written melody with meter that uses dotted rhythms and note values no less than 16th notes, the student will write in barlines and will write a slash over the beginning of each beat with 100% accuracy in five minutes or less.

8. Given 10 written perfect, major, and minor intervals, the student will write the names of the intervals with 80% accuracy in 5 minutes or less.

9. Given 4 major keys from 4 flats to 4 sharps, the student will write and play on the piano, 1 octave ascending and descending, the relative natural, harmonic, and melodic minor scales with 80% accuracy in 25 minutes or less.

10. Given 10 written songs, the student will write the key name for each with 80% accuracy in 10 minutes or less.

D. Harmony

1. Given 3 written major and 3 written minor scales, the student will write triads on the tonic, dominant, and subdominant with 100% accuracy in 3 minutes or less.

2. Given any key up to 4 sharps and 4 flats, the student will play on the piano either the tonic, subdominant, or dominant triad, as instructed. Required accuracy is at least 8 out of 10, allowing 15 seconds for each chord for pianists and 30 seconds for nonpianists.

3. Given 2 8-measure written melodies in the key of C major, the student will write a correct harmonization in block chords and play them on the piano within one class period.

4. Given an 8-measure written melody, including the bass line and the symbols $\frac{6}{3}$--$\frac{6}{4}$-- , the student will write the correct chord tones with 75% accuracy in 20 minutes or less.

5. Given written melodic cadences in the keys of C, F, and G major and their relative minor keys, the student will write and play on the piano 6 perfect authentic and plagal cadences, as instructed, with accuracy of at least 5, in 15 minutes or less.

Bibliography for Teacher-Training Module

TEXTS

Cass, Jeanette. *Rudiments of Music*. New York: Appleton-Century-Crofts, 1956.

Castellini, John. *Rudiments of Music*. New York: W. W. Norton, 1962.

Fischer, Hans. *Practical Harmony*. Boston: Allyn & Bacon, 1964.

Jones, George T. *Music Theory*. New York: Barnes and Noble, 1974

Ottman, Robert. *Elementary Harmony*. Englewood Cliffs, N.J.: Prentice-Hall, 1970.

Siegmeister, Elie. *Harmony and Melody*. Belmont, Calif.: Wadsworth, 1967.

Swift, Jonathan, *Elementary Theory*. New York: Belwin Mills, 1968.

PROGRAMMED TEXTS

Barnes, Robert. *Fundamentals of Music: A Program for Self-Instruction*. New York: McGraw-Hill, 1965.

Batcheller, John. *Musical Notation*. Chicago: Encyclopedia Britannica Educational Corporation, 1964.

Carlsen, James C. *Melodic Perception: A Program for Self-Instruction*. New York: McGraw-Hill, 1965.

Dallin, Leon. *Foundations in Music Theory*. Belmont, Calif.: Wadsworth, 1962.

Harder, Paul. *Basic Materials in Music Theory*. Boston: Allyn & Bacon, 1968.

Martin, Gary. *Basic Concepts in Music*. Belmont, Calif.: Wadsworth, 1969.

Text Evaluation for Bibliography for
Teacher-Training Module

Bibliographical data:

Is this book written in language that the high school student can understand?

Does this book provide adequate illustrations and musical examples?

Does this book provide material for homework?

Does this book provide material for review?

Does this book contain supplementary material such as bibliography and suggested activities?

How would you rate the organization and presentation of material in this book?

Will this book fulfill the stated objectives of the high school music theory course?

Would you use this book for such a course? State your reasons.

TEACHING STRATEGY 8.3

WEBER STATE COLLEGE
INDIVIDUALIZED PERFORMANCE-BASED
TEACHER EDUCATION PROGRAM
June 1981

WILKIT: The Language of Music
APPROXIMATE TIME TO COMPLETE: 10–14 hours
MATERIALS: Enclosures: (1) Check List;
(2) Programmed Book, *The Language of Music*

EXPERIENCES TO BE SCHEDULED IN ADVANCE:

1. One Seminar (Learning Experience 1)
2. Optional group sessions (Learning Experience 3)

Teaching Strategy 8.3 (cont.)

3. Conference with the faculty advisor (Proficiency Assessment)
All scheduled experiences in the WILKIT (seminars, faculty conferences, examinations) are made through the Operations Center unless otherwise indicated.

INTRODUCTION:

The purpose of this WILKIT is to help you master some basic music concepts necessary for teaching music in the elementary school. However, it is suggested that if you have had no previous music training that you enroll in one of the two music classes for elementary teachers that are taught each quarter in the music department. The course numbers of these classes are: Music 169 and Music 320.

Music is a very important part of the teaching day on the elementary school level. The state department of education requires that music be taught 150 minutes per week/per classroom. That amounts to two and one-half hours of music each week. Therefore, it is important and necessary that each elementary teacher education major be adequately prepared to teach music effectively to elementary classroom children.

The subject matter in the WILKIT is very limited and simplified in order to encourage you as well as appeal to you as an adult student. This WILKIT does not attempt to teach you methods of teaching music to children, but only provides you with learning experiences in basic music skills and music concepts which will help you understand and interpret written music.

SUMMARY OF CONTENT:

1. The Music Staff and Piano Keyboard
2. Time Signatures
3. Beat Patterns
4. Key Signatures
5. Glossary of Musical Terms and Symbols

PRE-ASSESSMENT:

If you can pass the Post-Assessment with a score of 100% you will not be required to take the WILKIT. The Post-Assessment consists of questions that deal with basic music theory and is designed for students who have had previous music training.

The WILKIT will not be required of any student who has credit in Music 169 or Music 320. However, the student who has had either of these classes or passes the Post-Assessment with a score of 100%, will discuss basic music theory with the faculty advisor during the proficiency check out for WILKIT 40.

INSTRUCTIONAL OBJECTIVES:

Upon completion of the Learning Experiences in this WILKIT, you will be able to:
1. Demonstrate your comprehension of the letter names of the music staff lines and spaces by writing the correct letter names on a blank music staff.
2. Demonstrate your knowledge of the treble clef note syllable names and the treble clef note letter names in the Key of C from the first ledger line below the staff to the first ledger line above the staff by writing the note syllable names on a staff of musical notes.
3. Apply our knowledge of the keyboard by writing the letter names on the

Teaching Strategy 8.3 (cont.)

piano keys of a drawing of the section of the paino keyboard from Middle C to two octaves above Middle C.

4. Analyze the given time signatures of the staff of notes by dividing, with written measure bars, each staff into correct measures according to the following time signatures:

$\frac{2}{4}$ $\frac{3}{4}$ $\frac{4}{4}$ $\frac{6}{8}$.

5. Analyze eight key signatures by drawing a whole note in the position of "do" in each of the 8 key signatures and by writing the name of the key under each key signature.

6. Demonstrate your knowledge of music terms and symbols by defining or identifying through multiple choice in a teacher-made test the musical terms and symbols described in this WILKIT.

7. Apply your knowledge of time beat patterns by drawing schematic figures indicating two-four, three-four, four-four, and six-eight time beat patterns and by numbering sequentially the beats in your figure.

LEARNING EXPERIENCES:

Note: Participation in both the seminar and the faculty-advisor check-out is required for credit for this WILKIT.

1. Attend a seminar (Scheduled Activity 39-1) with other students and the faculty advisor for discussion on how to proceed with the Learning Experiences in this WILKIT (All Instructional Objectives).

2. Study the programmed learning book, *Language of Music*, included in this WILKIT. It is divided into different colored sections by title. Section 1, Musical Staff, relates to Instructional Objectives 1, 2, and 3. Section 2, Time Signatures, relates to Instructional Objective 4. Section 3, Beat Patterns, relates to Instructional Objective 7. Section 4, Key Signatures, relates to Instructional Objective 5. Section 5, Glossary of Musical Terms and Symbols relates to Instructional Objective 6. (Instructional Objectives 1-7)

3. You may find it helpful to work with other students who are studying this WILKIT. Even if you choose to work alone, you may wish to meet in a seminar with other students who are working in this WILKIT. If so, you can sign up at the Operations Center. The Center will make the names of other students similarly interested available to you and you will then be responsible for making your own group meeting arrangements. (Instructional Objectives 1-7)

PROFICIENCY ASSESSMENT:

1. You will be required to pass a written examination on the material contained in the programmed learning book, *Language of Music*.

2. Schedule a conference (Scheduled Activity 39-2) with the faculty advisor. At this conference your written examination on the *Language of Music* will be evaluated with you.

Check List

Name _____	*Date*	*Completed*
Check out WILKIT—Operations Center	____	_____
Pre-Assessment	____	_____

Teaching Strategy 8.3 (cont.)

Learning Experiences:
1. Seminar (Scheduled Activity 39–1)   _____   _____
2. Reading—Programmed Book   _____
3. Group Study   _____

Proficiency Assessment:
1. Attendance at Seminar
    (Learning Experience 1)   _____   _____
2. Written Examination   _____
3. Faculty Conference
    (Scheduled Activity 39-2)   _____   _____

This Check List is designed as a tool for you. You can use it to schedule your time and keep track of your progress. No authorized signatures are required on this form.

Note. Copyright © WILKIT Educators Trust 1981.

2. Techniques exist to evaluate objectively whether or not a candidate actually has these competencies.
3. Research has shown which teacher competencies are related to children's learning.
4. Developing a competency system of preparation and evaluation is a relatively simple task and not likely to be more expensive than present systems.[4]

Carroll Gonzo, in his appraisal of CBTE, summarizes the need for a cautious approach to the subject:

CBE [CBTE] as a movement has rekindled self-examination of the teaching-learning process and has forced old and new questions into the academic and public arenas, and answers are wanting. It is important to raise such questions as 1. who is competent to judge competence, 2. what is competence, 3. what is basic, 4. where are the philosophical roots to justify CBE, 5. in what learning theory is it nested, and 6. what teaching theory embraces it. But asking and examining the questions as if to theoretically "blow away" CBE will not alter the fact that it is here and must be accommodated. Like all trends and movements in education, CBE is fraught with ambiguities and one would do well to consider them seriously. With the arrival of Competency Based Education, the pedagogical road to Eden has not unequivocally been found.[5]

Probably the most critical aspect of the relationship between CBTE and music education is the fact that an aesthetically based subject does not lend itself readily to the requirements of behavioral objectives. According to Schwadron,

Aesthetic matters were neatly placed in "affective domains." Considering the highly subjective nature of the arts, the covertness of the aesthetic experience, and the longitudinal factors critical to any true attempts at evaluation, the entire design looms up as a convenient misconception, musically and aesthetically fallacious and insensitive. First, the nature of music . . . does not lend itself to the immediacy of quantitative measures. Hence it is disappointing to hear from music educators that since the aesthetic response cannot be overtly observed, or objectively measured, *ergo* it cannot significantly contend with the "pressing" need for accountability. Second, it has been stated . . . that aesthetic responses cannot be taught. May I suggest . . . that if something is learned, *some* mode of teaching is responsible. . . . Finally, I truly hope that the time will draw near when we are willing to stand fast as sensitive educators *and* musicians to be counted among those who can recognize the totality of the musical arts and the consequent aesthetic import as antithetical to any extrinsic need for domains or taxonomies.[6]

Status of CBTE

CBTE and a variety of its offshoots are major factors in contemporary teacher education. Many states require what has by now become traditional competency-based teacher education programs, and others require some form of competency testing for selecting and certifying teachers. As of 1982, twenty-seven states had legislative or state department of education mandates to develop state-wide competency tests for teachers. Nine others were in a planning phase for competency testing. Thirty-six (including some of the above) were already involved to some degree in competency testing. Many states were assessing, or planning to assess, on-the-job performance.[7]

Regardless of the controversy stimulated by CBTE, and the difficulty of applying it to music education (and to the other arts), it has taken a firm hold in teacher education and certification. It appears that it will remain a factor, and will influence the education of music teachers in an increasing number of states in the future.

RESEARCH IN MUSIC EDUCATION

One of the areas of interest to which many music educators address themselves is research. The reasons for giving so much attention to an activity somewhat removed from the actual practice of teaching are numerous, but generally can be divided into three categories; (1) to discover solutions to practical problems in music education; (2) to satisfy personal curiosity about problems that can be solved only by the application of research techniques; and (3) to develop a body of knowledge about music education that can be utilized as needed by other researchers, practitioners, curriculum developers, and persons in such related professions as psychology, sociology, anthropology, and therapy, among others.

Research as a field of major interest is relatively new to the music education profession. Although music education research had been conducted for decades, it gained sufficient stature to be considered a serious aspect of the profession only when the *Journal of Research in Music Education (JRME)* began publication in 1953. From that time, MENC, which sponsors *JRME*, has been the main support for research activities in the United States outside of colleges and universities. Almost all music education research is done by faculty and graduate students, but MENC has provided various kinds of research events and outlets for publications that are beyond the means of institutions of higher education. Research is now the primary professional interest of many individuals serving on university faculties, and virtually all graduate music education students take at least one course in the subject. The purposes of such a course are to: (1) introduce students to the research process, including its rationale, techniques, and tools; (2) prepare students to become researchers in their own right, usually after they take more advanced courses in research, measurement, and statistical techniques; and (3) provide students with sufficient knowledge to be able to read research reports and articles knowledgeably and critically.

The Music Education Research Council

The impetus for MENC involvement in the sponsorship of research was the Educational Council. Established in 1918, it was the forerunner of the Music Education Research Council (MERC), the body that now governs MENC research activities. The publications of the Educational Council did not include the work of individual scholars as do current research journals. The Educational Council published bulletins, including curriculum guides, information on the training of music supervisors, and a variety of topics concerning music education. Most reports were based on survey data and included recommendations for the profession. One of the most significant reports of the Educational Council was *The Present Status of Music Instruction in Colleges and High Schools 1919–1920*, which was published as *Bulletin Number 9* by the U.S. Bureau of Education. The name of the Educational Council was changed in 1923 to the National Research Council of Music Education. The National Research Council continued to publish bulletins reporting on survey studies of various aspects of music education.

In 1932 the name of the National Research Council was changed again, this time to the Music Education Research Council (MERC), which has remained the research branch of MENC to the present day. MERC continued the research bulletin series, covering such topics as rural schools, music supervision, standard courses of study in music, basic programs of study, and music in the senior high school, among others.

The bulletin series was completed in 1940 with the publication of number 19. The best known of the bulletins is number 17, *Music Buildings, Rooms and Equipment*, which was written in 1934 and revised in 1949, 1955, and 1966.

The responsibilities of MERC are as follows:

1. To serve as the governing body of the SRME [Society for Research in Music Education] and implement the objectives of the society.
2. To organize and administer a suitable variety of research sessions at the national conventions of the MENC.
3. To coordinate and guide the work of the divisional and state research chairmen.
4. To cooperate, individually or collectively, with any agency or organization in any project likely to enhance the status of research in music education, improve the quality or increase the quantity of such research, or facilitate the application of the results of such research; and to support, encourage, and promote all types of research in music education and fields related to music education.
5. To advise and cooperate with the Curator of the MENC Historical Center and the University of Maryland in developing and administering the Center.
6. To function as a source of information, coordination, and communication in all matters affecting research in music education nationally and internationally.
7. To recommend for publication, position papers relating to research problems (evaluation, design, measurement, value of inferential statistics, bibliography, curriculum, etc.) with a view to establishing guidelines in research practices in music education.
8. To sponsor institutes and publish proceedings for the purpose of critically examining current research findings in specific subject areas with a view toward their application and implementation in educational practice.
9. To cooperate with the President, National Executive Board, publication committee, or any other MENC committee or unit in matters relating to research in music education.[8]

From 1940 until 1960, MERC was relatively inactive. It had lost its impetus and was searching for a sense of direction that would provide stability. By 1960 the *Journal of Research in Music Education* had been in operation for seven years and had achieved stature in the profession. *JRME* and MERC cosponsored some joint projects, including the following publications: *Bibliography of Research Studies in Music Education, 1949–1957; American Index to the Musical Quarterly, 1915–1957; Music Education Materials—A Selected Bibliography* (1954); and *Basic Concepts in Music Education* (1958). These publications and other projects helped to revitalize MERC by making it meaningful to the profession.

The Society for Research in Music Education

The Society for Research in Music Education (SRME) was established in 1960 under the governance of MERC. The objective of SRME is "the encouragement and advancement of research in those areas pertinent to music education." Its aims are as follows:

1. Sponsor meaningful sessions at MENC national conventions devoted to reports of research studies and relevant topics.
2. Through its divisional and state units, sponsor similar sessions at the divisional and state levels.
3. Provide an effective framework for the exchange of information among persons engaged in or interested in research in music education.
4. Encourage all research in music education and in fields related to music education.[9]

In 1963 the *Journal of Research in Music Education* became the official publication of SRME. Members of MENC who subscribe to *JRME* are automatically members of SRME.

Special Research Interest Groups

In 1978 several Special Research Interest Groups (SRIG) were formed at the MENC national convention. The SRIGs, which operate under the governance of MERC, are vehicles to serve music educators who share similar research interests. There is a SRIG for each of the following topics: creativity, learning and development, general research, measurement and evaluation, affective response, history, instructional strategies, perception, and early childhood. Each SRIG publishes a newsletter and meets at MENC national conventions for the purpose of discussing its particular research area and presenting research findings.

The MENC Historical Center

The MENC Historical Center was established at the University of Maryland, College Park in 1965. MENC and the University of Maryland share the support costs and governance of the center. The purpose of the MENC Historical Center is "to preserve the documents and materials that have reflected and influenced the history of musical instruction in the United States."[10] It is an outstanding archive of materials relevant to the history of MENC and to American music education in general. It shares its facility with the International Piano Archives and the archival collections of the American Bandmasters Association (ABA), the National Association of College Wind and Percussion Instructors (NACWAPI), the Music Library Association (MLA), and the International Clarinet Society.

The Journal of Research in Music Education

The *Journal of Research in Music Education* began publication in 1953 under the editorship of Allen P. Britton, whose title was Chairman of the

Editorial Committee. The original purpose of *JRME* was to publish "articles which report the results of research in any phase of music education." For a number of years, many of the articles were based on historical and descriptive research. In the early 1960s, music educators, like educators in other fields, began to value experimental methods, and articles based on that kind of research began to find their way into *JRME*. By the time Robert G. Petzold became editor in 1972, the majority of articles were based on experimental and descriptive research techniques. James C. Carlsen became editor in 1978, George L. Duerksen (acting editor) in 1981, and Jack A. Taylor in 1982. The journal now publishes "reports of research that clearly make a contribution to theories of music education." Included are experimental, descriptive, and historical research reports.

The Council for Research in Music Education

The Council for Research in Music Education (CRME) was founded in 1963 by the University of Illinois and the Illinois Office of the Superintendent of Public Instruction. The CRME *Bulletin* is published by the University of Illinois. Each issue of the *Bulletin* contains a few articles and several reviews by CRME members of doctoral dissertations. CRME also publishes indexes of music education doctoral dissertations in progress and of recently completed dissertations available for review in the *Bulletin*.

Other Research Journals

Although the *Journal of Research in Music Education* has been the major outlet for music education research for many years, other journals were established for specialized kinds of research or to provide more opportunity for persons in particular states to publish the results of their research.

The *Missouri Journal of Research in Music Education*, established in 1962, is a publication of the Missouri State Department of Education. The journal publishes "contributions of a philosophical, historical or scientific nature which reports the results of research pertinent in any way to instruction in music in the educational institutions of Missouri."

The *Bulletin of Research* was founded in 1963 and is sponsored by the Pennsylvania Music Educators Association. Its policy is as follows:

The Editorial board encourages and solicits written reports of innovative teaching efforts which show positive results in actual practice. Although some researchers feel that informality results in questionable validity and reliability, the Editorial Board of the Bulletin feels that many valuable projects go unrecognized. In our opinion, certain of these efforts are true research and deserve to be reported. The more formal and characteristic research reports are nonetheless important, and the Editorial Board feels a continued need to report them as well as applied research that may not conform to traditional research patterns. Articles which synthesize research studies from a variety of sources also are solicited.

Contributions to Music Education is the research journal of the Ohio Music Educators Association. It was started in 1972

to support scholarly work in Music Education conducted in Ohio primarily and in the field of Music Education as a whole secondarily. The intent of the journal is to provide a needed addition to the existing journals of research in Music Education in the United States. . . . *Contributions* contains research reports, speculations about research, book reviews, and discussions about knowledge in music education and research methodology. All forms of inquiry are to be included—descriptive, experimental, historical, and philosophical as well as unusual speculative articles.

The Bulletin of Historical Research in Music Education was founded in 1980 as an outgrowth of the newly established History Special Research Interest Group of MENC. It is published at the University of Kansas. It serves as a forum for historians in music education, an outlet for publication of research findings in the history of music education, and as a source of information pertinent to research in the history of the profession. In it is published "research of a philosophical and historical nature pertinent in any way to music education."

Update: The Applications of Research in Music Education, established in 1982, is published by the Department of Music of the University of South Carolina. It contains research articles reported in nontechnical language and articles about research. "All articles must be research-based." They may take the form of a "review of the literature or may report the findings of a single research study if that study is of sufficient scope." Emphasis is on interpretation and application in the classroom rather than on research procedures and statistics.

In addition to the above, there are several foreign journals that publish research articles pertinent to music education. The International Society for Music Education (ISME) sponsors several commissions, one of which is the Research Commission. It meets before each biennial general meeting of ISME to share research findings of international interest.

Other Research Activities

THE ANN ARBOR SYMPOSIUM

In 1978, 1979, and 1981 MENC sponsored the Ann Arbor Symposium on the Applications of Psychology to the Teaching and Learning of Music at the University of Michigan. The University of Michigan and the Theodore Presser Foundation were cosponsors. The purpose of the Symposium was to explore the relationship between research in certain areas of behavioral psychology and music education.

In Session I (1978), papers were presented by leading music education researchers to acquaint the participating psychologists with music education practices, and to present issues to which research psychologists might contribute their knowledge and expertise. Session II (1979) consisted of presentations of papers by the psychologists on the topics discussed by the music educators the year before. Each presentation in Session I was followed by a response from a psychologist, and in Session II by a music educator. The topics of the sessions are as follows:

Session I (1978)

Auditory Perception: Concerns for Musical Learning (James C. Carlsen)

Auditory Perception in Music Teaching and Learning (Jack J. Heller and Warren C. Campbell)

Psychomotor Skills (Steven K. Hedden)

Motor Learning in Music Education (Robert G. Sidnell)

Child Development (Robert G. Petzold)

Child Development and Music Education (Marilyn P. Zimmerman)

Music Learning and Learning Theory (Edwin E. Gordon)

Cognition and Musical Development (Gerard L. Knieter)

Children's Processing and Remembering of Music: Some Speculations (Henry L. Cady)

Music Information Processing and Memory (David Brian Williams)

An Operant Approach to Motivation and Affect: Ten Years of Research in Music Learning (R. Douglas Greer)

Motivation and Affect (Malcolm J. Tait)

Session II (1979)

Mental Structures Through Which Music Is Perceived (W. Jay Dowling)

Individual Differences in the Perception of Musical Pitch (Roger N. Shepard)

Perceptual and Motor Schemas in the Performance of Musical Pitch (David Laberge)

Culturally Defined Learning Experience (Jane A. Siegel)

Musical Illusions and Handedness (Diana Deutsch)

Music and Language (Roger Brown)

Music Ability and Patterns of Cognition (Ruth S. Day)

Toward a Linkage System Between Psychology and Music Education (Asahel D. Woodruff)

The Acquisition of Song: A Developmental Approach (Lyle Davidson, Patricia McKernon, and Howard E. Gardner)

Hedgehog Theory and Music Education (Edward L. Walker)

Motivational Determinants of Music-Related Behavior: Psychological Careers of Student, Teacher, Performer, and Listener (Joel O. Raynor)

Encounters: The American Child's Meeting with Music (William Kessen)

Session III (1981)

Presented "to provide further structured contacts with psychologists." The topics were as follows:

Task Involvement in Music (John G. Nicholls)

The Development of Continuing Interests in Music (Martin L. Maehr)

Directing Creativity: Marching with Different Drummers (Stanley S. Gryskiewicz)

Step-Path Theory and the Motivation for Achievement (Joel O. Raynor)

Creativity and Talent (Michael A. Wallach)

Children's Motivation to Study Music (Jacquelynne Eccles Parsons)

Aesthetics, Biography, and History in Musical Creativity (Dean Keith Simonton)

Musical Chairs: Who Drops Out of Music Instruction and Why? (Martin V. Covington)

Fostering Creativity and Problem Solving (Donald J. Treffinger)

THE WESLEYAN SYMPOSIUM ON THE APPLICATION OF SOCIAL ANTHROPOLOGY TO THE TEACHING AND LEARNING OF MUSIC

The Wesleyan Symposium was held in August 1984 under the sponsorship of Wesleyan University, MENC, and the Theodore Presser Foundation at Wesleyan University in Middletown, Connecticut. The titles of the presentations were as follows:

The Person as a Work of Art: Music and Dance in Hopi, Polynesian, and Other Cultures (Joann W. Keali'inohomoku)

Music Tradition as a Result of the Effect of Experience on Perception (Robert Garfias)

Paideia con Salsa (charles M. H. Keil)

Versus Gradus Novos ad Parnassum Musicum: Exemplum Africanum (John Blacking)

Ethnomusicology as an Instructional Tool (Gerald T. Johnson)

Music that Is Learned, but Not Taught: The Case of Bulgaria (Timothy Rice)

Tshiyanda na Ululi: Boundaries of Independence, Music Life and Education in Tshokwe Society (Barbara Schmidt-Wrenger)

Polynesian Music and Dance: Traditional Transmission and the Transmission of Tradition (Adrienne L. Kaeppler)

Processes of Transmission: Music Education and Social Inclusion (Carol E. Robertson)

Montana and Iran: Learning and Teaching in the Conceptions of Music in Two Contrasting Cultures (Bruno Nettl)

NOTES

1. Dennis M. Holt. "Competency Based Music Teacher Education: Is Systematic Accountability Worth the Effort?" *Bulletin* of the Council for Research in Music Education n. 40, Winter 1974, p. 1.

2. Robert Klotman, ed. *Teacher Education in Music: Final Report.* Washington, D.C.: Music Educators National Conference, 1973.

3. *Teacher Education in Music* (Washington, D.C.: Music Educators National Conference, 1972), pp. 4–7.

4. T. E. Andrews. "What We Know and What We Don't Know." In Houston (ed.), *Exploring Competency Based Education.* Berkeley, Cal.: McCutchan Publishing Company, 1979.

5. Carroll Gonzo, "A Critical Look at Competency Based Education." *Contributions to Music Education,* 1981/1982, p. 181.

6. Abraham A. Schwadron, "Music Education and Teacher Preparation: Pespectives from the Aesthetics of Music." *Journal of Musicological Research,* 1982, p. 181.

7. Task Force on Shortage/Surplus/Quality Issues in Teacher Education. *The Impact of Teacher Shortage and Surplus on Quality Issues in Teacher Education* (Washington, D.C.: American Association of Colleges for Teacher Education, 1983) p. 40.

8. "Handbook of the Society for Research in Music Education." *Journal of Research in Music Education* V. XIX n. 2, Summer 1971, p. 243.

9. Ibid., p. 239.

10. Ibid., p. 249.

BIBLIOGRAPHY

The Education of Music Teachers

American Association of Colleges of Teacher Education. *Performance-Based Teacher Education: An Annotated Bibliography.* Washington, D.C.: American Association of Colleges for Teacher Education, 1972.

Brookhart, C. Edward, ed. *Graduate Music Teacher Education Report.* Reston, Va.: Music Educators National Conference, 1982.

Burke, Caseel. *The Individualized Competency-Based System of Teacher Education at Weber State College.* Washington, D.C.: American Association of Colleges for Teacher Education, 1972. An overview of the rationale, structure, and techniques of a CBTE program in a school that bases its entire curriculum on CBTE principles.

Elam, Stanley. *Performance-Based Teacher Education: What is the State of the Art?* Washington, D.C.: American Association of Colleges for Teacher Education, 1971. An introduction to CBTE. This book provides a basic description and rationale for the philosophy and concepts of CBTE.

Elfenbein, Iris M. *Performance-Based Teacher Education Programs: A Comparative Description.* Washington, D.C.: American Association of Colleges for Teacher Education, 1972. A description and analysis of several CBTE programs as they exist at specific colleges. Included are several diagrams and flow charts of programs, a list of CBTE institutions, a selected bibliography, and a glossary of CBTE terms.

Gonzo, Carroll. "A Critical Look at Competency-Based Education." *Contributions to Music Education,* 1981/82, no. 5, pp. 77–84.

Madsen, Clifford K.; and Yarbrough, Cornelia. *Competency-Based Music Education.* Englewood Cliffs, N.J.: Prentice-Hall, 1980.

Mountford, Richard D. "Competency-Based Teacher Education: The Controversy and a Synthesis of Related Research in Music from 1964 to 1974." *Bulletin,* Council for Research in Music Education, no. 46, Spring 1976, pp. 1–12.

National Association of Schools of Music. *Handbook.* Reston, Va.: Contains National Association of Schools of Music, 1974. NASM standards and recommendations for collegiate music and music education programs.

National Commission on Accrediting. *Accreditation in Music.* Reston, Va.: National Commission on Accrediting, 1969. Report of the Commission.

Schwadron, Abraham A. "Music Education and Teacher Preparation: Perspectives from the Aesthetics of Music." *Journal of Musicological Research,* 1982, pp. 176–92.

Task Force on Shortage/Surplus/Quality Issues. *The Impact of Teacher Shortage and Surplus on Quality Issues in Teacher Education.* Washington, D.C.: American Association of Colleges for Teacher Education., 1983.

Teacher Education Commission. *Teacher Education in Music: Final Report.* Washington, D.C.: Music Educators National Conference, 1972.

Wolfe, Irving. *State Certification of Music Teachers.* Washington, D.C.: Music Educators National Conference, 1972. An overview of music teacher certification practices and requirements, and specific certification criteria for each state.

Research in Music Education

Barnes, Stephen H. *A Cross-Section of Research in Music Education.* Washington, D.C.: University Press of America, 1982.

Boisen, Robert. "Selected Recent Art Education Research: Its Implications for Research in Music Education." *Bulletin,* Council for Research in Music Education, no. 64, Fall 1980, pp. 1–11.

Deihl, Ned C.; and Kenneth C. Partchey. "Status of Research: Educational Technology in Music Education." *Bulletin,* Council for Research in Music Education, no. 35, Winter 1973, pp. 18–29.

Documentary Report of the Ann Arbor Symposium: Applications of Psychology to the Teaching and Learning of Music. Reston, Va.: Music Educators National Conference, 1981.

Documentary Report of the Ann Arbor Symposium Session III: Applications of Psychology to the Teaching and Learning of Music. Reston, Va.: Music Educators National Conference, 1983.

Documentary Report of the Wesleyan Symposium on the Application of Social Anthropology to the Teaching and Learning of Music. Reston, Va.: Music Educators National Conference, 1985.

Gonzo, Carroll. "Research in Choral Music: A Perspective." *Bulletin*, Society for Research in Music Education, no. 33, Summer 1973, pp. 21–33.

Grashel, John W. "Doctoral Research in Music Student Teaching: 1962–1971." *Bulletin*, Council for Research in Music Education, no. 78, Spring 1984, pp. 24–32.

Greenberg, Marvin. "Research in Music in Early Childhood Education: A Survey with Recommendations." *Bulletin*, Council for Research in Music Education, no. 45, Winter 1976, pp. 1–20.

"Handbook of the Society for Research in Music Education." *Journal of Research in Music Education* XIX, no. 2 (Summer 1971):238–52.

Heller, George; and Bruce Wilson. "Historical Research in Music Education." *Bulletin*, Council for Research in Music Education, no. 69, Winter 1982, pp. 1–20.

Hylton, John. "A Survey of Choral Education Research: 1972–1981." *Bulletin*, Council for Research in Music Education, no. 76, Fall 1983, pp. 1–29.

International Society for Music Education. Papers of the Second International Seminar on Research in Music Education. *Bulletin*, Council for Research in Music Education, no. 22, Fall 1970.

International Society for Music Education. Papers of the Sixth International Seminar on Research in Music Education. *Bulletin*, Council for Research in Music Education, no. 50, Spring 1977.

International Society for Music Education. Papers of the Seventh International Seminar on Research in Music Education. *Bulletin*, Council for Research in Music Education, no. 59, Summer 1979.

International Society for Music Education. Papers of the Eighth International Seminar on Research in Music Education. *Bulletin*, nos. 66–67, Spring-Summer 1981.

Jellison, Judith A. "The Frequency and General Mode of Inquiry of Research in Music Therapy, 1952–1972." *Bulletin*, Council for Research in Music Education, no. 35, Winter 1973, pp. 1–8.

Klemish, Janice. "A Review of Recent Research in Elementary Music Education." *Bulletin*, Council for Research in Music Education, no. 34, Fall 1973, pp. 23–40.

Lehman, Paul R. *Tests and Measurements in Music*. Englewood-Cliffs, N.J.: Prentice-Hall, Inc., 1968.

Leonhard, Charles; and Richard J. Colwell. "Research in Music Education." *Bulletin*, Council for Research in Music Education, no. 49, Winter 1976, pp. 1–30.

Madsen, Clifford K.; and Charles H. Madsen. *Experimental Research in Music Education*. Raleigh, N.C.: Contemporary Publishing, 1978.

———; and Randall S. Moore. *Experimental Research in Music* (workbook). Raleigh, N.C.: Contemporary Publishing, 1978.

Moog, Helmut. "Psychological Research in Music as the Basis of Music Education, Especially the Education of the Handicapped." *Bulletin*, Council for Research in Music Education, no. 62, Spring 1980, pp. 22–30.

Nelson, David J. "String Teaching and Performance: A Review of Research Findings." *Bulletin*, Council for Research in Music Education, no. 74, Spring 1983, pp. 39–48.

Phelps, Roger P. *A Guide to Research in Music Education*. 2nd ed. Metuchen, N.J.: The Scarecrow Press, 1980.

Rainbow, Edward. "Instrumental Music: Recent Research and Considerations for Future Investigations." *Bulletin*, Council for Research in Music Education, no. 33, Summer 1973, pp. 8–20.

Richardson, Carol Peterson. "Creativity Research in Music Education: A

Review." *Bulletin,* Council for Research in Music Education, no. 74, Spring 1983, pp. 1–21.

Saffle, Michael. "Aesthetic Education in Theory and Practice: A Review of Recent Research." *Bulletin,* Council for Research in Music Education, no. 74, Spring 1983, pp. 22–38.

Schwadron, Abraham A. "Philosophy in Music Education: State of the Research." *Bulletin,* Council for Research in Music Education, no. 34, Fall 1973, pp. 41–53.

Serafine, Mary L. "Piagetian Research in Music." *Bulletin,* Council for Research in Music Education, no. 62, Spring 1980, pp. 1–21.

Smith, Ralph A.; and Christiana M. Smith. *Research in the Arts and Aesthetic Education: A Directory of Investigators and Their Fields of Inquiry.* St. Louis: CEMREL, Inc., 1978.

Turrentine, Edgar. "Historical Research in Music Education." *Bulletin,* Council for Research in Music Education, no. 33, Summer 1973, pp. 1–7.

Wapnick, Joel. "A Review of Research on Attitude and Preference." *Bulletin,* Council for Research in Music Education, no. 48, Fall 1976, pp. 1–20.

Warren, Fred. "A History of the Music Education Research Council and The Journal of Research in Music Education of the Music Educators National Conference." Doctoral diss., University of Michigan, 1966. University Microfilms no. LC-66-14612.

Whybrew, William E. "Research in Evaluation in Music Education." *Bulletin,* Council for Research in Music Education, no. 35, Winter 1973, pp. 9–17.

Music Education Research Journals

Bulletin, Council for Research in Music Education. School of Music, the University of Illinois.

Bulletin of Historical Research in Music Education. Department of Art and Music Education and Music Therapy, the University of Kansas.

Bulletin of Research. Pennsylvania Music Educators Association.

Contributions to Music Education. Ohio Music Educators Association, Kent State University.

Journal of Research in Music Education. Reston, Va.: Music Educators National Conference.

Missouri Journal of Research in Music Education. Missouri State Department of Education.

Update. Department of Music, University of South Carolina.

INDEXES OF NATIONAL MUSIC EDUCATION RESEARCH JOURNALS

The Bulletin of Historical Research in Music Education

Vol. I, no. 1, July 1980

"The Music Educators National Conference and World War II Home Front Programs," Mark.

Vol. II, no. 1, Jan. 1981

"An Executive Secretary for the Music Educators National Conference: A Process of Organizational Change," Troth.

Vol. II, no. 2, July 1981

"Visionary of What Might Be: The Story of W. Otto Miessner," Miller.

Vol. III, no. 1, Jan. 1982

"The Founding of MENC: Reprints from *School Music Monthly*.

Vol. III, no. 2, July 1982

"Keokuk in 1907: More Reprints from School Music Monthly." "Music Education in the United States of America," Britton.

Vol. IV, no. 1, Jan. 1983

"The First Earned Doctorate in Music Education," Phelps.
"An Analysis of the Values Expressed in the Song Texts of an 1873 Music Education Book," Haack.

Vol. IV, no. 2, July 1983

"Music Reading Programs Established in Selected General Music Textbooks of the 1940's," Miller.
"The Effect of Eclecticism on American Music Education," Mark.

Bulletin of the Council for Research in Music Education

No. 1, 1963

"The Growth of Musical Awareness in Children," Kresteff.
"Music: An Important Subject for Learning Research," Spohn.
"Directions for Research in Music Education," Petzold.
"Newer Concepts in Learning Theory as They Apply to Music Education," Leonhard.
"Action Research Methodology," Pernecky.

No. 2, Winter 1964

"One Approach Toward the Development of an Individual Test For Assessing One Aspect of Instrumental Music Achievement," Gutsch.
"Automated Music Training," Ihrke.
"Information Theory and the Analysis of Musical Meaning," Reimer.
"Some Problems in the Evaluation of New Teaching," Shetler.
"Trends in Music Education Research," Ihrke.
"A Test of Musical Expression," Hoffren.

No. 3, Spring 1964

"Creativity, General Creative Abilities, and the Creative Individual," Ausubel.
"Patterning of Research Problems," Watson.
"The Synthesis of Music Education Research," Cady.
"Programs for Music in the U.S. Office of Education," Arberg.
"The Importance of Design in Research Studies," Colwell.
"To Know Or To Question," Spohn.

No. 4, Winter 1965

"The Development and Evaluation of Self-Instructional Materials in Basic Music Theory for Elementary Teachers," Hargiss.

"A Device to Facilitate Learning of Basic Music Skills," LaBach.

"Evaluation in Instrumental Music Performance: An Individual Approach," Gutsch.

"Implications of Recent Research Problems in Programmed Music Instruction," Carlsen.

"Aural and Visual Perception of Melody Presented in Tonal and Atonal Musical Environments," Sherman.

No. 5, Spring 1965

"Patterns of Meaning in Aesthetic Education," Smith.

"A Survey of American and British Solo Vocal Literature to Select and Evaluate Songs, the Musical and Technical Demands of Which do not Exceed the Abilities of Physical Limitations of High School Singers Whose Talents Range from Average to Excellent," Toms.

"The Theory of Expectation Applied to Music Listening," Colwell.

No. 6, Fall 1965

"Innovation and Experiment in Music Education," Turner.

"An Approach to Musical Understanding for Secondary School Students: A Curriculum Development Project," Wendrich.

"The Musical Aptitude Profile: A New and Unique Musical Aptitude Test Battery," Gordon.

"The Development of Specialized Programs for Singing in the Elementary School," Gould.

"A Study of New Concepts, Procedures, and Achievements in Music Learning as Developed in Selected Music Education Programs," Thomas.

No. 7, Spring 1966

"How Children Conceptually Organize Musical Sounds," Pflederer.

"Correlation of Musical Talents and Behavioral Traits in Elementary School Children," Greenberg, MacGregor.

"Automated Rhythm Training (Progress Report)," Ihrke.

No. 8, Fall 1966

"An Analysis of Student Attitudes Towards Contemporary American Music," Hornyak.

"Factors Affecting Pitch Discrimination," Bergan.

"Evaluation of Electronic Self-Instruction on Piano Keyboard," Lund.

"Development and Trial of a Basic Course in Music Theory Using Self-Instructional Materials to Supplement Training Received in High School Performance Groups," Andrews.

"Development and Trial of a Two Year Program in String Instruction," Rolland and Colwell.

"The Kodály System in the Elementary Schools," Richards.

"A Basis for Determining Structural Interest in Choral Music," Gerow.

"The Kodály Method for Choral Training," Darazs.

No. 9, Spring 1967

"Evaluation and Synthesis of Research Studies Relating to Music Education: 1930–1962," Schneider and Cady.
"Youth Concert Study: An Introduction and Progress Report," Hill.
"Symbols Used in Music Analysis: Final Report," Jones.
"The Effectiveness of the Use of Adjunct Programmed Analyses of Musical Works on Students' Perception of Form," Nelson.
"Developing Aesthetic Concepts Through Movement," Rowen.
"Improving Listening Through a Program of Keyboard Experience in Elementary Music," Lyke.

No. 10, Summer 1967

"The Development of Self Instructional Drill Materials to Facilitate the Growth of Score Reading Skills of Student Conductors," Sidness.
"The Development of a Planned Program for Teaching Musicianship in the High School Choral Class," Linton.
"A Study of the Development of Musicality in the Junior High School and the Contributions of Musical Composition to This Development," Kyme.
"Grass Roots Research: Its Strength and Weaknesses, Particularly in Considering New Media for Music," Vasil.
"The Identification of Excellence in Music Education Research," Cady.

No. 11, Fall 1967

"Computer-Assisted Teaching: A New Approach to Research in Music," Kuhn, Allvin.
"The Study and Evaluation of Certain Problems in Eartraining Related to Achievement in Sightsinging and Music Dictation," Thostenson.
"A Study of the Development of Musicality in the Junior High School and the Contributions of Musical Composition to this Development, Part II," Kyme.

No. 12, Winter 1968

"A Study of the Relationship Between the Perception of Musical Processes and the Enjoyment of Music," Duerksen.
"An Evaluation of Adequacy of Graduate Music Offerings at California Colleges and Universities," Morgan
"Development and Trial of a Basic Course in Music Theory Using Self-Instructional Materials to Supplement Training Received in High School Performance Groups," Andrews.
"Demonstration and Research Programs for Teaching Young String Players," Yarborough.
"The Contribution of Each Music Aptitude Profile Subtest to the Overall Validity of the Battery: A Note from the Author," Gordon.
"The State of the Program," Hargiss.

No. 13, Spring 1968

"Development of a Technique for Identifying Elementary School Children's Musical Concepts," Andrews, Deihl.
"A Plan for Developing Performance Materials in the Contemporary Idiom for the Early Stages of String Instruction," Farish.

"Improving and Extending the Junior High School Orchestra Repertory," Moore, Collier.

"Conservation-Type Responses of Children to Musical Stimuli, Pflederer, Sechrest.

"A Beginning Toward Diagnosing and Correcting Individual Deficiencies in Learning Music," Spohn.

"A Study of the Efficacy of General Intelligence and Musical Aptitude Tests in Predicting Achievement in Music," Gordon.

No. 14, Fall 1968

"Aural and Visual Perception of Melody in Tonal and Atonal Musical Environments." Sherman, Hill.

"Programed Analyses of Musical Works: An Experimental Evaluation," Nelson.

"A Survey of Music Education Materials and the Compilation of an Annotated Bibliography," Collins.

No. 15, Winter 1969

"Computer-Assisted Instruction: Potential for Instrumental Music Education," Deihl, Radocy.

"Seminar in State Music Supervision," Phelps.

No. 16, Spring 1969

"Factors Influencing the Development of Nonuniversity-Connected Schools of Music," Soucek.

"Accuracy of Recognition for Verbal and Tonal Stimuli Presented to the Left and Right Ears," McCarthy.

No. 17, Summer 1969

"An Approach to Aesthetic Education," Colwell.

"Developing Specialized Programs for Singing in the Elementary School," Gould.

"Cultural Enrichment Project," Brooks.

No. 18, Fall 1969

"The Computer and Music Research: Prospects and Problems," Lincoln.

"A Conference on Research in Music Education," Cady.

"The Effect of Reinforcement and Directional Scalar Methodology on Intonational Improvement," Madsen, Wolfe, Madsen.

"Public Higher Education and the Fees Charged for Applied Music Instruction," Desmond, Vanderwater.

No. 19, Winter 1970

"Children's Information Seeking About the Symphony," Clarke.

"Investigating the Effectiveness of Programed Listening in Secondary Instrumental Music Instruction," Simpson.

"Keyboard Computer-Assisted Music Instruction: Summary of the Project Plan," Kent.

"Philosophy in Music Education: Pure or Applied Research," Schwadron.

No. 20, Spring 1970

"Fulfilling the Need for Replication in Music Education Research," Prince.

No. 21, Summer 1970

"Harvard Project Zero: A Fresh Look at Art Education," Howard.
"The Relative Efficiency of Aural-Musical and Non-Musical Tests as Predictors of Achievement in Instrumental Music," Whellams.
"The Other Side of the Record," Mueller.
"Do Colleges and Universities Need an Automated Music Learning Center?" Allvin.

No. 22, Fall 1970

"Second International Seminar on Research in Music Education," papers from the Seminar.

No. 23, Winter 1971

"Institute in Music for Southeastern Kentucky Area Elementary Public School Teacher Aides," Linger.
"Inconsistencies in the Writing of James L. Mursell," Metz.
"A Longitudinal Study of Musical Achievement," Aurand.

No. 24, Spring 1971

"Music Performance Analysis," Heller, Campbell.
"The Arts Curriculum Project, ES ' 70," Stoddard.
"Self Esteem and Academic Achievement in Black Junior High School Students: Effects of Automated Guitar Instruction," Michel.

No. 25, Summer 1971

"Culture and Curriculum: A Note on the Gathering of an Idea Whose Time Has Come," Farrell.
"Integration of the Systems Approach and Electronic Technology in Learning and Teaching Music," Knuth.
"Establishment of Standards for the Indiana-Oregon Music Discrimination Test Based on a Cross-Section of Elementary and Secondary Students with an Analysis of Elements of Environment, Intelligence, and Musical Experience and Training in Relation to Music Discrimination," Long.

No. 26, Fall 1971

"Mini-electives for the Non-music Major," Tellstrom.
"A Study of the Effects of a Concept Teaching Curriculum on Achievement in Performance in Elementary School Beginning Bands: A Critical Evaluation of Robert F. Noble's Project No. 9-H-002," Edwards.
"The Discriminate Use of Music Listening as a Contingency for Improvement in Vocal Pitch Acuity and Attending Behavior," Greer, Randall, and Timberlake.
"Music Admission Policies and Practices: The Music Student Enters the NASM Accredited Institution of Higher Education," Motycka.

No. 27, Winter 1972

"Research Projects to Provide Materials for Teaching Asian Music in the United States Public Schools and Colleges," Curtiss.

"The Development of Content and Materials for a Music Literature Course in the Senior High School," Glidden.

"A Review of Recent Research in High School General Music," Glenn.

No. 28, Spring 1972

"Computerized Criterion-Referenced Testing of Certain Nonperformance Musical Behaviors," Radocy.

"A Course of Study and Curriculum Guide for School Bands," Haines.

"On Writing a Critical Review," Gonzo.

No. 29, Summer 1972

"Interim Report: Interdisciplinary Model Program in the Arts for Children and Teachers: An Interim Report on the Arts Impact Project," Lathrop, Boyle.

"Programing Principles in Automated Pitch Training," Ihrke.

"A Preliminary Report of the Effectiveness of a Preschool Music Curriculum with Preschool Head Start Children," Greenberg.

"The Dimensions of Research in Music Education," Sidnell.

No. 30, Fall 1972

"Symbolism, Art, and Education," Howard.

"A Predictive Investigation of Personality and Music Teaching Success," Krueger.

"The Logic of Assumptions," McCarthy.

No. 31, Winter 1973

"Evaluation of a CAI Program in Articulation, Phrasing and Rhythm for Intermediate Instrumentalists," Deihl, Zeigler.

No. 32, Spring 1973

"Evaluation of Instructional Objectives in Comprehensive Musicianship," Boyle, Radocy.

"Rebuttal 1," Whellams.

"Rebuttal 2—Logic and Assumption: A Report from a Quiet War Zone," Edwards.

No. 33, Summer 1973

"Historical Research in Music Education," Turrentine.

"Instrumental Music: Recent Research and Considerations for Future Investigations," Rainbow.

"Research in Choral Music: A Perspective," Gonzo.

"Multiple Correlation in Music Education Research Studies," Whellams.

"An Application of Guttman Facet Theory to Attitude Scale Construction in Music," Tunks.

No. 34, Fall 1973

"Exploring the Analysis of Variance," Whellams.
"A Review of Recent Research in Elementary Music Education," Klemish.
"Philosophy in Music Education: State of the Research," Schwadron.

No. 35, Winter 1973

"The Frequency and General Mode of Inquiry of Research in Music Therapy, 1952–1972," Jellison.
"Research in Evaluation in Music Education," Whybrew.
"Status of Research: Educational Technology in Music Education," Deihl, Partchey.
"Music Discrimination Training and the Music Selection Behavior of Nursery and Primary Level Children," Greer, Dorow, Hanser.

No. 36, Spring 1974

Special Issue: Accountability.

No. 37, Spring 1974

"James L. Mursell: A Developmental Philosophy of Music Education," Harvey.
"Changing Concepts of the Ear's Response to Tonal Stimuli: A Study of the Theories of Hearing," Tallarico.
"Treating the Uncertain Singer Through the Use of the Tape Recorder," Klemish.

No. 38, Summer 1974

"The Effect of Individualized Instruction on the Performance Achievements of Beginning Instrumentalists," McCarthy.

No. 39, Fall 1974

"A Study of the Three Phrase Concept of Memory: Its Musical Implications," Tallarico.

No. 40, Winter 1974

"Competency Based Music Teacher Education: Is Systematic Accountability Worth the Effort?" Holt.

No. 41, Spring 1975

"A Rebuttal," McCarthy.
"A Survey of Band Literature Performed by the High Schools and Colleges of Iowa and Nebraska from 1968–1972," Berry.

No. 42, Summer 1975

"A Multivariate Investigation of Reaction Profiles in Music Listeners and Their Relationships with Various Autochthonous and Experimental Characteristics": Author's Reply, Hedden; Reviewer's Reply, Edwards.
"Dissertations in Progress in U.S. Universities as of January 1975."

No. 43, Summer 1975

(Special Issue: CEMREL Aesthetic Education Program)

"The Aesthetics of Education: The CEMREL Aesthetic Education Program," Madeja.

"The Curriculum Development Game as Played by the Aesthetic Education Programs," Bocklage, Meyers.

"Through the Teacher to the Child: Aesthetic Education for Teachers," Rosenblatt, Trapaga.

"Formative Evaluation in the Aesthetic Education Program," Hall, Thuernau.

"The Role of Research in the Aesthetic Education Program, Bagenstos, LeBlanc.

"The Arts, A Natural Resource for Education," Sweda, Blaustein.

"Psychological Aspects of Aesthetic Education: Some Initial Observations," Smith.

No. 44, Fall 1975

"The Construction and Validation of the Smith-Ryan Musical Proficiency Teachers Examination Grades K–12," Smith.

No. 45, Winter 1976

"Research in Music in Early Childhood Education: A Survey with Recommendations," Greenberg.

No. 46, Spring 1976

"Competency-Based Teacher Education: The Controversy and a Synthesis of Related Research in Music from 1964 to 1974," Mountford.

"Preferences for Trumpet Tone Quality Versus Intonation," Madsen, Geringer.

"Influence of Distributional Redundancy in Rhythmic Sequences of Judged Complexity Ratings," McMullen.

No. 47, Summer 1976

"The Effects of Videotaped Feedback and Self-Evaluation Forms on Teaching Skills, Musicianship and Creativity of Prospective Elementary Teachers," Moore.

"The Discrimination of Musical Form Through "Conceptual" and "Non-Conceptual" Successive Approximation Strategies," Greer, Lundquist.

"An Investigation of Personality and Music Teaching Success," Krueger.

No. 48, Fall 1976

"A Review of Research on Attitude and Preference," Wapnick.

"A Multivariate Analysis of Factors in the Backgrounds of Wyoming Adults Related to Their Attitudinal Levels Concerning Music," Noble.

No. 49, Winter 1976

"Research in Music Education," Leonhard, Colwell.

No. 50, Spring 1977

Papers of the Sixth International Seminar on Research in Music Education.

No. 51, Summer 1977

"Strategy in Bennett Reimer's 'A Philosophy of Music Education,'" Lemmon.
"Philosophical Monism in Music Education: Some Thoughts in Response to Douglas Lemmon's Paper," Reimer.
"Musical Aptitude Stability Among Primary School Children," Schleuter, DeYarman.
"Computer Information Search and Retrieval: A Guide for the Music Educator," Williams, Beasley.

No. 52, Fall 1977

"Left-Right Ear Differences in the Processing of Instrument Tone Segments," Rushford-Murray.
"Music Education Choose-A-Title System," Melton.

No. 53, Winter 1977

"Applying an Instructional Development Process to Music Education," Eickmann, Lee.
"An Experimental Study of the Comparative Effectiveness of Harmonic and Melodic Accompaniment in Singing as It Relates to the Development of a Sense of Tonality," Hale.

No. 54, Spring 1978

"Systematic Musicology: Aspects of Definition and Academe," Schwadron, Hutchinson.

No. 55, Summer 1978

"The Nonmusical Outcomes of Musical Education: A Review of the Literature," Wolff.

No. 56, Fall 1978

"A Look at Some Data about Music Tests in National Testing Programs Geared to College-Level Courses," Humphry.

No. 57, Winter 1978

"How Basic is Aesthetic Education? or Is 'RT the Fourth R?'" Broudy.
"Music Education for the Mentally Handicapped: A Summary of Selected Related Literature with Conclusions and Recommendations," Krebs.
"Unified Curriculum Construction: The Icelandic-American Comprehensive Musicianship Framework Project," Woods.
"The Use of Omega Squared in Interpreting Statistical Significance," Tunks.
"A Review of Research on Observational Systems in the Analysis of Music Teaching," Dorman.

No. 58, Spring 1979

"State Arts Agencies: An Overview," Goekjian.
"A Description of Various Projects of the State Arts Councils," Murray.
"Amount of Money Allotted to Each Discipline by State."

No. 59, Summer 1979 (Special Issue: ISME)

Report of the Seventh International Seminar on Research in Music Education.

No. 60, Fall 1979 (Special Issue: The Yale Seminar)

No. 61, Winter 1980

"The Effects of Arts Education on Intellectual and Social Development: A Review of Selected Research," Hanshumaker.
"Outline of a Proposed Model of Sources of Variation in Musical Taste," LeBlanc.

No. 62, Spring 1980

"Piagetian Research in Music," Serafine.
"Psychological Research in Music as the Basis of Music Education, Especially the Education of the Handicapped," Moog.
"Relationships Between Musical Attitudes, Self-Esteem, Social Status, and Grade Level of Elementary Children," Vander Ark, Nolin, Newman.

No. 63, Summer 1980

"Toward A Contemporary Program of Music Education," Leonhard.
"Functions of Music in Music Education Since Tanglewood: A Ten-Year Report," Jones.
"Enrollment Trends in Secondary School Music Courses," Hoffer.
"Developmental Music Aptitudes Among Inner-City Primary Children," Gordon.

No. 64, Fall 1980

"Selected Recent Art Education Research: Its Implications for Research in Music Education," Boisen.
"Development of Music Listening Skills," Hedden.

No. 65, Winter 1981

"The Effect of Altering the Number of Choices Per Item on Test Statistics: Is Three Better Than Five?" Asmus.
"Music Listening Skills and Music Listening Preferences," Hedden.

No. 66–67, Spring–Summer 1981 (Special Issue)

Report of the Eighth International Seminar on Research in Music Education.

No. 68, Fall 1981

"A Composer's Study of Young Children's Innate Musicality," Pond.
"Implications of the Pillsbury Foundation School of Santa Barbara in Perspective," Wilson.
"Investigating the Musical Capabilities of Young Children," Shelley.

No. 69, Winter 1982

"Historical Research in Music Education: A Prolegomenon," Heller, Wilson.

No. 70, Spring 1982

"Music vs. Psychoacoustical Variables and their Influence on the Perception of Musical Intervals," Balzano.

"The Use of Self-Paced Televised Instructional Programming in Music and Its Implications for Australian Education," Rees.

No. 71, Summer 1982 (University of Western Ontario Symposium IV)

"Musical Expectancy: Some Perspectives," Carlsen.

"From Tone to Melody to Music: Some Directions for a Theory of Musical Cognition," Cuddy.

"Auditory Cognition: A Study of the Similarities in Memory Processing for Music Tones and Spoken Words," Williams.

"Connotative Responses to Musical Stimuli: A Theoretical Explanation," McMullen.

No. 72, Fall 1982

"Music Communication and Cognition," Heller, Campbell.

"Music's Proper Place: Trends in the Status of Music at Selected Institutions of Higher Education in America, 1870–1920," Levy.

"Creativity and Aging: The Black Musician's Perspective," Standifer.

No. 73, Winter 1983

"Cognitive Processes in Music: Discoveries vs. Definitions," Serafine.

"The Role of Private Music Instruction in the Development of High School Music Students' Ability to Describe Musical Events," Nierman.

"Conservation of Rhythmic and Tonal Patterns of Second Through Sixth Grade Children," Webster, Zimmerman.

"On the Significance of Significance: Addressing a Basic Problem in Research," Heller, Radocy.

No. 74, Spring 1983

"Creativity Research in Music Education: A Review," Richardson.

"Aesthetic Education in Theory and Practice: A Review of Recent Research," Saffle.

"String Teaching and Performance: A Review of Research Findings," Nelson.

"Characteristics of High School Chorus, Band and Orchestra Members as Described by the Strong Vocational Interest Blank," Roys.

No. 75, Summer 1983

"A Look at E. Gordon's Theories," Brink.

"A US-Poland Comparison of Scores Attained on the Aliferis College Entrance Test," Aliferis.

"Selecting Students to Music Instruction," Karma.

"The Validity of Certain Entrance Tests as Predictors of Grades in Music Theory and Ear Training," Arenson.

"Presenting a Method of Analyzing Mental and Emotional Processes in Secondary School Students While They are Listening to Music," Herberger.

No. 76, Fall 1983

"A Survey of Choral Education Research: 1972-1981," Hylton.
"Children's Perceptions of Horses and Melodies," Walker.
"The Arts/The Sciences, A Student Research Profile," Jackson.
"Quantitative Differences in Frequency Perceptions by Violinists, Pianists, and Trombonists," Parker.

No. 77, Winter 1984

"Music Education, Recent History, and Ideas," Miller.
"Educating in Thoughts Too Definite for Words," Walker.
"Measurement of Musical Awareness," Olson.
"Effects of Two Music Series Texts on Seventh Grade Students' Musical Perception and Musical Sensitivity," Smith.

No. 78, Spring 1984

"A Longitudinal, Predictive Validity Study of the Intermediate Measures of Music Audiation," Gordon.
"Doctoral Research in Music Student Teaching: 1962-1971," Grashel.
"A Survey of Music Performing Group Grading Practices in N.A.S.M. Member Colleges and Universities in Ohio and Four Neighboring States," Drake.
"Some Considerations of Difficulties Encountered in International Exchange of Music Education Research Information," Jetter.

Journal of Research In Music Education

Vol. I

"Administrative Policies for the College and University Band," Spring 1953, Boyd.
"Band Programs in Minnesota," Spring 1953, Ivory.
"A Comparative Study of Two Methods of Teaching Sight Singing in the Fourth Grade," Fall 1953, Hutton.
"Characteristics of First Year Conservatory Students," Fall 1953, Taylor.
"The Development of a College Entrance Test in Music Achievement, Fall 1953, Aliferis and Stecklein.
"The Determination of Musical Experiences Designed to Develop Musical Competencies Required of Elementary School Teachers in Maryland," Spring 1953, Fleming.
"The Easy Instructor (1798-1831): A History and Bibliography of the First Shape Note Tune Book," Spring 1953, Lowens and Britton.
"The Fulbright Program," Fall 1953.
"The History of the Flute and Its Music in the United States," Spring 1953, Giroux.
"A List of State Music Education Periodicals," Fall 1953, Weigand.
"The Organization and Development of the Sectional Conferences," Fall 1953, Molnar.
"The Role of Body-Awareness in the Emergence of Musical Ability: Its Application to Music Education, the College Basic Music Course, and Critic Teaching," Spring 1953, Brody.

"The Study of Music at the University of Oxford in the Middle Ages (to 1450),"
Spring 1953, Carpenter.
"The Value of Notated Examples in Learning to Recognize Musical Themes
Aurally," Fall 1953, Smith.

Vol. II

"General Education and the College Music Program," Spring 1954, Kintzer.
"Graduate Study in Music Education—A Report of the Committee on Graduate
Study in Music Education," Fall 1954.
"A History of Music Education in the Cincinnati Public Schools," Spring 1954,
Gary.
"John Tufts' Introduction to the Singing of Psalm-Tunes (1721-1744): The First
American Music Textbook," Fall 1954, Lowens.
"Microcard Publications in Music Education," Spring 1954.
"The Measurement of Musical Tone," Fall 1954, Stubbins.
"On Musical Expression," Spring 1954, Schoen.
"Music for the Preservice Classroom Teacher," Spring 1954, Linton.
"Music Reading Films," Fall 1954, Rea.
"Nineteenth Century Graded Vocal Series," Fall 1954, John.
"The Study of Music at the University of Paris in the Middle Ages," Fall 1954,
Carpenter.
"A Study of the Relationship of Music Reading and I.Q. Scores," Spring 1954,
King.
"Tonal Function and Sonority in the Study of Harmony," Spring 1954, Cadzen.

Vol. III

"Bibliography of Sources, 1930-1952, Relating to the Teaching of Choral Music
in Secondary Schools," Spring 1955, Modisett.
"Characteristics of Outstanding High School Musicians," Spring 1955, Garder.
"The Establishment of the Music Supervisors National Conference, 1907-1910,"
Spring 1955, Molnar.
"Factors Which Underlie the Development of a Research Program," Spring 1955,
Gaston.
"Leadership in Orchestral Conducting," Fall 1955, Woodbury.
"Lowell Mason and the Manual of the Boston Academy of Music," Spring 1955,
Ellis.
"Music in the Medieval Universities," Fall 1955, Carpenter.
"Psychological Problems in Musical Art," Spring 1955, Schoen.
"Research: Philosophy and Esthetics," Spring 1955, Leonhard.
"A Study of Community Attitudes Toward Music Education in the Public Schools
of Selected Communities in Missouri," Fall 1955, Burmeister.
"The Total Work-Load of High School Music Teachers in Michigan," Fall 1955,
Steg.
"Toward Cultural Definition," Fall 1955, McKay.
"Training of Secondary School Music Teachers in Western Colleges and
Universities," Fall 1955, Peterson.

Vol. IV

"Are Musical Tastes Indicative of Musical Capacity?" Spring 1956, Kyme.
"Basic Concepts in Music Education: A Symposium. A Pragmatic Approach to
Certain Aspects of Music Education," Fall 1956, McMurray.

"The Era of Beginnings in American Music Education (1830–1840)," Spring 1956, Sunderman.

"Esthetics for the Music Educator: The Maturation of Esthetic Sense," Fall 1956, Benn.

"Music Supervision in the Elementary Schools of New York State," Spring 1956, Banse.

"The Place of the Performance Area in Training High School Music Teachers," Spring 1956, Peterson.

"The Social Nature of Musical Taste," Fall 1956, Mueller.

"Studies in Music Appreciation: I. A Program of Testing II. Measuring the Listener's Recognition of Formal Music Structure III. Experimental Analysis of the Process," Spring 1956, Mueller.

"Treatise on Ornamentation by Guiseppe Tartini," Fall 1956, Babitz.

Vol. V

"Bibliography of Research Studies in Music Education, 1949–1956," Fall 1957, Larson.

"Certain Characteristics of Baton Twirlers," Spring 1957, Richardson and Lehman.

"Current Trends and New Directions in Educational Research," Spring 1957, Jones.

"A History of Music Education in Texas," Spring 1957, Bakkegard.

"The Relationship of Instrument to Music Achievement Test Scores," Spring 1957, Stecklein and Aliferis.

"A Study of Certain Practices in Music Education in School Systems of Cities Over 150,000 Population," Spring 1957, Ernst.

Vol. VI

"Americana Index to *The Musical Quarterly*," Fall 1958, Kinscella.

"Common Efforts of the Community Orchestra and the School Music Program in Providing Listening Experiences for School Students," Spring 1958, Hoffer.

"Did Puritanism or the Frontier Cause the Decline of Colonial Music: Debated in a Dialogue between Mr. Quaver and Mr. Crotchet," Spring 1958, Covey.

"Music Teaching Competencies," Spring 1958, Baird.

"The Need for Research in the History of American Music," Spring 1958, Johnson.

"Opinions and Practices of Supervisors of Student Teachers in Selected Music Schools," Spring 1958, Clarke.

"A Tentative Bibliography of Early Wind Instrument Tutors," Spring 1958, Riley.

Vol. VII

"Béla Bartók's *Mikrokosmos*," Fall 1959, Suchoff.

"Changing Aspects of American Culture As Reflected in the MENC," Fall 1959, Molnar.

"Fixed or Movable Do?" Fall 1959, Bentley.

"Music Education Materials: A Selected Bibliography," Spring 1959.

"Musical Intervals and Simple Number Ratios," Fall 1959, Cadzen.

"The Teaching of Music Appreciation," Fall 1959, Tischler.

Vol. VIII

"An Acoustical Analysis of Tones Produced by Clarinets Constructed of Various Materials," Spring 1960, Lanier.

"An Approach to the Quantitative Study of Dynamics," Spring 1960, Gordon.

"The Chapins and Sacred Music in the South and West," Fall 1960, Hamm.

"Christopher Tye and the Musical Dialogue in Samuel Rowley's "When You See Me, You Know Me," Spring 1960, Carpenter.

"Comparison of Solo and Ensemble Performances with Reference to Pythagorean, Just, and Equi-Tempered Intonations," Spring 1960, Mason.

"Elam Ives and the Pestalozzian Philosophy of Music Education," Spring 1960, John.

"An Experiment in Teaching Children to Read Music with Shape Notes," Spring 1960, Kyme.

"Logic and Language in Musical Criticism," Fall 1960, Chase.

"The Mendelssohn Quintet Club: A Milestone in American Music Education," Spring 1960, Phelps.

"Music in Arizona Before 1912," Fall 1960, Bakkegard.

"Music Instruction in Inca Land," Fall 1960, Stevenson.

"The Song Choices of Children in the Elementary Grades," Spring 1960, Blyler.

"The State Supervisor of Music," Fall 1960, Blakely.

Vol. IX

"Béla Bartók's Contributions to Music Education," Spring 1961, Suchoff.

"An Evaluation of Various Seating Plans Used in Choral Singing," Spring 1961, Lambson.

"The Development of a Music Reaction Test to Measure Affective and Aesthetic Sensitivity," Fall 1961, Lipton.

"Francis Henry Brown, 1818–1891, American Teacher and Composer, Spring 1961, Coolidge.

"Music in the Junior High School, 1900–1957," Spring 1961, Weigand.

"Soviet Music Instruction: Service to the State," Fall 1961, Krebs.

"A Study to Determine the Effects of Training and Practice on Drake Musical Aptitude Test Scores," Spring 1961, Gordon.

"A Study of the Musical Preferences of a Select Group of Adolescents," Fall 1961, Kelly.

"A Study of the Relation Between Certain Mental and Personality Traits and Ratings of Musical Abilities," Fall 1961, Cooley.

"A Study of Score Reading Ability of Musicians," Fall 1961, Lansen.

"The Teacher-Training Program in Music at Chautauqua Institution, 1905–1930," Spring 1961, Troth.

"The Teaching Load and Related Activities of Music Teachers in Indiana Public Schools, 1953–1954," Fall 1961, Colbert.

Vol. X

"The Acquisition of Sight Singing Ability in Piano Classes for Students Preparing To Be Elementary Teachers," Spring 1962, Hargiss.

"Classification of Reaction Patterns in Listening to Music," Fall 1962, Yingling.

"Comparative Study of Two Methods of Developing Music Listening Ability in Elementary School Children," Spring 1962, Andrews.

"The Concertos for Clarinet," Spring 1962, Tuthill.

"Criteria of Choral Concert Program Building as Related to an Analysis of the Elements of Music Structure," Summer 1964, Gerow.

"Curriculum Planning in Music Education," Fall 1964, Farwell.

"Doctoral Dissertations in Music and Music Education, 1957–1963," Spring 1964, Gordon.

"Factors Affecting the Development of the Orchestra and String Program in Minnesota Secondary Schools, 1940–1960," Fall 1964, Fergus.

"The Function of Sociability in the Sociology of Music and Music Education," Summer 1964, Riedel.

"Improving Facility in Music Memorization," Winter 1964, Ross.

Index to Volumes XI and XII, Winter 1964.

"Music Activities of High School Graduates in Two Communities," Summer 1964, Claire Ordway.

"Music at the Hohe Karlsschule, 1770–1794," Summer 1964, Longyear.

"Piano Study in Soviet-Russian Schools of Music," Fall 1964, Robert.

"Programmed Instruction in Music Fundamentals for Future Elementary Teachers," Fall 1964, Barnes.

"Programed Learning in Melodic Dicatation," Summer 1964, Carlsen.

"The Relationship Between Musical and Social Patterns in American Popular Music," Winter 1964, Etzkorn.

"The Responses of Children to Musical Tasks Embodying Piaget's Principle of Conservation," Winter 1964, Pflederer.

"Skills of Piano Performance in the Preparation of Music Educators," Summer 1964, Buchanan.

"The Status of Music in the Negro High Schools in South Carolina," Summer 1964, Bryant, Deloach.

"Teaching Clarinet Fingerings with Teaching Machines," Winter 1964, Woelflin.

"Teaching Composition Via Schenker's Theory," Winter 1964, Silberman.

Vol. XIII

"Causes of Elementary Instrumental Music Dropouts," Fall 1965, Martignetti.

"A Comparative Study of Elementary Music Instruction in Schools of the United States and Great Britain," Summer 1965, Anderson.

"The Construction, Validation, and Standardization of a Test in Music Perception for High School Performance Groups," Winter 1965, Fluke and Sparks.

"Development of a Method for Analysis of Musical Compositions Using an Electronic Digital Computer," Winter 1965, Roller.

"Doctoral Dissertations in Music," Spring 1965, Gordon.

"The Early Clarinet Concertos," Fall 1965, Titus.

"Effects of Music Education: Implications from a Review of Research," Fall 1965, Reimer.

"Eighteenth Century Keyboard Instruction Practices as Revealed in a Set of Master Lessons," Spring 1965, Bostrom.

"An Evaluation of Achievement in Auditory-Visual Discrimination Resulting from Specific Types of Musical Experiences Among Junior High School Students," Winter 1965, Colwell.

"Experimental use of Pre-Instrumental Music Melody Instruments," Winter 1965, Anastasiow and Shambaugh.

"The Formation of A Cappella Choirs at Northwestern University, St. Olaf College, and Westminster Choir College, Winter 1965, Van Camp.

"The Relationship of Intelligence to Creativity," Winter 1966, Moore.
"A Selective List of Choral and Vocal Music with Wind and Percussion Accompaniments," Winter 1966, Vagner.
"The Sonatas for Clarinet and Piano," Fall 1966, Tuthill.
"The Third Edition of Tufts' 'Introduction to the Art of Singing Psalm-Tunes'," Fall 1966, Finney.
"The Tone-Word System of Carl Eitz," Summer 1966, Jones.
"Unaccompanied Woodwind Solos," Spring 1966, Merriman.
"The Use of Programed Instruction to Teach Fundamental Concepts in Music Theory," Fall 1966, Ashford.
"Vocal Growth in the Human Adolescent and the Total Growth Process," Summer 1966, Joseph.

Vol. XV

"The Aesthetic Gap Between Consumer and Composer," Summer 1967, Mueller.
"An Analysis of In-Service Teacher Evaluations of Their Preparatory Curriculum in Elementary Classroom Music," Winter 1967, Logan.
"An Investigation of the Use of the Musical Aptitude Profile with College and University Freshman Music Students," Winter 1967, Lee.
"Computer-Assisted Teaching: A New Approach to Research in Music," Winter 1967, Allvin and Kuhn.
"Conservation Laws Applied to the Development of Musical Intelligence," Fall 1967, Pflederer.
"Cooperative Research in Programed Learning: Taped Interval Discrimination Drills," Fall 1967, Spohn and Tarratus.
"Doctoral Dissertations in Music and Music Education," Spring 1967, Gordon.
"Early Public School Music in Columbus, Ohio, 1845–1954," Fall 1967, Kapfer.
"The Effects of Order of Presentation and Knowledge of Results on the Aural Recognition of Melodic Intervals," Fall 1967, Jeffries.
"The Evaluation of Clarinet Tone Quality Through the Use of Oscilloscopic Transparencies," Spring 1967, Small.
"Factors Relating to Carryover of Music Training into Adult Life," Spring 1967, Dachinger and Lawrence.
"A Formula, Nomogram, and Tables for Determining Musical Interval Relationships," Summer 1967, Mason.
"Implications for the Use of the Musical Aptitude Profile with College and University Freshman Music Students," Spring 1967, Gordon.
"Johann Conrad Beissel and Music of the Ephrata Cloister," Summer 1967, Blakely.
"Listening to the Audience," Winter 1967, DeJager.
"Music Education and Experimental Research," Spring 1967, Colwell.
"Music in Israel's Primary Schools," Spring 1967, Greenberg.
"Operant Training of Aural Musical Discriminations with Preschool Children," Fall 1967, Fullard.
"The Phenomenological Analysis and Description of Musical Experience," Winter 1967, Pike.
"The Place of Music in German Education from the Beginnings Through the 16th Century," Winter 1967, Livingstone.
"The Professional Role and Status of Music Educators in the United States," Spring 1967, White.
"Programed Part Writing," Summer 1967, Fink.

"The Relationships among Pitch Identification, Imagery for Musical Sounds, and Musical Memory," Summer 1967, Bergan.

"Tests and Measures in Higher Education," Summer 1967, Cady.

"The Use of 8mm Loop Films to Teach the Identification of Clarinet Fingering, Embouchure, and Hand Position Errors," Fall 1967, Collins and Diamond.

"The Use of Notated Examples in Fifth-Grade Music Appreciation Classes," Winter 1967, Oberdin.

Vol. XVI

"An Approach to the Measurement of Music Appreciation (I)," Fall 1968, Crickmore.

"An Approach to the Measurement of Music Appreciation (II)," Winter 1968, Crickmore.

"An Attempt to Modify the Musical Preferences of Preschool Children," Spring 1968, Schuckert and McDonald.

"A Cinfluorographic Investigation of Brass Instrument Performance," Spring 1968, Merriman and Meidt.

"The Development and Validation of a Test of Listening Skill," Spring 1968, Bailey.

"Doctoral Dissertations in Music and Music Education, 1963–1967," Summer 1968, Gordon.

"Effect of Delayed Auditory Feedback on Musical Performance, Winter 1968, Havlicek.

"An Experimental Study of the Role of Expectation and Variation in Music," Fall 1968, Simon and Wohlwill.

"An Experimental Study of Selected Variables in the Performance of Musical Durational Notation," Winter 1968, Drake.

"James L. Mursell: An Annotated Bibliography," Fall 1968, Simutis.

"Musical Activity Preferences of a Selected Group of Fourth-Grade Children," Winter 1968, MacGregor.

"The Norfolk Musical Society 1814–1820: An Episode in the History of Choral Music in New England," Winter 1968, Nitz.

"Observations on Music Dictation Programing," Fall 1968, Trythall.

"The Philosophy of Universal Music Education," Fall 1968, Gehrkens.

"Recognition of Repeated and Altered Thematic Materials in Music," Spring 1968, Duerksen.

"A Research Study of a Technique for Adjusting Clarinet Reeds," Spring 1968, Intravaia and Resnick.

"Some Long-Range Effects of Programed Instruction in Music," Winter 1968, Ashford.

Vol. XVII

"Auditory Perception by Children," Spring 1969, Petzold.

"A Cinefluorographic Investigation of Selected Clarinet Playing Techniques," Summer 1969, Anfinson.

"Comparative Music Education," Spring 1969, Cykler.

"A Comparison of Orff and Traditional Instructional Methods in Music," Fall 1969, Siemens.

"Developing Aural Perception of Music in Context," Spring 1969, Carlsen.

"Development of Children Aged Seven to Eleven," Spring 1969, Taylor.

"Doctoral Dissertations in Music and Music Education," Fall 1969, Gordon.

"Educational and Social Factors," Spring 1969, Cleak.

"Electronic Graphs of Musical Performance: A Pilot Study in Perception and Learning," Summer 1969, Heller.

"An Encoding Algorithm and Tables for the Digital Analysis of Harmony (I)" Fall 1969, Mason.

"An Encoding Algorithm and Tables for the Digital Analysis of Harmony (II), Winter 1969, Mason.

"Encyclopedia Favoritism Toward Native Composers," Winter 1969, Farnsworth.

"Entrance Test Validity," Spring 1969, Frazen.

"Evaluation of Bentley Measures," Spring 1969, Rowntree.

"Experimental Investigation of Absolute Pitch," Spring 1969, Sergeant.

"Experimental Research in Germany," Spring 1969, Eicke.

"An Experimental Study Comparing Programed Instruction with Classroom Teaching of Sightsinging," Summer 1969, Kanable.

"Foreword to the Papers of the International Seminar on Experimental Research in Music Education," Spring 1969, Bentley.

"Individualizing Instruction Through New Media Research," Spring 1969, Spohn.

"The Influence of Selected Factors on Interval Identification," Fall 1969, Buttram.

"Intelligence vs. Progress in Music Education," Spring 1969, Holmstrom.

"Intercorrelations Among Musical Aptitude Profile and Seashore Measures of Musical Talents Subtests," Fall 1969, Gordon.

"Investigation of Kinesthetics in Violin Playing," Spring 1969, Jacobs.

"An Investigation of the Primary Level Musical Aptitude Profile for Use with Second and Third Grade Students, Winter 1969, Harrington.

"Is It Research?" Spring 1969, Franzen.

"James L. Mursell: An Annotated Bibliography—Addendum" (Letters to the Editor), Summer 1969, O'Keefe.

"Measurement of Music Appreciation (Summary)," Spring 1969, Crickmore.

"Members of the Seminar on Experimental Research in Music Education," Spring 1969.

"The Monotone Problem," Spring 1969, Joyner.

"The Optimum Length of the Musical Aptitude Profile Subtests," Summer 1969, Brown.

"The Philosophy of Julia E. Crane and the Origin of Music Teacher Training," Winter 1969, Claudson.

"The Predictive Measurement of Musical Success," Spring 1969, Lehman.

"Psychological Testing in Hungarian Music Education," Spring 1969, Kokas.

"Report of an Informal Symposium on the Organization and Administration of Music Education Degree Programs," Fall 1969, Henke.

"Research in the United States," Spring 1969, Britton.

"Rhythmic Training and its Relationship to the Synchronization of Motor-Rhythmic Responses," Winter 1969, Groves.

"Scandinavian Research," Spring 1969, Jensen.

"The Secular Cantata in the United States: 1850–1919," Winter 1969, Stopp.

"A Selected Bibliography of Works on Music Testing," Winter 1969, Lehman.

"Sociological Conditions which Contributed to the Growth of the School Band Movement in the United States," Summer 1969, Whitehill.

"Some Preverbal Concepts in Music," Spring 1969, Hickman.

"Some Problems in Musical Learning," Spring 1969, Carlsen.

"Some Problems in Psychology of Music," Spring 1969, Schuter.

"Some Research Interests and Findings," Spring 1969, Bentley.

"The Status of Elementary Special Music Teachers in California Public Schools," Winter 1969, McQuerrey.

"A Study in the Development of Music Listening Skills of Secondary School Students," Summer 1969, Haack.

"Summary of Discussions at the International Seminar on Experimental Research in Music Education," Spring 1969, Shuter and Taylor.

"Tonality as a Basis for Musical Talent," Spring 1969, Franklin.

"Vocal Growth Measurements in Male Adolescents," Winter 1969, Joseph.

Vol. XVIII

"An Analysis of State Requirements for College or University Accreditation in Music Education," Fall 1970, Raessler.

"A Bibliography of Materials on Programmed Instruction in Music," Summer 1970, Rogers and Almond.

"Brief Focused Instruction and Musical Concepts," Spring 1970, Zimmerman and Sechrest.

"Chamber Music in Boston: The Harvard Musical Association," Summer 1970, Paige.

"A Comparative Study of Traditional and Programed Methods for Developing Music Listening Skills in the Fifth Grade," Summer 1970, Rives.

"A Comparative Study of Two Methods of Teaching Music Reading to First-Grade Children," Winter 1970, Klemish.

"A Comparative Study of Two Response Modes in Learning Woodwind Fingerings by Programed Text," Spring 1970, Bingham.

"Compositional Technique and Musical Expressivity," Spring 1970, Levy.

"The Development of Music Reading Skills, Summer 1970, Bobbitt.

"Development of a Technique for Identifying Elementary School Children's Musical Concepts," Fall 1970, Andrews and Diehl.

"Doctoral Dissertations in Music and Music Education," Fall 1970, Gordon.

"The Effect of Prescribed Rhythmical Movements on the Ability to Read Music at Sight," Winter 1970, Boyle.

"The Effects of Four Profiles of Oboe Reeds on Intonation," Fall 1970, Wehner.

"Effects on Aesthetic Sensitivity of Developing Perception of Musical Expressiveness," Summer 1970, Standifer.

"Eighteenth-Century Conducting Practices," Winter 1970, Camesi.

"First-Year Results of a Five-Year Longitudinal Study of the Musical Achievement of Culturally Disadvantaged Students," Fall 1970, Gordon.

"Franz Liszt as Pedagogue," Winter 1970, Gervers.

"A Further Investigation of Certain Learning Aspects in the Aural Recognition of Melodic Intervals," Winter 1970, Jeffries.

"The German Male Chorus of the Early Nineteenth Century," Spring 1970, Brinkman.

"A History of the High School A Cappella Choir," Winter 1970, Kegerreis.

"Instructions Concerning the Teaching of Masterpieces of Art: Introduction and Translation," Spring 1970, Turrentine.

"An Investigation and Analysis of the Public Junior College Music Curriculum with Emphasis on the Problems of the Transfer Music Major," Winter 1970, Belford.

"A Music Theory Approach to Beginning Piano Instruction for the College Music Major," Spring 1970, Trantham.

"Musical Achievement and the Self-Concept, Spring 1970, Greenberg.

"On Religion, Music, and Education," Summer 1970, Schwadron.

"Opinions of Music Teachers Regarding Professional Preparation in Music Education," Winter 1970, Taylor.

"Elementary Music Education Program," Fall 1970, Picerno.
"Pedagogical Philosophy, Methods, and Materials of American Tune Book Introductions: 1801–1860," Spring 1970, Perrin.
"The Prediction of Academic Success of College Music Majors," Fall 1970, Ernest.
"Principles of Neglected Musical Repertoire," Summer 1970, Longyear.
"The Relationship Between Pitch Recognition and Vocal Pitch Production in Sixth-Grade Students," Fall 1970, Pedersen and Pedersen.
"The Relationship of Self-Concept and Selected Personality Variables to Achievement in Music Student Teaching," Fall 1970, Wink.
"The Republican Harmony (1795) of Nathaniel Billings," Winter 1970, Link.
"The Role of the Elementary Classroom Teacher and the Music Specialist: Opinions of the Music Supervisor," Summer 1970, Picerno.
"A Study in Aural Perception," Winter 1970, Sherman.
"A Study Involving the Visual Arts in the Development of Musical Concepts," Winter 1970, Haack.
"Systems of Scale Notation in Nineteenth-Century Tune Books," Fall 1970, Perrin.
"Vocal Music in the Common Schools of Upper Canada: 1846–1876," Winter 1970, Trowsdale.

Vol. XIX

"Affective Outcomes of Musical Education," Fall 1971, Lewy.
"An Analysis of Factors Related to Choral Teachers' Ability to Detect Pitch Errors While Reading the Score," Gall 1971, Gonzo.
"The Appropriateness of Young Audience Music Programs for Primary Grade Children," Fall 1971, Kyme.
"Automated Music Training: Final Report on Phase I," Winter 1971, Ihrke.
"A Bibliography on Research on the Evaluation of Music Teacher Education Programs," Spring 1971, Mathison.
"Children's Duplication of Rhythmic Patterns," Fall 1971, Gardner.
"The Computer and Bartók Research in America," Spring 1971, Suchoff.
"Computer-Assisted Instruction and Instrumental Music: Implications for Teaching and Research," Fall 1971, Diehl.
"Computer-Assisted Music Instruction: A Look at the Potential," Summer 1971, Allvin.
"Current Practices in the Evaluation of Student Teachers in Music," Summer 1971, Panhorst.
"Development and Evaluation of a Visual-Aural Program in Conceptual Understanding of the Basic Elements of Music," Spring 1971, Michalski.
"The Development and Experimental Application of Self-Instructional Practice Materials for Beginning Instrumentalists," Fall 1971, Puopolo.
"Early Twentieth-Century Singing Schools in Kentucky Appalachia," Spring 1971, Graham.
"Edward MacDowell's Critical and Historical Essays (1912)," Spring 1971, Lowens.
"The Effect of Musical and Extramusical Information upon Musical Preference," Fall 1971, Larson.
"Effect of the Timing of Supplementary Materials on Programed Learning in Music," Winter 1971, Kohn.
"Effects of a Concept Teaching Curriculum on Performance Achievement in Elementary School Beginning Bands," Summer 1971, Noble.

"Electronic Video Recording as a New Resource in Music Education," Winter 1971, Skapski.

"An Examination of Musical Process as Related to Creative Thinking," Fall 1971, Vaughan-Myers.

"Handbook of the Society for Research in Music Education," Summer 1971.

"An Investigation of Growth in Musical Facts and Concepts, Musical Discrimination, and Vocal Performance Proficiency as a Result of Senior High School Music Experiences," Winter 1971, Flom.

"An Investigation of Relationships Between Personality Characteristics and Success in Instrumental Study," Fall 1971, Sample and Hotchkiss.

"Measuring Attitude and Value Changes in Selected Humanities and Human Relations Programs," Winter 1971, Meeker.

"Mouth Air Pressure and Intensity Profiles of the Oboe," Spring 1971, Anastasio and Bussard.

"Music Education in the Private Schools of Vermont in the Nineteenth Century," Summer 1971, Keene.

"Musical Interest of Certain American Literary and Political Figures," Fall 1971, Johnson.

"Patterns of Teacher-Student Interaction in Selected Junior High School General Music Classes," Fall 1971, Nolin.

"A Pilot Study in the Use of a Vertically-Arranged Keyboard Instrument with the Uncertain Singer," Summer 1971, Jones.

"The Place of Music in German Education Around 1600," Summer 1971, Livingstone.

"A Program for Developing Aural Discrimination of Instrumental Tone Colors Using a Videosonic Teaching Machine, Spring 1971, Greenberg and Huddleston.

"Programed Instruction in Score Reading Skills," Winter 1971, Costanza.

"The Relationally Analytic and the Impressionistically Concrete Components of Western Music," Winter 1971, Northrop.

"The Relationship Between Academic Preparation and Professional Responsibilities of Secondary School Music Teachers in South Carolina," Winter 1971, Franklin.

"Repetition as a Factor in the Development of Musical Preferences," Fall 1971, Bradley.

"The Role of Musical Aptitude, Intelligence, and Academic Achievement in Predicting the Musical Attainment of Elementary Instrumental Music Students," Winter 1971, Young.

"A Scale to Measure Attitudes Toward Music," Summer 1971, Edwards and Edwards.

"Self-Instructional Drill Materials for Student Conductors," Spring 1971, Sidnell.

"Simulations for Music Education," Winter 1971, Swift.

"Solmization and Pitch Notation in Nineteenth-Century American School Music Textbooks," Winter 1971, Blum.

"Some Implications for Music Education in the Work of Jean Piaget," Spring 1971, Larsen and Boody.

"A Study of Two Approaches to Ear Training for Elementary School Children," Summer 1971, Deutsch.

"A Suggested Taxonomy of Music for Music Educators," Summer 1971, Biggs.

"Using MAP Scores in the Instruction of Beginning Students in Instrumental Music," Spring 1971, Froseth.

"Verbal Description of Aural Musical Stimuli," Fall 1971, Zimmerman.

Vol. 20

"Abstracts of Research Reports from MENC National Convention," Summer 1972, John.

"Beat Elimination as a Means of Teaching Intonation to Beginning Wind Instrumentalists," Winter 1972, Miles.

"A Comparison of First and Third Position Approaches to Violin Instruction," Winter 1972, Cowden.

"A Comparison of Two Computer Assisted Instructional Programs in Music Theory," Fall 1972, Hullfish.

"Concertos for Clarinet: Annotated Listings," Winter 1972, Tuthill.

"A Consideration of the Perceptual Process in the Evaluation of Musical Performance," Summer 1972, Schmalstieg.

"Disadvantaged Junior High School Students Compared with Norms of Seashore Measures," Winter 1972, Dawkins and Snyder.

"Doctoral Dissertations in Music and Music Education," Winter 1972, Gordon.

"Duties and Activities of Music Supervisory Personnel in California," Fall 1972, McQuerrey.

"Effect of Interval Direction on Pitch Acuity in Solo Vocal Performance," Summer 1972, Edmonson.

"The Effect of Rhythmic Notation Variables on Sight-Reading Errors," Winter 1972, Gregory.

"Effect on Student Musical Preference of a Listening Program in Contemporary Music," Fall 1972, Bradley.

"Effects of Musical Aptitude, Instruction, and Social Status on Attitudes Toward Music," Fall 1972, Williams.

"The Emergence of Simple Instrument Experiences in Early Kindergartens," Summer 1972, Mathis.

"Familiarity-Frequency Ratings Melodic Intervals," Fall 1972, Jeffries.

"A Guided Listening Program in Twentieth-Century Music for Junior High Students," Fall 1972, Zumbrunn.

"Model Computer-Assisted Information Retrieval System in Music Education," Winter 1972, Edwards and Douglas.

"Music Instruction in the Education of American Youth: The Early Academics" Winter 1972, Fouts.

"Music Aptitude Profile Norms for Use with College and University Nonmusic Majors," Fall 1972, Young.

"National School Band Contests Between 1926 and 1931," Summer 1972, Moore.

"A Paradigm for Research on Music Listening," Winter 1972, Prince.

"Performance Technique on Brass Instruments During the Seventeenth Century," Fall 1972, Fromme.

"A Phenomenological Analysis of Emotional Experience in Music," Summer 1972, Pike.

"Polish Research on the Psychology of Music," Summer 1972, Polakowski.

"The Relationship of Musical Instrument Preference to Timbre Discrimination," Summer 1972, Bernier and Stafford.

"Relative Effectiveness of Contrasted Music Teaching Styles for the Culturally Deprived," Winter 1972, Reid.

"Roles of Music Supervisors in Selected School Districts," Fall 1972, Dawson.

"Some Effects of Expectation of Evaluation of Recorded Music Performance," Summer 1972, Duerksen.

"Sonatas for Clarinet and Piano: Annotated Listings," Fall 1972, Tuthill.

"A Study of Gaston's 'Test of Musicality' as Applied to College Students," Winter 1972, Yoder.

"A Study of Student Correlations Between Music and Six Paintings by Klee," Winter 1972, Peretti.

"Use of Positive and Negative Examples in Teaching the Concept of Musical Style," Winter 1972, Haack.

Vol. 21

"Adult Approval and Students' Music Selection Behavior," Winter 1973, Greer, Dorow, Wachhaus, and White.

"Attitudinal Growth Patterns Toward Elementary School Music Experiences," Summer 1973, Nolin.

"The Bentley 'Measures of Musical Abilities': A Congruent Validity Report," Spring 1973, Young.

"Career Patterns and Job Mobility of College and University Music Faculty," Summer 1973, Aurand and Blackburn.

"Developing a Music Education Thesaurus," Spring 1973, Edwards, Douglas, and John.

"Development and Validation of a Clarinet Performance Adjudication Scale," Fall 1973, Ables.

"Effect of Contingent Music Listening on Increases of Mathematical Responses," Summer 1973, Madsen and Forsythe.

"Effect of Repeated Listenings on Structural Discrimination and Affective Response," Winter 1973, Bartlett.

"The Effect of Training on the Harmonic Discrimination of First-Grade Children," Spring 1973, Hair.

"Effectiveness of Chamber Music Ensemble Experience," Spring 1973, Zorn.

"Evaluation of a Sight-Reading Test Administered to Freshman Piano Classes," Spring 1973, Sowder.

"Feasibility of Tracking Musical Form as a Cognitive Listening Objective," Fall 1973, Smith.

"The First Cry of the Newborn: Basis for the Child's Future Musical Development," Fall 1973, Fridman.

"Formative Evaluation of a Kindergarten Music Program Based on Behavioral Objectives," Summer 1973, Piper and Shoemaker.

"Guido d'Arezzo: Medieval Musician and Educator," Fall 1973, Miller.

"The Hindman Settlement School and its Music," Summer 1973, Chambers.

"A History of the College Band Directors National Association," Spring 1973, Lasko.

"An Introduction to Seventeenth-Century Spanish Music Theory Books," Spring 1973, Forrester.

"Levels of Conceptual Development in Melodic Permutation Concepts Based on Piaget's Theory," Fall 1973, Larsen.

"Listeners' Responses to Music in Relation to Autochthonous and Experiential Factors," Fall 1973, Hedden.

"Meaning of the Concept of Music Teacher to High School Musicians," Winter 1973, Hedden.

"Measurement of Pitch Discrimination," Spring 1973, Sergeant.

"MENC Historical Center Acquires CMP Library and Files," Fall 1973, Willoughby.

"Music and Self-Esteem: Disadvantaged Problem Boys in an All-Black Elementary School," Spring 1973, Michel and Farrell.

"Music in the Educational Philosophy of Martin Luther," Winter 1973, Tarry.

"Musical Abilities and Sex Differences in the Analysis of Aural-Musical Capacities," Spring 1973, Whellams.

"A Musical Investigation of the Kamin Effect," Summer 1973, Tallarico.

"Osbourne McConathy: American Music Educator," Summer 1973, Platt.

"The Performance of William Billings' Music," Winter 1973, Crawford and McKay.

"Piano Learning and Programed Instruction," Summer 1973, Wagner, Piontek, and Teckhaus.

"Predicting Choral Achievement Through Use of Musicality and Intelligence Scores," Fall 1973, Helwig and Thomas.

"Relationship Between Teaching Incidents and Taba's Theoretical Construct," Summer 1973, Dorman.

"A Report of the Third International Seminar on Research in Music Education," Summer 1973, Petzold.

"A Review of Measures of Musico-Aesthetic Attitude," Winter 1973, Bullock.

"The Roots of Music Education in Baltimore," Fall 1973, Fisher.

"Simple Instrument Experiences in School Music Programs from 1900," Fall 1973, Mathis.

"Use of Music Training to Actuate Conceptual Growth in Neurologically Handicapped Children," Winter 1973, Pirtle and Seaton.

Vol. 22

"Acquiring Conservation of Melody and Cross-Modal Transfer Through Successive Approximation," Fall 1974, Botvin.

"Automated Aural-Visual Music Theory Instruction for Elementary Education Majors," Winter 1974, Roach.

"Design and Trial of a Computer-Assisted Lesson in Rhythm," Spring 1974, Placek.

"Development of Aural and Visual Perception Through Creative Processes," Fall 1974, Bradley.

"Discrimination of Modulated Beat Tempo by Professional Musicians," Winter 1974, Kuhn.

"Doctoral Dissertations in Music and Music Education," Summer 1974, Gordon.

"Effect of Jaw-Thrust Instruction on Trumpet Performance and Overjet of Young Players," Fall 1974, Testa.

"Effect of Melodic Parameters on Ability to Make Fine-Tuning Responses in Context," Winter 1974, Swaffield.

"Effects of Various Instructional Modes on Children's Performance of Music Concept Tasks," Fall 1974, Taebel.

"Effect of Vocalization on the Sense of Pitch of Beginning Band Class Students," Summer 1974, Elliot.

"Effects of Guided Listening on Musical Enjoyment of Junior High School Students," Spring 1974, Prince.

"Effects of Music on Anxiety as Determined by Physiological Skin Responses," Winter 1974, Peretti, Swenson.

"Effects of Music on Physiological Response," Landreth, Landreth.

"Electromyographic Analysis of Embouchure Music Function in Trumpet Playing," Winter 1974, White, Basmajian.

"Environment—A Factor in Conceptual Listening Skills of Elementary School Children," Fall 1974, McDonald.

"Influence of Number of Different Pitches and Melodic Redundancy on Preference Responses," Fall 1974, McMullen.

"Investigation of the Relationships Between Music Perception and Music Performance," Spring 1974, Marciniak.

"Music Instruction in Early Nineteenth-Century American Monitorial Schools," Summer 1974, Fouts.

"Music Listening Preferences of Elementary School Children," Winter 1974, Greer, Dorow, Randall.

"Musical Development in Preschool Disadvantaged Children," Fall 1974, Young.

"Pilot Study of Performance Practices of Twentieth-Century Musicians," Spring 1974, Papich, Rainbow.

"Predicting Success in Beginning Instrumental Music Through Use of Selected Tests," Spring 1974, Hufstader.

"Preferences for Single Tone Stimuli," Hedden.

"Self-Instructional Program for Musical Concept Development in Preschool Children," Summer 1974, Romanek.

"Study of a Behaviorally Oriented Training Program for Aural Skills," Fall 1974, Harriss.

"Use of Standardized Musical Aptitude Tests with University Freshmen Music Majors," Winter 1974, Schleuter.

Vol. 23

"Amzi Chapin: Frontier Singing Master and Folk Hymn Composer," Summer 1975, Scholten.

"Association of Hearing Acuity, Diplacusis, and Discrimination with Music Performance," Winter 1975, Sherbon.

"Attacks and Releases as Factors in Instrument Identification," Spring 1975, Elliott.

"Effect of Magnitude of Conductor Behavior on Students in Selected Mixed Choruses," Summer 1975, Yarbrough.

"Effect of Music and Biofeedback on Alpha Brainwave Rhythms and Attentiveness," Spring 1975, Wagner.

"Effect of Notational Values, Age, and Example Length on Tempo Performance Accuracy," Fall 1975, Gates, Kuhn.

"Effects of Music Literature on Developing Aesthetic Sensitivity to Music," Spring 1975, Anderson.

"Effects of Training in Conservation of Tonal and Rhythmic Patterns on Second-Grade Children," Winter 1975, Foley.

"Efficacy of a Self-help Program in Music for Disadvantaged Preschools," Summer 1975, Young.

"Increased Difficulty of Pitch Identification and Electroencephalographic Desynchronization," Fall 1975, Carlson, Chu Wang, Marple.

"Influence of Loudness on the Discrimination of Musical Sound Factors," Spring 1975, Haack.

"Judge-Group Differences in the Rating of Secondary School Trumpet Performances," Fall 1975, Fiske.

"Melodic Memory Tests: A Comparison of Normal Children and Mental Defectives," Spring 1975, Zenatti.

"Music Reading Ability of Beginning Wind Instrumentalists After Melodic Instruction," Spring 1975, MacKnight.

"Naive Minority of One and Deliberate Majority Mismatches of Tonal Stimuli," Summer 1975, Radocy.

"Poor Pitch Singing: Response of Monotone Singers to a Program of Remedial Training," Winter 1975, Roberts, Davies.

"Short-Term Retention of Pitch Sequence," Spring 1975, Williams.

"Student Perception of Characteristics of Effective Applied Music Instruction," Summer 1975, Abeles.

"Study of Two Approaches to Developing Expressive Performance," Spring 1975, Marchand.

"Verbal Behavior Analysis as a Supervisory Technique with Student Teachers of Music," Fall 1975, Verrastro.

"Villa-Lobos as Pedagogue: Music in the Service of the State," Fall 1975, Vassberg.

Vol. 24

"Changing Inservice Teachers' Self-Perceptions of their Ability to be Effective Teachers of the Arts," Winter 1976, Boyle, Thompson.

"Developing and Using Videotapes to Teach and Rehearse Techniques and Principles," Spring 1976, Gonzo, Forsythe.

"Development of the Child's Conception of Meter in Music," Fall 1976, Jones.

"Effect of Differential Teaching Techniques on Achievement Attitude, and Teaching Skills," Summer 1976, Moore.

"Effect of Music via Television as Reinforcement for Correct Mathematics," Summer 1976, Madsen, Dorow, Moore, Womble.

"Effects of Authority Figure Biases on Changing Judgments of Musical Events," Fall 1976, Radocy.

"Graduate Level Listening Test in Music History and Analysis," Summer 1976, LeBlanc.

"Longitudinal Comparison of Four Music Achievement and Music Aptitude Tests," Fall 1976, Young.

"Music Attitude Scale for Use with Upper Elementary School Children," Summer 1976, Shaw, Tomcala.

"Musical Tasks Related to the Development of the Conservation of Metric Time," Winter 1976, Perney.

"Perception of Tonality in Short Melodies," Winter 1976, Taylor.

"Preference and Interest as Functions of Distributional Redundancy in Rhythmic Sequences," Spring 1976, McMullen, Arnold.

"Process of Musical Creation: Interviews with Eight Composers," Spring 1976, Bennett.

"Relative Effectiveness of Two Approaches to Rhythm Reading for Fourth-Grade Students," Fall 1976, Palmer.

"Responses of Kindergarten Children to Musical Stimuli and Terminology," Spring 1976, Van Zee.

"Student Participation in Decision-Making Processes Concerning Musical Performance," Winter 1976, Petters.

"Tuning Preferences in Recorded Orchestral Music," Geringer.

Vol. 25

"Description of Tonal Direction on Verbal and Nonverbal Tasks by First Grade Children," Fall 1977, Hair.

"Effectiveness of Simulation Techniques in Teaching Behavior Management," Summer 1977, Brand.

"The Effect of Multiple Discrimination Training on Pitch-Matching Behaviors of Uncertain Singers," Spring 1977, Porter.

"The Effect of Teacher Approval/Disapproval Ratios on Student Music Selection and Concert Attentiveness," Spring 1977, Dorow.

"Effects of Dynamics, Halves of Exercise, and Trial Sequences on Tempo Accuracy," Fall 1977, Kuhn.

"The Effects of Pitch Interval on Brainwave Amplitudes," Summer 1977, Wang.

"Elementary Student Attending Behavior as a Function of Classroom Activities," Fall 1977, Forsythe.

"A Facet-Factorial Approach to Rating High School Choral Music Performance," Summer 1977, Cooksey.

"The Influence of Personality Composition in Applied Piano Groups," Fall 1977, Suchor.

"An Investigation of a Learning Sequence of Music Listening Skills," Fall 1977, Hufstader.

"Johann Gottfried Schmauk: German-American Music Educator," Summer 1977, Wolf.

"Mainstreaming: Needs Assessment through a Videotape Visual Scale," Winter 1977, Stuart, Gilbert.

"Measuring Discrimination of Complex Musical Events," Prince.

"A Multivariate Analysis of Factors in Attitudinal Levels of Wyoming Adults Toward Music," Spring 1977, Noble.

"Perceptions of Role Expectations and Performance of the Music Coordinator," Spring 1977, Heller, Quatraro.

"Physical Effects and Motor Responses to Music," Dainow.

"Relationship of Selected Factors in Trumpet Performance Adjudication Reliability," Winter 1977, Fiske, Jr.

"The Relationship of Selected Observational Variables to the Teaching of Singing," Summer 1977, Froelich.

"Relationships Between Melodic Error Detection, Melodic Dictation, and Melodic Sightsinging," Winter 1977, Larson.

"Relationships Between Pitch Memory in Short Melodies and Selected Factors," Winter 1977, Long.

"Review and Survey of MENC Research Training Institutes," Spring 1977, Nelson, Williams.

"A Systematic Approach to Aural-Visual Identification Instruction in Music for Young Children," Spring 1977, Jetter.

"Values and Personalities of Selected High School Choral Educators," Winter 1977, Slack.

Vol. 26

"Administrators' Ratings of Competencies for an Undergraduate Music Education Curriculum," Spring 1978, Stegall, Blackburn, Coop.

"Auditory Laterality Effects for Melodic Stimuli among Musicians and Non-musicians," Spring 1978, Franklin, Baumgarte.

"Cerebral Dominance for the Perception of Arpeggiated Triads," Winter 1978, Aiello.

"The Cognitive Flexibility Claim in the Bilingual and Music Education Research Traditions," Summer 1978, Bain.

"A Comparison of the Singing Formant in the Voices of Professional and Student Singers," Winter 1978, Magill, Jabobson.

"Computer-Based Recognition of Perceptual Patterns in Harmonic Dictation Exercises," Summer 1978, Hofstetter.

"The Development of a Measure of Attitude toward Instrumental Music Style," Summer 1978, Chalmers.

"Doctoral Dissertations in Music and Music Education, 1972–1977," Fall 1978, Gordon.

"Effects of Certain Lateral Dominance Traits, Music Aptitude, and Sex Differences with Instrumental Music Achievement," Spring 1978, Schleuter.

"Effects of Televised Instruction on Student Music Selection, Music Skills, and Attitudes," Winter 1978, Brown.

"Expressive Qualities in Music Perception and Music Education," Winter 1978, Levi.

"An Instructional Model for Teaching Identification and Naming of Music Phenomena to Preschool Children," Summer 1978, Jetter.

"Intersensory and Intrasensory Transfer of Melodic Contour Perception by Children," Spring 1978, Olson.

"Intonational Performance and Perception of Ascending Scales," Spring 1978, Geringer.

"Perception and Analysis of the Difference Tone Phenomenon As an Environmental Event," Summer 1978, Asmus, Jr.

"Repetition Effects Depend on Duration and Are Enhanced by Continuation of Interrupted Music," Winter 1978, Coppock.

"The Sex Stereotyping of Musical Instruments," Summer 1978, Ables, Porter.

"Testing Music Hearing in Right and Left Ears of Children Ages Ten, Eleven, and Twelve," Spring 1978, Gollnick.

Vol. 27

"Acquiring Relative Pitch Perception as a Function of Age," Winter 1979, Litke, Olsen.

"Comparison of the Unit Study and Traditional Approaches for Teaching Music through School Band Performance," Fall 1979, Garofalo, Whaley.

"Comparisons of Beginning Versus Experienced Elementary Music Educators in the Use of Teaching Time," Summer 1979, Wagner, Strul.

"Effect of Videotape Feedback Techniques on Performance, Verbalization, and Attitude of Beginning Conductors," Summer 1979, Yarbrough, Wapnick, Kelly.

"Elementary School Children's Vocal Range," Wassum.

"Evaluation of a Competency-Based Approach to Teaching Aural Interval Identification," Winter 1979, Hofstetter.

"Fray Pedro de Gante: Pioneer American Music Educator," Spring 1979, Heller.

"Generic Style Music Preferences of Fifth-Grade Students," Winter 1979, LeBlanc.

"Grade/Age Levels and the Reinforcement Value of the Collative Properties of Music," Summer 1979, Eisenstein.

"The Influence of Peer Imitation on Expressive Movement to Music," Fall 1979, Flohr, Brown.

"Instrumental Music Instruction as a Contingency for Increased Reading Behavior," Summer 1979, Gordon.

"Modulated Beat Discrimination among Musicians and Nonmusicians," Summer 1979, Madsen.

"Music History and Appreciation in the Two-Year College Curriculum," Spring 1979, Friedlander.

"Programmed Instruction Using Band Literature to Teach Pitch and Rhythm Error Detection to Music Education Students," Fall 1979, Ramsey.

"Relationship between Creative Behavior in Music and Selected Variables as Measured in High School Students," Winter 1979, Webster.

"Relationship of Music Ability and Intelligence to Auditory and Visual Conservation of the Kindergarten Child," Spring 1979, Norton.

"Replication of a Study on Teaching Singing in the Elementary General Music Classroom," Spring 1979, Froelich.

"Strategies for Using Popular Music to Teach Form to Intermediate Instrumentalists," Fall 1979, Grashel.

"The Theoretical Relationship between Item Difficulty and the 'In Doubt' response in Music Tests," Fall 1979, Levendusky.

"Undergraduate Nonmusic Major Vocal Ranges," Summer 1979, Kuhn, Wachaus, Moore, Pantle.

"The Use of Videotape Recordings to Increase Teacher Trainees' Error Detection Skills," Spring 1979, Stuart.

"Using a Vertical-Keyboard Instrument with the Uncertain Singer," Fall 1979, Jones.

Vol. 28

"An Acoustical Study of Individual Voices in Choral Blend," Summer 1980, Goodwin.

"An Assessment of Motor Music Skill Development in Young Children," Fall 1980, Gilbert.

"A Comparison of Scalar and Root Harmonic Aural Perception Techniques," Winter 1980, Alvarez.

"Computer-Based Recognition of Perceptual Patterns in Chord Quality Dictation Exercises," Summer 1980, Hofstetter.

"Divergent Production Abilities as Constructs of Musical Creativity," Spring 1980, Gorder.

"The Early Childhood Song Books of Eleanor Smith: Their Affinity with the Philosophy of Friedrich Froebel," Summer 1980, Alper.

"The Effect of Appropriate and Inappropriate In-Class Song Performance Models on Performance Preference of Third- and Fourth-Grade Students," Spring 1980, Baker.

"The Effect of Group Size on Individual Achievement in Beginning Piano Classes," Fall 1980, Jackson.

"The Effects of a Creative-Comprehensive Approach and a Performance Approach on Acquisition of Music Fundamentals by College Students," Summer 1980, Dodson.

"Effects of Dark-Bright Timbral Variation on the Perception of Flatness and Sharpness," Spring 1980, Wapnick, Freeman.

"Elementary School Children's Concept of Tonality," Wassum.

"Empirical Testing of an Affective Learning Paradigm," Fall 1980, Asmus.

"Evaluation of Three Types of Instructional Strategy for Learner Acquisition of Intervals," Winter 1980, Canelos, Murphy, Blomback, Heck.

"Hemispheric and Directional Asymmetry of Pitch Discrimination," Winter 1980, Murray.

"Individualized Instruction, Student Achievement, and Dropout in an Urban Elementary Instrumental Music Program," Spring 1980, McCarthy.

"Interrelationships among Music Aptitude, IQ, and Auditory Conservation," Winter 1980, Norton.

"Music in Special Education before 1930: Hearing and Speech Development," Winter 1980, Solomon.

"On the Existence of Combination Tones as Physical Entities," Summer 1980, White, Grieshaber.

"Pitch, Tempo, and Timbral Preferences in Recorded Piano Music," Fall 1980, Wapnick.

"Public School Music Teachers' Perceptions of the Effect of Certain Competencies on Pupil Learning," Winter 1980, Taebel.

"Relationships among Ensemble Participation, Private Instruction, and Aural Skill Development," Fall 1980, May, Elliott.

"Selected Indexes of the Academic and Professional Preparation of Music Supervisors in Canada," Summer 1980, Jorgensen.

"Teaching Effectiveness among Teaching Competency Measures, Pupil Product Measures, and Certain Attribute Variables," Winter 1980, Taebel, Coker.

"Thomas Harrison's Patented Numeral Notation System," Winter 1980, Elward.

Vol. 29

"An Ascending Music Stimulus Program and Hyperactive Children," Summer 1981, Haack, Radocy.

"Computer-Based Recognition of Perceptual Patterns and Learning Styles in Rhythmic Dictation Exercises," Winter 1981, Hofstetter.

"Course Entry Affect and its Relationship to Course Grade in Music Education and Music Therapy Classes," Spring 1981, Asmus.

"Development and Validation of a Music Education Competency Test," Spring 1981, Beazley.

"Dimensionality in High School Student Participants' Perception of the Measuring of Choral Singing Experience," Winter 1981, Hylton.

"Discrimination between Tone Quality and Intonation in Unaccompanied Flute/Oboe Duets," Winter 1981, Madsen, Geringer.

"The Effect of Melodic Context on Students' Aural Perception of Rhythm," Fall 1981, Boisen.

"Effects of Sequencing, Classifying, and Coding on Identifying Harmonic Functions," Summer 1981, Alvarez.

"Effects of Style, Tempo, and Performing Medium on Children's Music Preference," Summer 1981, LeBlanc.

"E. Thayer Gaston: Leader in Scientific Thought on Music in Therapy and Education," Winter 1981, Johnson.

"Factors Influencing Pop Music Preferences of Young People," Spring 1981, Boyle, Hosterman, Ramsey.

"The Gamut and Solmization in Early British and American Texts," Spring 1981, Grashel.

"Instrument Association Skills: Children in First and Second Grades," Spring 1981, Wooderson, Small.

"Interval and Pitch Recognition in and out of Immediate Context," Summer 1981, Shatzkin.

"Lateralization of Components of Melodic Stimuli: Musicians versus Non-musicians," Fall 1981, Baumgarte, Franklin.

"Mainstreaming: Music Educators' Participation and Professional Needs," Spring 1981, Gilbert, Asmus.

"Moravian Music Education in America, ca. 1750 to ca. 1830," Fall 1981, Hall.

"Music Abilities and Experiences as Predictors of Error-Detection Skills," Summer 1981, Brand, Burnsed.

"Music Lessons and Books as Reinforcement Alternatives for an Academic Task," Summer 1981, Madsen.

"On a Choice-Based Instructional Typology in Music," Jorgensen.

"Praise and Corrective Feedback in the Remediation of Incorrect Left-Hand Positions of Elementary String Players," Summer 1981, Salzberg, Salzberg.

"Prediction of Performer Attentiveness Based on Rehearsal Activity and Teacher Behavior," Fall 1981, Yarbrough, Price.

"Relationships between Motivation Variables and Selected Criterion Measures of High School Band Directing Success," Fall 1981, Caimi.

"The Role of the Federal Government in Support of the Arts and Music Education," Winter 1981, Barresi.

"Sex-Role Associations of Music Instruments and Occupations by Gender and Major," Spring 1981, Griswold, Chroback.

"Short-Term Music Instruction and Young Children's Developmental Music Aptitude," Fall 1981, Flohr.

"Verbal Identification of Music Concepts," Spring 1981, Hair.

Vol. 30

"An Assessment of Anxiety in Instrumental and Vocal Performances," Summer 1982, Hamann.

"Comparison of Two Approaches to Teaching Beginning Band," Winter 1982, Whitener.

"Discrimination of Pitch Direction by Preschool Children with Verbal and Nonverbal Tasks," Schlentrich, Webster.

"The Effect of Disc Jockey, Peer, and Music Teacher Approval of Music on Music Selection and Preference," Fall 1982, Alpert.

"The Effect of Keyboard Learning Experiences on Middle School General Music Students' Achievement and Attitudes," Fall 1982, Boyle, Wig.

"The Effect of Peer Approval and Disapproval on Improvement of Pitch Matching and Group Behavior," Spring 1982, Hanser.

"The Effect of Subdivision Activity on Rhythmic Performance Skills in High School Mixed Choirs," Spring 1982, Major.

"The Effects of Conducting Experience and Programmed Materials on Error Detection Scores of College Conducting Students," Fall 1982, DeCarbo.

"Effects of Student Teaching on the Classroom Management Beliefs and Skills of Music Student Teachers," Winter 1982, Brand.

"Effects of Traditional and Simplified Methods of Rhythm-Reading Instruction," Summer 1982, Bebeau.

"The Evolution of Music Education Philosophy from Utilitarian to Aesthetic," Spring 1982, Mark.

"Froebelian Implications in Texts of Early Childhood Songs Published Near the Turn of the Century," Spring 1982, Alper.

"A History of Music Education in the Black Community of Kansas City, Kansas, 1905-1954," Summer 1982, Buckner.

"Music Aptitude Profile Scores in a Noninstitutionalized Elderly Population," Spring 1982, Gibbons.

"On Early Applications of Psychology in Music Education," Fall 1982, Rideout.

"Preferences of Elderly Individuals for Selected Music Education Experiences," Winter 1982, Beal, Gilbert.

"Prediction of Music Achievement in the Elementary School," Spring 1982, Hedden.

"The Relationships Among Instrumental Sight-Reading Ability and Seven Selected Predictor Variables," Spring 1982, Elliott.

"Same/Different Discrimination Techniques, Readiness Training, Pattern Treatment, and Sex on Aural Discrimination and Singing Ability of Tonal Patterns by Kindergarteners," Winter 1982, Jordan, DeCarbo.

"Significant Developments in Choral Music Education in Higher Education between 1950-1980," Summer 1982, White.

"A Study of High School Music Participants' Stylistic Preferences and Identification Abilities in Music and the Visual Arts," Winter 1982, Haack.

Vol. 31

"Art and Music in the Pestalozzian Tradition," Fall 1983, Elfand.

"Carl Busch: Danish-American Music Educator," Summer 1983, Lowe.

"A Comparison of the Motor Music Skills of Nonhandicapped and Learning-Disabled Children," Summer 1983, Gilbert.

"Comparison of Two Approaches to Teaching Beginning Band," Spring 1983, Whitener.

"A Comparison of Rhythm Pattern Perception and Performance in Normal and Learning-Disabled Readers, Age Seven and Eight," Winter 1983, Atterbury.

"Discrimination and Interference in the Recall of Melodic Stimuli," Spring 1983, Madsen and Staum.

"Discrimination of Modulated Music Tempo by Music Majors," Spring 1983, Wang.

"The Effect of Conductor Academic Task Presentation, Conductor Reinforcement, and Ensemble Practice on Performers' Musical Achievement, Attentiveness, and Attitude," Winter 1983, Price.

"The Effect of Instruction in Vocabulary and Listening on Nonmusicians' Descriptions of Changes in Music," Fall 1983, Flowers.

"The Effect of Male and Female Vocal Modeling on Pitch-Matching Accuracy of First-Grade Children," Fall 1983, Small and McCachern.

"Effects of Music Loudness on Task Performance and Self-Report of College-Aged Students," Fall 1983, Wolfe.

"Effect of Tempo on Children's Music Preference," Winter 1983, LeBlanc and McCrary.

"Effects of Tempo and Performing Medium on Children's Music Preference," Spring 1983, LeBlanc and Cote.

"The Effects of Age, Singing Ability, and Instrumental Experiences on Preschool Children's Melodic Perception," Summer 1983, Ramsey.

"Effects of Rhythmic and Melodic Alterations on Rhythmic Perception," Summer 1983, Sink.

"Engineering Change in Music Education: A Model of the Political Process Underlying the Boston School Music Movement (1829–1838)," Spring 1983, Jorgensen.

"Montessorian Music Method: Unpublished Works," Fall 1983, Rubin.

"Multivariate Analysis of Degree Persistence of Undergraduate Music Education Majors," Winter 1983, Brown and Alley.

"Music Education, and Community in Nineteenth-Century Kansas Euterpe, Tonnies, and the Academy on the Plains," Summer 1983, Haack and Heller.

"Peer Tutoring Effects on the Music Performance of Tutors and Tutees in Beginning Band Classes," Spring 1983, Alexander and Dorow.

"The Relationship of Pitch-Matching and Pitch-Discrimination Abilities of Preschool and Fourth-Grade Students," Summer 1983, Geringer.

"The Snedden-Farnsworth Exchanges of 1917 and 1918 on the Value of Music and Art in Education," Fall 1983, Lee.

Finale

Part IV

9

The National Assessment of Educational Progress

Until recently, there has been no means of evaluating the results of music education on a national scale. American education methods, standards, and goals are extremely diversified; a nationwide evaluation would be complicated and expensive. The need for a national assessment of education became apparent in the early 1960s, when the education reform movement was well under way. No means had been developed to correlate the enormous resources being invested in education with the results of education. The tremendous increase in education expenditures in the late 1950s and early 1960s was for education input (personnel, teacher retraining, curriculum development, equipment, and facilities) because it was assumed that increased input would produce a corollary output, although there was no conclusive evidence that such was the case. Standardized achievement tests, which had been in use for decades, indicated how well students achieved in relation to each other, but did not indicate what they actually learned, and therefore, could not be used for a national assessment of educational results.

In 1963 Dr. Francis Keppel, U.S. Commissioner of Education, initiated several conferences to explore ways of obtaining the needed information. The result was the formation of a committee called the Exploratory Committee on Assessing the Progress of Education (ECAPE) in 1964. The purpose of ECAPE was "to examine the possibility of conducting an assessment of educational attainment on a national basis."[1] ECAPE decided that such an assessment would be feasible, and that ten areas of education would be covered initially—art, career and occupational development, citizenship, literature, mathematics, music reading, science, social studies, and writing. The committee in charge of the project was called the Committee on Assessing the Progress of Education (CAPE). CAPE began its work in 1969 under the auspices of the Carnegie Corporation, but later in the same year, control was shifted to the Education Commission of the States, which still operates it. The U.S. Office of Education (USOE), now the U.S. Department of Education, provides funds and monitors the National Assessment of Educational Progress (NAEP).

Keppel, in a meeting with representatives of all educational disciplines, was made aware of the inherent danger of misinterpreting data from the first assessment and of the fact that great care must be taken in reporting to the public. The first assessment could only establish a basis by which future ratings could be measured and have relevance. Unfortunately, not enough caution was shown in this regard, and the press often neglected to mention that the data from the first assessment would have meaning only in relation to those following. The raw data was published and was usually accompanied by negative headlines. This dealt a blow to American education by shaking the confidence of the public. The second music assessment was done in 1978 and 1979. It provided the comparison with the first that was called for in the 1960s.

THE GOALS OF NAEP

NAEP provides information to educational decision makers and teachers that can be used to establish educational priorities and to determine the national progress in education. Its goals are as follows: (1) to measure changes in the educational attainments of young Americans; (2) to make available on a continuing basis comprehensive data on the educational attainments of young Americans; (3) to utilize the capabilities of NAEP to conduct special interest "probes" into selected areas of educational attainment; (4) to provide data, analyses, and reports understandable to, interpretable by, and responsive to, the needs of a variety of audiences; (5) to encourage and facilitate interpretive studies of NAEP data, thereby generating implications useful to educational practitioners and decision makers; (6) to facilitate the use of NAEP technology at state and local levels when appropriate; (7) to continue to develop, test, and refine the technologies necessary for gathering and analyzing NAEP achievement data; (8) to conduct an ongoing program of research and operational studies necessary for the resolution of problems and refinement of the NAEP model.[2]

METHODOLOGY OF NAEP

The first NAEP asked questions of respondents at four age levels; the second queried respondents at three age levels. Each question, or task (called an exercise), reflects a previously defined educational goal or objective. The exercises are administered to scientifically selected samples that take into account demographic factors—the size of the community and socioeconomic status of the respondents—as well as ethnic categories (the latter only for the second assessment). Respondents from all parts of the country are included. Students are sampled at three age levels that represent educational milestones attained by most students: age 9, when most students are near the completion of their primary education; age 13, when most students have completed their elementary school education; and age 17, when most students are still in school and completing their secondary education. The first assessment also sampled 17-year-olds not in school in order to gain a more accurate picture of skills, knowledge, and attitudes of that age level; this group was not sampled in the second assessment. Another group, young adults (ages 26 to 35), was included in the first assessment (but not the second) in order to learn what the educational results were for people who have completed their formal education and have been away from school for years.

NAEP does not score or rank the individual respondents. It determines how groups at the four age levels perform on specific exercises and, within each age level, how groups of individuals perform, taking into consideration demographic and sociological variables. It is unnecessary for each respondent to take every exercise. The exercises are divided into booklets; each respondent takes only one booklet. The samples for each booklet are statistically equivalent, so group comparisons can be made across booklets. This allows NAEP to assess performance on more exercises than would be possible in the usual testing situation.

Most exercises are multiple-choice questions; there are also open-ended exercises that require responses from a few words to a long essay. Some employ the use of pictures, tapes, films, or practical everyday items as stimuli. Individual interviews, the manipulation of appropriate apparatus to solve a problem, and observations of the respondents' problem-solving techniques supplement the paper-and-pencil tasks. For example, in music, respondents were asked to sing a song or perform on an instrument; in science, to conduct a small experiment; in math, to make change from a change drawer; in social studies, to interpret an election ballot. Positive attitudes toward, or opinions about, the various learning areas, are considered important educational attainments.

Therefore, affective exercises and attitude survey questions are also included.

NAEP exercises are administered either to individuals or to small groups (not larger than twelve) by specially trained personnel. Individuals are not ranked according to their performance. Because the aim of NAEP is to describe attainment, exercises that require high discrimination power are not emphasized. The exercises cover the entire spectrum of difficulty, from very easy tasks to the most difficult.

NAEP differs from standardized achievement tests in several ways. Achievement tests are norm-referenced; NAEP is content- or objective-referenced. In standardized achievement tests, all respondents take every exercise, are scored for their performance, and are ranked with respect to a reference group; with NAEP, no respondent takes all of the exercises, receives a score, or is ranked because emphasis is placed on the performance of groups. Standardized tests are usually mass-administered; NAEP exercises are administered to individuals or small groups. Standardized tests are usually limited to the multiple-choice format; NAEP utilizes a variety of exercise formats. Standardized tests usually focus on the cognitive domain; NAEP includes exercises relating to the affective domain as well. Respondents to standardized tests are required to read the items for themselves; NAEP exercises are read to respondents by a paced tape or by the exercise administrator in an interview situation (except during the reading assessment). Finally, it is most unusual for the items on standardized tests to be made public; NAEP releases half of the exercises used so the public will understand its methods.[3]

NAEP IN MUSIC

Prior to constructing assessment instruments for each subject area, NAEP had to specify its objectives. Basic guidelines were set up for the development of objectives: (1) objectives must be acceptable to scholars in the discipline of each locale, most educators in that locale, and to thoughtful lay citizens; and (2) objectives must be stated in behavioral terms. Four organizations that had had considerable experience in test construction were contracted to bring together scholars, teachers, and curriculum specialists to develop objectives and prototype exercises. The Educational Testing Service (ETS) of Princeton, New Jersey, was awarded the contract for developing music objectives in 1965. A group of experts was invited to assist ETS in the job. The results of the committee's work were then circulated to research organizations and various individuals for recommendations. The broad categories of objectives at which the committee arrived are as follows:

  I. Perform a piece of music
      A. Sing (technical proficiency not required)
      B. Play or sing (technical proficiency required)
      C. Invent and improvise (technical proficiency required)
 II. Read standard musical notation
      A. Identify the elements of notation, such as clefs, letter names of notes, duration symbols, key signatures, and dynamic markings
      B. Identify the correct notation for familiar pieces
      C. Follow notation while listening to music
      D. Sight-sing
III. Listen to music with understanding
      A. Perceive the various elements of music, such as timbre, rhythm, melody and harmony, and texture
      B. Perceive structure in music
      C. Distinguish some differing types and functions of music
      D. Be aware of (and recognize) some features of historical styles in music
 IV. Be knowledgeable about some musical instruments, some of the terminology of music, methods of performance, some of the standard literature of music, and some aspects of the history of music
      A. Know the meanings of common musical terms to be used in connection with the performance of music, and identify musical instruments and performing ensembles in illustrations
      B. Know standard pieces of music by title, or composer, or brief descriptions of the music, or of literary–pictorial materials associated with the music from its inception
      C. Know something of the history of music
  V. Know about the musical resources of the community and seek musical experiences by performing music
      A. Know whether or not there are music libraries and stores in the community, and know where concerts are given
      B. Seek to perform music by playing, singing, taking lesons, joining performing groups, etc.
 VI. Make judgments about music, and value the personal worth of music
      A. Distinguish parodies from their models
      B. Be able to describe an important personal "musical" experience.[4]

The 1978–79 assessment provided a measure of change in performance since the 1971–72 assessment. About half of the exercises in the first assessment were repeated in the second under roughly identical administrative conditions. The objectives of the first assessment were revised for the second, and additional exercises were included to cover them. The second assessment involved approximately 20,000 9-year-olds, 25,000 13-year-olds and 22,000 17-year-olds.[5] The objectives of the 1978–79 assessment were as follows:

I.   Value music as an important realm of human experience
    A.   Be affectively responsive to music
    B.   Be acquainted with music from different nations, cultures, periods, genres, and ethnic groups
    C.   Value music in the life of the individual, family, and community
    D.   Make and support aesthetic judgments about music

II. Perform music
    A.   Sing (without score)
    B.   Play (without score)
    C.   Sing or play from a written score
    D.   Play or sing a previously prepared piece

III. Create music
    A.   Improvise
    B.   Represent music symbolically

IV. Identify the elements and expressive controls of music
    A.   Identify the elements of music
    B.   Identify the relationships among elements in a given composition
    C.   Demonstrate an understanding of a variety of musical terms, expression markings, and conducting gestures in a musical context

V.   Identify and classify music historically and culturally
    A.   Identify and describe the features that characterize a variety of folk, ethnic, popular, and art music
    B.   Identify and describe the music and musical style of the various stylistic periods in Western civilization (e.g., Medieval, Renaissance, Baroque, Classical, Romantic). Identify representative composers of each period.
    C.   Cite examples of ways in which people utilize music in their social and cultural life.[6]

Musical Achievement: First Assessment

In 1971 and 1972, NAEP measured the level of musical achievement. The first music assessment contained fifteen performance exercises, some of which included several parts. The exercises were divided into five groups: singing familiar songs, repeating unfamiliar musical material, improvising, performing from notation, and performing a prepared piece. Special methods were required for administration and scoring. An exercise administrator read the instructions to each individual, played the stimulus on one tape recorder, and recorded the response on another tape recorder. Individuals were encouraged to record their voices before the administration actually began in order to minimize anxiety caused by singing into a microphone. After the responses were taped, a group of music professionals listened to samples of the responses and constructed scoring guidelines that were comprehensive enough to encompass the wide variety in the quality of performances, and objective enough to ensure that any given performance would receive the same score from any scorer. It is not within the scope of this chapter to report all of the results. Instead, an overview will be provided.

PERFORMANCE

Singing Familiar Songs.

About 20 percent of the 9-year-olds, 30 percent of the 13-year-olds, and 40 percent of the 17-year-olds and adults gave performances rated "good" in the unaccompanied singing of "America." Singing with accompaniment, approximately 93 percent of all four age levels were able to keep an acceptable rhythm. Acceptable pitch ranged from 70 percent for adults to 50 percent for 9-year-olds. Success levels were relatively similar for singing a familiar round, but were considerably lower. Forty-five percent of the adults were able to perform a familiar round acceptably.

 Repeating unfamiliar musical material. About half of the older groups and 30 percent of the 9-year-olds were able to repeat a rhythm pattern successfully. Success in repeating a four-measure melodic pattern ranged from 2 percent for 9-year-olds to 9 percent for adults. Acceptable repetition of a harmonic pattern was performed by 8 percent of the 13-year-olds and by 15 percent of adults. This was not administered to 9-year-olds.

 Improvising. Success in improvising a rhythmic accompaniment to a short jazz selection of moderate tempo was achieved by from 70 to 90 percent of the various age groups of respondents, but fewer than 20 percent in any age group added embellishments. Success in improvising a complementary melody to a given one ranged from less than 50 percent to about 60 percent. Those judged "good" ranged from about 20 to 40 percent. Only about 10 percent of the 13-year-olds and adults were able to improvise a harmonic accompaniment acceptably. Many individuals did not attempt to respond to this exercise.

Performing from notation. Four sight-reading exercises were administered. In the simplest, not more than 12 percent of any age group was successful in overall quality, although there were higher success rates for the separate aspects of rhythm and pitch.

Performing a prepared piece. Twenty-five percent of the 9-year-olds, 35 percent of the 13-year-olds, 25 percent of the 17-year-olds, and 15 percent of the adults claimed to play a musical instrument. Approximately half played a prepared piece for the assessment, and about half of those performed a simple piece acceptably. About 60 percent of the respondents were successful in singing a selection of each individual's choice. Females did slightly better than males in all age groups. There was little difference between blacks and whites in overall performance, although variations occurred in many exercises. In rhythm exercises, for example, 9-, 13-, and 17-year-old blacks attained percentages of 7 or 8 points higher than whites of the same ages. Black adults were even with or above the national average in the familiar song, rhythm, melody, and harmony exercises. Children of parents with some post–high school education attained percentages from 5 to 20 points higher than respondents whose parents had no high school education. As far as geographical location was concerned, respondents from the central United States did slightly better than those from other regions, but regional differences were slight. Respondents from rural communities scored lower, especially at the adult level, in improvising and instrumental performance. The younger groups in inner city areas scored considerably lower than the national average, although 9-year-olds in this group attained percentages 7 or 8 points higher than the rest of the nation in tapping out a rhythm. The suburban group performed consistently well on practically all of the exercises at every age level. The conclusion of the NAEP report was:

If there is a pattern emerging from all this, it is that people can enjoy and perform music in a rudimentary way but that they are not familiar with the more technical aspects of music. They can sing, and they like to sing; they hear enough music to recognize the instruments, and they like to listen to music. Only the technical skills and the specialized vocabularies that have been constructed to describe music are lacking from the musical background of most individuals. The majority of Americans do enjoy listening to music and can perform music in a rudimentary way.[7]

KNOWLEDGE OF MUSICAL NOTATION AND TERMINOLOGY

Vocabulary. Between 90 and 95 percent of each age group were able to identify which musical element changed in a certain place in a recorded piece of music. Given a choice of "louder," "softer," "slower," or "exactly the same," most respondents correctly identified "louder." This was the only vocabulary exercise in which a majority chose the correct response. Approximately 60 percent of the 17-year-olds, 50 percent of the 13-year-olds, and 25 percent of the 9-year-olds were able to identify correctly a four-phrase structure. But when asked to identify changes in rhythm, melody, and harmony in a heard piece, less than 60 percent identified rhythm, and less than 50 percent identified melody and harmony.

Basic notation. About 60 percent of the 13-year-olds and 40 percent of the adults were able to identify the note D from a list of five choices. Less than 30 percent of any group knew that two 8th notes are equal to a quarter note in duration. In score reading, when asked to mark in the score the place where the recorded music stopped, less than 20 percent of the 9-year-olds were successful, but about 50 percent of the 13-year-olds, 70 percent of the 17-year-olds, and 55 percent of the adults were successful. Not more than 30 percent of any group was able to identify a discrepancy between a heard melody and a printed score.

LISTEN TO MUSIC WITH UNDERSTANDING

Aural recognition: All groups achieved high percentages in identifying the timbres of various instruments. All groups scored about 90 percent in identifying a keyboard instrument. There were also high success rates in identifying a trumpet and a piccolo. Respondents had more difficulty in identifying instrumental timbres in a jazz idiom. About 60 percent of the upper age groups were able to identify the tone of a violin and cello. In visual recognition tests, approximately 80 percent of the upper three age levels were able to identify a picture of a trumpet among other instruments. The success rate was about 40 percent in visual identification of cellos and bassoons.

MUSIC HISTORY AND LITERATURE

The music history and literature section tested knowledge about music history, genres, styles, and literature. Included were traditional Western art music, popular, folk, and electronic music, and music of earlier periods.

Periods in Music History:

Approximately 60 percent of the respondents were able to identify the correct chronological order of five historical periods. When asked to

FIGURE 9.1. Sample NAEP Exercises: Singing Rounds

Exercise 1C was administered only to 9-year-olds. It required children to sing one part in the round "Are You Sleeping?" A corresponding unreleased exercise, Exercise 1c, required individuals from the older three age groups to sing a part in a similar round. The subsequent paragraphs discuss the results of both the released and unreleased exercises involving rounds, although, strictly speaking, the two exercises are not directly comparable.

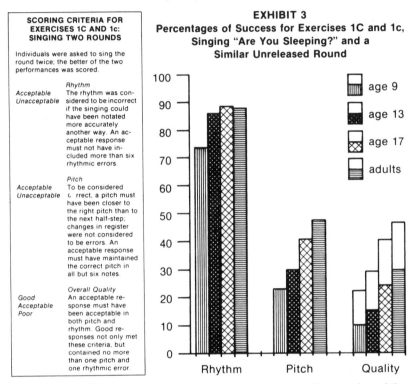

SCORING CRITERIA FOR EXERCISES 1C AND 1c: SINGING TWO ROUNDS

Individuals were asked to sing the round twice; the better of the two performances was scored.

Rhythm
Acceptable / Unacceptable — The rhythm was considered to be incorrect if the singing could have been notated more accurately another way. An acceptable response must not have included more than six rhythmic errors.

Pitch
Acceptable / Unacceptable — To be considered correct, a pitch must have been closer to the right pitch than to the next half-step; changes in register were not considered to be errors. An acceptable response must have maintained the correct pitch in all but six notes.

Overall Quality
Good / Acceptable / Poor — An acceptable response must have been acceptable in both pitch and rhythm. Good responses not only met these criteria, but contained no more than one pitch and one rhythmic error.

EXHIBIT 3
Percentages of Success for Exercises 1C and 1c, Singing "Are You Sleeping?" and a Similar Unreleased Round

age 9 / age 13 / age 17 / adults

Rhythm / Pitch / Quality

There are notable similarities in response patterns between the rounds and the "America" exercises. Individuals at all age levels were much more capable of maintaining the rhythm than maintaining the pitch. And, as in the "America" exercises, adults demonstrated a considerable improvement over the 17-year-old percentage, 17-year-olds demonstrated an improvement over the 13-year-old percentage and so on.

However, the percentages for Exercises 1C and 1c were significantly lower than those for the "America" exercises. Although 70% of the adults gave an acceptable performance of "America," only about 45% were able to give an acceptable performance of the round.

Since rounds are by their nature more difficult to perform than monophonic music, the lower percentages in Exercises 1C and 1c are understandable. But one similarity holds for all the exercises that involve singing familiar songs: almost all individuals were able to maintain rhythmic patterns, while relatively few were accurate in pitch.

Note. Example provided by National Assessment of Educational Progress, 1860 Lincoln Street, Denver, Colorado.

FIGURE 9.2. Sample NAEP Exercises: Improvising Melody

In Exercise 1H, individuals were asked to listen to the following phrase and then improvise a concluding phrase (m.m. 152):

An acceptable phrase was one which complemented the first phrase and ended with a cadence. About half of the individuals from all four age groups attained acceptable scores. Percentages of good responses were lower, ranging from about 20% for 9-year-olds to about 40% for adults, but criteria for good responses were far more stringent.

**SCORING CRITERIA
FOR EXERCISE 1H,
IMPROVISING MELODY**

Good
Acceptable
Poor

Three basic criteria separated the acceptable responses from the poor responses. To be considered acceptable, a response must have begun within two measures of the end of the stimulus, must not have deviated in tempo by more than 10% and must not have contained more than two unidentifiable pitches (pitches a little sharp or flat were acceptable).

Three other criteria separate good responses from other acceptable responses:

A good response must have lasted at least two measures, while other acceptable responses could have been as short as one measure.

Good responses maintained the key, while other acceptable responses could establish and retain a new tonal center in a closely related key (dominant, subdominant, relative minor or parallel minor). Temporary dominant modulation with return to the tonic was not considered to be a change of key.

A good response must have ended on the first, third or fifth degree of the tonic chord with a definite feeling of finish, while other acceptable responses could end on any note in the same key in a clear cadence or half-cadence.

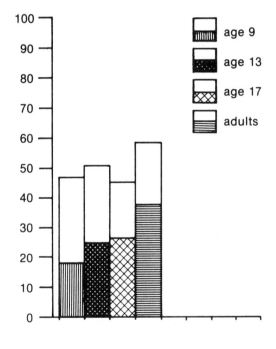

**EXHIBIT 8
Percentages of Success for Exercise 1H,
Improvising Melody**

Note. Example provided by National Assessment of Educational Progress, 1860 Lincoln Street, Denver, Colorado.

FIGURE 9.3. Sample NAEP Exercises: Musical Genres

Exercise 5E

Exercise 5E was administered individually to 9-year-olds, 13-year-olds, 17-year-olds and adults. Administrators read from and recorded responses on pages like the following.

A. Are there any kinds of music that you like to listen to?

	Age Level			
	9	13	17	Adult
Yes (Go to B)	83%	96%	99%	99%
No (Go to D)	16	4	1	1
No response (After 10 seconds, go to D)	1	0	0	0

B.*What one kind of music do you MOST like to listen to?

If no response is given in 10 seconds, go to D.

If respondent names more than one kind of music or says "ALL kinds" ask, *Which kind do you MOST like to listen to?* If respondent gives a general response such as "Popular" or "Classical," ask, *What TYPE of (popular, classical, etc.) music?* Probe to find out the specific kind of music such as rock, blues, opera, symphonic, etc. If respondent names a performer or composer, ask, *What kind of music do you MOST like by that person?*

Go to C.

	Age Level			
	9	13	17	Adult
Instrumental art (e.g., classical, symphonic)	3%	4%	5%	12%
Vocal art (e.g., opera)	1	0	0	1
Jazz	4	5	4	6
Folk	4	2	4	5
Rock	32	57	62	14
Country-western	8	7	5	29
Soul	1	3	5	0
Popular ballads (e.g., barbershop, male vocalists, romantic)	2	2	2	8
Blues	1	1	2	2
Background music	0	0	0	3
Other popular	3	5	4	8
Other types (e.g., unclassifiable responses)	17	7	6	11

C. What other kinds of music do you like to listen to?

(1) _____   (6) _____
(2) _____   (7) _____
(3) _____   (8) _____
(4) _____   (9) _____
(5) _____   (10) _____

If respondent answers "None" OR no response is given in 10 seconds, go to D.

If respondent pauses after first response ask, *What other kinds do you like to listen to?* Probe to find out the specific kinds of music, as in B.

Stop after 10 responses OR when respondent answers "None" OR no response is given in 10 seconds.

	Age Level			
	9	13	17	Adult
At least one additional type named	40%	73%	85%	92%
At least two additional types named	11	38	51	66
At least three additional types named	3	14	26	37

D. Are there any kinds of music that you do NOT like to listen to?

	9	13	17	
⬭ Yes (Go to E)	62	73	78	82
⬭ No (End the exercise)	36	26	22	18
⬭ No response (After 10 seconds, end the exercise)	2	1	0	0

E.*What one kind of music do you LEAST like to listen to?

If no response is given in 10 seconds, end the exercise.

If respondent names more than one kind of music or says "ALL kinds," ask, *Which kind do you LEAST like to listen to?* If respondent gives a general response such as "Popular" or "Classical," ask, *What TYPE of (popular, classical, etc.) music?* Probe to find out the specific kind of music such as rock, blues, opera, symphonic, etc. If respondent names a performer or composer, ask, *What kind of music do you LEAST like by that person?*

Go to F.

	Age Level			
	9	13	17	Adult
Instrumental art (e.g., classical, symphonic)	4%	9%	14%	9%
Vocal art (e.g., opera)	5	16	15	24
Jazz	2	4	4	7
Folk	2	3	2	1
Rock	8	7	11	25
Country-western	6	12	18	10
Soul	1	1	2	1
Popular ballads (e.g., barbershop, male vocalists, romantic)	4	3	1	0
Blues	1	1	2	1
Other popular	3	5	2	3
Other types (e.g., unclassifiable responses)	18	7	4	1

Note. Example provided by National Assessment of Educational Progress, 1860 Lincoln Street, Denver, Colorado.

identify the periods of a variety of musical selections, success varied among 17-year-olds from 60 percent (Tchaikovsky) to less than 10 percent (Schoenberg). For adults, the range was from approximately 54 percent to 10 percent. Vivaldi was recognized by fewer adults than was Schoenberg.

Musical Genres and Styles:

When asked to recognize style similarities, about 60 percent of the three upper age groups were successful. Approximately the same percentage was able to correctly classify jazz pieces as ragtime, boogie-woogie, Chicago school, or modern when they heard boogie-woogie and Dave Brubeck. Between 30 percent and 40 percent identified the styles of Cannonball Adderly, Earl Hines, and Scott Joplin.

Music Literature:

"America the Beautiful" was recognized by approximately 40 percent to 50 percent of the respondents of the three upper age groups. Success in recognizing "This Land Is Your Land" and "When the Saints Go Marching In" was considerably higher. The three upper levels were less successful in recognizing several "familiar" classical selections (from 3.1 percent to 38.6 percent). Success in matching composers and compositions ranged from 3.6 percent (13-year-olds, Prokofiev's *Peter and the Wolf*) to 52.5 percent (adults, Sousa's "Stars and Stripes Forever").

ATTITUDES TOWARD MUSIC

Musical achievement is important, but it is only a means to the development of aesthetic sensitivity. Because aesthetic sensitivity is the ultimate goal of music education, it was necessary for it to be included by NAEP. The national assessment included exercises designed to elicit information about attitudes toward music. The attitude exercises do not actually measure sensitivity (which cannot be done under the survey conditions of NAEP); rather, they measure "approach tendencies," which are assumed to correlate to aesthetic sensitivity. It was found that a majority of people in all four age groups seek out and listen to music at least once a week (many people do so more often) on televisions, radio, or recordings. Most people attend live musical programs outside of school, although not frequently. The kind of music that 9-, 13-, and 17-year-olds most like to listen to is rock. The greatest percentage of adults (29%) prefer country and western. Fourteen percent of the adults prefer rock and 12 percent instrumental art music. Lower percentages expressed preferences for vocal art music, folk, soul, popular ballads, blues, background music (3% of adults and no others), other popular, and other types that were unclassifiable. A large majority of respondents at all age levels said that they like to sing "very much" or "somewhat." Twenty percent of the 9-year-olds, 40 percent of the 13-year-olds, and 30 percent of the 17-year-olds most enjoy singing rock. Adults most enjoy singing folk (10%), country and western (13%), and popular ballads (12%). The data indicate that fewer people in each successively higher age group play instruments, and that there is a decrease in the amount of time spent playing in each successive group. This is true of all instruments except keyboard and strings, which remain fairly stable through the adult group. A majority of each age level (sometimes a large majority) indicated that they "strongly agree" or "somewhat agree" that singing and/or playing an instrument with a large or small group is enjoyable. This exercise indicated a growing interest in small group participation, which may have implications for music education programs. In response to the exercises concerning membership in musical groups, 22 percent of the 9-year-olds, 27 percent of the 13-year-olds, 20 percent of the 17-year-olds, and 5 percent of the adults indicated that they belonged to a school or community vocal group. Membership in school and community instrumental groups included 8, 17, 10, and 1 percent of the age groups, respectively. Generally, females of all ages expressed more positive attitudes toward music than did males. Blacks expressed more positive attitudes toward music than did whites; blacks listen more often and enjoy musical participation more. Children of parents with some post-high school education enjoy singing and playing more, and were more willing to participate in musical groups than children of parents with no high school education. There is little difference in attitudes between various types of communities. The greatest differences were in the suburban areas, where there is more playing of instruments, and in the rural areas, where there is more participation in musical groups.

After the results of the first music assessment were tabulated, the MENC Executive Board appointed a six-member panel to meet with the National Assessment staff to study the implication of the survey. The panel members, Paul Lehman, Jo Ann Baird, William English, Richard Graham, Charles Hoffer, and Sally Monsour, discussed each group of exercises and identified implications that were "to be interpreted not as statements of fact, but as hypotheses which need further testing." Three statements were offered as a guide to interpretation of the results.

1. The assessment results are based on a random sample of the entire population regardless of musical background or preparation. The data provide valuable insights into the musical competence of the "average" citizen; however, a study of persons with some degree of training or interest in music would presumably produce quite different findings.

2. Not all of the musical knowledge and skills assessed are directly attributable to formal instruction in schools. Television, radio, and social environments play major roles in developing musical knowledge as well as in influencing musical tastes and attitudes. Thus, the ability of the music teacher to influence the results is limited.

3. Each exercise represents a single, specific skill from a broad array of

related skills. It is tempting but hazardous to generalize from one or two discrete bits of information to a more sweeping conclusion. Although certain patterns of results may appear to emerge, the validity of any generalization must be considered in light of a number of related skills assessed and the extent to which they are representative of the generalized array of skills. The variety of skills included in the assessment is so great that the number of exercises devoted to each skill must be very small. As a result, attempts to generalize should be undertaken with the greatest caution.[8]

The Second Music Assessment

The highlights of the second assessment findings are as follows.

ACHIEVEMENT RESULTS FOR THE 1978-79 ASSESSMENT

Around three-fourths of the students at each age appear to have positive feelings about music and appear able to make simple judgments about it. Many students have some knowledge of the elements and expressive controls of music. On 45 questions about elements and controls, the average success rate for 9-year-olds was 52 percent; on 50 questions, the average for 13-year-olds was 61 percent; and on 49 questions, the average for 17-year-olds was 57 percent. However, students appear strongest at identifying the elements and controls and weakest at identifying the relationships among them in a given composition. Knowledge about music history and style is less widespread: on 18 exercises assessing these areas, the average success rate for 9-year-olds was 58 percent; on 55 items, the average success rate for 13-year-olds was 36 percent; and on 61 such exercises for 17-year-olds, the average success rate was 39 percent.

CHANGES IN ACHIEVEMENT

Fewer 9- and 17-year-olds were successful in answering their respective exercises in the 1978-79 assessment than in the 1971-72 assessment. The decline between assessments for 9-year-olds was 3.3 percent; for 17-year-olds, it was 2.5 percent. The percentage of 13-year-olds able to respond correctly to the music exercises was about 41 percent in both assessments. Fewer 9- and 17-year-olds in the second assessment were successful on exercises that required knowledge of the elements and expressive controls of music than in the first assessment. The decline between assessments was 3.4 percent for 9-year-olds and 4.9 percent for 17-year-olds. Knowledge about music history and style did not decline between assessments among 9-, 13-, or 17-year-olds.

EXPOSURE TO MUSIC

Nine-year-olds who indicated they had been taught music in school for two years (1977–78/1978–79) performed about 4 percentage points higher on all music exercises than those who had been taught music in school for only one year, and 6 percentage points higher than those who had not been taught music in school in either year. Seventy-four percent of the 9-year-olds indicated that they "listen to music," 45 percent indicated that they "sing just for fun," and nearly 30 percent indicated they "play a musical instrument just for fun" in the school music class. More 13- and 17-year-olds indicated participation in general music classes than in choir, band, or orchestra. However, approximately 28 percent of the 13-year-olds and 18 percent of the 17-year-olds had never taken a general music class or music appreciation. Forty-eight percent of the 13-year-olds and 46 percent of the 17-year-olds had never enrolled in choir, chorus or glee club; 50 percent of the 13-year-olds and nearly 52 percent of the 17-year-olds had never taken band or instrumental music; and a bit more than 90 percent of the 13- and 17-year-olds had never taken orchestra. Those 13- and 17-year-olds who had participated in school musical activities and classes performed better on the achievement exercises than those students who had not. Achievement results were 12 to 13 percentage points different between students who had had no band or orchestra experience and those who had had at least three years of participation in this activity. Achievement results also are 6 to 9 percentage points different between students who had not participated in choir or glee club and those who had participated for at least three years.[9]

Comparative Results of the Two Assessments

The exercises common to both assessments provided a basis for comparison over a period of several years. Data on students' abilities to perform and to create music were not collected during the second assessment because of funding limitations. The comparative results indicate the following. Fewer 9- and 17-year-olds were successful in answering their respective exercises in the 1978–79 assessment than in the 1971–72 assessment. The decline between assessments for 9-year-olds able to respond correctly to the music exercises was about 41 percent in both assessments. Achievement results on the objectives indicate that: fewer 9- and 17-year-olds in the second assessment were successful on exercises that required knowledge of the elements and expressive controls of music than in the first assessment; the decline between assessments was 3.4 percent for 9-year-olds and 4.9 percent for 17-year-olds; and knowledge about music history and style did not decline between assessments among 9-, 13-, or 17-year-olds.

FIGURE 9.4 National Mean Percentages and
Changes in Correct Responses for 9-, 13- and
17-Year-Olds in Two Music Assessments

	Mean % Correct 1971–72	Mean % Correct 1978–79	Change in Mean % Correct 1971–72, 1978–79
Age 9 Total exercises—25	53.6	50.3	−3.3*
Age 13 Total exercises—69	41.8	41.3	−0.5
Age 17 Total exercises—80	45.7	43.2	−2.5*

*Asterisk indicates percentages statistically significant at the
0.5 level

Note. Music 1971–79: Results from the Second National
Music Assessment, no. 10-MU-35, National Institute
of Education (pamphlet).

NAEP also gathered data on the musical training background of students. All students participating in the 1978–79 music assessment were asked the same questions about their exposure to musical activities outside of school. Here are some of the results.

More 13- and 17-year-olds than 9-year-olds listen to music, sing just for fun, and sing with friends for fun. However, percentages for 9- and 13-year-olds are more similar to each other than to percentages of 17-year-olds who sing with friends for fun. Conversely, more 9-year-olds than 13- or 17-year-olds indicated that they sing in a church or community music group. Percentages of 9-, 13-, or 17-year-olds who do at least one of the singing activities are very similar. More 13- and 17-year-olds than 9-year-olds play a musical instrument alone for fun, while more 9-year-olds than 13- or 17-year-olds indicated that they play a musical instrument with friends for fun and play a musical instrument in a community group. In addition, more 9-year-olds than 13- or 17-year-olds indicated at least one activity involving playing an instrument. More 9-year-olds than 13- or 17-year-olds take music lessons and make up their own music.[10]

Response to the Second Assessment by Music Educators

Following the second assessment, the National Assessment staff met with three music educators who had participated in its development.

They were Dr. Richard M. Graham of the University of Georgia; Dr. Kevin J. McCarthy of the University of Colorado; and Dr. Diana V. Owen, an independent music education specialist. The group identified reasons for the results and needs of the music education profession that appeared to be related to the assessment. The statements are too lengthy to be reported in this chapter and do not lend themselves to abridgement. Music educators are strongly advised to read the transcripts of the panels that addressed themselves to both the first and second assessments in order to bring them into perspective. The reader will be made aware of societal factors that affect the musical development of children but which are often beyond the influence of music educators in the schools.

The information contained in the National Assessment reports is of great potential value to the profession of music education. Music educators should be aware of the NAEP findings, but should also be aware that it is raw data that needs to be interpreted in relation to the greatly varying local circumstances of education in general, and music education in particular.

NOTES

1. National Assessment of Educational Progress, *National Assessment of Educational Progress: General Information Yearbook*, report no. 0304 SGY (Washington, D.C.: U.S. Office of Education, 1974), p. 1.
2. *NAEP: General Information Yearbook*, p. 2.
3. Ibid.
4. Ibid.
5. NAEP, Education Commission of the States, *Procedural Handbook: 1978–79 Music Assessment*, December 1981, report no. 10-Mu-40, p. xi.
6. Ibid., pp. 2, 3.
7. National Assessment of Educational Progress, *The First National Assessment of Musical Performance*, report no. 02-MU-01 (Washington, D.C.: U.S. Government Printing Office, 1974), p. 29.
8. National Assessment of Educational Progress, *A Perspective on the First Music Assessment* (Washington, D.C.: U.S. Government Printing Office, 1974), p. 2.
9. NAEP, Education Commission of the States, *Music 1971–79: Results from the Second National Assessment*, November 1981, report no. 10-MU-01, p. xiii.
10. NAEP, Education Commission of the States, "Music 1971-79: Results from the Second National Music Assessment," (brochure), no. 10-MU-35.

BIBLIOGRAPHY

A Perspective on the First Music Assessment. Report no. 03-MU-02, 1971–72 Assessment. Denver: National Assessment of Educational Progress, Education Commission of the States, 1974. ERIC no. ED 097 276.

An Assessment of Attitudes Toward Music. Report no. 03-MU-03, 1971–72 Assessment. Denver: National Assessment of Educational Progress, Education Commission of the States, 1974. ERIC no. ED 099 270.

Music Objectives. No. 03-MU-10, 1971–72 Assessment. Denver: National Assessment of Educational Progress, Education Commission of the States, 1970. ERIC no. ED 063 197.

Music Objectives, Second Assessment. No. 10-MU-10, 1978–79 Assessment. Denver: National Assessment of Educational Progress, Education Commission of the States, 1980. ERIC no. ED 183 434.

Music Technical Report: Exercise Volume. Report no. 03-MU-20, 1971–72 Assessment. Denver: National Assessment of Educational Progress, Education Commission of the States, 1975. ERIC no. ED 120 086.

Music Technical Report: Summary Volume. Report no. 03-MU-21, 1971–72 Assessment. Denver: National Assessment of Educational Progress, Education Commission of the States, 1975. ERIC no. ED 114 348.

Procedural Handbook: 1978–79 Summary Assessment. Report no. 10-MU-40. Denver: National Assessment of Educational Progress, Education Commission of the States, 1981.

The First Assessment: An Overview. Report no. 03-MU-00, 1971–72 Assessment. Denver: National Assessment of Educational Progress, Education Commission of the States, 1974. ERIC no. ED 097 275.

The First National Assessment of Musical Performance. Report no. 03-MU-01, 1971–72 Assessment. Denver: National Assessment of Educational Progress, Education Commission of the States, 1974. ERIC no. ED 155 126.

The Second Assessment of Music, 1978–79 Released Exercise Set. No. 10-MU-25. Denver: National Assessment of Educational Progress, Education Commission of the States, 1980.

For a list of article reprints and miscellaneous documents about NAEP, see the "NAEP Publications List," which can be ordered from:

National Assessment of Educational Progress
1860 Lincoln, Suite 700
Denver, Colorado 80203

10
Contemporary Music Education: A Summary

ARE WE SUCCESSFUL?

It is difficult to evaluate the success of music education in the United States; in fact, it is probably impossible to provide an accurate assessment based on empirical data. Success is measured by a number of criteria. Assessment may be based on observation of performing organizations at a school music festival; statistics that indicate how many students in one or many school systems are enrolled in music courses; the number of music teachers in service at a given time; student achievement on tests; music department budget increases; public displays of participation (concerts, festivals, parades, football games); amount and quality of publicity given the music department; praise from parents, colleagues, and administrators; and any of a number of other factors.

Such yardsticks may measure success in some aspects of local or regional programs but they do not provide evaluative measures for music education on a national scale. There are factors that make nationwide success difficult, if not impossible, to assess. One reason is that there are no national curricula, goals, or standards because the state is the highest level of education authority in the United States. The diversity in education authority is even more bewildering because much control is in the hands of local boards of education, which may adhere to the minimum levels of quality determined by the state or may insist on higher levels. In effect, there are thousands of decision-making bodies that have the legal authority to establish education policies. If the goals set for a music program in a community are achieved, then that program may be deemed successful, at least in terms of its own goals. But that does not mean that it is more successful than programs in other communities which may have different assessment standards and practices (if any at all). In many cases, success is not measured by what or how much children learn. There is little uniformity of program content or assessment among the states and among school districts within the same state.

Another factor that makes national assessment of music education difficult is that most music instruction in American elementary schools is provided by classroom, rather than music, teachers. In most cases, elementary classroom teachers have the major responsibility for music instruction. Sometimes they supplement the teaching of music specialists who work directly with the children on an infrequent basis; in other cases, they may work with music resource people who provide assistance for music instruction. The amount of success varies from teacher to teacher and depends on such variables as talent, training in music, confidence in one's ability to teach music, and conviction about the importance of music in education. A 1963 survey by the National Education Association (NEA) produced the following information.

The practice reported by . . . about 40 percent [of the schools] was to have the classroom teacher teach music with help from a music specialist. . . . The elementary-school classroom teacher had to teach music on his/her own in almost as large a percent of schools in grades 1, 2, and 3, but in grades 4, 5, and 6, the teacher carried the full responsibility for music in less than a third of the schools. Music specialists alone did the teaching in about one-fifth of the schools in grades 4–6, and in 12 to 15 percent of the schools in grades 1–3.[1]

There are no recent surveys to indicate the present state of affairs, but various estimates indicate that there has been little change, at least in elementary general music. In situations where there is no music specialist, there is usually no program as such. Instead, the quality and quantity of music instruction varies from teacher to teacher. Lack of precise information about who teaches music and how it is taught makes it difficult, if not impossible, to assess success.

For these reasons, the success of American music education can only be discussed in general terms. It is simply too broad and diversified a subject to be considered as a single entity for evaluative purposes. The NAEP offers some clues, but, for their data to be helpful, it must be interpreted in the light of actual music education situations rather than a nonexistent national program. To learn the true meaning of the data, we must correlate it with information that we do not have about music education on a national scale. Music educators must evaluate the information they have and draw their own conclusions.

CHANGE AND MUSIC EDUCATION

As can be seen from the preceding chapters, there was much developmental and evolutionary activity in the profession from the late 1950s to the present. Living and working in a time of change, music educators have made valiant attempts to keep up with the times, to modernize the curriculum, and to achieve relevancy for the many students whom they influence. Obviously, change is not unique to music or education; it is a strong force in all public institutions, including the military, government, industry, and other facets of American life. The process of change in American society and schools has become a way of life; many young people are more oriented to change than to the status quo.[2]

The decade of the 1960s was characterized by demands for faster change. The demands came in the form of civil rights sit-ins and marches, student riots, and other kinds of protests. When the air cleared in the early 1970s, society had begun to move toward more openness, which led to more equitable treatment for most Americans, including educational opportunities. The results of the 1960s protest activities are manifested in music education in the form of diversity of viewpoints and approaches, as well as tolerance of new ideas. Until recently, music was taught by more or less traditional methods that had evolved slowly from nineteenth-century practices. Musical materials have also undergone an evolutionary process; previously, they had provided many excellent performing and listening experiences, but not a sense of cultural identification for students. The problem was partially solved by the acceptance of popular and ethnic music in the curriculum. In the late 1960s, when the profession began its long and earnest process of introspection, it became clear that radical change was necessary if music education was to have an impact on American society. The development of philosophy (as expressed at Yale and Tanglewood) and innovation went hand in hand. The 1960s was a time of generous government funding; some of the funds were used to develop new curricula. Although many of the curricular innovations of the 1960s have not survived, they helped the profession become receptive to new methods and provided many new materials and techniques.

The new methods created an atmosphere conducive to change and progress. American music teachers have often lacked the resources to adopt a new teaching method, or have been in professional situations that make adoption undesirable. Therefore, they have often adopted only those aspects of other methods that they consider useful, thereby creating an eclectic methodology. The wealth of new materials now being offered by publishers provides further stimulation for trying new methods. Workshops for teacher training and retraining are available in all parts of the country. Music educators must remember, however, that change should be approached cautiously and with foresight. Allen Britton, expressing his concern for the casual acceptance of change, observed:

Many American music educators have demonstrated what may be considered an easy readiness to climb aboard any intellectual bandwagon which happened to be near by, and to trust it to arrive at destinations appropriate for music educators, or worse, to adopt its destinations as their own without careful enough scrutiny of the intellectual properties involved.[3]

As time goes on, there will be more and more choices to make in regard to change. Teachers must be aware of philosophies, methods, techniques, and materials in order to be sure that they make the best possible choices. This will allow them to provide the highest quality services, which in turn will keep the profession viable, dynamic, and sensitive to the needs of society.

SUMMARY

The decade of the 1970s contrasts sharply with that of the 1960s. Although there were many important developments in music education, one generally associates the 1960s with ascent and the 1970s with decline. There was little music curriculum development of importance in the 1970s. The resources available to music educators, in the form of students enrollment, facilities, and funding, diminished. Indeed, the number of music educators and music programs also fell. From an objective view of the two decades, it appears that the 1970s provided a balance to the 1960s, which was a time of unusual richness that could not be sustained. In other words, the seventies brought us back to a more normal level. Most of the new developments during that decade were in response to causes external to the profession, and were not conducive to extensive curriculum or philosophical development.

The 1970s should not be viewed too negatively, however. It was a decade in which the use of the new curricula was refined. Music teachers who learned to utilize the new methods were more effective because the time that had elapsed since the sixties had given them more practice in their use. Time also helped to work out the bugs in the curricula, and adaptations became more effective. The 1970s was also a time of the development of excellent materials to support the new curricula.

Surveying the 1960s and 1970s, one sees a reiteration of the historical swing from one ethos to another. Throughout history there have been periods of creativity, richness of ideas, and material comfort, always followed by times in which conditions have levelled out. Such antonyms as liberal/conservative, classical/romantic, and Apollonian/Dionysian describe this rhythm that history has often displayed. Its pendulum usually serves to compensate and adjust for any excesses of a previous period. The constant swing from one to another can be seen as a method by which nature attempts to prevent us from taking directions that might prove dangerous in the future.

The beginning of the 1980s is similar in character to the late 1950s. There is strong concern on the part of the general public and educators that excellence be restored to education. Generally, this is healthy for music education because most people realize that a truly superior education must include the arts. Music educators, like other educators, will have to change with the times, although that is often difficult to do. As long as their response to the demand for excellence is excellence in music education, however, there is every reason for optimism for the future.

CODA

It is important for music educators to remember that each crisis in the past has proven, in time, to be an opportunity. Music education has not only survived its hard times but has always been strengthened by them because music educators found new and better ways for their profession to serve children. In doing so, they took advantage of crisis situations by treating them as opportunities. The same phenomenon appears to be recurring in the 1980s. It is up to music educators to take advantage of the new opportunity to strengthen music education for their students and for themselves.

Despite many trials and setbacks, music has been a vital part of the school curriculum in the United States for a long time and will continue to be so. President Kennedy made a statement that describes the need for the arts in our country, and which gives credibility to arts education. The words are inscribed in marble in the John F. Kennedy Center for the Performing Arts in Washington, D.C.:

This country cannot afford to be materially rich and spiritually poor. To further the appreciation of culture among all people, to increase respect for the creative individual, to widen the participation by all in the processes and fulfilments of art—this is one of the fascinating challenges of these days.

NOTES

1. *Music and Art in the Public Schools*, Research Monograph 1963-M3 (Washington, D.C.: Research Division, National Education Association, 1963), p. 12.

2. Alvin Toffler, *Future Shock* (New York: Random House, 1970), pp. 7–17.
3. Allen P. Britton, "Music in Early American Public Education: A Historical Critique," National Society for the Study of Education, *Basic Concepts in Music Education*, ed. Nelson B. Henry (Chicago: University of Chicago Press, 1958), p. 107.

Index